Deserts

Deserts

Michael Allaby

Facts On File, Inc.

Deserts

Facts On File, Inc.
11 Penn Plaza
New York NY 10001

Library of Congress Cataloging-in-Publication Data

Allaby, Michael
    Deserts/Michael Allaby
        p. cm.—(Ecosystem)
    Includes bibliographical references (p.)
    ISBN 0-8160-3929-1 (alk. paper)
    1. Deserts. I Title. II. Series.
QH88 .A45 2000
577.54—dc21   00-041749

Facts On File books are available at special discounts when purchased in bulk quantities for businesses, associations, institutions or sales promotions. Please call our Special Sales Department in New York at (212) 967-8800 or (800) 322-8755.

You can find Facts On File on the World Wide Web at http://www.factsonfile.com

Text design by Cathy Rincon and Sandra Watanabe
Cover design by Cathy Rincon
Illustrations by Richard Garratt

Printed in Hong Kong

Creative FOF 10 9 8 7 6 5 4 3 2 1

This book is printed on acid-free paper.

Contents

Seen from space, the Earth is blue and green, with patches of white cloud, and it shines brilliantly in the light of the Sun. It is breathtakingly beautiful, and astronauts have told how they have stared at it transfixed, no matter how many times they have seen it before. Our planet is blue because of the oceans that cover more than three-quarters of its surface and because of the air, which is blue—the reason a cloudless sky is blue. It is green because of the plants that grow on the surface—the vast forests of the Tropics and the northern taiga, the grasslands, and the farmed lands that provide our food.

Usually we look no farther. We admire the beauty we see, unaware of all that remains hidden. Orbiting satellites take photographs of the Earth that reveal more. Cameras on satellites are sensitive to light beyond the visible spectrum, especially in the infrared, and they can photograph what our eyes cannot see. Their "eyes" are able to penetrate cloud and distin-

Naukluft National Park, Namibia (Gerry Ellis / ENP Images)

guish different types of vegetation and different types of land surface. They transmit radio messages to receiving stations on the surface that are processed by computers to form pictures rich in information. The pictures are still beautiful, but with a beauty that tells us what the surface of the Earth is really like.

Desert Covers Nearly Half the World

Satellite pictures reveal that although forests, grasslands, and farms cover more than half the land surface, it is barely more than half. Over about 48 percent of the land, plants are widely scattered, with bare ground between them, and in some regions there are no plants at all. These areas are classified as dry (10 percent), semiarid (18 percent), arid (12 percent), or hyperarid (8 percent). The arid and hyperarid areas are deserts and the remaining areas are dry enough to resemble deserts at least some of the time. These inhospitable areas are vast, and about 13 percent of all the people in the world live in them.

Deserts are also different, one from another. Some are hot, some cold, and some are covered with great oceans of sand piled into high dunes. Some are frozen and thickly covered with ice. All deserts are dry, even those buried beneath thousands of feet of ice, but this does not necessarily mean they are far from the sea. There are coastal deserts, bordered by the ocean. Other deserts lie in the heart of Asia, thousands of miles from the sea, or in the rain shadow of mountain ranges, such as the Rockies.

Desert Geography

This book is about deserts. It begins, as it must, by describing where on Earth deserts are found and the ways in which one type of desert differs from another. PART 1, Geography of Deserts, discusses the processes through which deserts appear and disappear over long periods. They are produced by climatic conditions and climates change. During ice ages, for example, deserts expand.

Having established the locations and general types of deserts, the part continues with a more detailed account of the most important deserts. These include the hot deserts, such as the Sahara; the cold continental deserts, such as the Gobi; and the coastal deserts, such as the Namib and Atacama, as well as the North American Deserts. PART 1 also describes the polar deserts, with their ice sheets and glaciers.

Desert Surfaces and Landforms

Deserts have a variety of surfaces. Some are sandy, others covered with gravel or bare rock. PART 2 of the book, Geology of Deserts, explains how these surface types and shapes are produced and describes what they are like. It explains, for example, why sand dunes have particular shapes—each with its own name.

Dryness is the one feature all deserts share. The section continues by describing how water moves in a desert and it explains how oases are formed. The movement of water results from the rain that falls occasionally in most deserts or that drains into a desert from elsewhere. Rain is a meteorological phenomenon, and PART 3 of the book, Atmosphere and Deserts, is about climate. It describes how the circulation of the atmosphere produces desert climates in certain places and also explains some of the spectacular types of desert weather, including whirlwinds, dust devils, and sandstorms.

Desert Plants and Animals

We are right in thinking that deserts are barren, but this does not mean they are devoid of life. There are many plants and animals that have evolved to tolerate the harsh conditions of even the hottest, coldest, windiest, and driest deserts. PART 4 of the book, Biology of Deserts, is concerned with desert life. It describes how plants and animals economize in their use of water and how some species can remain alive but dormant for years, then come to life when a rare opportunity occurs for them to complete their life cycles. When this happens, the desert blooms and within hours is ablaze with the color of flowers that vanish as rapidly as they appeared.

Some desert animals are especially famous—or notorious. PART 4 describes camels and locusts as well as the wolf, wolverine, and polar bear of the Far North. It also describes animals of the polar seas and shores—the walrus, seals, fishes, and penguins.

Desert Peoples

With its description of desert plants and animals the first section of the book draws to a close. The second section deals with people. It tells of how human societies have thrived in and beside deserts for thousands of years; of how it was there, in Egypt and the land between the Euphrates and Tigris Rivers, that Western civilization was forged. It describes how desert dwellers managed their water supply; the dangers that accompany the irrigation of fields in a hot, dry climate; and how, in Mexico, those dangers were avoided in one of the most successful, and remarkable, of all methods of irrigation and cultivation, the *chinampas,* or "floating gardens."

If this is how life in the desert has been made possible, what is it actually like? PART 5, History and the Desert, continues with a series of accounts of a number of desert peoples. Some are famous, such as the Berber and Tuareg peoples of

North Africa, the Mongol peoples of Central Asia, the Inuit of the Far North, and the Hopi and other Pueblo peoples of North America; others are less well known. The section also describes the Silk Road, which formed a communications link between Europe and China, and tells of the explorers who were the first outsiders to penetrate these difficult and unmapped regions.

Deserts Today

The final three sections of the book discuss the deserts as they are today, dealing with the economics of desert nations and industries (PART 6), the possibilities of climatic change (PART 7), and the management of desert lands (PART 8). They include an account of the development and impact of the oil industry in Africa and the Middle East and of the opportunities for tourism. In discussing climate change, the book explains the climatic effect of changes in the orbit and rotation of Earth and in energy output from the Sun. It also explains the ways in which local weather, though not climates, can sometimes be manipulated.

No book about deserts can ignore the widespread fear that at least some of the world's deserts are spreading. Here you will read about the way deserts do indeed expand—and also how they contract again. The danger to farming arises much more from poor land management that leads to overgrazing and the resulting degradation of land than from desert expansion itself. Land degradation is described, together with its causes.

Moving water from one place to another can have catastrophic consequences. Egyptian culture has always depended on the Nile. The book describes the river itself, the way its water is used, and the effect of damming the river at Aswān and continues with the story of irrigation in the arid lands of the former Soviet Union and its effect on the Aral Sea.

From ancient artificial oases made by building underground water channels to methods used to make sea water drinkable the book shows how life in the desert can be improved successfully. It also warns of the risk of conflict over access to water but points out that, so far water has not been used as a reason for going to war.

Ecosystems: Deserts contains a large amount of scientific and technical detail, but the information is presented clearly and should not be difficult to follow. So far as possible, technical terms are avoided, and where they cannot be avoided, they are defined in simple language. To follow the text, readers will need to understand no more than the most elementary mathematics. At the end of the book there is a list of sources for further information, including many on the World Wide Web.

Deserts

PART 1

Geography of Deserts

Location of the World's Deserts

Wherever you look there is nothing but sand, rocks, and gravel. The landscape seems to have no features, nothing from which you could take your bearings, nothing you could be sure to recognize were you to see it again. Only the Sun can guide you and it beats down mercilessly.

This is the desert. At least, it is the desert we see in movies. Movies need the desert to be hot and harsh; the story demands it. So screenwriters exaggerate, but only a little. The desert really is an inhospitable place. The problem is that the deserts movies depict are all the same, and, except at the widely scattered oases and for the nomadic travelers moving from one oasis to the next, they are all lifeless. As you will see, deserts are not lifeless and they are not all the same. They are not all equally harsh—some are hotter and drier than others—nor equally barren.

It is true, though, that deserts are typically hot, dry regions. Part of the reason for this is obvious. A glance at the map of the world shows that most deserts lie within the Tropics. These are the regions on each side of the equator, bounded by latitude 30°. Latitude 30° N is the tropic of Cancer; 30° S is the tropic of Capricorn (the names refer to those lines of latitude). Within these latitudes the Sun appears directly overhead at noon on at least one day in the year. To the north or south of them, the Sun is never directly overhead.

Imagine the amount of solar radiation in a narrow beam. Obviously, any beams of equal width will contain the same amount of radiation. Now picture how two beams of the same width size affect people living in two different parts of the world, one group in the Far North, say in

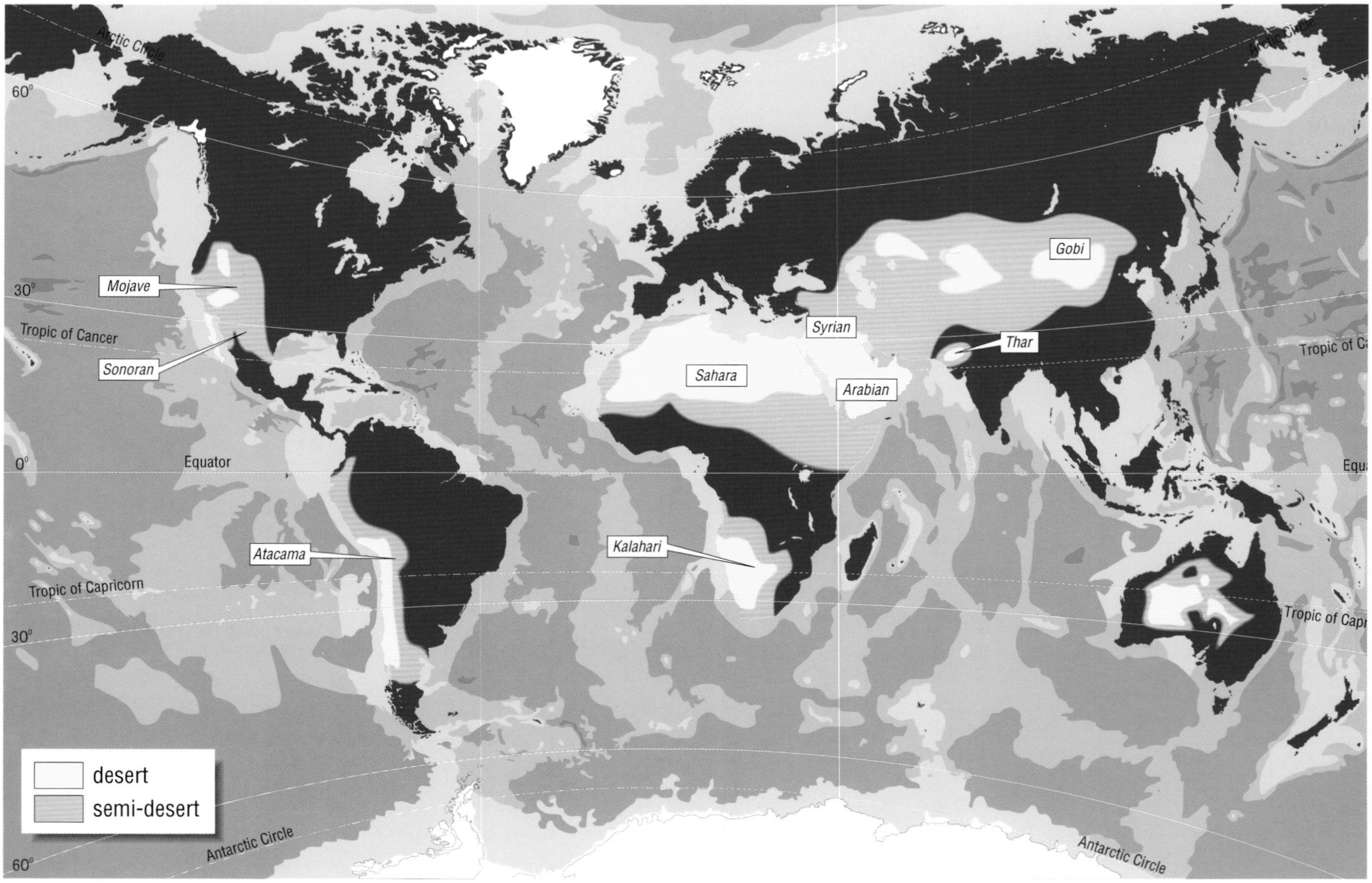
Arctic Circle
60°
Mojave
30°
Tropic of Cancer
Sonoran
Equator
0°
Atacama
Tropic of Capricorn
30°
Gobi
Syrian
Thar
Sahara
Arabian
Kalahari
desert
semi-desert
Antarctic Circle
60°
Antarctic Circle

Greenland, and the other near the equator, say in southern Mexico. The figure (right) shows these effects. For the people in the south, the noonday Sun is almost overhead, because they are on the part of the Earth that directly faces the Sun. There, the sunlight shines nearly vertically downward, so the beam illuminates a quite small area, because of the angle at which it strikes the surface. To the Greenlanders, the Sun appears much lower in the sky, so its light reaches them not vertically, as it does the Mexicans, but at a low angle. The beam is the same width as the one shining on Mexico, but it illuminates a much bigger area. Since both beams are the same width, they both deliver the same amount of light and heat. In Mexico, that light and heat are concentrated into the small area the beam illuminates, and in Greenland it illuminates a much bigger area. So the Mexicans receive their solar energy in a much more concentrated form than do the Greenlanders.

Continental Interiors

Deserts occur in or very close to the Tropics. That is why they are hot. Many of them also occur in the center of continents, a very long way from the sea. This has two consequences. The first is that continental interiors experience extremes of temperature (page 18), the second that their distance from the ocean means their climates are dry. New York City, for example, is at latitude 40.7° N and Des Moines, Iowa, is at 41.6° N. In New York, the difference between the highest and lowest temperatures ever recorded (over 46 years of records) is 117°F (65°C) and the average annual precipitation (rain and snow) is 43 inches (1,086 mm), spread evenly through the year. In Des Moines the difference between the highest and lowest temperatures recorded over 52 years is 139°F (77°C) and the average annual precipitation is 32 inches (811 mm) with the wettest months in the summer. Des Moines is not surrounded by desert, of course, but it is near the center of the continent and a long way from the sea.

The World's Principal Deserts

In North America, the deserts are in the west. California's Mojave Desert lies to the southeast of the Sierra Nevada, approximately between latitudes 34° N and 37° N, with the most extreme conditions in Death Valley. Desert conditions also occur west of the Great Salt Lake, Utah, centered on latitude 40° N, and desert continues in the southwest with the Sonoran Desert, in Baja California.

A region of northern Colombia, on the Gaujira Peninsula, is desert, and there are arid conditions in northeastern Brazil, inland from the forested coastal strip.

The principal South American desert, however, is the Atacama. It runs through northern Chile as a north-south strip from about 5° S to 30° S, covering an area of about 140,000 square miles (363,000 sq km).

Across the Atlantic, the world's largest desert is the Sahara, covering most of Africa north of about latitude 15° N. Altogether the Sahara covers an area of about 3.5 million square miles (9.1 million sq km). It seems much larger, because the desert continues through part of Ethiopia as the Denakil Desert, and into Sudan. Farther east, across the Red Sea, lies the Arabian Desert, covering the whole of the Arabian Peninsula, an area of about 1.6 million square miles (3 million sq km) from about 30° N to 12° N. North of the Arabian Desert there lies the Syrian Desert, which occupies much of the Middle East.

South of the equator, the Kalahari Desert covers 275,000 square miles (712,250 sq km) from the tropic of Capricorn to about 27° S. On its western side the Kalahari merges into the Namib Desert, one of the world's driest. This runs along the coast for a distance of 1,200 miles (1,930 km) and extends up to 100 miles (160 km) inland.

Europe and Asia together form the continent of Eurasia, which is by far the biggest of all continents. Not surprisingly, its interior is dry, with several deserts. The most famous is the Gobi, unusual

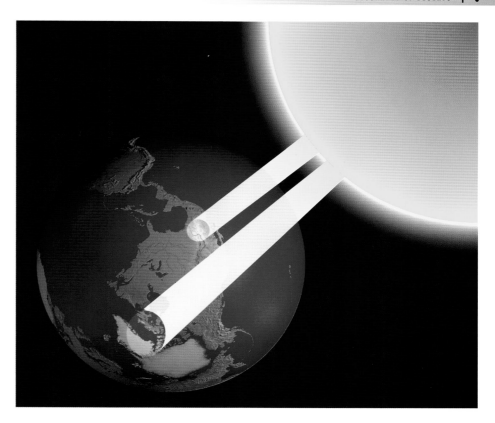

Latitude and warmth

because it lies outside the Tropics, latitude 40° N passing approximately through its center. It extends in some places for 1,000 miles (1,610 km) from east to west and 600 miles (970 km) from north to south. To the east, the Gobi continues as the Ordos Desert. Farther west lies the Takla Makan, or Taklimakan, Desert. Between the Tien Shan in the north and Kunlun Mountains in the south it occupies about 115,000 square miles (297,850 sq km) consisting mainly of drifting sand dunes.

Across the mountains in the south, there is the Thar, or Great Indian, Desert about 500 miles (805 km) long and 300 miles (485 km) wide.

Finally, there is the Australian Desert, covering much of the western side of the interior. In fact it is not a single desert, but several, formed in depressions between large, uplifted highland areas.

Deserts cover a substantial part of the Earth's land surface. Those mentioned previously are the hot deserts of the Tropics or cool deserts of continental interiors. There are also cold deserts. Away from the coasts, Greenland and Antarctica are as dry as any sandy desert. This sounds paradoxical, given that they lie beneath thick ice sheets, but the ice sheets exist not because there is heavy snowfall, but because such little snow as falls fails to melt.

What Makes a Desert?

Some deserts are hot, some are cold, but all deserts are dry. It is aridity that defines a desert. You might think, therefore, that a desert is a place where it never rains, but you would be wrong. True, there are deserts, or parts of deserts, where no rain has fallen throughout the whole of human history, but these are very exceptional. It rains sometimes in most deserts. What matters is not whether or not it rains, but what happens to the rain as it is falling and once it reaches the ground.

Water consists of molecules of hydrogen oxide, H_2O, in which one hydrogen atom is bonded to two atoms of oxygen. In the liquid phase, water molecules are linked together by hydrogen bonds, forming small groups. These are constantly breaking and reforming and groups can slide past one another. Given enough energy, however, molecules start breaking free. These energetic molecules escape into the air and as more and more of them do so, the amount of liquid water diminishes. This is evaporation.

While this is happening, however, some of the water molecules already in the air and moving very fast in all directions collide with the water surface. This traps them, because they dissipate their energy in the impact of the collision, form hydrogen bonds with the molecules around them, and are then part of the liquid water mass.

These events take place just outside the boundary between the liquid and the air—just outside a water droplet or above the surface of a pool of water. Here, energetic water molecules are both leaving and joining the liquid. If the number leaving is greater than the number joining the liquid, water will evaporate, and if the number joining the liquid is equal to the number leaving, the liquid will not evaporate. The rate at which the liquid evaporates depends on the number of water molecules in this boundary layer of air. The more water molecules the air contains, the more slowly the liquid will evaporate, and it will evaporate faster the fewer airborne molecules there are.

Partial Pressure

Air exerts a pressure on the surface of water, which is due to the weight of all the air in a column above an area on the surface all the way to the top of the atmosphere. Its weight is the sum of the weights of all its constituent gases, and so each of these contributes proportionally to the surface pressure. This is called the *partial pressure* for each gas. If the pressure is, say, 1,000 millibars (mb), then the partial pressure of nitrogen will be about 781 mb and that of oxygen about 209 mb, because air consists of 78.1 percent nitrogen and 20.9 percent oxygen. Water vapor is also a gas and it, too, exerts a partial pressure. The partial pressure water vapor must exert to prevent more water from evaporating is called the *saturation*

Sand dunes, southern Utah (Gerry Ellis/ ENP Images)

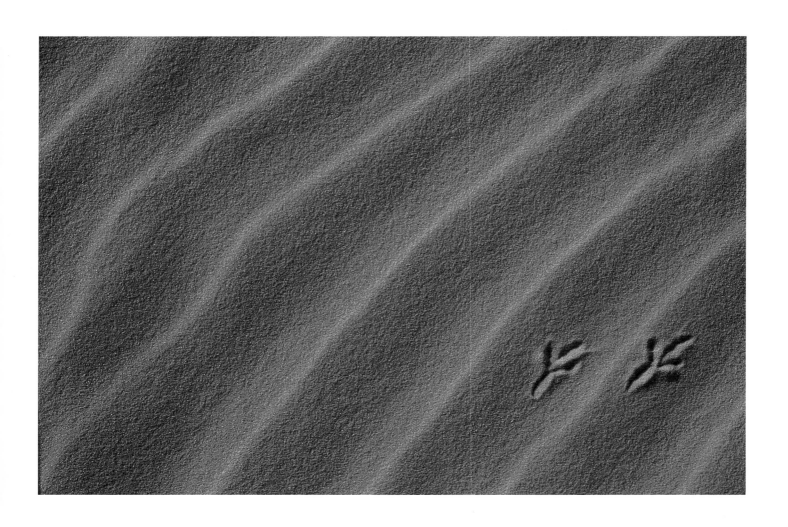

vapor pressure. When that pressure is reached, the water vapor is saturated and no additional water molecules can join it. We are used to thinking of the air as saturated, not the water vapor, and that is the way the word *saturation* will be used henceforth, but strictly speaking it is incorrect.

How many water molecules a given volume of air can contain depends on the temperature. The warmer the air, the more molecules it can hold: the difference air temperature makes is dramatic. Very warm air, say at 95°F (35°C) will be saturated when the saturation vapor pressure reaches 56.236 mb, meaning water vapor accounts for about 5.6 percent of the total mass of the air. In much cooler air, say at 14°F (-10°C), saturation vapor pressure is reached at 2.597 mb, with water vapor accounting for about 0.26 percent of the mass of the air. In other words, a fall in temperature of 81°F (45°C) reduces the water-holding capacity of the air by 53.639 mb. This is, perhaps, an extreme change, but even a quite small drop in temperature, say from 77°F to 75.2°F (25°C to 24°C), reduces the saturation vapor pressure from about 31.7 mb to 29.8 mb.

Saturation and Humidity

Saturation is measured and reported in several ways. The ratio of the mass of water vapor to a unit mass of dry air (as grams of water vapor per kilogram of air, for example) is called the *mixing ratio.* The mass of water vapor to a unit mass of air including the water vapor is called the *specific humidity.* The mass of water vapor present in a unit volume of space (as grams of water vapor per cubic meter of air, for example) is called the *absolute humidity.*

Relative humidity is the measure most often used, however. This is what weather forecasters mean when they talk simply of humidity and the figure they quote is always a percentage. Relative humidity is calculated as the amount of water vapor in the air divided by the amount of water vapor needed to saturate the air at that temperature, multiplied by 100. Or, to put it another way, it is the actual vapor pressure expressed as a percentage of the saturation vapor pressure.

Warm air can hold much more water vapor than cool air, so much more water vapor is needed to saturate it. In other words, the warmer the air, the less likely it is to be saturated and, therefore, the more readily water will evaporate (or vaporize) into it. As you know, water evaporates much faster from a saucer left close to a heater than from one left somewhere cool.

Evapotranspiration

Think what this means for hot deserts. As a raindrop falls from its cloud it enters unsaturated air. At once it starts to vaporize. If the cloud base from which it falls is high enough, probably the droplet will have evaporated completely before it reaches the ground. You can see this happening, even in temperate latitudes. Look for a gray, almost transparent sheet extending for some distance below the base of a cloud. Called *virga,* it is rain that evaporates before reaching the ground.

If the rain does reach the ground, it will soak a little way into the surface, finding its way through the tiny spaces between sand or other mineral grains. These spaces are filled with air, and, like the air above, it is warm and dry. The water will evaporate into it.

A desert will form if the amount of rain that falls is less than the amount that evaporates. Obviously, rain must fall before it can evaporate, so measuring the rate at which water actually evaporates is not much help. Instead, the measure to use is the rate at which water would evaporate into air at the existing temperature were there an unlimited supply of water available. This is a quantity that can be measured fairly easily. Plants take water from the ground and release it as vapor into the air. The process is called *transpiration* (page 60). In practice it is almost impossible to measure transpiration separately from evaporation, so the two are usually combined, as *evapotranspiration,* and this is what is measured. The maximum amount of water that will evaporate and be transpired if the supply is unlimited is called the *potential evapotranspiration (PE).* If *PE* is greater than rainfall, desert will develop.

An occasional downpour will not bring an end to desert conditions, although plants and animals will be quick to take advantage of it. A place in the Thar Desert of India once received 33.5 inches (850 mm) of rain in 2 days, but it was a very long time before it rained again. Such water as falls soon disappears and the ground remains dry. The desert will remain desert until such time as the annual rainfall exceeds the annual *PE.* Anywhere in the world, an annual rainfall of less than about 10 inches (250 mm) will produce a desert.

Polar Deserts

A hot climate and low rainfall will produce a desert, but how does an extremely cold climate achieve this? The answer lies in the relationship between the temperature of air and the amount of water vapor it can hold.

Air moving toward the polar regions (page 44) travels at a high altitude, where the air temperature is very low. Because it is so cold, its water vapor condenses and falls as precipitation in the course of its journey. By the time the air reaches the polar regions, where it descends to surface level, it is very dry indeed. Occasionally snow falls, just as rain falls in the tropical deserts, but this does not alter the fact that the climate is extremely arid. The air is so dry that despite the low temperature some water molecules will escape into it from snow surfaces without the snow's melting first (this is called *sublimation*). Near the South Pole, in latitudes 70–90° S, an average of about 2.8 inches (71 mm) of snow (measured as the equivalent amount of rain) falls each year, and about 1.2 inches (30.5 mm) sublimes, leaving about 1.6 inches (40.6 mm) to accumulate.

The relationship between air temperature and saturation also effects long-term climate changes. During ice ages (page 26), average temperatures were lower than they are today. This meant the air could hold less water vapor and, therefore, climates were drier than they are now. Indeed, one way scientists identify past ice ages is by the dust trapped in layers of polar ice laid down long ago. So, if the world climate grows cooler, we should expect it also to grow drier, and if it grows warmer, the amount of rainfall and snowfall will increase.

Climatic Optima and Minima

Walk slowly and observantly, with your eyes on the ground, kicking up the dust, stones, and sand to see what may be hiding beneath, and who knows what you may discover. You can do this in a desert as well as anywhere else, and if you were to do it in some parts of the Sahara you might be surprised. Look in the right places and you may find fish bones. These are not the remains of someone's lunch, but of fish that died when a sea dried up so all that remained was a lake, known today as *Lake Chad* (or Tchad).

Lake Chad lies just to the south of the Sahara Desert, in the region known as the Sahel. It is where four countries meet—Niger, Chad, Cameroon, and Nigeria. As the map shows, the lake is still large. It covers an area of 10,000 square miles (25,900 sq km). Its appearance on the map is deceptive, however, because during the dry season the area is sometimes as little as 4,000 square miles (10,360 sq km) and the lake is very shallow. Nowhere is it more than 20 feet (6 m) deep, and in the shallower northwest the depth in places is only 3 feet (1 m).

The fish, whose remains can still be found, lived when Lake Chad was an inland sea, in places more than 150 feet (45 m) deep. As well as fish bones, it is possible to identify the former shores of that sea. The sea existed about 5,000 years ago,

and, as well as the sea and its fish, there were elephants, giraffes, and rhinoceroses, although these were already becoming rare. Hannibal, the Carthaginian general whose armies used elephants in their assault on Rome, obtained the animals from Algeria, where they were still living in the wild, isolated from the main elephant population south of the desert.

In the Tibesti Mountains, on the border of northern Chad and southeastern Libya, there are caves containing wall paintings between 7,000 and 8,000 years old. The people who painted them were hunters and the pictures depict the game they pursued. There are pictures of elephants, rhinoceroses, hippopotami, antelopes, deer, giraffes, buffalo, and crocodiles. There are even pictures of people traveling in a kind of canoe. Farther east, there were settlements in the heart of what is now the Arabian Desert.

Obviously, at that time the Sahara had a climate much wetter than the one it experiences now. In the driest part of the Sahara, where nowadays it rarely rains at all, the average annual rainfall about 8,000 years ago is believed to have

---

Lake Chad

been 8–16 inches (200–400 mm). The Lake Chad area received much more than that, and rivers flowed all year round from the Tibesti Mountains. Lake Turkana (also known as *Lake Rudolf*), with an area of 2,741 square miles (7,100 sq km), in the Rift Valley, mainly in Kenya with a part across the border in Ethiopia, held much more water than it does now and discharged some of it into the Nile.

Flooding of Ancient Cities

Nor was the Sahara unique. Around the world, lands in the same latitude as the Sahara had a wetter climate then. In parts of Asia, the rains brought by the summer monsoon were so heavy they probably gave rise to the flood legends that form part of the tradition of many cultures. Certainly there is archaeological evidence of flooding between about 6,000 and 4,400 years ago at Ur, Nineveh, and other ancient cities.

Around 4,000 years ago, melons, dates, wheat, and barley were being grown in the region we know as the Thar Desert, in northwest India, where the rainfall was 16–32 inches (400–800 mm). Many parts of Australia had a much wetter climate than they do now, before about 4,500 years ago, when the Australian climate became drier.

Wet weather is also warm weather. When the weather is warm, more water evaporates from the oceans, there is more cloud, and rainfall increases. During cold periods the opposite happens, and climates become drier. A prolonged period of weather that was wetter and warmer than present-day weather is called a *climatic optimum* and its opposite, a period of cold, dry weather, a *climatic minimum*. It was a climatic optimum that allowed hunters to travel the Sahara in search of game, sometimes traveling by boat, without fear of failing to find water to drink.

Tree Rings

The period from about 10,000 to 4,000 years ago was not the only climatic optimum, although it may have been the warmest and longest since the end of the last ice age (page 26). Climate records for more recent times are obtained from the annual growth rings in trees, and especially in the bristlecone pines (*Pinus longaeva*) growing in the mountains of California. Some of these trees are more than 4,600 years old, and when growth rings in living trees are used in conjunction with those from dead trees nearby, they record growing conditions over the last 8,000 years.

NIGER

Lake Chad

CHAD

NIGERIA

☐ N'Djamena

Maiduguri ○

lake during dry season
lake after rains

CAMEROON

Dating past events from tree rings is called *dendrochronology*. It is based on the observation that unless the weather is so bad that a tree does not grow at all, every year the trunk and branches of a woody plant, such as a tree, grow thicker by laying down a layer of new cells around the cells formed in previous years. The cells produced in spring are large and have thin walls. Those produced in late summer are smaller, with thicker walls. This growth pattern produces each year a pale ring with a thinner, dark ring inside it. There is generally one pair of rings for every year of the plant's age. But the rings reveal more than that, because plants do not always grow at the same rate. If the weather in a particular year is especially favorable, the plant grows more and produces a wider annual growth ring than it does in a year when the weather is bad. In very good years a plant may even lay down two pairs of rings, and in very bad years it may put down none. This means, for dating purposes, tree-ring records must be checked against records of other kinds, but it also means tree rings provide a faithful record of the weather.

Tree-ring records show a global climatic optimum that peaked around 3,100 years ago, leading to a minimum about 2,500 years ago. This was followed by another optimum, lasting much longer. Starting from the 2,500-year-ago minimum, the next optimum reached its peak about 2,000 years ago, and although there were relatively warm and cool episodes within it, the European climate did not start cooling until about 300 C.E. In North America the cooling began up to 150 years earlier.

That was the climatic optimum that coincided with the maximum extent of the Roman Empire, when the Romans introduced vine growing in Britain and Germany. Britain was developed by the Roman authorities into a major exporter of metals and, most of all, of cereals. North Africa was also farmed intensively at that time, and the outlines of fields can still be seen from the air in what is now desert.

Eventually the climate cooled, but only to grow warmer again. The Middle Ages was another period of warm, wet weather. It began around 900 C.E. in Europe, a little later in North America, and it ended in the 13th century. While it lasted, Britain was an important wine-producing country.

Within these long periods of relative warmth there were shorter episodes, lasting a few years or decades, when the average weather was a little warmer or cooler. Similar fluctuations occur now—and are sometimes mistakenly thought to be evidence of longer-term climatic change.

The Little Ice Age

By about 1300, though, the climate was growing cooler. Wine harvests started failing in northern France. Several winters in the 1430s were very severe in Europe and from all over northern Europe there are reports of wolves approaching close to villages and farms as their natural prey starved and disappeared. In parts of Scandinavia falling crop yields due to the bad weather triggered a major movement of people from the countryside into the cities and farmers were deserting their holdings in England and Germany as well.

Average temperatures were falling toward a climatic minimum known as the *Little Ice Age*. In *Love's Labour's Lost* (act V, sc. ii), probably written in 1590 or 1591, Shakespeare described a winter that would have been familiar to his audience:

> When icicles hang by the wall,
> And Dick, the shepherd, blows his nail,
> And Tom bears logs into the hall,
> And milk comes frozen home in pail . . .

Between 1500 and 1550 the river Thames at London froze over at least three times—and that was a relatively mild period. There was worse to come. The average summer temperature between 1690 and 1699 was about 2.7°F (1.5°C) cooler than the average between 1920 and 1960. It was a time when glaciers descended farther into their valleys and the Arctic sea ice extended farther south. During the 1580s there were some winters when it completely blocked the Denmark Strait between Iceland and Greenland.

The Little Ice Age affected the whole of the Northern Hemisphere. In Maine, the weather was so severe in the winter of 1607–8, many people died, both Europeans and Native Americans. There were bitter frosts in Virginia, and there was ice along the edges of Lake Superior in June 1608.

It is not easy to say precisely when a climatic period begins and ends. The Little Ice Age may have started around 1200 and was certainly established by the first quarter of the 15th century. It ended around 1850 or, perhaps, 1900.

Characteristics of the Sahara and Arabian Deserts

There is an Arabic word, *sahrá,* which means "wilderness." Arabic speakers apply it to the barren emptiness of the world's largest desert, also known as the Great Desert. It is the desert we know as the Sahara and it occupies more than 3.5 million square miles (9.1 million sq km) in North Africa—not far short of the area of the United States, 3.7 square miles (9.5 million sq km).

The Sahara is bounded in the west by the Atlantic Ocean, in the north by the Atlas Mountains and Mediterranean Sea, and in the east by the Red Sea. In the south it is bounded partly by the river Niger. Elsewhere the boundary is climatic, as the desert gives way to the semiarid lands known as the *Sahel.* Conventionally the desert is divided into the sections shown in the map: the Atlantic, Northern, Central, Southern, and Eastern Sahara. The Eastern Sahara, which is very large, is subdivided into the Libyan Desert in the west and the Nubian Desert to the east of the Nile River in Sudan. The region to the east of the Nile in Egypt is considered part of the Arabian Desert.

Structure of the Sahara

Much of the Sahara is a plateau with an elevation varying from 1,300 to 1,600 feet (395–490 m) above sea level. It comprises sedimentary rocks, some more than 2,500 million years old, that have been folded by movements of the Earth's crust and then eroded, after which further sediments have been deposited on top of them. In places, volcanic rocks have been intruded into the sedimentary structure. Several of the highest mountains, such as Mount Tousidé—10,712 feet (3,265 m)—in the Tibesti Mountains, are extinct volcanoes.

At various times what is now the desert lay beneath the sea. This led to the deposition of sand and calcareous deposits that now form sandstone and limestone. Other sediments were deposited on dry land by wind or rivers. Dry river valleys (called *wadis*) still cut through the sedimentary rocks, but there are also deep gorges caused by episodes of uplifting—when movement deep below the surface thrust a large block of rock upward—and subsequent erosion.

Despite being a plateau, the Sahara is far from level. Large areas of it are below 600 feet (183 m) and some are below sea level. To the west of Cairo, for example, the elevation of the Qattara Depression averages 440 feet (134 m), but parts of it are more than 400 feet (122 m) below sea level. This is a land of soft sand, salt lakes, and marshes. There are other salt lakes, called *chott,* south of

Biskra, Algeria, one of which, the Chott Melrhir, also lies below sea level.

Such low-lying areas contrast with mountains. The Atlas range lies along a southwest-northeast line. In the Central Sahara the Ahaggar Mountains reach almost 10,000 feet (3,050 m). They extend into a range of hills to the southwest, then rise again to form the Tibesti Mountains in Chad and extending into southern Libya. There is low-lying land in northeast Chad, but then the ground rises again, into the mountains of western Sudan, and continues again as the mountains of Ethiopia. Together, these mountains form a ridge crossing the Sahara from west to east.

Sand Dunes and Sandstorms

There are three types of land surface in the Sahara: erg, reg, and hammada. Ergs are "sand seas," composed of dunes that have formed in basins and depressions from sand carried into them by rivers of earlier times. In some places the dunes are still shifting; in others they have stabilized. The large areas of dunes, the ergs, are in the Northern Sahara, extending across the Libyan Desert and into Egypt. The Great Western and Great Eastern Ergs are in Algeria, between Béni-Abbès in the west and Gadàmes (or Ghudāmis) just across the border in Libya. These two towns are both at latitude 30° N. The other principal ergs are Erg Iguidi, to the southwest of the Great Western Erg, and Erg Chech to the east of Erg Iguidi.

It is the wind that makes sand dunes shift, but it can act more dramatically. Average-sized sand grains can be lifted by a wind of 12 mph (19 km/h) and desert winds frequently exceed this speed. The winds are produced either by strong surface heating during the day or by low-pressure systems. During the hottest part of the day, the desert surface can reach temperatures as high as 180°F (85°C). Air, heated by contact with the surface, expands and rises. This produces an area of very low pressure near ground level. Denser air rushes in to compensate and its movement causes strong, gusty winds. These are called *thermal* winds because they are caused by temperature differences. Low-pressure weather systems are much bigger. They affect much larger areas and can generate stronger winds than those due to daytime heating.

A wind that carries sand can cause a sandstorm. These are common. Their winds need not be blowing with the force of a gale: a 35-mph (56-km/h) wind is sufficient. That is about the

speed of the wind, called the *khamsin,* that closed the Suez Canal and Cairo Airport in March 1998. It reduced visibility to about 200 yards (180 m) and affected Lebanon and Jordan as well as Egypt.

The khamsin is a hot, dry wind that blows from the southeast at regular 50-day intervals in later winter and early spring. *Khamsin* means "fifty." As well as sand, it brings air temperatures between 100°F and 120°F (38–49°C). Khamsins are caused by the passage of low-pressure systems, and similar winds, though not always so hot, occur widely in North Africa and in countries bordering the Mediterranean. The wind is called *ghibli* in Libya, *leveche* in Spain, and *sirocco* (or *scirocco*) across the Mediterranean—and brings wet weather, not dry, to southern Europe.

Reg

Reg is the name given to ground covered by boulders and gravel. The reg is fairly level, with gradients as low as 1:5,000 in some places. These areas are bleak, windswept, and monotonous.

Reg is formed by wind action. Small particles are blown from around and between the larger, heavier stones. The process, called *deflation,* keeps the reg swept clean. Indeed, it keeps the surface very clean, because the finest particles are often carried very long distances. Saharan dust has been identified in the United States.

Where the stones are a little larger and mixed with some sand, the surface is called *serir.* There are areas of serir in Libya and Egypt. The Sarīr Tibesti is a large expanse of serir in southern Libya, extending across the border into Chad. Serir occurs on fairly level ground and formed originally from material deposited by rivers flowing along entwined, braided channels or by water flowing in sheets across the surface. Subsequently the climate changed and dry winds gradually altered the surface into the condition found today.

Hammada

Hammada (or hamada) is the rocky desert. It has no small particles at the surface, of sand or anything else. There is just rock, either as large boulders or exposed bedrock. Stony hammada forms the jagged, broken surface of crystalline rocks—igneous rocks formed by volcanic activity. Pebbly hammada forms over sedimentary rocks. As the name suggests, it consists of pebbles mixed with broken fragments of bedrock.

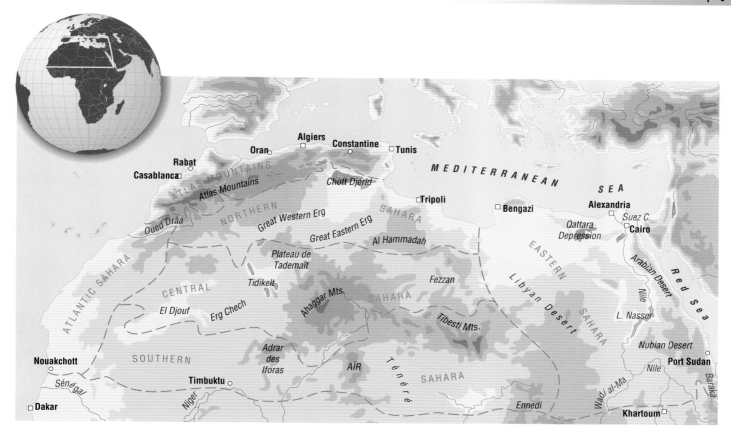

Sahara Desert

This type of desert surface is widespread. There is a very large area of it in northern Libya, called the *Hammāda al-Hamrā.* Where it comprises nothing more than exposed bedrock, hammada resembles a vast and rather uneven parking lot. It is probably the most inhospitable type of desert surface. Very little can live on it.

Saharan Climate

The Sahara is a hot desert. At Tamanrasset, in southern Algeria, the mean temperature ranges from 54°F (12°C) in January to 84°F (29°C) in July, but average temperatures can be misleading. Summer daytime temperatures exceed 90°F (32°C) for 8 months of the year and often exceed 100°F (38°C). At Al-'Aziziya, in Tripolitania, northern Libya, a temperature of 136.4°F (58°C) was once recorded, making this the hottest place on Earth.

At night, however, the temperature at Tamanrasset drops sharply, by as much as 50°F (28°C). Nights can be cold, and temperatures often fall below freezing in winter.

Rainfall is sparse, of course. The annual total amounts to less than 2 inches (51 mm).

The Arabian Desert

In the east the Sahara extends over virtually all of the Arabian Peninsula. Geologically, the Arabian Peninsula lies above ancient, hard rocks (called the *shield*) in the west and sedimentary rocks in the east. These slope down into the basin in which much of the Middle Eastern desert lies.

A range of mountains dominates the western side of Arabia. The mountains run parallel to the eastern coast of the Red Sea, the highest peaks rising to more than 9,000 feet (2,745 m). In some places two mountain ranges run parallel to each other, separated by a plateau. The northern section of the coastal belt, from Aqaba in the north to a point about 200 miles (320 km) south of Mecca, is called *Hejaz,* which means "the barrier." The southern section is called *Asir,* meaning "difficult."

East of the mountains, the central part of the Arabian shield is known as *Najd* ("highland"). It is marked by wadis running toward the east. They carry water during the rainy season, from January to May.

The biggest sand desert in the world lies to the south of the Najd. It is called *Rub' al-Khali,* the "empty quarter"—although the Bedouin who live there know it as *Ar Ramlah,* "the sand"—and it covers about 230,000 square miles (595,700 sq km). Despite its name, it includes watering places, so crossing it is not too dangerous for those familiar with the desert. The second biggest desert is more difficult to cross and has fewer watering places. Covering about 26,000 square miles (67,300 sq km) it is called *An Nafud* and lies to the north of the Najd.

The two deserts are linked by Dahna, a stream of sand 800 miles (1,290 km) long that is flowing slowly southward. Several roads and a railroad cross it, and during the rainy season it provides some grazing for livestock. In many places its sands are a reddish color and they form parallel ridges up to about 150 feet (45 m) high.

Climate of Arabia

Arabia has a desert climate, but in places the relative humidity can be high, making conditions clammy, especially at night. Rainfall is low, however, averaging no more than 4 inches (100 mm) a year. In Riyadh, the average is 3.2 inches (81.3). It is hot. December and January are the coolest months, with an average temperature of 70°F (21°C) during the day and 46°F (8°C) at night, although the averages conceal a wide range of extremes. A daytime temperature of 87°F (31°C) has been recorded in December and a nighttime minimum of 19°F (-7°C) in January.

From May to September the average daytime temperature is between 100°F (38°C) and 107°F (42°C), but 113°F (45°C) has been recorded. At night the temperature falls to between 72°F (22°C) and 78°F (26°C).

Characteristics of the Gobi, Takla Makan, and Thar Deserts

The Sahara and Arabian Deserts lie mainly within the Tropics. They are hot deserts produced by descending air on the poleward side of Hadley cells (page 42). This produces a belt of fairly permanent high pressure. Farther north, the deserts of Central Asia are also caused by persistent high pressure, but they are well clear of the Tropics and much cooler.

There are no towns in the Gobi Desert, but the capital of Mongolia, Ulan Bator (or Ulaan-baatar), lies not far from its northern margin. In July, the hottest month of the year, the average daytime temperature in Ulan Bator is 71°F (22°C), falling to 51°F (11°C) at night. The highest July temperature recorded was 92°F (33°C), but there has also been a July nighttime temperature of 34°F (1°C). January temperatures average -2°F (-19°C) during the day and -26°F (-32°C) at night, with a record high of 21°F (-6°C) and low of -47°F (-44°C).

Precipitation falls mainly in the summer. Ulan Bator has an average annual precipitation of about 8 inches (203 mm). This is typical for the northern and southeastern margins. In the center, the desert receives 1–2 inches (25–50 mm) a year.

Only the southeastern part of the desert is completely without water.

Defining the Gobi

There is some confusion about the definition of the *Gobi*. Mongolians often apply the word *gobi* to the bottoms of basins. These are usually level and sometimes marshy or covered with grass. Adding to the confusion, the Chinese name for the desert is *Sha-mo,* which means "sand desert," although sand dunes are confined to quite small areas.

With these qualifications, the location of the Gobi is shown on the map. The desert extends for about 1,000 miles (1,600 km) from west to east and about 600 miles (970 km) from north to south. It is bounded on its eastern side by the Da Hinggan Ling (Greater Kinghan Mountains), to the south by the Altun Shan and Qilian Shan (Nan Shan) Mountains, to the west by the Tien Shan Mountains, and to the north by the Altai, Hangayn Nuruu, and—across the border in Russia—Yablonovy Mountains. Surrounded by

mountains, the desert occupies a plateau at a height of 3,000 feet (914 m) in the east and rising to 5,000 feet (1,524 m) in the west.

The surface is bare rock or gravel over most of the desert, forming rolling plains with isolated hills and low ranges of hills with tops that have been flattened by erosion. About three-quarters of the area supports sparse vegetation consisting of grass, shrubs, and thornbushes.

The Takla Makan

West of the Gobi, in the Sinkiang Uighur (Xinjiang Uygur) Autonomous Region of China,

Gobi Desert

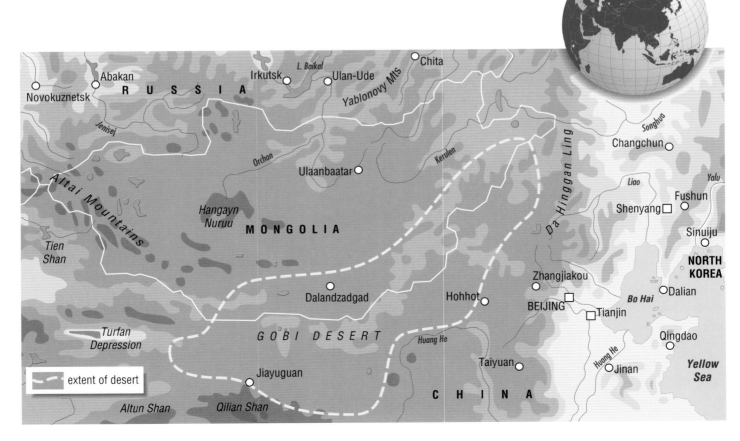

there is another desert, the Takla Makan (or Taklimakan). It occupies the center of the Tarim Basin, a low-lying area adjoining the river Tarim, on the northern edge of the desert.

Extending about 600 miles (970 km) from east to west and 250 miles (400 km) from north to south, the Takla Makan is a much more barren place than the Gobi. In winter the temperature falls to about -11°F (-24°C) and in summer it rises to about 86°F (30°C). The climate is extremely dry because air must cross high mountains to reach the desert and in doing so it loses the moisture it carries.

This is a sandy desert, especially in the south and southwest, where there are great expanses of shifting dunes interspersed with small, eroded hills and bare ground, swept clear by the incessant wind. Sandstorms are frequent and often last for days on end. There is some vegetation near the eastern and western edges, where there are permanent rivers, but nothing lives in the interior.

The Great Indian, or Thar, Desert

The Thar, or Great Indian, Desert covers about half of the Indian state of Rajasthan and part of eastern Pakistan. As this map shows, the desert is bordered to the south by the area of salt marsh in the delta of the Indus River known as the *Rann of Kutch* and to the west by the plain across which the Indus flows. In the southeast, the desert ends at the Aravalli Range of mountains, and in the northeast it gives way to less arid conditions in Punjab state. The distance from its southwestern to northeastern margins is about 500 miles (805 km) and from the southeast to northwest is about 300 miles (485 km).

This is a tropical desert—the tropic of Cancer passes through the Rann. In July the afternoon temperature can reach 127°F (52.8°C), but in January frosts can occur at night, although the mean January nighttime temperature is 55°F (12.7°C). The daytime temperature in January averages 70°F (21°C). Dust storms are common in April and May and again in October. There is little rain. The total ranges from about 10 inches (254 mm) a year in the east to about half that in the west, near the Indus. Rain falls mainly during the summer monsoon season, from June to September.

Air pressure over the Thar Desert is usually low. During winter, the mean daytime temperature is high enough to cause air to rise, producing low pressure near the surface. The air flowing in to fill the low is drawn from the regions of high pressure to the northwest. The high-pressure region extends over much of central Asia and its air is very dry. It produces offshore winds, carrying air

away from the land. During summer, the intertropical convergence zone (ITCZ, page 46) moves to a position where it lies to the north of the desert at ground level and to the south of the desert at a height of about 10,000 feet (3,000 m). This allows some moist air to enter from the sea, but at high altitude and at ground level in the east, air is still flowing from the continental landmass.

At its boundary with the Arvalli range, the Thar Desert is at an elevation of about 1,500 feet (457 m). From there it slopes to about 200 feet (61 m) near the Rann and the Indus Plain.

Thar Desert

It is a sandy desert. The name *thar* means "sandy waste." There are rock outcrops, but the surface consists mainly of rolling sandhills. In places the sand is mixed with silt and fine soil. Crops can be grown where irrigation is provided, although salt-laden dust is also carried into the area from the Indus River Delta and the Rann.

Characteristics of the Kalahari and Namib Deserts

South of the equator there are tropical deserts matching those of the north. They are smaller, but only because there is less land in the Southern Hemisphere than in the Northern. The two deserts of southern Africa are the Kalahari and the Namib.

The Kalahari Desert covers an area of about 275,000 square miles (712,250 sq km) in southwestern Botswana, northern South Africa, and southeastern Namibia, mostly between latitudes 20° S and 28° S. The map shows its general location. Its southern boundary is the Orange River in Cape Province. In the north it ends at valley of the Okovango River in Botswana. It merges into the Namib Desert in the northwest, but down the remainder of its western side the two deserts are separated by two ranges of hills, the Nama and Namara. On its eastern side the Kalahari gradually gives way to cultivated land.

Ngamiland and the Makarikari Pan

The northern edge of the Kalahari, near the Okovango River, is low-lying. After heavy rain the river overflows into this basin, producing extensive mud flats and swampy areas. Although the flow of water is irregular, the river terminates in an inland delta with an area of about 4,000 square miles (10,360 sq km) in a region called *Ngamiland*.

Lake Ngami, a little way to the south of the river, was discovered by David Livingstone in 1849. It is 40 miles (64 km) long and between 6 and 10 miles (10–16 km) wide, but very shallow and often dry. It receives water from several of the delta channels, but in 1887 the channel that until then had been the main source of its supply, called the Taokhe, became blocked by papyrus beds and since then no water has entered the lake by this route. Water reaches the head of the delta in March and arrives at the northeastern end of the lake by July or August, but the amount varies greatly from year to year. There is no natural outlet from the lake, so if it were to fill, two valleys would be inundated.

To the west of Lake Ngami there are salt flats in the Makarikari Pan, formed by the inflow and evaporation of water from the Okovango. The river water carries dissolved mineral salts. These remain as evaporite deposits when the water evaporates.

The Makarikari Pan is in the lowest part of the basin. Elsewhere the elevation is fairly uniform. The Kalahari occupies part of the wide southern African tableland that covers much of

the interior of Africa south of the equator. The average height is about 3,000 feet (900 m) in the west, rising to about 4,000 feet (1,220 m) in the east, and sloping into the low-lying Ngamiland region in the north.

It lies on rocks of Archaean age—formed more than 2.5 billion years ago. These are covered by more recent material. In most places the desert surface consists of red, sandy soil. Sand dunes are found in the drier parts, especially in the east.

Climate of the Kalahari

Despite being a desert, most of the Kalahari supports at least some vegetation, and, except in the most arid parts, it is more accurate to describe it as poor scrub, rather than desert. In the north the annual rainfall averages 25 inches (635 mm) and in the south 10 inches (254 mm). The climate is barely dry enough to produce a desert, but the rate of evaporation is high enough to remove much of the surface water before it can be absorbed by the ground, and in

the east the rainfall is only about 5 inches (127 mm) a year.

Average daytime temperatures range from about 90°F (32°C) in summer to 70°F (21°C) in winter, but frosts are fairly common on winter nights and summer temperatures can exceed 104°F (40°C). Francistown, Botswana, at an elevation of 3,294 feet (1,004 m) to the east of the Makarikari Pan near the Zimbabwean border, has a typical Kalahari climate. The average daytime temperature varies little through the year. June is the coolest month, with a temperature of 74°F (23°C), and October is the warmest, when the temperature averages 90°F (32°C). Night temperatures average 41°F (5°C) in midwinter and 65°F (18°C) in midsummer. Francistown receives an average 18 inches (457 mm) of rain a year, but most of this falls in summer, between November and March, and little or no rain falls from May to the end of September.

Kalahari Desert

The Namib

To the west, along the coastal strip between the hills lining the edge of the tableland, the Namib Desert is much drier than the Kalahari. It receives an average of about 2 inches (51 mm) of rain a year. Walvis Bay, on the Atlantic coast of Namibia and 24 feet (7 m) above sea level, has a total of 0.8 inches (20 mm) of rain a year and for 7 months no rain at all can be expected. The climate is not especially hot, however. At Walvis Bay the average daytime temperature is between 66°F (19°C) and 75°F (24°C) throughout the year. At night the temperature falls to 46–60°F (8–16°C).

The Benguela Current

Walvis Bay lies just miles north of the tropic of Capricorn, where it might be expected to have a much warmer and more markedly seasonal climate. That it does not is due to the Benguela Current—Benguela is a town on the coast of Angola.

This is a cold current that flows northward along the coast, moving slowly, at about 5.6 mph (9 km/h). It flows from the edge of the Antarctic Ocean as a stream of water blown in an easterly direction by the West Wind Drift and turning north just south of the African continent. For part of its journey the current flows beneath the warmer, less dense water, but there are many upwellings, where cold water reaches the surface.

Land Breezes, Sea Breezes, and Fog

In this part of Africa the prevailing winds are the very dependable southeasterly trade winds, but land and sea breezes are more evident along the coast. At about 10 A.M. on most days the sea breeze begins as the land warms, air over the land rises, and cool air blows in from the west to fill the low pressure. Despite having crossed the ocean, this air brings no rain, because it was chilled as it crossed the cold water of the Benguela Current and its water vapor condensed. It does produce cool conditions over land, however. During the course of the day the wind

direction changes slowly from west to south-southwest. The sea breeze is often strong, especially south of the Orange River, where its speed exceeds 30 mph (48 km/h) for most of the afternoon, driving sand and dust inland.

Soon after sunset the wind drops. The land cools very quickly and the calm air soon changes into a gentle land breeze blowing from the north. This continues through the night. Easterly winds, called *berg* winds, are also fairly common, carrying warm, very dry air. They occur mainly on winter mornings, as the sea breeze overpowers them in the afternoon.

Warm, moist air from the tropical Atlantic is cooled as it crosses the Benguela Current. Its water vapor condenses, but as low cloud and fog rather than rain and fog—known in Angola as *cacimbo*—the most characteristic feature of the Namibian climate. At night it is cool enough for the cloud and fog to drift over the coast and there is often a fine drizzle. The sky soon clears in the morning. In Walvis Bay there is fog on an average of 55 days a year.

Sea fog across coastal Namib (Gerry Ellis/ENP Images)

Dimensions of the Namib

The northern margin of the Namib Desert is some distance south of Luanda, Angola. Luanda, at 8°49' S, receives an average of 13 inches (330 mm) of rain a year. The Angolan seaport of Namibe, at 15°12' S, receives 2 inches (50 mm). Farther south the rainfall is even lower. The desert extends southward for about 1,200 miles (1,930 km), across the Orange River and into Cape Province, South Africa. Nowhere is it more than about 100 miles (160 km) wide.

Over the northern part of the Namib the surface is covered mainly with gravel. The ground is level, but with isolated, steep-sided hills called *inselbergs*. In the south there is more sand, with large dunes shaped into parallel lines by the sea breezes and berg winds.

Characteristics of the Atacama Desert and Patagonia

If the Namib Desert is dry, its South American counterpart may be even drier. In parts of the Atacama Desert (Desierto de Atacama), in Chile, the average annual precipitation amounts to about 0.4 inches (10 mm) and it arrives as fog, not rain. Rain can be expected no more than two to four times a century. Over a period of 21 years the town of Iquique received an average 0.06 inches (1.5 mm) of rain a year. This was not spread evenly. There was one 5-year period during which no rain at all fell for the first 4 years and in July of the fifth year—July is in the "rainy" season!—a single shower delivered 0.6 inches (15 mm). Showers have been known to deliver 2.5 inches (64 mm), however. Although rain is rare, Iquique is on the coast and the relative humidity is usually about 75 percent—bare iron rusts rapidly there. Arica, in the north, received an average of less than 0.03 inches (0.75 mm) a year over a 19-year period. Antofagasta and Copiapó each receive 0.6 inches (14 mm) a year, in the case of Antofagasta, a 22-year average. Rainfall increases toward the southern end of the desert. La Serena, at 30° S, receives 5.6 inches (142 mm), and Valparaíso, at 33° S, receives 19.7 inches (500 mm). Local people say that an earthquake is much more likely than a week of rain.

Perhaps the driest desert in the world, the Atacama covers about 140,000 square miles (363,000 sq km) in northern Chile, mainly in the Antofagasta and Atacama Regions. The tropic of Capricorn passes through its center, so it lies farther north than the Namib. It is a narrow desert, running parallel to the coast for about 600 miles (965 km). The map shows its location.

Moderate Temperatures and a Cold Current

Despite its tropical location, the desert climate is not hot. The average temperature is about 65°F (18.3°C) and, because the latitude is tropical, it varies little through the year. At Antofagasta January and February are the warmest months, with daytime temperatures averaging 76°F (24°C). In August, the coolest month, the average daytime temperature is 62°F (16.6°C). Nor is there much difference between daytime and nighttime temperatures, which range from about 51°F (11°C) to 63°F (17°C).

A cool, very dry climate in a coastal region suggests the presence of a cool ocean current, and South America has its equivalent of the Benguela Current. It is called the *Peru Current,* or some-times the *Humboldt Current,* after the German traveler and scientist Friedrich Heinrich Alexander von Humboldt (1769–1859). Von Humboldt measured the sea temperature in the current in the course of his exploration of South America between 1800 and 1804.

The Peru Current flows northward close to the coast, turning to flow westward as it meets the "bulge" of South America. It originates in the Antarctic Ocean, as the Benguela Current does, and although it flows beneath warmer, therefore less dense, surface water, there are frequent upwellings that carry cool water to the surface. These occur because the prevailing tropical winds, the southeast trade winds, drive the Equatorial Current, which carries warm water away from the South American coast and toward Asia, where it forms a deep pool in the region of Indonesia. Off the South American coast the layer of warm water is kept thin enough by this constant removal of surface water for the cooler water to break through. During an El Niño–Southern Oscillation (ENSO) episode the pattern changes and heavy rain falls in Peru, where the climate is usually dry, but this change does not help the Atacama. It receives no benefit from the El Niño rains.

The prevailing wind is from the southwest during the day. At night, land breezes blow from the northeast or east. Gales are rare north of 30° S—south of this latitude their frequency increases toward the "roaring forties." Warm air is chilled as it crosses the Peru Current, and low cloud and fog are common, just as they are along the Namibian coast.

A High Plateau

There the similarity ends, because most of the Atacama Desert lies a little farther inland and is separated from the coast by mountains. Coastal cliffs are 2,000–3,000 feet (610–915 m) high and the coastal mountains rise to about 9,000 feet (2,745 m). Inland from the mountains, the desert lies in a depression, but still at an average elevation of about 2,000 feet (610 m). Its height contributes to the moderate temperatures. On its eastern side the desert is bordered by high mountains, such as the Cordillera de Domeyko range, that form part of the Andes chain.

Air reaching the coast from the ocean loses most of its moisture at sea, where it is chilled. It is dry when it arrives. Any remaining moisture is lost as the air rises to cross the coastal ranges, forming cloud that rarely brings rain, although sometimes it may be low enough to be called fog. Air from the southwest crosses the South American continent, then loses such moisture as it carries during its ascent over the Andes. This is the combination of geographical circumstances that makes the Atacama so extremely arid.

The aridity continues on the eastern side of the Domeyko Mountains, where the desert rises to a height varying from 7,000 feet (2,100 m) to 13,500 feet (4,100 m). The high, bleak Andean plateau is known generally as the *altiplano* and in this part of Peru and Chile as the *puna.* The desert region is called the *Puna de Atacama.* Within the Puna there is another region, the Salar de Atacama, where there are basins rich in mineral salts.

Away from the influence of the ocean current, temperatures are higher, despite the elevation, and the diurnal variation is greater. In summer the temperature can rise to 90°F (32°C), but on winter nights often falls to below freezing as the ground loses its heat by radiation and fog forms.

Bolsons and Minerals

The desert is not level. The mountains were formed by movements of crustal rocks that caused much faulting, with blocks being thrust upward and leaving deep basins between the faulted blocks (page 28). Such a basin is called a *bolson;* in the Atacama their surfaces are 2,000–3,000 feet (610–915 m) below the level of the equivalent rocks in the raised blocks. The structure produces a characteristic surface. In the center there is a level plain, called a *playa* or *salina.* Near its edges it begins to slope gently upward, in a region called the *pediment,* and is covered with broken rock.

Nothing lives in the Puna de Atacama. There is just brown earth and dust. In the lower desert, west of the Domeyko Mountains, some tough grasses and a small amount of other vegetation manage to survive. There is some very sparse vegetation on the coastal strip. In general, though, the Atacama is one of the bleakest, most forbidding places on Earth.

Despite this, in the last century Chile and Bolivia fought for the part of the Atacama Desert that lies between latitudes 23° S and 26° S. The War of the Pacific lasted from 1879 until 1884 and ended with Chile in control of the area. The treaty confirming this was signed in 1904 and made Bolivia into an entirely landlocked country. The war was not fought simply for control of a worthless desert. The Salar de Atacama, in the bolsons, contains some of the richest deposits of sodium nitrate and copper in the world. At first the attraction was the nitrate deposits, the raw material for fertilizer and explosive manufacture. Then, from about 1920, after the introduction of the Haber process for manufacturing ammonia industrially, the mining companies switched their effort to the copper reserves. The Haber process, discovered by the German chemist Fritz Haber (1868–1934), produces ammonia (NH_3) from atmospheric nitrogen. Nitrate (NO_3) can be made cheaply from ammonia.

Patagonia

Far to the south, there is another South American desert that lies between the mountains and a cold ocean current. Patagonia is the whole of Argentina lying to the east of the Andes and south of the Colorado River at latitude 39° S. Its total area is about 300,000 square miles (777,000 sq km), making it the biggest desert in either North or South America.

It is also unique. There is no other desert in the world lying on the eastern side of a continent in a latitude north of 40° S. It is far less arid than the Atacama Desert, but nowhere is the average annual rainfall as high as 10 inches (254 mm), the precipitation threshold below which a desert will form regardless of the temperature. Sarmiento, a town near the center of Patagonia, at 45°36' S, has a climate that is fairly typical of the region. The wettest months are in winter, from April to August, but barely more than 5 inches (127 mm) of rain falls in an average year. The average daytime temperature ranges from 45°F (7°C) in July to 78°F (26°C) in January.

A Series of Terraces

Patagonia occupies high ground, most of it more than 2,000 feet (610 m) above sea level, and rises like a series of terraces from the high coastal cliffs in the east to the Andes in the west. The terrain is broken by deeply incised valleys that are aligned from west to east. Some of the valleys are dry, rivers flow through others for part of the year, but few carry rivers that flow all the time. Hills rise from the plain, made from hard rocks resistant to the weathering that has eroded the material around them. On the western side, where the plateau meets the Andean foothills,

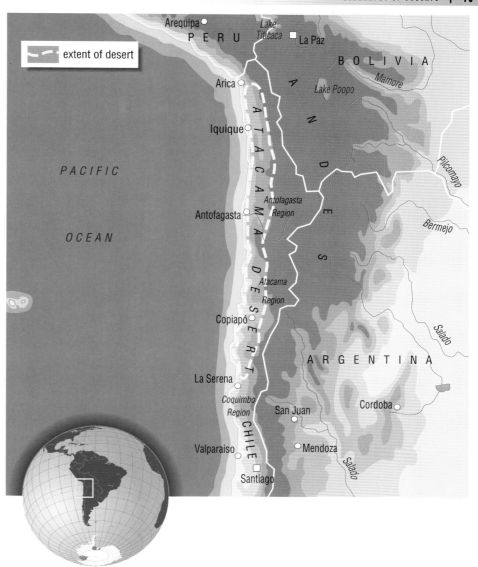

there are lakes, sealed on one side by glacial moraines and extending westward into deep mountain canyons.

The Falkland Current

Patagonia is far enough south to lie in the belt of westerly prevailing winds. These carry air over the Andes, where it loses its moisture. Patagonia is in the rain shadow of the high mountain range. Winds blowing from the sea must cross a cold ocean current. Along the northern edge of the Antarctic Ocean, the West Wind Drift drives a surface current. Part of this current turns north in the Pacific, forming the Peru Current, and

Atacama Desert

another part turns north in the Atlantic, forming the Benguela Current, but there is a smaller part that turns north south of the tip of South America. This branch flows north along the eastern coast, between the coast and the Falkland Islands. This is the Falkland Current, chilling air that approaches Patagonia from the east.

The Patagonian Desert is bleak, but not all of it is barren. In the north there are tough grasses and shrubs, and the grasses provide pasture for sheep. There is little vegetation farther south, where the climate is colder as well as drier.

Characteristics of the Australian Desert

The tropic of Capricorn passes across the center of Australia. This means the country lies close enough to the trade wind latitudes for the prevailing winds to be from the southeast. These bring maritime conditions, with abundant rain, to the coast of New South Wales and Queensland. Brisbane, Queensland, for example, enjoys an average annual rainfall of about 45 inches (1,136 mm). Sydney, New South Wales, receives about 46 inches (1,183 mm). In both cities the rainfall is distributed fairly evenly through the year.

Inland from the densely populated coastal strip there is a range of mountains, the Great Dividing Range, that runs the entire length of the country parallel to the eastern coast (and continues into Tasmania). Consequently, lands to the west of the mountains lie in a rain shadow. A second mountain range extends along an approximately southwest—northeast line from the Yorke Peninsula, South Australia, until it merges with the Great Dividing Range at about the tropic of Capricorn. The southern part of this range is called the *Main Barrier Range* and the northern section is the *Grey Range*.

Rainfall

There are thus two lines of high ground over which air must rise as it moves inland and where the southeasterly trade winds lose moisture. The 20-inch (500-mm) isohyet (line on a map joining places of equal rainfall) runs along the Great Dividing Range. To its west is the 15-inch (380-mm) isohyet, and to the west of the second range is the 10-inch (250-mm) isohyet. An average rainfall of 10 inches a year is the limit below which desert usually forms regardless of the average temperature.

Most of the interior of Australia is either semiarid or desert. Of all the continents, Australia is by far the driest.

To Australians the figure that matters is not so much the amount of rainfall as its usefulness to farmers. If the amount of rain that falls during a month is greater than one-third of the amount that would evaporate from an open water surface during the same period, the rain is said to be *effective*—precipitation exceeds potential evaporation from the soil. If there is an effective amount of rain for at least 5 months of the year agriculture is possible. With less than 5 months of effective rain the only crops that can be grown are those that mature rapidly in valley bottoms and other depressions, where the water table is within reach of their roots. The 5-month line runs across the north of the country on the southern side of Arnhem Land to the Gulf of Carpentaria. From the western side of the Cape York Peninsula in the north it runs southeast about to the tropic, then south-southwest to approximately the latitude of Sydney, and then west more or less parallel with the coast as far as Perth. Most of the land enclosed by this line is semiarid and much of it is desert. Alice Springs, just south of the tropic and almost exactly at the center of Australia, has an average rainfall of just under 10 inches (250 mm) a year.

Continental Climate

Australia is an island, but an island the size of a continent, and, away from the coasts, it has a continental climate—dry and with extremes of temperature, compared with the moister, milder climate of an island. A large proportion of the total area of Australia experiences a continental climate because of the shape of the continent. It is very compact, especially along its west–east axis, with no deep embayments to bring the ocean closer to the center of the landmass and extend its climatic influence inland. This combines with the rain-shadow effect to increase the aridity, partly by increasing the extremes of temperature.

Alice Springs is in the foothills of the Macdonnell Ranges, the highest of which is Mount Ziel, at 4,954 feet (1,510 m), and the town itself is at 1,901 feet (579 m). The hottest month is January, with an average daytime temperature of 97°F (36°C), but the temperature usually exceeds 90°F (32°C) from November through March. In midwinter the temperature falls to about 67°F (19°C). These are averages, however, and the temperature can fall below freezing in winter and in summer has been known to reach 111°F (44°C). Kalgoorlie, Western Australia, is at a similar elevation (1,247 feet [370 m]) farther south, to the west of the Great Victoria Desert and Nullarbor Plain. It receives an average of 9.7 inches (246 mm) of rain, about the same as Alice Springs, and its temperatures are also fairly similar. In January the average daytime temperature is 93°F (34°C), but 115°F (46°C) is not unknown. In July the daytime temperature averages 62°F (17°C) but has been known to reach 81°F (27°C). High temperatures increase the rate of evaporation.

Plateaus, Tablelands, and Lowlands

Geologically, Australia is a very ancient continent, in the sense that its rocks were not affected by movements of the Earth that elsewhere raised great mountain ranges such as the Himalayas, Atlas, Alps, and American Cordillera (page 28). Much of it lies on rocks of Precambrian age, (more than 570 million years old) and, except in the east, typical Australian landscapes are those of plains and plateaus. Where rugged features do occur they are due to ravines or steep-sided valleys cut through the plateaus by rivers that flowed in the remote past. Even the ranges of hills are rounded, but there are also isolated, flat-topped hills, the larger ones called *mesas* and the smaller ones *buttes*. Only about 7 percent of the total land area is more than 2,000 feet (610 m) above sea level, and the average elevation is between 1,000 and 1,500 feet (305–460 m).

The main platform of Precambrian rock—the shield—is broken into a number of distinct blocks separated by lowland areas. It is in the lowland regions that the deserts have formed.

The Five Deserts

Australia has not one desert but five. Four are on the western side of the country and the fifth is approximately in the center. In the northern part of Western Australia is the Great Sandy Desert. It lies partly in the Canning Basin, less than 600 feet (183 m) above sea level. Nowhere does the Great Sandy Desert rise above (1,200 feet (370 m).

To its south on slightly higher ground, there is the Gibson Desert, lying right on the tropic north of the aptly named Lake Disappointment. The tableland rises to the south of the Gibson Desert. In the lowland still farther south the Great Victoria Desert stretches across nearly half the width of Western Australia and to halfway across South Australia.

The Nullarbor Plain lies immediately to the south of the Great Victoria Desert. It is not called a desert, but the plain is a very arid and virtually uninhabited limestone plateau.

The Macdonnell Ranges lie to the east of the Gibson Desert, with Alice Springs in their southeastern foothills. On low ground to the southeast of the ranges the Simpson Desert, less than 500 feet (150 m) above sea level, occupies the southeastern corner of the Northern Territory and part of northern South Australia and western Queensland. It lies to the north of Lake Eyre, one of the largest of a number of salt lakes and the lowest point on the continent, about 60 feet (18 m) below sea level. Despite being called a lake, Lake Eyre most of the time is a sheet of

salt, 90 miles (145 km) long and 40 miles (64 km) wide, that is firm enough to drive a truck across.

Desert Surfaces and Vegetation

The desert surfaces vary. In places it is bare rock, elsewhere gravel or pebbles shaped by the wind. These small stones are called *gibber* in Australia and a large expanse of them is a *gibber* *plain*. There are sand dunes in the Simpson Desert.

The deserts are not lifeless, except locally. In some areas the desert is bordered by a savanna type of vegetation comprising grasses and *Acacia* scrub, called *mulga,* in others by dwarf eucalyptus scrub, called *mallee.* There are also areas of *Acacia* scrub, called *brigalow.* Over most of the Great Sandy, Gibson, and Great Victoria Deserts the soil is sandy and the principal vegetation

Pinnacle formations, Nambung National Park (Gerry Ellis/ENP Images)

consists of various species of porcupine grasses (*Triodia* species) and cane grass (*Spinifex paradoxus*). Farther south and southeast the soil is salty and supports saltbushes and other salt-tolerant plants.

Characteristics of the North and Central American Deserts

It is one of the hottest places on Earth. In July the average temperature is 116°F (47°C), and it has been known to rise to 134°F (57°C) in the shade. At night the temperature falls to an average 87°F (31°C). Winter temperatures are much lower, but 85°F (29°C) has been known in January, the coldest month. It is dry and often windy. Sandstorms and whirling dust devils are common. The average rainfall amounts to no more than 2 inches (50 mm) a year.

Death Valley, California, was named in 1849. That was the year a party of 30 settlers used it as a shortcut to the California gold fields and 12 of them perished. By the end of the last century, however, the valley had become a winter resort.

The valley is hotter and drier than anywhere else in the United States. It is also lower. About 4.75 miles (7.6 km) west of Badwater there is the lowest point on the North American continent—282 feet (86 m) below sea level. The region is a national park with an area of 5,315 square miles (13,765 sq km), and about 550 square miles (1,425 sq km) of that area lies below sea level.

In the lowest parts of the valley the surface comprises salt flats. It is not devoid of water. There are springs, marshes, and pools, but the water is salt—in many places it is much saltier than seawater. Despite this the pools support several species of pupfish, one of which, the Devil's Hole pupfish (*Cyprinodon diabolis*), is found nowhere else in the world. On higher ground there is a mixture of salt and sand grains. Cacti and other succulent plants grow in the valley, and when there is sufficient rainfall annual herbs appear in the early spring. Lizards, snakes, rabbits, rodents, and foxes live in the valley throughout the year.

Mojave Desert

Death Valley lies between two mountain ranges. Part of the Amargosa Range forms its eastern boundary, and in the west it is bounded by the Panamint Range. To the southwest, beyond the mountains, is the much larger Mojave Desert, covering an area of 15,000 square miles (38,850 sq km).

The Mojave Desert lies to the south and east of the Sierra Nevada, extending south to the San Bernardino Mountains and the Colorado River. Both it and Death Valley are in the rain shadow of the mountain ranges to the west. Maritime air crossing the mountains from the ocean is forced to rise—the process is called *orographic lifting*—and this causes it to expand, cool to below its dew point temperature, and lose most of its moisture as rain. By the time it reaches the lee side of the mountains the air is very dry. The average rainfall is less than 5 inches (127 mm).

Occasionally the precipitation falls as snow, and frosts are fairly common on winter nights, when the temperature falls to 15–30°F (-2.8 to -34.4°C). Winter days are mild, however, with temperatures of about 55°F (12.8°C). In summer, daytime temperatures often exceed 100°F (37.8°C).

Surrounded by mountains, the Mojave's scenery is dramatic. The mountains are rugged and rise steeply from level basins where the surface is of gravel and sand. In the center of the desert there are salt flats from which a variety of chemical compounds are extracted.

Cattle graze on part of the Mojave and in the mountains there are open juniper and piñon woodlands. Elsewhere the vegetation consists of low shrubs (page 70).

Colorado Desert

The San Bernardino Mountains mark the southern boundary of the Mojave Desert. Beyond the mountains, starting at the San Gorgonio Pass, the Colorado Desert extends into Baja California, Mexico. As well as the San Bernardino Mountains, the Chocolate, Chuckwalla, and Cottonwood ranges separate the Colorado and Mojave Deserts. The map shows where these and the other North American deserts lie in relation to each other.

The Colorado Desert is about 200 miles (320 km) long and 50 miles (80 km) wide, much of it below sea level. The Salton Sea is a brackish lake, the bed of which is 235 feet (72 m) below sea level. The Imperial and Coachella Valleys are also low-lying.

Rainfall rarely exceeds 4 inches (102 mm) a year and temperatures can change rapidly, from 32°F (0°C) to 115°F (46.1°C). Between May and September daytime temperatures average 90°F (32°C), and they can reach 125°F (52°C). There

Mojave Desert (Michael Durham/ENP Images)

are shifting sand dunes in the northwest and among the sandhills to the east.

Surprisingly, the soils of the Imperial Valley are very fertile and irrigation is supplied from a canal leading from the Colorado River. The valley is renowned for its cotton, vegetables, and fruit.

Painted Desert

To the northeast, near the upper end of the Grand Canyon, the Little Colorado flows into the Colorado River. The Painted Desert, in Arizona, stretches for about 150 miles (241 km) along the northeastern side of the Little Colorado. It is between 15 and 50 miles (24–80 km) wide and covers an area of about 7,500 square miles (19,425 sq km). Part of the eastern region of the Painted Desert lies within the Petrified Forest National Park.

Lieutenant Joseph C. Ives is said to have given the desert its name. An explorer employed by the government, he visited the desert in 1858 and was struck by the brilliant colors of its rocks. These include shales, sandstones, and marls and have bright bands of red, yellow, blue, white, and lavender. Navajo and Hopi people, who live in the desert, use its colored sands for their ceremonial sand paintings. On its northern side the desert is bounded by vermilion cliffs that are the sides of large mesas.

This desert lies on high ground, with elevations ranging from 4,500 feet (1,373 m) to 6,500 feet (1,983 m). Isolated buttes rise from a generally rolling surface. It is a colorful place, but barren. The annual rainfall varies from 5 to 9 inches (127–229 mm) and temperatures are extreme. They can fall to -25°F (-32°C) and rise to 105°F (41°C).

Sonoran (Yuma) Desert

Yuma is a town in southern Arizona, very near the Mexican border, and it gives its name to the largest desert in North America, the Yuma Desert. This is not its only name. It is also called Carson Plains and the Sonoran Desert. *Sonora* is the name of a state in Mexico. The desert lies mainly in southwestern Arizona, southeastern California, and northwestern Sonora. On its western side the desert borders the Gulf of California. On its other

sides it borders other deserts or semiarid regions—the Mojave Desert to the northwest, the dry Arizona highlands to the northeast, and the Sierra Madre Occidental, in Chihuahua, Mexico, to the east. In all, the desert covers 119,692 square miles (310,000 sq km).

Most of the desert is low-lying, with an average elevation of about 1,000 feet (305 m), but mountains rise steeply from the floors of the broad basins, where the surface is of sand and gravel. There are salt flats in the lowest basins, especially in the Coachella–Imperial Valley in the northwest, which lies below sea level. The Chocolate and Chuckwalla Mountains of California, Kofa and Harquahala Mountains of Arizona, and Mount Pinacate in Mexico are within the desert.

Few parts of the desert receive more than 10 inches (254 mm) of rain a year, and the annual rainfall is often only about 5 inches (127 mm). Frosts can occur in winter, but the climate is typ-

Deserts of the western United States

ically warm in winter and hot in summer. Winter temperatures rise to 60–70°F (15.5–21°C) by day and fall to 40–50°F (4–10°C) at night. In summer the daytime temperature often exceeds 110°F (43°C).

There is a variety of vegetation. Tall shrubs and trees grow along dry riverbeds, creosote bushes and sage in the basins, and cacti, including the giant saguaro, on higher ground. The desert also provides habitat for many reptiles, including at least six species of rattlesnakes and the venomous lizard the Gila monster (*Heloderma suspectum*).

Much of the area is protected. There are several wildlife refuges and the Joshua Tree and Saguaro National Parks lie within the desert. Its mild winters have long made Palm Springs, Tucson, and Phoenix popular resorts.

Cold Deserts

As this map shows, most of Antarctica receives less than 8 inches (200 mm) of precipitation a year and a substantial area at the center of the continent receives less than 2 inches (50 mm). Near the South Pole, the average precipitation is probably no more than 1 inch (25 mm) a year.

Visitors usually travel no farther than the coastal strip or the tip of the long Antarctic Peninsula. They see a different type of weather, with warmer temperatures and much more precipitation. In summer, which is the only season when the continent is easily accessible, the temperature near the coast can rise to 32°F (0°C). This is not warm enough to melt the ice and snow but is comfortable enough for visitors, provided there is only a light wind.

There is abundant snow. Precipitation near the coast averages about 15 inches (380 mm) a year. It will seem to be much more, because snow is about 10 times bulkier than liquid water and precipitation is always measured as its equivalent in rain.

Winds are often fierce. Air crossing the ocean gathers moisture and is warmer than air over the land. Where the two types of air meet, huge storms are produced. These generate strong gales and heavy precipitation. They are confined to the coastal area, however, and tend to travel fairly quickly around the edge of the continent.

Blizzards

Inland, the weather is different. There, precipitation is light, but the winds are at least as strong. Gales have been known to blow at 200 mph (320 km/h). Strong winds produce blizzards, but these are not blizzards of falling snow. The fine, powdery snow they carry has been lifted from the ground and is being transported. Blizzards in the Antarctic interior are the equivalent of the sandstorms and dust storms of tropical deserts.

Some of the snow is lost by *ablation*. This is a fairly general term describing losses by melting and evaporation and sublimation. Although the air temperature rarely rises above freezing, even at the coast, the surface layer of snow can absorb enough solar warmth for a little of it to melt, and the resulting liquid water evaporates quickly in the very dry air. Inland, where the air carries very little water vapor, some snow can vaporize directly.

Losses by sublimation are very small, however, and most of such little snow as does fall inland becomes permanently trapped. This is how a land receiving less precipitation than the Sahara can lie buried beneath such a thick layer of ice.

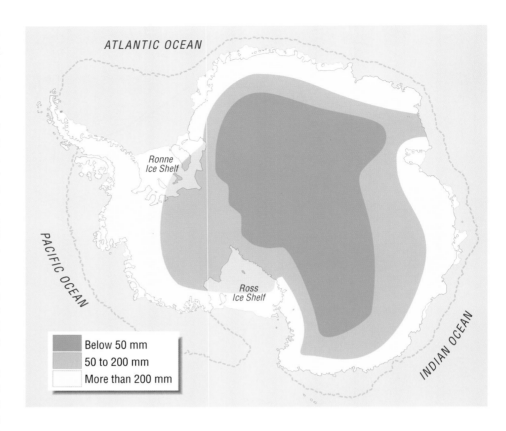

ATLANTIC OCEAN

PACIFIC OCEAN

INDIAN OCEAN

Ronne Ice Shelf

Ross Ice Shelf

Below 50 mm
50 to 200 mm
More than 200 mm

Antarctica: precipitation

Why Antarctica Is Cold and Dry

It does not explain why Antarctica is so cold and so dry. There are several reasons for this.

The first and most obvious explanation is astronomical. Antarctica receives only diffuse sunlight (page 22), and even in summer the Sun never rises high above the horizon. Summer is a time of almost constant daylight—the "midnight Sun"—and winter of almost constant darkness. Climatically, this means that any warmth the ground absorbs during the long days of summer is lost during the long nights of winter, and during winter there is little or no direct heating of the surface by the Sun.

When the Sun does shine, most of its light and heat are reflected. The reflectivity of a surface is called its *albedo* and it can be measured. Freshly fallen snow has an albedo of 75–95 percent. That is the proportion of solar radiation it reflects. Dry sand also has a fairly high albedo, but of only 35–45 percent. For comparison, a field of grass has an albedo of 10–20 percent.

Antarctica is the fifth largest continent. Its total area, of about 4.8 million square miles (12.4 million sq km), is more than half that of North America and considerably more than that of Australia. Its center is a long way from the ocean and

air has ample opportunity to lose any moisture it may be carrying long before it arrives there.

It is also the highest of all the continents. The average elevation of the rock surface, beneath the ice, is about 8,000 feet (2,440 m) above sea level and there are several mountain ranges. The highest point on the continent is the Vinson Massif, in the Ellsworth Mountains of West Antarctica at 16,860 feet (5,139 m). The continent is divided into distinct eastern and western parts by the Transantarctic Mountains. The height of its surface makes the climate even colder, because air temperature decreases with height. The actual surface is higher, because of the ice. A person standing on the ice will be about 14,900 feet (4,545 m) above sea level.

Over both North and South Poles cold, dense air is subsiding, producing areas of permanently high surface atmospheric pressure. Air flows outward from areas of high pressure. This increases the aridity, because moist air is unable to penetrate the region at low level.

In Antarctica, it is the outward movement of air that produces the constant winds. High pressure near the center of the continent pushes sur-

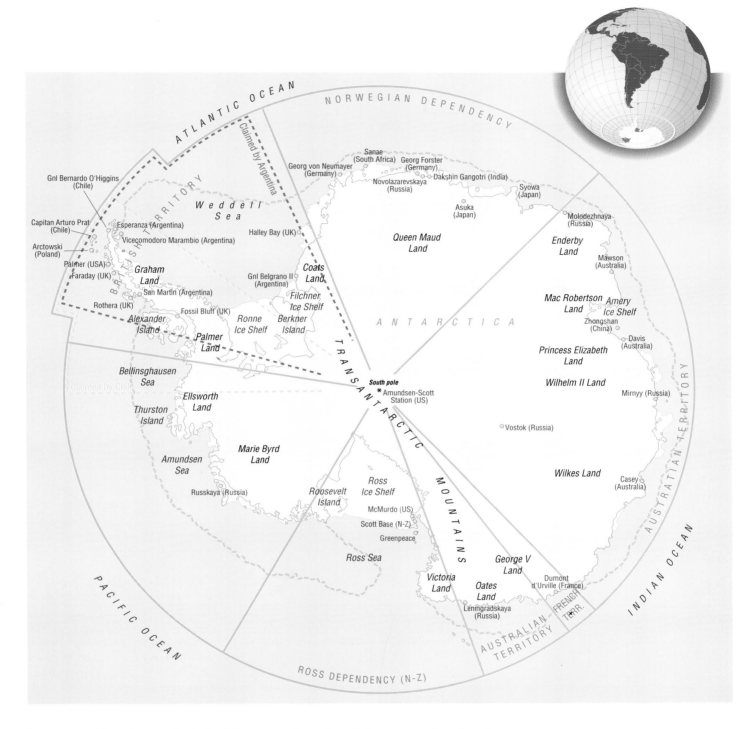

Antarctica

face air outward, but as it moves the air also sinks toward lower ground. This accelerates the gravitational flow, often producing winds of hurricane force (speeds greater than 75 mph, [121 km/h]).

Arctic Weather

Cold, dense air is also sinking over the North Pole, producing an Arctic region of permanently high atmospheric pressure similar to that in the Antarctic. Air flows outward from it, but the cli-

mate it produces is less extreme than that of Antarctica.

Spitzbergen, Norway, is at latitude 78°04' N. In July, the average temperature is 45°F (7°C). January and February are the coldest months, with average temperatures of 19°F (-7°C) by day and 7°F (-14°C) by night.

There are colder places. The coldest place in the Northern Hemisphere—known as the *cold pole*—is Verkhoansk, Siberia, where -90.4°F (-68°C) has been recorded. The lowest temperature ever recorded in North America was -85°F (-65°C) at Snag, Yukon.

Both these places lie well within the Arctic Circle and illustrate the fact that the Antarctic is much colder than the Arctic. It is also drier, although most of the region enclosed by the Arctic Circle also has a desert climate. The difference between the two arises from the fact that Antarctica is a large continent with a high elevation and the Arctic region is not. The North Pole lies beneath the Arctic Ocean.

Ice Sheets and Glaciers

Most of the continent of Antarctica—about 98 percent of its total surface area—lies beneath a layer of ice averaging about 6,900 feet (2,100 m) in thickness and containing about 90 percent of all the world's ice and about 98 percent of all the fresh water on Earth. Such a large volume of ice can exist in a region where the annual rate of precipitation is so low only if that rate of precipitation is nevertheless higher than the rate at which water is lost and if the ice has been accumulating for a long time.

At the Vostok Station scientists have drilled out cores of ice in order to study details of past climates. Much can be learned about climates from the chemical composition of tiny bubbles of air that were captured between ice crystals as the ice formed, and from the ratio of oxygen isotopes (the ratio of $^{16}O{:}^{18}O$). They have drilled to a depth of more than 6,500 feet (2,000 m) and recovered ice that formed more than 150,000 years ago.

This suggests the ice has been accumulating at an average rate of about half an inch (1 cm) a year. Some years ago scientists also drilled ice cores near a research station called Byrd, in Marie Byrd Land, at about latitude 80° S, that has since closed. They calculated that ice at a depth of 1,000 feet (300 m) had formed from snow that fell 1,600 years ago, a formation rate of about 0.6 inch (1.8 cm) a year. The rate of accumulation is not constant over very long periods. When the world climate is cool, and especially during ice ages, it is also dry. Precipitation decreases (*see page 5*) and polar ice accumulates more slowly. During warm periods the reverse happens and climates become wetter.

Snow into Ice

Place some water in a freezer to make ice cubes and as its temperature falls the water changes into ice. Its molecules move toward one another and form crystals.

A water molecule consists of two atoms of hydrogen (H_2) and one atom of oxygen (O), making the familiar H_2O. These atoms are arranged in a V shape, with the oxygen at the bottom of the V and the two hydrogen atoms separated by an angle of 104.5°. The bond holding the molecule together is covalent: that is, it is based on the attraction between the positive electric charge on the protons in the atomic nuclei and the negative charge on the electrons surrounding the nuclei but with the atoms sharing electrons.

ISOTOPES

The nucleus of an atom comprises two types of particle. There are protons, which carry a positive electromagnetic charge, and neutrons, which are neutral. The number of protons in the nucleus determines the chemical characteristics of the atom, so all atoms of any chemical element contain the same number of protons in their nuclei. Neutrons do not affect the chemical behavior of the atom and atoms of an element may contain different numbers of neutrons. Varieties of an element that have different numbers of neutrons in their atomic nuclei are called isotopes of that element. All the isotopes of an element are identical chemically, but because of the different number of neutrons their nuclei contain their atoms have different masses.

Oxygen has three isotopes, oxygen-16, oxygen-17, and oxygen-18. These are usually written as ^{16}O, ^{17}O, and ^{18}O. Oxygen consists of 99.7 percent ^{16}O, 0.04 percent ^{17}O, and 0.2 percent ^{18}O. Ordinarily, air contains 1 atom of ^{18}O to every 499 atoms of ^{16}O.

When hydrogen is oxidized to form water ($2H_2 + O_2 \rightarrow 2H_2O$) this ratio continues, but molecules containing ^{16}O ($H_2{}^{16}O$) are lighter than those containing ^{18}O ($H_2{}^{18}O$). This means they travel faster and are better able to escape into the air from liquid water. When the water vapor condenses, therefore, the liquid contains a slightly higher proportion of ^{16}O (about 7 parts per thousand [0/00] more) than is present in the water from which it evaporated, and that water is left slightly depleted of ^{16}O (or enriched in ^{18}O).

The ratios of ^{16}O to ^{18}O present in air and water reflect the amount of evaporation, so they provide an indication of temperature. Polar ice and the air bubbles in it record the temperature at the time the original snow fell. If air and ice have more than 499 atoms of ^{16}O to every atom of ^{18}O, the weather was warm. Water was evaporating and falling as precipitation. Fossil seashells can be used in the same way. They are made from calcium carbonate ($CaCO_3$) that is taken from the sea. Analyzing the shells reveals the temperature of the water in which the animals lived. During an ice age they contain about 2 parts per thousand (0/00) more ^{18}O than they do at other times.

A hydrogen atom has only one proton and one electron, however, and in a water molecule both the hydrogen electrons are pulled to the oxygen side of their atoms. This leaves the molecule with a slight positive charge on the hydrogen side, away from the electrons, and a slight negative on the oxygen side, due to the excess of electrons. A molecule of this type, which has a charge at either end but is neutral overall, is called *polar*.

Water molecules are attracted to one another. The positive charge on the hydrogen end of one molecule can form a bond with the negative charge on the oxygen end of another. This is called a *hydrogen bond*. It is weaker than an ionic bond, but it causes the molecules in liquid water to link together in short strings. Heating a substance imparts energy to its molecules. Heat water sufficiently and the energy its molecules absorb will cause the hydrogen bonds to start breaking. First the strings of molecules will

become shorter and then free molecules will be able to escape from the liquid. In other words, the water will start to vaporize.

Cool the water and the strings grow longer as more hydrogen bonds form. Having less energy, the molecules move more slowly. The volume of the liquid decreases as gradually they are drawn together. Finally, the groups form links and the water crystallizes. Uniquely it then expands, because the crystals that water forms have an open structure.

This is how ice forms in a freezer. The ice in a polar ice sheet forms rather differently, because it starts not as liquid water but as snow. Warm air rises and as it rises it cools. As its temperature falls below a particular value, called the *dew point*, water vapor present in the air will start to condense into droplets and a cloud will form. Within the cloud vertical air currents will carry the tiny droplets to a height at which the temperature is below freezing. They will freeze and water vapor condensing at that height will do so as ice, not liquid water. The change from vapor to solid without passing through a liquid phase is called *sublimation*.

Ice crystals collide, adhere to one another, and form snowflakes. These fall, and if they fall into a region where the temperature is above freezing, they melt into drops of water. If snowflakes or water drops are too heavy to be carried aloft by air currents, they will fall from the bottom of the cloud. Snowflakes may still melt as they fall toward the ground if the air below the cloud is warmer than about 39°F (4°C). Most of the rain that falls in middle latitudes is melted snow—even in summer.

The amount of snow that falls in polar regions is small, but the snow rarely melts. On January 12, 1958, the warmest summer's day ever recorded at the South Pole, the temperature rose to 5°F (-15°C). Each fall lies on top of the preceding fall and even if the surface does thaw briefly it quickly freezes again.

Large, soft snowflakes form only where the air temperature is higher than about 23°F (-5°C). In colder air the snow falls as much smaller ice crystals. In middle latitudes this powdery kind of snow falls only during really severe winter cold. In the Arctic and Antarctic it is the most common type of snow.

Ice crystals can have many shapes. There is an international system for classifying them that recognizes 10 basic shapes. They do not stack well, so a mass of ice crystals of various shapes scattered randomly form a loose arrangement. Powdery snow is easily lifted from the ground—by a kick or by the wind, which can cause a blizzard. Snow is heavy, however, and at the base of a thick accumulation the weight of the layer crushes the crystals, packing them tightly together. Cars and trucks driving over a snow-covered road have a

similar effect. They pack the snow down hard, making it almost solid. Beneath the much greater weight of a thick snow layer underlying snow becomes solid. It is packed into ice.

This is not the way ice forms in a freezer or on the surface of a pond in winter, and the resulting ice looks different. It is white rather than transparent. This is because crushing the ice crystals together traps large numbers of tiny air bubbles. These are the bubbles scientists release from ice cores and then capture for analysis.

Ablation, Ice Sheets, and Glaciers

Some of the snow is lost. Where the air is extremely dry, as it is in the interior of Antarctica, ice can sublime directly. The amount involved is small, however. Fine, powdery snow can also be lifted by the wind—and Antarctica is a very windy continent. It will fall again, of course, but a small proportion of it will be carried over the coast and dropped into the sea. Losses by wind and sublimation are called *ablation*.

Most of the snow remains close to the place where it fell and is compacted into ice. It forms the ice sheet. An ice sheet is an expanse of ice covering an area of at least 20,000 square miles (52,000 sq km).

At the base of the ice sheet, compaction has a further effect. The ice is squeezed to the sides, away from the center, and very, very slowly it begins to flow. The pressure from the center is sufficient to force the moving ice over small hills, but generally the ice moves down slopes. Where there is a natural valley, or soft rock that is easily eroded, the moving ice will be confined by the valley walls. It is then called a *valley glacier* and conforms to the popular impression of a glacier. In fact, though, there is no clear distinction

between an ice sheet and a glacier. Both consist of ice and in both cases the ice moves.

Ice Shelves and Icebergs

West of the Transantarctic Mountains, the smaller section of Antarctica is low-lying and its coast has large bays and offshore islands. Where the flowing ice sheet reaches a bay on a low-lying coast it does not halt. The flow continues into the sea. It is secured to the land on either side of the bay and inshore it is in contact with the sea floor. Farther from the shore, in deeper water, it is not supported from below. There is water beneath the ice.

This extension of the ice sheet is an ice *shelf*, and the Antarctic ice shelves are big, especially the Ronne and Filchner Ice Shelves in the Weddell Sea and the Ross Ice Shelf in the Ross Sea. At the outer margin of the shelves the ice is floating on water that moves and from time to time large blocks of ice break free. These are icebergs. Antarctic icebergs enter the Antarctic Ocean from the Weddell and Ross Seas. They are flat-topped and can have surface areas of 1,200 square miles (3,100 sq km) or more—the size of Rhode Island. An iceberg that broke away (the technical term is *calved*) from the Ross Ice Shelf in October 1987 had an area of 1,834 square miles (4,750 sq km) and was at least 825 feet (250 m) thick.

We should not be overly alarmed, therefore, at reports of large blocks breaking away from the Antarctic shelves. On April 17, 1998, the Larsen B Ice Shelf, off the Antarctic Peninsula, calved a block 75 square miles (194 sq km) in area. This was reported as an indication of global warming that heralded the imminent collapse of the ice shelves and possibly of the ice sheet. It was nothing of the kind. Such calvings are perfectly normal events.

Greenland, or Kalaallit Nunaat

Like Antarctica, Greenland is mountainous. Mountains running down the east coast rise to about 7,000 feet (2,100 m) and down the western side of the country there are mountains 5,000–6,000 feet (1,525–1,830 m) high. The highest mountain is Mount Gunnbjørn, the peak of which is at 12,139 feet (3,700 m). It is on the eastern coast, south of the Arctic Circle.

Between them, the interior of the country is a high plateau covered by an ice sheet averaging 5,000 feet (1,525 m) in thickness and on the highest ground, west of Ittoqqortoormiit (Scoresbysund) on the western coast, raising the surface to about 10,000 feet (3,050 m) above sea level. At its deepest point the ice sheet is more than 8,000 feet (2,440 m) thick. It is a remote, empty place and several early attempts to cross it failed. The first to succeed was in 1888, when a team of six people led by the Norwegian explorer Fridtjof Nansen (1861–1930) crossed from east to west at about latitude 64°25' N. They set out from the east coast on August 16 and reached the west coast on September 26. Scientists now visit the interior, but Greenlanders live near the coast, where most earn their living.

The Ice Sheet

The ice sheet covers an area of 670,272 square miles (1,736,095 sq km), more than the areas of Oregon and Alaska combined and equal to 85 percent of the area of the country. It is 1,550 miles (2,500 km) from north to south and about 620 miles (1,000 km) from east to west, and it contains about 10 percent of all the freshwater in the world. In addition, local ice caps and glaciers cover a smaller area of approximately 18,763 square miles (48,599 sq km)—more than the combined areas of Vermont and New Hampshire.

This leaves 15 percent of the country ice-free. This area amounts to 135,100 square miles (350,000 sq km)—an area considerably larger than New Mexico and eight times that of Denmark—located around the coasts.

Place-Names and Geographic Links

Greenland, known in Danish as *Grønland* and in Inuit as *Kalaallit Nunaat,* is the largest island in the world. The population is 53,000 of which approximately 45,000 are Inuit and 8,000 European, mainly Danish. It is a self-governing dependency of Denmark, and since it was granted self-rule the Inuit names of its towns and villages have replaced the Danish names. Older maps still show

the Danish names, however, so at the first mention of a place with two names the modern name is given here with the Danish name in parentheses—for example, Qaanaaq (Thule). Subsequent references to the place give only the modern name, in this case Qaanaaq.

Geographically Greenland forms part of the North American continent. The rocks beneath the ice sheet are ancient—some of them as old as the planet itself—and related to those in adjacent Canada. In the north only the 25-mile- (40-km-wide) Smith Sound separates Greenland from Ellesmere Island, Canada. The earliest traces of life on Earth are also found in rocks from Greenland.

Cape Farewell, the southernmost tip of Greenland, is at latitude 59°46' N and the Arctic Circle passes a short distance to the south of the town of Sisimiut (Holsteinsborg). Most of the country lies inside the Arctic Circle. The northernmost point, Cape Morris Jesup, is at 83°39' N.

Temperatures

Over the ice cap the average winter temperature is about -27°F (-33°C) and it can fall much lower. In 1930–31 German scientists of the Alfred Wegener Expedition recorded an average February temperature of -52.9°F (-47.2°C) and an average temperature in July of 12.8°F (-10.7°C). Several times during the winter they spent there the temperature fell to -85°F (-65°C) and in summer it never rose above 26.6°F (-3°C). At the same time as the German expedition, a British expedition was recording similar weather conditions 300 miles (483 km) to the south. Several more teams of meteorologists visited the ice sheet during the 1930s and 1940s, and in the 1950s French scientists confirmed the earlier temperature records.

These temperatures demonstrate the effect of elevation on climate. At sea level it is much warmer. In South Greenland, described as "lush" by Greenlanders, about 100 families earn their living raising sheep and growing vegetable crops. The capital, Nuuk (Godthåb), at 51°43' N, has an average winter (November through March) daytime temperature of about 23°F (-5°C). Much farther north at 68°49' N, the average daytime temperature during the same 5 months at Qaanaaq is about 1.5°F (-17°C). In summer (May through August) the daytime temperature averages 40°F (4.4°C) at Qaanaaq and 48°F (9°C) at Nuuk.

The East Greenland Current, a branch of the Gulf Stream, flows northward parallel to the western coast. This gives the coast a milder cli-

mate than that of Baffin Island on the western side of the Davis Strait separating Greenland from Canada. The cold Labrador Current flows southward on the Canadian side of the strait and influences the climate. The western coast of Greenland also has a milder climate than the eastern coast, which is also affected by a cold current. Consequently, most of the towns and villages are located along the western coast.

There is another factor that contributes to the mild coastal climate. Light and heat are reflected strongly from the surface of the snow, which has an albedo of 75–95 percent (*see page 20*). This maintains the low temperature over the ice sheet, since only 5–25 percent of the incoming solar energy is absorbed by the surface. Air immediately above the surface is chilled. Cold, dense air flows out from the ice sheet and down the glacial valleys. As it descends from the high interior the air is compressed and grows warmer, sometimes producing warm, dry winds at the coast. These are called *föhn* winds (originally this was the name of a local wind in the Swiss Alps).

Precipitation

Rainfall is moderate in the southwest. Nuuk receives an average 23.5 inches (597 mm) a year, distributed fairly evenly through the year, although August and September are somewhat wetter than other months. Qaanaaq is much drier. It receives an average of only 2.5 inches (63.5 mm) of rain a year, of which 1.6 inches (41 mm) falls between June and September. Much of the precipitation falls as snow, of course, but precipitation is always measured as rainfall or its equivalent; 1 inch (25 mm) of rain is roughly equivalent to 10 inches (254 mm) of snow, but the volume of a given weight of snow can vary considerably. Snow that does not melt in summer and is eventually turned into glacier ice is called *firn* or *névé.*

Qaanaaq probably has a climate quite similar to that in the uninhabited center of the country, on the ice sheet. There almost all of the precipitation falls as snow and on average is equal to about 0.3 inch (8 mm) of rain a year, or approximately 3 inches (8 cm) of snow, giving the interior of Greenland a climate that is dry even by desert standards. The snow accumulates, ice forms, and in the 1990s the ice sheet overall was found to be growing thicker by about 0.8 inch (2 cm) a year.

Glaciers and Icebergs

Pressure exerted by the weight of ice at the center squeezes the ice outward. At the edges of the ice sheet, ice is forced through the mountain valleys, where it moves as glaciers. Near the coast the glaciers enter fjords. These are deep, U-shaped valleys open to the sea, where the glaciers partly melt. They formed by erosion and were flooded when the sea level rose.

The Humboldt Glacier is the biggest. It is more than 62 miles (100 km) wide and enters the sea in the north, presenting a wall of ice more than 300 feet (118 m) high. Some of the glaciers in the west move rapidly. The fastest have been known to advance 100 feet (40 m) in 24 hours, but this rate was not sustained. A movement of 97 feet (38 m) in 24 hours has been sustained, however. Eastern glaciers move more slowly.

As it enters the sea, the forward edge of a glacier begins to float and become unstable. Sections of ice calve from it as icebergs. These differ from Antarctic icebergs because the ice originates in valley glaciers rather than ice shelves. Arctic icebergs—most of which come from Greenland—are smaller and more irregularly shaped than Antarctic ones. When they first calve they are often more than 200 feet (60 m) high and

*Ice field meeting the sea, Antarctica
(Gerry Ellis/ENP Images)*

extend down to 800 feet (244 m) below the sea surface, but they are rarely more than about 0.5 mile (0.8 km) long. They carry rock fragments and soil scoured by their parent glaciers from the base and sides of their valleys, and this composition makes them darker in color than Antarctic icebergs. It was with an iceberg from the Illulissat (Jakobshavn) Glacier, on the western coast of Greenland, that the ocean liner *Titanic* collided on the night of April 14–15, 1912.

When Northern America, Europe, and Asia Were Cold Deserts

In 1836 and 1837 Louis Agassiz spent his vacations exploring glaciers in his native Switzerland. At that time, Agassiz—his full name was Jean Louis Rodolphe Agassiz (1807–73)—was professor of natural history at the University of Neuchâtel, in Switzerland, and was already famous as a leading authority on fossil fish. Glaciers had come to fascinate him, because they presented a puzzle.

Boulders lying on the ground at various places on the plains of eastern France as well as in Switzerland itself were made of rock quite different from that beneath the soil on which they lay. Such "misplaced" rocks are called *erratics*. The puzzle was how they had arrived in the localities where they were found. The boulders resembled rocks found in other parts of Switzerland, and a number of scientists had suggested that they might have been transported by glaciers. It seemed rather unlikely and Agassiz was deeply suspicious.

For that to happen, glaciers would have to move. At some time in the past they would also have to have extended very much farther than they did in the early 19th century—to account for the present location of the erratics. There was no proof that glaciers move, it was difficult to believe they were formerly much more extensive, and the origin of the erratics could be explained in other ways. A popular view was that they had been carried in icebergs drifting in a sea that once covered much of Europe and were deposited when the sea retreated. Glacial deposits were called *drift* deposits, referring to the idea of drifting icebergs, and the word is still used, even today.

Nevertheless, in 1836 Agassiz and his colleagues built a hut on the Aar Glacier to use as a base for their studies. They quickly observed that the sides of the glacier were lined with broken rocks and there were also broken rocks at the lower end of the glacier. The most reasonable explanation for their presence was that the glacier had torn them from the sides of its valley, smashed them into smaller fragments, and then pushed them ahead of itself. This suggested glaciers might move after all.

Two years later, in 1839, he found another hut that had been built on the glacier in 1827. There was a record of its original position, but when he found it the hut was almost 1 mile (1.6 km) from that location. To check that it really was the glacier that had carried the hut, Agassiz drove a straight line of stakes firmly into the surface of

the ice, from one side of the glacier to the other. When he returned in 1841 to check them he found they were no longer in their original positions. Nor were they in a straight line. The stakes had moved and now formed a U shape. They had all moved, but those in the center had moved farther than those at the sides—presumably because friction between the ice and valley walls slowed the movement of the ice at the edges.

The Ice Age

Agassiz was forced to conclude that glaciers do indeed move. He then linked this movement to the distribution of boulders and other *erratics*—deposits of gravel and smaller rocks that were unrelated to the rocks on which they lay. If glaciers move and if they scour rocks from the valley walls on either side and from the ground over which they move, dragging and pushing these rocks along with them, then at one time the glaciers must have extended over much of western Europe.

He described his studies of Swiss glaciers and the conclusions he had reached in a book, *Études sur les glaciers,* which he published in 1840. His principal conclusion was that in the geologically recent past Switzerland lay beneath a single ice sheet and that ice sheets similar to those still found in Greenland once covered all those regions where erratic boulders and other deposits are found. There had been, in fact, an ice age.

In 1846 he was invited to the United States to deliver a series of lectures at the Lowell Institute, in Boston, followed by more lectures in several other cities. The welcome he received and his fascination with the natural history of North America persuaded him to remain. In the course of his travels he found signs that the Ice Age had affected North America just as it had Europe.

He was appointed professor of zoology at Harvard University in 1848 and became an American citizen. Louis Agassiz was elected to the Hall of Fame for Great Americans in 1915.

Quaternary Glacials

The Ice Age Agassiz identified began about 1.64 million years ago and marks the beginning of the Quaternary era of geologic time. Most of the Quaternary comprises the Pleistocene epoch,

which ended about 10,000 years ago. We are now living in the Holocene (or Recent) epoch of the Quaternary.

The recent Pleistocene glacial discovered by Agassiz turned out to be not one ice age, as he supposed, but many. By the early 20th century geologists had identified four separate glacials in countries adjacent to the European Alps. There were also glaciations in New Zealand and South America.

These episodes of extreme cold were interspersed with warmer periods, called *interglacials*. The interglacials lasted for an average of between 10,000 and 20,000 years, the glacials about 100,000 years.

Scientists now know that there have been many episodes of cold and warm conditions and that climates are constantly changing. These fluctuations have not ceased and the era of ice ages has not come to an end. We are now living in an interglacial (called the *Flandrian*) that began about 10,000 years ago and it is very likely that one day the ice sheets will start expanding once more.

Last Glacial Maximum

Around 18,000 years ago the ice sheets covered a larger area than at any other time during the Quaternary. This period is often called the *Last Glacial Maximum* (LGM). As the map shows, at that time North America lay beneath ice that extended from southern Alaska to south of the Great Lakes. The ice formed several distinct sheets, spreading in the directions indicated by the arrows. The largest ice sheets were the Laurentide, covering the whole of the eastern side of the continent, and the Cordillera, in the west. Greenland lay beneath its own ice sheet, as it does still. Sea ice covered all of the ocean north of the latitude of Newfoundland.

Europe also lay beneath ice, the Fennoscandian ice sheet. This covered the whole of Scandinavia, all but the southernmost parts of Britain, and mainland Europe as far south as the Alps. In Russia it extended as far east as the Laptev Sea, at approximately latitude 110° E. There were smaller ice sheets in eastern Siberia and central Asia, but in general these areas remained free of ice because their climates were too dry.

Over the ice sheets covering so much of the Northern Hemisphere the climate would have

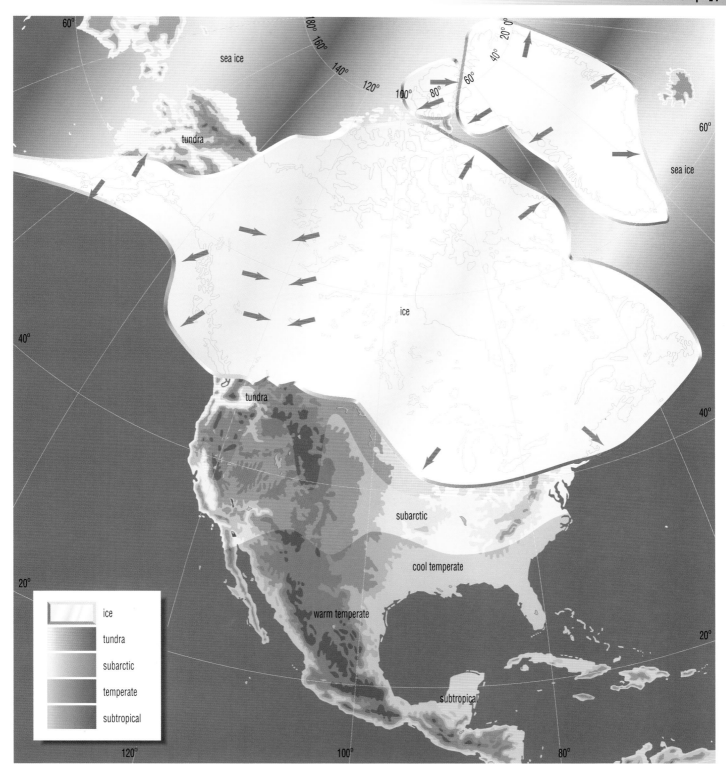

Pleistocene Ice Sheet in North America

been very similar to the present climate of central Greenland (*see* page 24). Temperatures would rarely have risen above freezing, and precipitation would have been very low. Most days would have brought clear blue skies, bitter cold, and fierce winds. The region was a very dry desert.

Beyond the ice there was tundra. In North America this covered most of Alaska and a broad belt across the continent in about latitude 40°N. Denver, Kansas City, and Cincinnati would probably have enjoyed weather much like that in the present-day Northwest Territories of Canada.

At one time, therefore, a large part of North America and Europe were cold, dry deserts. To the south of the ice sheets, the climate was semi-arid. The Last Glacial Maximum was about 18,000 years ago, a very remote, distant time, long before the dawn of the earliest civilization. Compared with the 4.6-billion-year age of the Earth, however, the interval between then and now is very short indeed. One day it is likely the ice, and the arid climate associated with it, will return.

Plate Tectonics and Orogenies

The county of Devon in the south of England is renowned for its gently rolling pastures and coastal vacation resorts. Along some parts of the coast there are distinctive cliffs formed, like all sea cliffs, by erosion as the sea has cut into what were once low hills. The cliffs are distinctive because of their color: they are brick red, made from what geologists call *old red sandstone*. Identical rock is found in northeastern North America, Ireland, Scotland, and Scandinavia.

Red sandstone is rock made from desert sand grains. Devon is not a desert now, but once, a very long time ago, what is now the south of Devon formed a large river delta, rather like the Nile Delta today, where a major river flowed across a very dry desert.

The rocks of Devon have given their name to an entire period of Earth history, the Devonian, which began about 408.5 million years ago and ended about 362.5 million years ago. The map shows the location in Wales and southwest England of rocks of Devonian age.

Obviously, Devon experienced a very different climate in the Devonian from the one it enjoys today. It was a dry, sandy desert again later, during part of the Permian period, which lasted from 290 to about 248 million years ago, and the shapes of dunes can still be discerned in the sandstone.

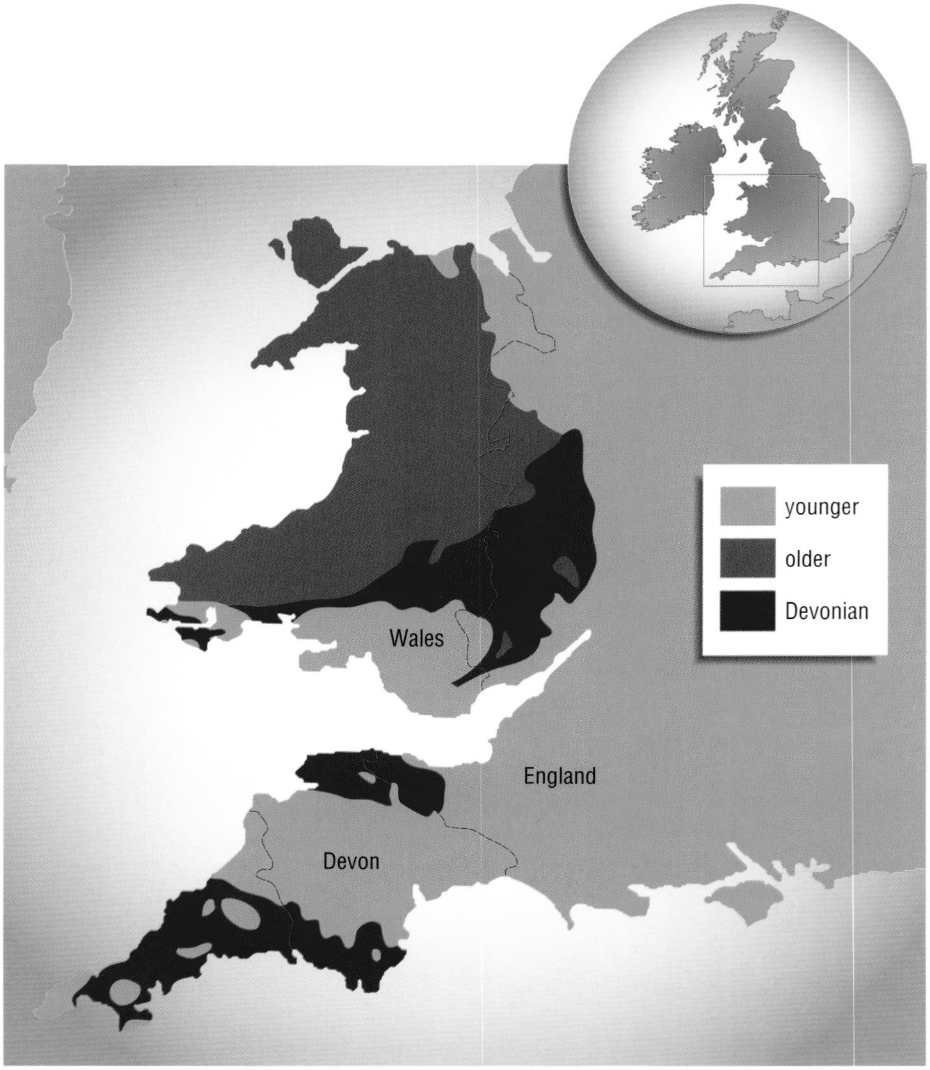

Continental Drift

The search for an explanation began in the last century with attempts to account for the curious fact that the west coast of Africa looks as though it ought to fit snugly against the east coast of South America. There were many theories, all of them based on the idea that the continents have not always been in the positions they occupy today.

Then, in 1912, a German meteorologist, Alfred Wegener (1880–1930), began giving lectures in which he expounded his own ideas. He described these in detail in a book, *Die Entstehung der Kontinente und Ozeane,* which was first published in 1915 and then expanded in later editions. It was not until the third edition appeared in 1922 that the book was translated into English. The translation was published in 1924, as *The Origin of Continents and Oceans.*

Wegener summarized all the evidence for continental drift that had been accumulating over several decades and added observations of his own. He showed that not only did the coastlines on either side of the Atlantic fit together, but the actual rock formations matched. Fossils in those rocks were of the same organisms, species that

younger
older
Devonian

Wales

England

Devon

Devonian rocks in Wales and southwest England

had evolved into distinct American and African forms after the split had occurred. He found evidence that parts of South America, Africa, India, and Australia had experienced glaciations (ice ages) around 270 million years ago.

All these strands of evidence made sense, Wegener argued, if all the continents had once been joined together around the South Pole and then had drifted northward. As they crossed the equator they would have experienced equatorial climates, evidence of which is widespread. Wegener called this huge continent *Pangaea,* from Greek words meaning "all Earth." He thought the mountain ranges running down the western side of North and South America were due to crumpling of the Earth's crust as the continents were pushed westward and that the Himalayas were also formed by crumpling, caused by the collision between India and Asia. The continents, he suggested, were made from rocks that are less dense than the material beneath them, so they floated like rafts.

Seafloor Spreading and Plate Tectonics

Few geologists supported these ideas, although Wegener was widely respected. Geologists hesitated to support the hypothesis of continental drift because neither Wegener nor anyone else had suggested a convincing mechanism that could move continents. Several geologists attempted to explain how this could happen—after all, there was a large mass of evidence to support the idea that, somehow, continents had moved. One of these explanations came close to what is now believed to be the case, but it was largely ignored. Arthur Holmes (1890–1965), a British geophysicist, became convinced that heat generated by the decay of radioactive elements deep below the Earth's surface produces masses of hot rocks within the mantle that rise slowly upward, spread out and cool, then sink once more. By the middle 1920s Holmes was proposing that this motion results in convection currents powerful enough to move the cold, solid rock above them.

During the late 1940s and 1950s new evidence began arriving. Research ships were fitted with drilling equipment to take rock samples and sensing equipment to map the seabed. For the first time, oceanographers were able to study the floor of the oceans. What they found indicated that ocean basins are constantly spreading to either side of ridges running down their centers. Finally, in 1967, Dan McKenzie (born 1942) unified the theories of continental drift and seafloor spreading within a new theory, that of *plate tectonics.* *Tectonic* derives from a Greek word meaning "deforming."

McKenzie proposed that the Earth's crust is composed of a number of large blocks, called *plates.* Some of these are relatively thin and made from dense rock. They form the floors of the oceans. Other plates are much thicker and made from rocks that are less dense. These form the continents, rising above the sea. The plates of the ocean floor and of the continents move in relation to each other. The map shows the major tectonic plates and the directions in which they are moving. They are still moving. North America and Europe are moving apart by roughly 0.8 inch (2 cm) a year, for example. The illustration also shows the ridges, where new crust is forming, and trenches, where crust is being removed by sinking back with the mantle. Hot spots, also marked on the map, are places where convection currents carry hot mantle material into the base of the crust. This tends to break through in volcanic eruptions and to form volcanic islands.

Lithospheric plates and mantle hot spots

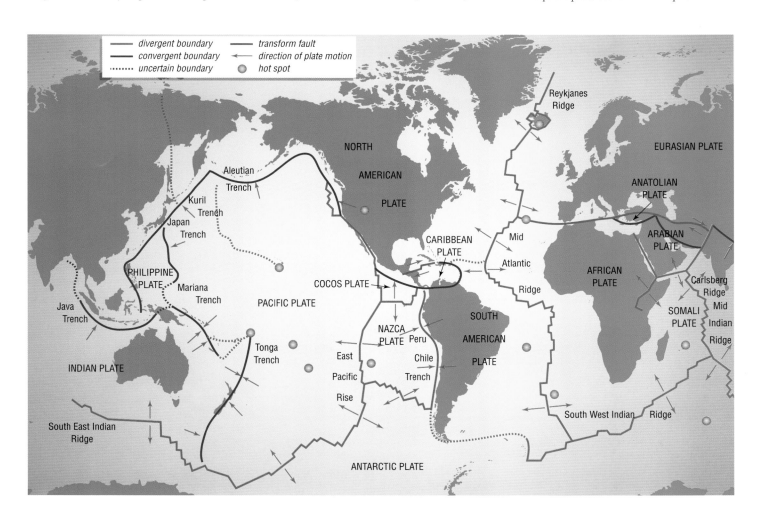

The Formation, Development, and Aging of Soils

From the moment rocks are exposed to the air they start to erode, to wear away. Picture a range of mountains about 10,000 feet (3,050 m) high. If these are worn away at a rate of 0.10 inch (about 3 mm) a year during a human lifetime, of about 75 years, their average height will have been reduced by about 7.5 inches (190 mm). No one would notice such a small amount of erosion, but compared with the life span of the Earth, which was formed about 4.6 billion years ago, 75 years is but an instant. At this rate of erosion it would take a little more than 1 million years for the mountains to be worn away altogether. The landscape they once dominated would be a level plain. Yet even 1 million years is a very short time in the history of the Earth. If you compare its 4.6 billion years to the human span of 75 years, 1 million years is equivalent to slightly less than 6 days.

That erosion, caused by sunshine, wind, and water, is called *weathering*. Contributing to it there are also chemical reactions between minerals in rocks and substances, mainly acids, present in water. All rain and snow is naturally slightly acid, because carbon dioxide, sulfur dioxide, and oxides of nitrogen dissolve into it, producing acid solutions. Some of the compounds present in rocks are soluble in water, so they dissolve to form solutions that engage in reactions with other mineral constituents. These processes are known as *chemical weathering* and form part of the overall weathering.

Sunshine weakens rocks, especially in warm climates. During the day they are heated by the Sun, sometimes so strongly it can be painful to walk across them with bare feet. Rocks are not very good conductors of heat, however, so it is only the surface layer that grows hot. Inside, the rock remains cool. As it warms, the outer layer of rock expands, but the cool, inner part of the rock remains the same size. Then, at night, the rock cools again, and contracts. Repeated day after day, expansion and contraction produce tiny cracks in the rock and cause flakes to separate and fall away.

In colder climates water freezes in winter. This also shatters rock. Liquid water penetrates all the small fissures in a rock, then freezes there. Water expands with great force when it freezes—as when the plumbing in a home freezes, the force of expansion is strong enough to burst metal pipes. This widens and extends the fissures. The ice thaws and the enlarged cracks fill with liquid water. The next time this freezes the gaps widen still more. Eventually adjacent fissures join and pieces of rock fall from the surface. Then,

detached fragments are washed and blown by water and wind. They are rolled along the ground, thrown against each other and against solid rock surfaces—knocking off yet more fragments—until they have been shattered, ground, and battered to grains, some so small as to be barely visible to the naked eye.

The First Organisms

Among the chemical compounds that are released from rocks by the processes of weathering there are some that can nourish bacteria. Bacterial colonies arrive and establish themselves in sheltered crevices where they are protected from direct exposure to heat, wind, and rain. The bacteria absorb substances from the rock and water, their own cells forming a layer, thin but rich in nutrients, on which other organisms can grow. Lichens arrive. A lichen is a kind of double organism. It consists of a fungus that lives in intimate association with an alga—a very simple green plant—or cyanobacterium—a type of bacterium that used to be called a "blue green alga." The fungal partner (called the *mycobiont*) absorbs mineral nutrients from the rock, and the alga or cyanobacterium (the *phytobiont*) carries out photosynthesis, the process in which sunlight provides the energy to drive reactions that produce sugars from water and carbon dioxide (see page 56).

Lichens grow across rock surfaces and as their cells die and are renewed, opportunities for other organisms to take hold begin to appear. Perhaps a moss will arrive. This is a more complex plant; beneath the green mat it presents to the world it forms a layer consisting of mineral grains, decaying plant material, and organic acids.

At first the layer is thin, but as it fills small depressions in the surface it thickens until finally a wind-borne seed lands and is able to germinate. A blade of grass appears, or a tiny herb, and when it dies its own tissues decompose and join the layer of organic matter.

One blade of grass is joined by another and then another, and more and different herbs arrive, until what had been bare rock bears patches of vegetation that slowly spread to cover wider areas of rock surface and eventually to join as a single continuous covering. Beneath the plants there is now a thin layer of soil. Soil consists of mineral grains mixed with organic material in varying stages of decomposition. It is made by the combined actions of physical and chemical weathering and biological activity.

Soil Formation

At this stage there is only a thin surface layer of soil. Soil formation—the technical term is *pedogenesis*—has only just begun and the soil is in its infancy. Over the years and centuries that follow, generation after generation of plants will contribute to its further development. Animals will arrive to feed on plant material and each other. Some of them will live on the surface or above it, among the plants. Many will live below the surface, in the soil itself, where they will also help with the formation of the soil. Tunnels made as they move through the soil will allow air and water to circulate. By feeding on dead plant and animal material they will break large pieces into small fragments and their own wastes and dead bodies will provide food for fungi and bacteria. These will complete the processes of decomposition, converting large, complex organic molecules into simple compounds with molecules small enough to be absorbed by plant roots.

As life proliferates in and upon the soil, the soil itself accumulates. No longer a mere film clinging to bare rock, it becomes a deeper layer that is not the same at every level. Cut a trench through it, with vertical sides all the way to the underlying rock, and the color and general appearance of the soil vary, so it is possible to make out distinct layers. A vertical cut of this kind is called a *soil profile* and the layers are called *soil horizons*. Soils vary according to the kind of rock from which they develop, the kind of plants that grow in them, and their age. A young soil that has only recently started to form will be thin and will have no horizons. A mature soil may have a number of horizons. Scientists identify soil horizons by letters and numbers that represent subdivisions of the two or more main horizons found in most soils.

The chart shows how this is done. The O horizons consist of twigs, leaves, and other plant and animal material that is lying at or just below the surface. Material lying on the surface is often called *litter*, so the O1 horizon is sometimes called the *L layer* or *litter layer*. Where that is done, the O2 horizon is called the *F layer* if the organic material can still be recognized and the *H layer* if it has decomposed into a mass of unidentifiable matter. At the bottom of the O2 horizon the organic material is partly decomposed. Lift the leaves lying on the ground in a forest and beneath them you will find partly rotted leaves.

Organic matter continues to decompose in the A horizons, and as it does so the soluble chemical compounds that are released drain downward. The loss of compounds by vertical draining is called *eluviation,* so together the A horizons comprise the *eluvial zone.* The eluvial zone is also what farmers and gardeners call the *topsoil.*

Beneath the eluvial zone there is the *illuvial zone,* the region into which the eluviated compounds drain and where they accumulate. This is also the subsoil and it comprises the B horizons. Here, the soil consists mainly of mineral particles. Below this region there is the partly weathered mineral material from which the overlying soil has developed—the soil parent material. The bedrock itself is sometimes included as well and called the *R horizon.*

Additional information about horizons can be included in these designations, as subscripted lowercase abbreviations. Ap, for example, describes an A horizon that has been disturbed by plowing, and B3ca is a B3 horizon that is enriched with calcium carbonate.

How Soils Age

This full complement of horizons develops slowly as a soil matures and is present in what soil scientists call a *virile* soil. As the soil ages further, material in the C horizon becomes increasingly weathered. Soluble compounds released from it by weathering are drawn upward to replace water that evaporates from the surface (see page 38) and are absorbed by plant roots, but more and more are lost in water that drains out of the soil altogether. Eventually flowing water transports the plant nutrients to the sea. In the *senile* stage to which a virile soil progresses, only the less soluble mineral nutrients remain, and in its final stage anything that can dissolve has dissolved.

The soil is then very deep, but very infertile even though it may continue to support luxuriant plant growth. This is possible where the nutrients are held mainly in the living plants themselves. Roots absorb nutrients as fast as the decomposition of organic material releases them. Ancient, exhausted soils of this kind are widespread in the humid tropics, where nevertheless they support rain forests.

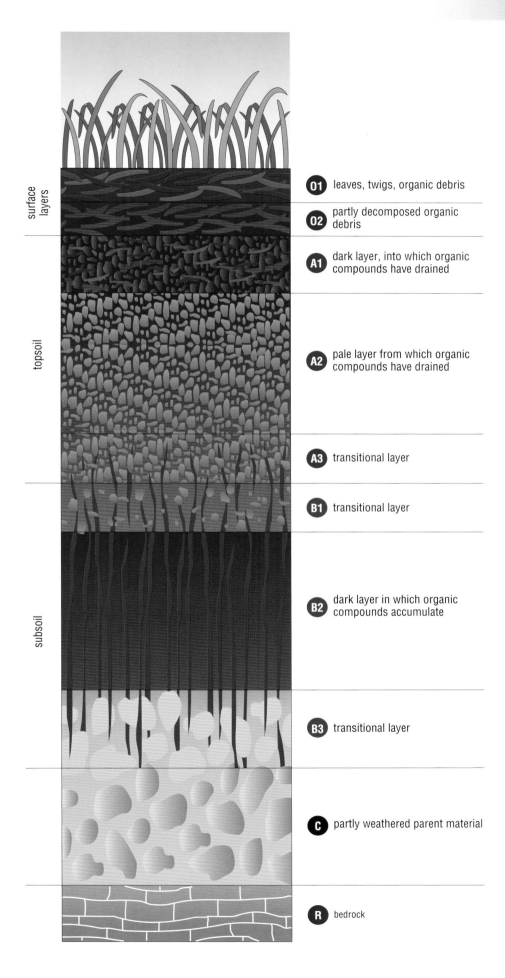

surface layers	**O1** leaves, twigs, organic debris
	O2 partly decomposed organic debris
	A1 dark layer, into which organic compounds have drained
topsoil	**A2** pale layer from which organic compounds have drained
	A3 transitional layer
	B1 transitional layer
subsoil	**B2** dark layer in which organic compounds accumulate
	B3 transitional layer
	C partly weathered parent material
	R bedrock

Soil horizons

Desert Soils

Soils result from the weathering of rock, in other words, from the action of sunshine, wind, and water. The time it takes for a mature soil to develop, with a full complement of horizons, varies greatly from place to place. The soils over much of the northern United States and northern Europe have developed since the end of the last glaciation (see page 26). Moving glaciers scour away the soil, so when the ice retreats bare rock and gravel are exposed. These mature soils are, therefore, no more than about 10,000 years old, because that is the length of time that has elapsed since the glacial retreat.

Obviously, this is a maximum time that takes no account of when the soils first covered the surface and supported deep-rooting plants. There are mature soils in Alaska that are known to be about 1,000 years old, and in some circumstances soils can develop much more quickly even than this. The reclamation of the huge piles of waste produced by mining provides a good example. Heaps of waste from the mining and processing of china clay, or kaolin, consist mainly of mineral grains, material that is very deficient in the soluble nutrient compounds needed by plants. Most of these heaps have been reclaimed by spraying onto them, using a machine resembling a water cannon, a mixture of water, fibrous organic material to bind the mineral particles together, and plant seeds, followed by an application of fertilizer. Within a few years the heaps were covered with vegetation and soil was starting to develop, although no horizons had yet formed.

With a little help from added fertilizer, soil was produced on the waste heaps by plants and other living organisms. They were able to colonize and root into material that was already finely fragmented. Fine fragmentation is ordinarily the result of weathering, so the waste tips consisted of the equivalent of weathered rock. Soils that began forming as the last ice age drew to its close were able to do so because rock was exposed to the forces of weathering.

Water and Warmth

For soils to develop, weathering and biological colonization must take place. They can do so only if certain criteria are met. Water must be available. Indeed, it should be abundant. The reactions that chemical weathering comprises take place in aqueous (water) solutions. It is water that transports the compounds from which plants derive nourishment and it is in solution that those compounds enter plant roots. Plants also need water to transport nutrients within their own tissues and to perform their own metabolic activities (see page 60).

Living organisms also require warmth. Many are able to survive periods of extreme cold, but they do so by slowing their life processes to the barest minimum. In Antarctica there are some species of moss that continue to photosynthesize down to 14°F (-10°C) and lichens that do so down to 1.4°F (-17°C), but for most plants photosynthesis (see page 56) is not possible at temperatures below about 21°F (-6°C), and at that temperature it proceeds very slowly. Between about 32°F (0°C) and 95°F (35°C) the rate of photosynthesis approximately doubles for every 18°F (10°C) rise in temperature. What is true for photosynthesis also obtains for most of the biochemical reactions on which living organisms depend, although there are many variations and this is very much a generalization. It is true, though, that falling temperature slows life processes and, up to a limit, rising temperature accelerates them.

Polar Soils

In polar regions, thick ice sheets cover most of the ground and there is no soil at all. Beyond the edge of the permanent ice of Antarctica there are ice-free areas where bare rock and gravel support a few lichens, liverworts, and other small plants that survive in places sheltered from the wind by growing during the few weeks in summer when the temperature rises above freezing.

These ice-free areas are known as *dry valleys* or *oases,* and their total area amounts to about 2,200 square miles (5,700 sq km). They are certainly exposed to physical weathering, but soil development has barely begun. The low temperature severely restricts biological activity and, although they are called oases, precipitation is very low. Their extreme dryness inhibits both plant growth and chemical weathering.

Except for the outermost tip of the Antarctic Peninsula, all of Antarctica lies within the Antarctic Circle and the continent is surrounded completely by the Antarctic Ocean. From the tip of the peninsula it is approximately 600 miles (965 km) to Tierra del Fuego, the southernmost point of South America, the nearest continent.

Conditions around the edge of the Arctic Circle are quite different. The South Pole is located near the center of a vast continent; the North Pole is at sea, albeit a permanently frozen sea, and instead of the land's being surrounded by ocean, in the north it is the ocean that is surrounded by land. Away from the region of permanent ice, in northern Canada, Alaska, Scandinavia, and Siberia, there is a belt of tundra vegetation, bordered by the sea or permanent ice to the north and by the coniferous boreal forest, or taiga, to the south.

Tundra Soil

The word *tundra* comes originally from *tunturi,* a Lappish or Finnish word that describes a hill on which there are no trees. In fact, there are a few trees, including black spruce (*Picea mariana*) in North America and dahurian larch (*Larix dahurica*) in northeastern Siberia. They are able to grow because their roots are quite shallow, extending to the sides rather than vertically. Most woody plants are no bigger than shrubs, however. In places dwarf willow (*Salix* species) forms forests that are only knee high. Dwarf birch (*Betula nana*) and dwarf juniper (*Juniperus sibirica*) are common, growing to a height of about 12 inches (30 cm). There are also a few flowering herbs and sedges, but the most abundant plants are lichens and mosses.

The tundra, too, is a dry desert. It covers a vast area—amounting to 15 percent of the land area of Russia, for example—and its climate is not the same everywhere. In western Eurasia, where the North Atlantic Drift (page 50), a branch of the Gulf Stream, washes the coast, the climate is wetter and milder than it is farther east. Precipitation everywhere is between 8 inches and 12 inches (200–300 mm) a year and the ground is not covered by snow. Heavy falls are uncommon and the perpetual wind quickly blows away any snow that does fall. Winds can reach 90 mph (145 km/h). In central and eastern Siberia, winter temperatures often fall to -58°F (-50°C) and in summer the average temperature is only about 40°F (4°C).

Permafrost

Surprisingly, perhaps, considering the low annual precipitation, much of the level, low-lying tundra is swampy. Water is trapped at the surface because, below, groundwater in the soil is permanently frozen. This frozen material, which may be sand, gravel, clay, or rock as well as soil, is known as *permafrost.* It forms an impermeable layer through which surface water cannot drain and in places the permafrost layer is up to 3,000 feet (900 m) thick. Permafrost covers nearly 3 million square miles (7.8 sq km).

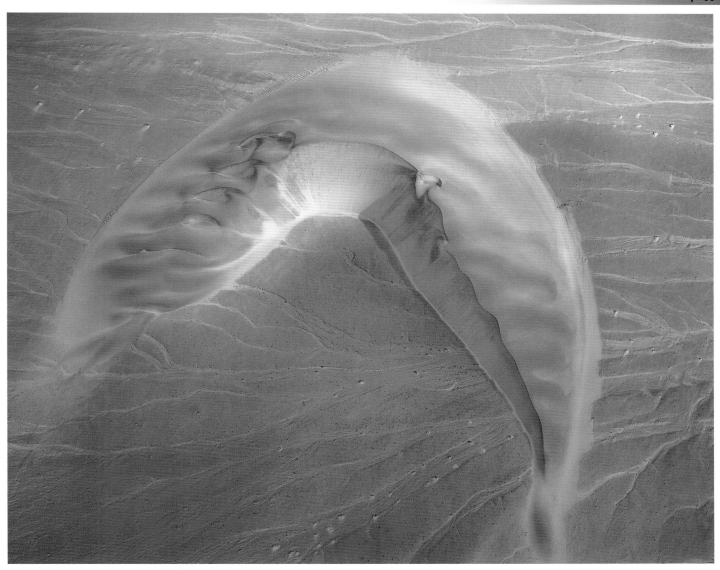

Above the permafrost, in the *active layer,* the ground thaws during the brief summer. Plant roots can absorb water only as liquid. Ice is useless to them, but in summer the trapped surface water becomes available. So in the tundra it is the low temperature that imposes the main restriction on biological activity, not the availability of water. In some places the active layer is up to 16 inches (40 cm) deep, but in others it is no more than 4 inches (10 cm) thick.

The summer thaw allows plants to grow, but the low soil temperature greatly slows the rate at which organic material decomposes. Consequently, tundra soil usually contains a large amount of organic matter in the shallow surface layer. No horizons form in it and it is classified as a soil at the very beginning of its development. Pedologists (soil scientists) classify soil types, and tundra soils are placed in the order Inceptisols, a name derived from the Latin *inceptum,* which means "beginning."

Soils of Hot Deserts

Soils of hot deserts are also placed in an order with a descriptive name. They are classified as Aridisols—arid soils. Aridisols are the most widespread of all soil types, occupying rather more than 19 percent of the land surface of the world, nearly 10 million square miles (26 million sq km).

They are very different from Inceptisols, because it is lack of water that restricts plant growth in hot deserts, not extremes of temperature. There is vegetation, of course, but it is sparse and the soil contains little organic matter. Deserts are windy places where soil, dry as dust, is blown from place to place, burying such plant debris as there is. There are no soil horizons.

Unlike the Inceptisols of the tundra, Aridisols are not beyond redemption. In many places they contain plant nutrients, so if water is supplied it is possible to cultivate them (page 174), and with

Slip face of barchan dune, Namibia (Gerry Ellis/ENP Images)

sustained cultivation they will eventually mature into soils more like those of the savanna grasslands, classified as Mollisols. It is fairly easy to remedy a lack of water, but there is no practical way to raise the average temperature (although should global warming occur this might happen [page 156]). This makes it impossible to cultivate the Inceptisols. If they were to thaw, over large areas they would turn into equally uncultivable swamp and marsh. Such wetlands are of great value to wildlife and worthy of protection. But if we did decide to cultivate them—probably to grow coniferous forests—they would first have to be drained to remove the surplus water and over so large an area this process would be prodigiously expensive.

Ergs and Sand Dunes

Think of a desert and the image most likely to spring to mind is of high sand dunes stretching endlessly in all directions devoid of life, empty, desolate, and still, on which the Sun beats down mercilessly from a clear, blue sky.

Deserts are not like this everywhere. Many are mainly mountainous and others are rocky. In parts of the southwestern United States, and extending into the desert, there are large areas in which movements in the Earth's crust have raised huge blocks of rock and lowered others, forming what is called a *basin-and-range* topography. There are similar landscapes in the Gobi and Kalahari Deserts.

Elsewhere, the surface is rocky, consisting of exposed horizontal bedrock, in places partly covered by boulders or smaller rocks. This surface is widespread in the Sahara and is known by its Arabic name of *hammada*.

There is sand, of course, and where it is plentiful it does form dunes. It is in the Sahara and Arabian Deserts that the dunes are biggest and there that sand covers the greatest area. For much of the Carboniferous period (362.5–290 million years ago) what is now the Sahara formed the bed of a sea—and coal formed around the edges of that sea. That is when the sand of the seabed was compressed into sandstone. Parts of it were covered by the sea again later, about 70 million years ago. When the sea retreated, erosion wore away at the sedimentary, seabed rocks. Sand and dust are the products of that erosion. Sand is abundant.

Draas and Ergs—Seas of Sand

The biggest dunes form ridges or chains more than 1,000 feet (300 m) high and from about 0.5 mile to 3 miles (0.8–5 km) apart. Landscape features produced by the wind are known as *bedforms*. Each of these very large desert bedforms is called a *draa*. A draa is so big that there are smaller dunes on its surface and ripples across the surfaces of the dunes.

Draas move up to about 2 inches (5 cm) a year. Dunes also move and where the sand covers a large area, as it does in the Sahara and in the Rub'al-Khali, the "Empty Quarter" of Arabia, it resembles a sea, with the dunes as waves. A "sand sea" is called an *erg;* the biggest ergs extend for up to almost 200,000 square miles (518,000 sq km).

It is the wind that builds sand dunes, just as it is wind that pushes water at the sea surface into waves. Although the image of a desert as sandy is partially correct, it is quite wrong to suppose it a place of stillness. Deserts are windy places and the wind seldom abates.

How Dunes Form

A light wind is enough to lift sand grains, provided they are dry and not sticking to one another. Whenever the wind speed exceeds 12 mph (19 km/h) grains will start moving. This is a moderate breeze. Along city streets it is strong enough to blow small pieces of paper and loose leaves about.

The wind is strong enough to lift sand grains, but not to keep them airborne for more than a few seconds. They quickly fall again. Some collect in a particular place, making a small mound, and then grains begin moving in little jumps up one side of the mound, as shown in the diagram.

What happens next is determined by gravity. If you have a supply of dry sand—it must be really dry—try pouring it to make the highest possible mound. You will find the height of the mound is limited by the angle of the sides. It is impossible for dry sand to form a mound with sides steeper than about 35°. At that angle, additional grains simply roll down the slope to the bottom. It is called, appropriately, the *angle of repose* for dry sand.

Sand grains are driven by the wind up one side of their mound. The other side is sheltered from the wind, so gravity is the only force acting on the grains there. As grains reach the top of the

mound they roll down the other side. Sand accumulates at the bottom of that side until the pile is level with the top of the mound. The side away from the wind has a slope of about 35°. That is as steep as it is possible for the slope to be. Consequently, a sand dune usually has a long, gradual slope on the side across which the wind blows and a slope of about 35° on the other, sheltered side, and the dunes move in the direction of the wind. The mechanism is the same regardless of the height of the dune. Dunes grow bigger by accumulating sand on the shallow-slope side, and the angle of slope on the steeper side is always close to the angle of repose.

Of course, this supposes the wind blows mainly from a particular direction. It is a reasonable supposition. Desert winds usually blow more from one direction than from others, although there are exceptions and a wind that is generally from one quarter may well vary to either side.

Dune Types

Wind blows sand into dunes and it also shapes the dunes, different winds acting on varying amounts of sand to produce particular types of dune. The figure illustrates some of the most common dune shapes.

If there is a virtually limitless supply of sand and the wind almost always blows from one particular direction, transverse dunes will form. These are long, with the gradual slope on the side facing the wind and the line of the dunes is at right angles to the wind direction. If the wind blows steadily from the south, the transverse dunes will be aligned east-to-west. Transverse

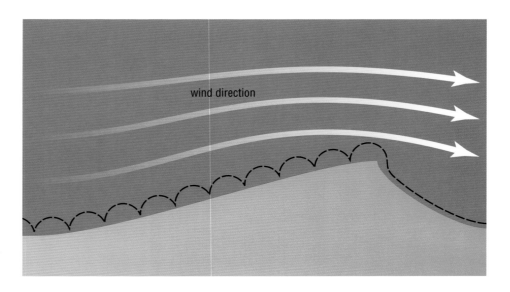

wind direction

How sand dunes form

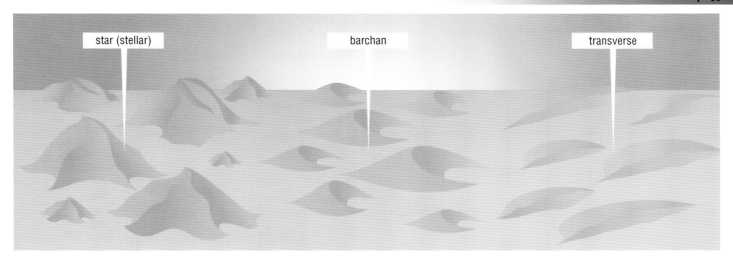

star (stellar)　　　barchan　　　transverse

dunes can be up to 60 miles (96 km) long and up to 300 feet (90 m) high and they move downwind at up to about 80 feet (25 m) a year.

Transverse dunes are not always straight. As a result of small irregularities in the wind they can also develop wavy crests, so the face of the dune faces alternately into and away from the wind direction. Wavy dunes of this type are called *aklé* dunes.

The southerly wind may not blow precisely from the south at all times. Sometimes it may be from the south-southwest, sometimes from the south, and sometimes from the south-southeast. Provided there is an abundant supply of sand, this wind pattern will produce longitudinal dunes. The sand is blown first from one side then from the other so longitudinal dunes are aligned in the average direction of the wind—in this case from south to north—and the slope is at the angle of repose on both sides.

Longitudinal dunes have long, sharp, sinuous crests. In some places, especially in the western Sahara, the biggest of them are known as *seif*

dunes. Seif dunes can stretch for hundreds of miles.

Where the supply of sand is limited, winds blowing from either side of a predominant direction will blow the sand into a crescent shape, with the "horns" pointing downwind. If the crescent is narrow, so the horns are close together, this is called a *parabolic* dune. If they are fairly wide, so the crescent is open, it is a *barchan*. Barchans are up to about 100 feet (30 m) high and the tips of their "horns" are up to 1,200 feet (370 m) apart.

Where there is enough sand, adjacent barchans may join to form an aklé dune, and sometimes one limb of a barchan can be blown away altogether, leaving the remaining limb as a seif dune.

Winds may not blow mainly from one direction. There are places where there are as many days when the wind blows from the west as when it blows from the east, south, and north. Such variable winds blow the sand into star-shaped, or *stellar* dunes. Dunes of this shape can also form where other dunes intersect. A dune of this inter-

Sand dunes

secting type is called a *rhourd*. Intersecting draas also form rhourds.

It seems there is a name, in English, Arabic, or French, for every shape it is possible for a large heap of sand to adopt. This has generated a list of names that may appear bewildering. Order can be brought to it, however, because these dune shapes resolve themselves into just two or three principal types, of which the others are variants. Dunes may be long, more or less straight, and arranged parallel to each other. These are the transverse, longitudinal, and seif dunes and they constitute one main type, or two types if transverse and longitudinal dunes are considered separately. Alternatively, dunes may be crescent-shaped. These are of the second (or third) type and include barchans and parabolic dunes. Stellar dunes and rhourds are derived from these shapes.

Desert Pavement, Erosion, and Varnish

Despite their vast seas of sand, the ergs, sand dunes cover no more than about 30 percent of the Arabian Desert and 11 percent of the Sahara. There are dunes in the North American desert, but only in about 2 percent of the total area.

Dunes used to be more widespread. During ice ages (page 26), when climates are drier, deserts extend farther and there are more dunes. Traces of these "fossil" dunes show that around 18,000 years ago during the last glacial maximum they extended more than 350 miles (563 km) south of the edge of the present Sahara, into West Africa. In Venezuela and northern Brazil sandy deserts once occupied what are now savanna grasslands.

Although sand may be abundant the supply is not limitless and wind that moves it also removes it. Some sand moves by rolling along the surface. This is called *creep*. *Deflation* is the lifting of grains by the wind and their removal downwind in a series of short hops. Smaller particles, of silt and clay, are lifted more easily and carried higher and farther. They can cause dust storms (page 54). Continued long enough, these eolian (wind) processes remove all the small particles from one place and pile them up in another.

Fluvial processes—those involving transport by water—also remove small mineral particles. Rain is infrequent in deserts, but when it falls it often does so torrentially. Water flows across the surface, washing clay, silt, and sand particles into ephemeral streams that carry them away, eventually depositing them where the stream descends to level ground. Material transported by water is called *alluvium,* and when the stream dries the transported particles remain as an *alluvial fan.* These deposits may then be moved farther by the wind.

The effect of wind and water is to remove the smaller material, leaving a surface of bare rock or one covered by stones that are too big and heavy to be transported. These remains compose what is known as a *lag deposit* and there are several types. A stony desert surface is sometimes called a *reg,* but the term is used more precisely to describe a level or slightly sloping gravel surface, made from rounded pebbles. Where gravel is mixed with sand the surface is called *serir.*

Desert Pavement

A rocky surface, including a surface consisting of exposed bedrock, is called *hammada* or *desert pavement.* Exposed bedrock is fairly rare, but desert pavement made from a covering of closely packed stones is one of the most common desert surfaces and occurs widely in the North Ameri-

can deserts. It sometimes forms as a result of deflation. Wind removes the small particles, causing the bigger rocks to sink onto the rocks beneath them until there are only large stones at the surface and the fine material below them is protected from further erosion.

If the pavement is the result of eolian processes, the material beneath it should be well mixed. As the figure shows, however, the surface stones often lie above a layer of sand, silt, or a mixture of the two and, below that, a layer of gravel. There are no stones mixed with the sand or silt and this layer is usually from about 1 inch (2.5 cm) to 1 foot (30 cm) deep. This sorting of particles according to their size cannot have been due to the action of wind. A different process has been at work.

At one time the stones were mixed with the fine particles and over a long period they have risen to the surface. It seems strange to think that big, heavy stones can float upward through a mass of much finer particles, but that is what happens. If you place a few dry pebbles at the bottom of a jar, half fill the jar with very dry sand, then shake the jar for some time, the pebbles will rise to the top. The small particles fall around the bigger ones and fill any spaces that appear beneath them, but then pack together so the pebbles cannot sink downward. Little by little this pushes the pebbles to the top. No one shakes deserts, of course, but occasionally the ground may be soaked with water and in some deserts water below ground may freeze. Some types of clay expand when they are soaked and water expands when it freezes. Expansion pushes upward, producing a bulge at the surface. When the clay dries or ice melts the bulge subsides, but as it does so the small grains fall or are washed beneath the stones, just as they do in the shaken jar. Given enough time—and the surface of a desert has thousands of years in which to form—the stones accumulate at the surface to form a desert pavement.

Ventifacts

Sandblasting is an industrial process used to clean stone and metal surfaces by driving a high-velocity stream of sand grains at them from a nozzle. When billions of sand grains strike an object at high velocity they are extremely abrasive. Desert rocks are subjected to a natural form of sandblasting, and, not surprisingly, they erode rapidly but also unevenly. The softest rocks are removed first, leaving behind the more resistant rocks, as stone

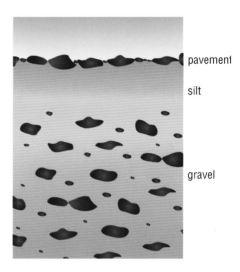

Desert pavement

and metal remain after sandblasting has removed the dirt.

It is not only large rock formations that experience this treatment. So do smaller rocks lying on the surface. The effect is to polish the exposed faces. Stones that are polished in this way are called *ventifacts.* A stone with a single polished facet is called an *einkanter* (German for "one edge") and one with three facets is a *dreikanter.* The dreikanter form is believed to develop as the wind polishes one facet, but at the same time removes sand from beneath the stone until it topples. The wind then repeats the process on a second, and then a third facet.

Mesas, Buttes, and Inselbergs

There are many places where sedimentary rocks, such as sandstone and limestone, form approximately horizontal strata through which harder, igneous rocks have been intruded upward at some time in the past, as magma from the Earth's mantle has penetrated the crust and then cooled and solidified. Erosion often levels the surface of a landscape formed in this way, producing an extensive plain. Further erosion then reduces the plain until isolated fragments of the igneous rock are left standing. They look like steep-sided hills with large, flat tops. Such a fragment of plain is called a *mesa,* which is the Spanish word for "plateau." Erosion continues and a mesa grows steadily smaller in area and height. Eventually all that remains is a flat-topped tower of rock. This is called *a butte,* which is an old word meaning "hill" or "mound."

Where hard igneous rock, such as granite, has been intruded into softer sedimentary rock, the softer rock may be eroded away, leaving the core. This forms a large hill standing alone on the plain called by the German name *inselberg,* which means "island mountain."

Salt Weathering

Salts can also cause weathering in areas where they are plentiful in the rocks or near the ground surface. When it rains, salts dissolve. High temperatures and almost constant wind cause water to evaporate very rapidly, and the salts are left behind. They recrystallize, expanding as they do so and splitting rocks. Crystalline salts also expand and contract in response to changes in temperature to a much greater extent than rocks.

This type of weathering—called *salt weathering*—can produce single rocks standing on top of other rocks to which they are joined by a narrow column of rock. These are known as *pedestal rocks* and the narrow column begins as an *alcove* eroded from around the rock along a shelf in which water can accumulate. Salts dissolve in the water, then crystallize on the rock surface when the water evaporates. This also separates sand grains from the rock. Grains and crystals are then blown away by the wind. Together, salt weathering and wind erosion also produce cuplike hollows, "water pockets" in which water collects as it does in the formation of alcoves, and honeycombs of holes, or pits, in vertical or nearly vertical rock faces. This can leave the rock looking like Swiss cheese. Large holes are called *tafoni* and small ones *alveoles.* The figure illustrates some of these features.

On a much larger scale, some of the rivers that flow after the rains deliver water to shallow lakes that fill depressions in low-lying land. Water then rapidly evaporates from them and as it does so the remaining water becomes increasingly saline. The lake may dry completely, leaving a surface salt deposit. Deposits resulting from the evaporation of water, called *evaporite deposits,* are

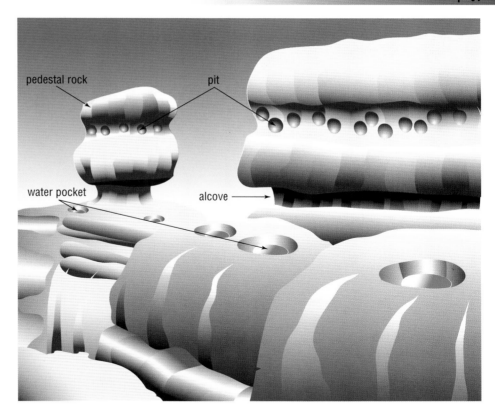

sometimes extensive. They form salt deserts in which very little can survive. Salt lakes that periodically evaporate entirely can also be large. When it is full, the surface area of Lake Eyre, South Australia, is about 3,000 square miles (7,800 sq km).

Desert Varnish and Weathering Rind

As well as salt weathering, desert rocks are affected by other chemical processes. In some places rocks have a black or orange coating, called *desert varnish.* This patina is made from iron and manganese oxides and clays that contain them. Those that are rich in manganese are black, those poor in manganese are orange, and the patina is less than 0.04 inch (1 mm) thick.

Erosional features

The oxides and clays that become desert varnish are carried by the wind and adhere to the surfaces they coat. Scientists believe microorganisms play an important part in the conversion of the coating into varnish. Once formed, the varnishes are highly durable. Some are many thousands of years old.

Rocks may also be covered in a thicker layer of red, orange, or yellow material. This resembles varnish, but is called *weathering rind* and forms differently. The layer, which can be 1 inch (2.5 cm) thick or more, is produced by the weathering of the rock surface. The colors derive from the products of the oxidation of minerals containing iron.

Deserts and Water

Evaporation, Water Flow, Drainage

Sprinkle water onto a dry sponge and the water will quickly soak downward into the sponge. Before long the surface will be dry again. Leave the damp sponge in a dry place and soon it will be completely dry once more. Place a dry sponge onto a wet surface and water will rise into the sponge, leaving the surface drier than it was before.

Soils, even desert soils, behave in very much the same way. After it has rained the ground dries again quickly. The water has disappeared, but obviously it cannot simply have vanished. It must have gone somewhere.

Most of it has returned to the air. It has evaporated, some of it during its fall from the base of a cloud, so it never reached the ground.

Terminal Velocity of Falling Rain

How much of the rain fails to reach the ground depends on the dryness of the air and the length of time the rain takes to pass through it. Drizzle, for example, consists of droplets less than 0.02 inch (0.5 mm) in diameter—and although desert rainfall often takes the form of heavy storms, drizzle and light showers also occur. In a severe storm the raindrops may be about 0.12 inch (4 mm) in diameter. This is close to the upper size limit for a falling water drop. Drops larger than this break into two or more smaller drops.

When a drop of water, or any other body, falls through the air it will accelerate until the gravitational force pulling it toward the center of the Earth is balanced by the resistance to its fall due to frictional force exerted by the air. When this

Thunderhead over desert pan, Amboseli National Park (Gerry Ellis/ENP Images)

point is reached the drop is falling at its terminal velocity and it will maintain this rate of fall until it strikes the ground. The terminal velocity of a falling body is related to its size and shape, because these are what determine the frictional resistance it experiences (gravitational acceleration is a constant, so in a vacuum all bodies accelerate at the same rate). A droplet of drizzle has a terminal velocity of about 8 mph (3.5 m/s) and that of a large raindrop is about 20 mph (9 m/s). In both cases the drops attain this velocity after they have fallen just a few feet. If the cloud base is at, say, 800 feet (244 m) a droplet of drizzle will take about 70 seconds to reach the ground and a large raindrop will take about 27 seconds. Both are losing water by evaporation during the whole of their fall, so it is much more likely that the drizzle will fail to reach the ground than that the big raindrops will. Not only does the drizzle have longer to evaporate, its droplets are much smaller.

Flowing by Gravity

Big drops falling at about 20 mph (9 m/s) strike the ground with considerable force. Small mineral particles, such as those of silt and clay, can be packed tightly together by the impact of raindrops so they form an impervious cap over the surface. The rainwater then flows across the surface, downhill, into a channel if there is one and otherwise spreading, dispersing, and at the same time slowing, as it soaks into the ground. Gentler rain or drizzle falling onto finely particulate material will soak downward and even heavy rain will soak into sand, because its grains are too big to be packed together into a cap. On a desert pavement most or all of the water flows horizontally, across the surface, until it reaches material it can penetrate.

It is gravitational force that causes water to soak into the ground. The water is continuing to fall, flowing through the tiny spaces between mineral grains. Its downward movement continues until it reaches a layer that it cannot penetrate because there are no spaces by which it can pass.

Descending water accumulates at the top of this impermeable layer, filling all the spaces between particles and thus saturating the ground. Water in the saturated region is known as *groundwater* and the upper margin of the saturated zone is the *water table*.

Capillarity and Polar Molecules

Water can also move upward between the mineral particles and there is a partly saturated region known as the *capillary fringe* immediately above the water table. *Capillary* is from the Latin *capillus,* which means "hair," and it describes a very fine tube or channel. Water is able to move upward through capillaries because of the shape of the water molecule.

As everyone knows, water is H_2O. This means a water molecule consists of one atom of oxygen (O) joined to two atoms of hydrogen (H). The bond joining them is said to be *covalent.* This means the atoms share electrons. A hydrogen atom has one electron but will readily accept a second one. An oxygen atom has six electrons but will readily accept two more. As the figure illustrates, two hydrogen atoms each share their electron with an oxygen atom and

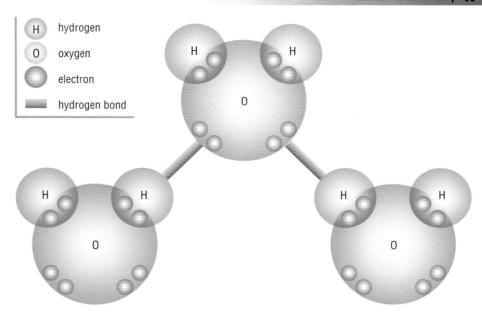

Water molecule

the oxygen atom shares two of its electrons with the hydrogen atoms. Each hydrogen atom then has access to the two electrons it needs to be stable and the oxygen atom has access to the eight electrons it requires. The resulting molecule is stable.

The nucleus of any atom carries a positive electric charge. This is neutralized by the negative charge on the electrons that surround the nucleus. In the water molecule the positive and negative charges balance, so the molecule as a whole carries no charge. To achieve its stable configuration, however, both hydrogen atoms are held on the same side of the oxygen atom; the angle between them is 104.5°. The electrons stabilizing the hydrogen atoms are on the oxygen side and four of the electrons stabilizing the oxygen atom are on the side away from the two hydrogen atoms. This leaves the molecule with a slight positive charge on the hydrogen side and a slight negative charge on the oxygen side. The molecule has two poles, one positive and one negative, and is said to be *polar.*

Its polarity allows the hydrogen atoms on one water molecule to form a fairly weak bond to the oxygen side of another. These are called *hydrogen bonds.*

Hydrogen bonds can also form between water molecules and solid surfaces. Hydrogen bonding between some water molecules and the solid material brings other water molecules within close enough range for them to form hydrogen bonds with the solid at a slightly higher level. This allows more molecules to bond higher still and in this way the water is drawn up the tube—or the narrow, tubelike spaces between mineral particles. The process continues until the weight of the water in the tube is equal to the capillary attraction drawing water up the tube.

The narrower the diameter of the tube, the less water it can hold and, therefore, the less weight the water will have and the higher it can climb.

Evaporation

Molecules of liquid water move freely in their small groups and the more energy they possess, the faster they travel. At a water surface—the boundary between liquid water and air—water molecules are breaking the hydrogen bonds holding them to their groups and escaping into the air. At the same time molecules of gaseous water—water vapor—present in the air are colliding and merging with the liquid and forming hydrogen bonds with other molecules.

If air in the layer, about 0.04 inch (1 mm) thick, above the water surface is holding as many water molecules as it can, molecules escaping from the liquid will immediately be replaced by molecules entering the liquid. The molecules in the layer of air exert a pressure on the liquid, and if that pressure is sufficient to prevent any net migration of molecules from the liquid to the air, the volume of liquid will remain constant.

Whether or not water evaporates depends on whether the vapor immediately above the water surface is saturated. The amount of water vapor air can hold is proportional to the air temperature: the warmer the air, the more water it can hold. A given volume of air at 85°F (29°C) holds more than three times more water vapor than a similar volume of air at 50°F (10°C). This is why water evaporates rapidly into hot desert air.

Aquifers, Oases, and Wells

Rainwater that drains vertically and avoids immediate evaporation will sink fairly slowly through the soil. If there are plants growing where the rain falls, their roots will capture some of the water as it passes and return it to the air (page 60). Water that is not captured will move all the way down to the saturated zone and become part of the groundwater.

In the world as a whole, the water that is above ground as rivers, lakes, and inland seas amounts to about 55,300 cubic miles (230,000 cu km). The water below ground amounts to about 2,016,000 cubic miles (8,398,000 cu km). This volume vastly exceeds that of the surface water, although ice sheets and glaciers contain very much more water than surface liquid water and groundwater combined, and the oceans hold more than 97 percent of all the water on Earth.

Groundwater is not static. It flows downhill, although it moves very slowly as it makes its way between mineral particles that are packed fairly tightly together. Its speed varies according to the porosity and permeability of the material through which it travels. Through most materials it moves at speeds ranging from a few feet per day to a few feet per month, but through clay it may travel no more than 1 foot (30 cm) in a century.

Porosity and Permeability

Porosity and permeability are not the same, although the words are often used interchangeably. *Porosity* is the proportion of a volume of material that consists of spaces, or pores. This can range from 0.5 percent, as fractures in a hard rock such as granite, to 50 percent in some soils.

In a particulate material such as soil porosity has little to do with the size of the particles. You can demonstrate this by placing the same measured volume of gravel, sand, and fine soil into jars and measuring the amount of water needed to saturate each, so water lies on the surface. The volume of water needed for saturation is a measure of the total pore space, the porosity. Express it as a percentage of the volume of each type of particle and you will find there is little difference.

This does not mean water will flow with equal ease through each material. The bigger the particles, the bigger the spaces between them and water flows more easily through a few big spaces than it does through many small spaces, even though the total volume of space is the same. *Permeability* is a measure of the ease with which water moves through a material. This depends on both the porosity and the size of pore spaces. The

shape of particles also affects permeability. Sand grains are very angular, so they do not pack together very closely. This means the spaces between them are bigger than they are in other materials with similar porosity, such as clay. Clay particles are extremely small and flat, like tiny flakes, so they tend to stack on top of each other. Clay and sand are equally porous, but sand is by far the more permeable.

Aquifers, Aquitards, and Aquifuges

Permeable and porous material through which water flows is called an *aquifer*. Aquifers can be huge. Sandstones form a vast aquifer beneath northeastern Africa and part of the Sahara. Another aquifer beneath much of Queensland,

Aquifers

Australia, and extending into the Northern Territory, South Australia, and the northern part of New South Wales is called the *Great Artesian Basin*.

Material such as some types of clay, shale, and silt slows the movement of water, and a mass of such material is called an *aquitard*. Impermeable material that halts the flow is called an *aquifuge* or *aquiclude*. The lower boundary of an aquifer consists of a layer of impermeable material. If all the material between the water table and the ground surface is permeable, the aquifer is said to be *unconfined*. A *confined* aquifer is bounded by impermeable layers both above and below. It can happen that a second aquifer forms above the impermeable layer forming the upper boundary of a confined aquifer. This second aquifer, completely isolated from the aquifer below, is called a *perched* aquifer. The figure illustrates these three types.

Water "finds its own level." That is to say, if two bodies of water are connected and unconfined the surfaces of both will be at the same level with respect to a certain datum, usually sea level. Consequently, the water table—the upper margin of the groundwater—tends to be at the same height above sea level over the entire area of an unconfined aquifer. Ground level, on the other hand, is determined by quite different forces and varies greatly. There are places, therefore, where the water table intersects the ground surface. At these places, depending on the terrain, water either seeps out, wetting the ground, or emerges more vigorously as a spring.

Oases and Wells

Where a natural depression in the ground surface penetrates the aquifer, water will lie on the surface as a lake. Such depressions occur in deserts, and if their water is not too salty they form oases, a word derived from the two Coptic words *oueh,* meaning "to dwell," and *saa,* meaning "to drink." The figure shows how an oasis of this type is formed and, as the drawing suggests, the provision of water is all that is required to stimulate the growth of plants. Other types of oasis are watered by rivers flowing down from adjacent mountains. Oases of this kind are found in the Atacama Desert at the foothills of the Andes and near the edge of Asian deserts, where they are fed by rivers flowing from the Himalaya and Karakorum Mountains.

Dig a hole all the way down to below the water table and the bottom of the hole will fill with water. This is a well and the water in it usually rises above the level of the water table. This is because most aquifers flow across an incline, so wells fill to approximately the level of the highest point in the aquifer. It is another example of water's finding its own level, although the water may be a long way below ground level. Most wells are less than 100 feet (30 m) deep, but some have been sunk to 500 feet (150 m). Drilling equipment for making wells was used in China a little over 2,000 years ago to sink shallow wells to obtain drinking water and also to recover saline water from depths of about 5,000 feet (1,525 m)—salt was obtained from the salt water. Using modern equipment, some wells in Australia have been sunk to about 6,000 feet (1,830 m).

Digging a well is extremely hard work and it is also dangerous. The material that is excavated has to be lifted to the surface, a task that becomes increasingly arduous as the well deepens, and the hole must be large enough for at least one and often more than one person to work. This means it must be at least 3 feet (90 cm) in diameter and the diameter is more likely to be up to 8 feet (2.4 m); some dug wells are 30 or even 40 feet (9–12 m) across. The first danger is that the sides may collapse. The second is that when the water table is penetrated, water may rise so rapidly in the well that the workers have no time to escape.

Once the well has been dug, water is removed either by lowering a bucket on a rope or, nowadays more commonly, by pumping it to the surface. A pumped well can be sunk by drilling a narrow borehole with pumps installed at intervals. This is quicker, simpler, and safer than digging a well by hand and usually cheaper.

Artesian Wells

There are places where no pumping is necessary, because as soon as the borehole crosses the water table water gushes to the surface of its own accord. The first well of this kind was made, probably by drilling, in 1126 C.E. at the small town of Lillers, to the west of Lille in northwestern France. In those days that part of France formed the province of Artois—in modern France it forms part of two départements and the name *Artois* is no longer used. The Latin name for Artois was *Artesium,* so the well at Lillers was said to be of an *artesian* type. There are many artesian wells in the Great Artesian Basin, in Australia.

An artesian well taps into water that is held under pressure. The bottom drawing in the figure shows how this pressure arises in a confined aquifer that is depressed into a hollow. Outside the depression the aquifer is at a higher level than the ground surface inside the depression. If a well is drilled from ground level and through the upper impermeable layer, water will rise to find its own level and, because that level—where the water table would be were the aquifer unconfined—is above ground level, water will flow from the well without pumping.

Oasis

lake

aquifer

impermeable layer

Hadley Cells

Trade used to mean "path," "way," or "track." It implied a constant direction and its modern meaning, of "commerce," is derived from the older meaning.

When European sailing ships began exploring the world in search of exotic goods to sell at home that the ship-owners could buy with goods produced in their own countries, mariners noticed a curious phenomenon in the seas near the equator. The winds, notoriously variable in northern waters, were very dependable. To the north of the equator the winds were almost always from the northeast and south of the equator they blew from the southeast. Using the word in its old sense, sailors called them the *trade winds*.

Although the sailors simply exploited the trade winds, back in Europe there were people who found them a puzzle and sought explanations for their regularity. Why should the wind blow for so much of the time from these two directions and why only in that part of the world? It took a long time to find the answers and those answers explained much more than the trade winds, useful though that was. They also explained why a belt of deserts extends through the tropics and subtropics, encircling the Earth in both hemispheres, and it provided the first clues about what it is that produces the weather.

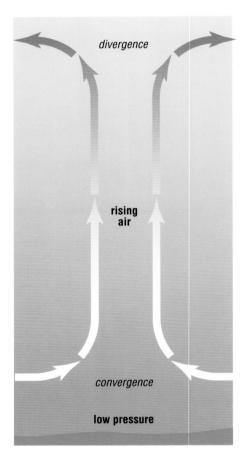

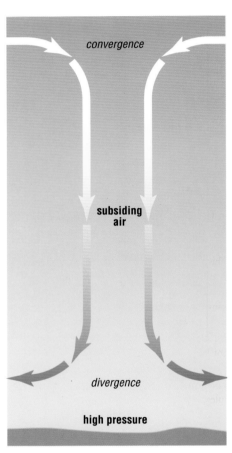

Convergence and divergence

Explaining the Trade Winds

It was not until 1686 that the first serious attempt at an explanation was made. Edmund Halley, the British astronomer, proposed that air is heated more strongly at the equator than anywhere else. The warmed air rises and cooler air flows toward the equator to take its place. This movement of cooler air from higher latitudes accounts for the trade winds.

Edmund Halley (1656–1742) had broad interests and had experienced the trade winds. Two years later, he drew the first meteorological map. In November 1676 he sailed in a ship of the

East India Company to St. Helena, a remote island in the South Atlantic, on an expedition to catalog stars (he cataloged more than 300). That was the first of several voyages he undertook for purely scientific purposes. In 1682 a comet appeared prominently. Halley calculated its orbit and predicted it would return in December 1758. That comet now bears his name. In 1703 he was appointed professor of geometry at the University of Oxford and in 1720 he became Astronomer Royal.

Eminent though he was, Halley was only partly right about the trade winds. The movement he suggested would produce winds blowing

from due north and south, not from the northeast and southeast. He had failed to explain this easterly component.

It was an honorable failure, because no one else did any better for nearly half a century. Then, in 1735, a reason was advanced for the easterly component. Warmed air rises at the equator, just as Halley thought, and is replaced by cooler air from higher latitudes, but while this air is flowing toward the equator the Earth itself is also turning.

The land and sea surface is moving beneath the wind, and it is this motion that swings the moving air, making it reach the equator from the northeast and southeast.

This was the idea of the British meteorologist George Hadley (1685–1768). He had trained to become a lawyer, but found science much more interesting. His proposal set out to do more than explain the trade winds. He thought about where the rising equatorial air went and discovered a way heat might be transferred from the equator to the Poles.

The warm, rising air must move away from the equator in order to make room for more air that is rising to follow it. It flows all the way to the Poles. There it sinks once more and flows back toward the equator. Warm, equatorial air moves into high latitudes. As it does so it makes the regions it crosses warmer than they would be otherwise. By the time it reaches the Poles the air is cold, and it is cold, polar air that moves back to the equator, making tropical regions cooler than they would be otherwise. This is *convection*—the transport of heat through a fluid (gas or liquid) by the movement of the fluid itself.

Convection and Convection Cells

In fact, convection is caused by gravity. When a fluid is heated its molecules acquire energy. They move faster and space themselves farther apart. This causes the fluid to expand, so a given mass of the fluid occupies a greater volume. To put it another way, a given volume of warm fluid contains fewer molecules and therefore less mass than a similar volume of cold fluid. The volume with less mass weighs less. Fluid around it, which has not been warmed and therefore is heavier, sinks beneath the lighter volume, pushing it upward. This is why warm fluid rises. As it rises its molecules lose energy and the fluid cools. Its molecules move more slowly, move closer together, and the fluid becomes denser—the mass of a

given volume increases. Being heavier the fluid now sinks. If there is a source of heat at the bottom, rising warm fluid and sinking cold fluid will establish a vertical circulation. This is called a *convection cell* and Hadley had described a convection cell operating on a huge scale. To this day it is called a *Hadley cell*.

George Hadley made a very important contribution to our understanding of the atmosphere and weather. Unfortunately, he was only partly correct.

He assumed that his convection cell accounted for all air movement and that the atmosphere was otherwise unperturbed. In fact, local variations due to a host of factors mean no single convection cell could remain stable. In fact there is not one Hadley cell, but several.

More seriously, his cells do not extend all the way from the equator to the Poles. This means the air movement generating the trade winds operates over a shorter distance than Hadley supposed and over that shorter distance the effect of the rotation of the Earth is insufficient to account for the easterly deflection. That was explained more than 120 years later, by the American meteorologist William Ferrel (1817–91). Any fluid moving over the surface of the Earth will tend to follow a circular path about a vertical axis—as water does when it flows out of a bathtub—and once it starts to swing, the rotational motion will be maintained. Ferrel proposed in 1856 that it is this rotational movement that swings the air moving toward the equator and produces the northeasterly and southeasterly trade winds. Ferrel also discovered the midlatitude cells named after him. Scientists now accept this as the correct explanation. In all, formulating it took 170 years!

Hadley Cells and Climate

As warm air rises it cools and as air cools its capacity to hold water vapor decreases (page 38). Equatorial air is very moist. Oceans cover most of

the equator and the high equatorial surface temperature allows large amounts of water to evaporate. So it is not simply warm air that rises at the equator: it is warm, *moist* air. As it rises it cools and its water vapor condenses. Clouds form and the water returns to the surface as rain. Equatorial regions have wet climates.

Now cold and dry, the equatorial air moves away from the equator, but not all the way to the Poles. Between latitudes 25° and 30° in both hemispheres it encounters warmer, less dense air and sinks beneath it, subsiding all the way to the surface. Just as rising air expands and cools, so descending air is compressed and becomes warmer. By the time extremely cold air at an altitude of about 50,000 feet (15.25 km) has sunk to ground level its temperature has risen considerably. It is now warm air, but no water has evaporated into it and so it is still very dry.

Imagine a column of air extending from an area on the ground all the way to the top of the atmosphere. If air is subsiding, it must spread out when it reaches the ground and at high altitude air must be entering the column, drawn downward by the divergence at low level. This produces high atmospheric pressure at ground level. Conversely, rising air produces convergence at low level, divergence at high level where air is leaving the column, and low pressure at the ground surface. The diagram illustrates this.

Dry, warm air subsides over the tropics and diverges at low level to complete the Hadley cells. Its divergence generates a general low-level air movement away from the tropics, preventing air from entering the region except from above. Moist maritime air cannot penetrate. Consequently, the Hadley cell produces the humid equatorial climate and the arid tropical climate. In seeking to account for the trade winds George Hadley also explained why there are deserts in the tropics and subtropics of all continents and both hemispheres.

General Circulation of the Atmosphere

Subsiding air and divergence at the surface produce the hot desert climates of the tropics and subtropics. There, surface atmospheric pressure is usually higher than the global average sea-level pressure of 14.7 lb per square inch—sometimes expressed as 30 inches (760 mm) of mercury, 1 atmosphere (1 atm), 1013.25 millibars (mb), or, in international scientific units, as 101.325 pascals (Pa).

Air flows out from this high-pressure region. Some of it flows back toward the equator as the easterly trade winds. The remainder flows away from the equator, also at low level. This air produces generally westerly winds.

At the North and South Poles, air is also subsiding and flowing away from the polar regions at low level. This movement produces polar easterly winds. This air is dry, like the subsiding air in the Tropics, and it produces the cold deserts of the Arctic and Antarctic.

As the air subsides it is compressed and warmed in the same way as tropical air, but polar climates remain cold because the solar radiation they receive is much more diffuse than that which warms the Tropics (page 2). Nevertheless, harsh though they are, polar climates are somewhat milder than they would be without that warming.

Arctic and Antarctic air flows toward middle latitudes, where it meets tropical air moving in the opposite direction from the descending side of the Hadley cell. Air converges and rises, producing a belt of generally low surface pressure. The rising air diverges, some flowing toward the Pole and some toward the equator.

In this way the two main systems of convection cells—the low-latitude Hadley cells and the Arctic and Antarctic cells—drive a third, midlatitude system. This was first described by William Ferrel (page 43) and so these are called *Ferrel cells.*

Together, these three systems of cells provide a very approximate description of the way air circulates over the Earth or, to give it its scientific name, the general circulation of the atmosphere. It is called the *three-cell model*—there are three cells in each hemisphere—and the diagram illustrates it, together with the belts of surface pressure and wind systems it produces.

Troposphere, Tropopause, and Stratosphere

The illustration greatly exaggerates the height of the cells in order to make them easier to see. In fact, there is a ceiling that air rising by convection can penetrate only if it is ascending extremely vigorously, as it does at the top of some really violent storm clouds.

The lower part of the atmosphere, in which all the weather systems reside, is called the *troposphere.* The Greek word *tropos* means "turning." In the troposphere air temperature decreases with increasing height by an average 3.6°F per 1,000 feet (6.5°C/km). Above the troposphere lies the stratosphere—*strato-* is from *stratum,* which is the past participle of the Latin verb *sternere,* meaning "to strew." Throughout most of the stratosphere the temperature remains constant or even increases with height. Air rising through the troposphere encounters air at the base of the stratosphere that is at the same temperature as itself, or warmer. The density of the overlying air is equal to or lower than that of the rising air, so the air can rise no farther.

The boundary between the troposphere and stratosphere is called the *tropopause.* Its height varies seasonally and with latitude, averaging about 10 miles (16 km) at the equator and 5 miles (8 km) at the Poles. Because air temperature decreases with height in the troposphere and the tropopause is higher over the equator than it is over the Poles, the temperature at the equatorial tropopause is lower than that at the polar tropopause. Over the equator it is usually between -95°F and -120°F (-71 to -84°C) and over the Poles -60– -75°F (-51– -59°C).

The wind systems balance, with the energy of the easterly winds equal to that of the westerlies. We can be certain this is so, because winds blowing across the surface of land and sea exert pressure. We feel this pressure when walking on a windy day. If, over a long period and over the world as a whole, either westerly or easterly winds predominated, the Earth would be accelerated or slowed in its rotation by that pressure.

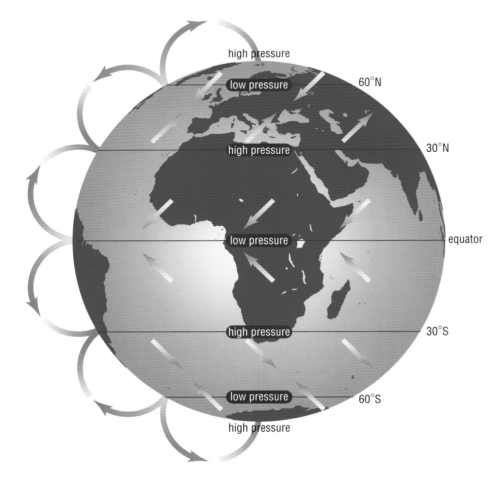

General circulation of the atmosphere

Heat Transport

Incoming solar radiation is not distributed evenly over the Earth. In fact, the equator receives about 2.5 times more energy from the Sun than do the North and South Poles. Were it not for the fact that the general circulation of the atmosphere transfers heat from low to high latitudes, and so has a moderating influence on climate, the temperature difference between low and high latitudes would be much greater than it is.

In fact, though, the atmosphere transfers heat very inefficiently. Solar radiation warms the surface of the Earth and air is warmed by contact with the warmed surface. In the air, convective movement (page 43) converts heat energy into kinetic energy—the energy of motion—but kinetic energy eventually dissipates through friction with the surface and in small eddies. Heat is also transferred through the horizontal movement of air masses (page 46), by ocean currents (page 50), and through the evaporation and condensation of water.

Vorticity and the Conservation of Angular Momentum

It was the American meteorologist William Ferrel who discovered it is the tendency of moving fluids to rotate about a vertical axis that accounts for the easterly component of the trade winds. Known as *vorticity*, this is also the reason for the westerly component in midlatitude winds. Both arise because the Earth and its atmosphere are rotating.

A body that is rotating about an axis possesses angular momentum. This is proportional to the mass of the body, the square of its distance from the axis (the rotational radius), and the rate at which it turns (its angular velocity). Providing no outside force acts to alter any of these, angular momentum remains constant—it is said to be conserved. In other words, if one component changes, one or both of the others will also change to ensure the angular momentum remains the same.

Earth rotates and the atmosphere rotates with it. If a mass of air moves to a different latitude, its distance from the axis of the Earth's rotation will change, because Earth is a sphere. The mass of the air cannot change, so as its rotational radius changes its angular velocity must change to conserve angular momentum. If the air moves away from the equator it will rotate faster and if it moves toward the equator its angular velocity will decrease. This deflects the wind systems associated with the convection cells to the east if the winds are moving away from the equator and to the west if they are blowing toward it. These directions are the same in both hemispheres.

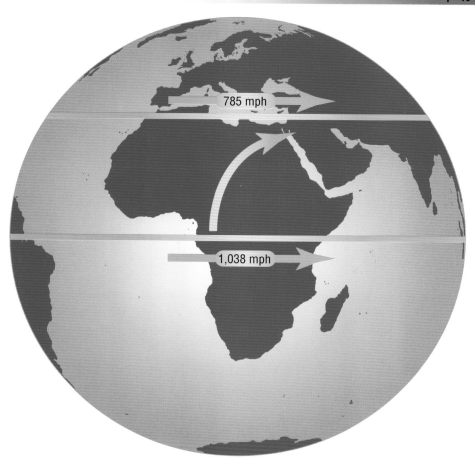

Coriolis Effect

Vorticity is not the same as the Coriolis effect (or force, though no force is involved), the phenomenon first explained in 1835 by the French engineer and mathematician Gaspard Gustave de Coriolis (1792–1843).

The Coriolis effect occurs because we measure positions in relation to points on the surface of the Earth—as being in New York, for example, or Cape Town—without taking account of the fact that the Earth is a rotating sphere. The Earth turns from west to east, completing one rotation every 24 hours. To achieve this, a point on the equator is moving east at approximately 1,038 mph (1,670 km/h) and a point in the latitude of New York is traveling at about 785 mph (1,263 km/h). This is illustrated in the figure.

Suppose an airplane were to take off from an airport on the equator and fly due north to somewhere in the latitude of New York on a journey that takes, say, six hours. Suppose also that the navigator steers by a coordinate system outside the Earth, ignoring completely the position of the airplane with regard to the ground below. As it stands on the runway waiting to take off, the airplane is traveling to the east, because the runway, which is fixed to the

Coriolis effect

Earth, is traveling to the east, and the airplane is still traveling to the east after it has taken off. Away from the equator, however, the ground below the airplane is moving more slowly, but the airplane is still traveling to the east at its original equatorial speed. It is drifting at a rate equal to the difference between the speed a point on the equator moves and the speed a point beneath the airplane moves and the further north it flies the slower the eastward movement of the ground beneath the plane. Consequently, the plane will follow a track over the ground that curves to the east. During its 6-hour flight it will move 6,228 miles (10,021 km) east in relation to the Earth's surface. During that same period, its destination also travels east, but by only 4,710 miles (7,578 km). At the end of the journey, instead of being at its destination airport, the airplane arrives 6,228 - 4,710 = 1,518 miles (2,442 km) to the east of it (no doubt with the navigator trying hard to explain to the passengers where they are and how they come to be there). This is the Coriolis effect.

Intertropical Convergence Zone, Monsoons, and Jet Streams

Air converges where the northeasterly and southeasterly trade winds meet, in an area called the *Intertropical Convergence Zone* (ITCZ). Air rising strongly produces low air pressure near the Earth's surface and, because the rising air carries much moisture, this is the region of intense tropical rainfall. The low-pressure region is not like the depressions that bring wet weather to middle latitudes. Air does not flow around them, because in the Tropics the Coriolis effect (page 45) is very weak, and at the equator it does not exist at all.

As the map at the bottom of this page shows, the ITCZ is not always in the same place. Because the Hadley cell circulation is driven by warmth from the Sun absorbed at the surface, its center moves with the seasons as the Earth's tilted axis turns first one and then the other hemisphere toward the Sun. Despite the seasonal movement, however, the map shows that the ITCZ, and its associated rainfall, never moves far enough to reach the subtropical deserts, much less the deserts of the cool continental interiors.

The contrast between the humid equatorial and arid tropical climates is intensified by a situation that develops as the tropical air flows back across the ocean. Initially dry, the trade winds collect moisture and this cools the air at low level. Above this layer of air, subsiding air is warmed as it descends. This results in a layer of cool, moist air lying beneath a layer of dry, warm air. The moist air cannot rise through the warmer air above. It is trapped beneath a temperature inversion—a condition in which warm air lies above cool air. This

is called the *trade wind inversion*. Because the moist air cannot rise, it cannot cool below its dew point temperature, which is the temperature at which its water vapor will condense, so it remains dry. It is not until the low-level air reaches the ITCZ and is forced to rise through the inversion that it cools and releases its moisture.

Local conditions can alter this pattern. Off the coast of Namibia, for example, the trade-wind air crosses the cool waters of the Benguela Current, and off the coast of Peru and northern Chile it crosses the cool Peru (or Humboldt) Current. The small cooling this causes is enough for water vapor to condense into fog offshore. Sometimes, especially in the Namib Desert, the fog drifts ashore, but the amount of moisture it delivers is very small. The inversion is also broken where the air crosses high mountains.

The amount of water vapor air can contain varies according to the temperature (page 38), and the amount of moisture present in the air is known as the *humidity* of the air. This can be measured in several ways. The *mixing ratio* or *humidity mixing ratio* is the measure scientists find most useful. This is the ratio of the mass of water vapor to a unit mass of dry air—air containing no water vapor. It is usually measured in grams of water vapor per kilogram of dry air. The mass of water vapor in a given mass of air including the water vapor is the *specific humidity*. The total mass of water vapor in a given volume of air, usually expressed in grams per cubic meter, is the *absolute humidity* of that air.

The figure used in weather forecasts is the *relative humidity*, often abbreviated as *RH*. This is the amount of water vapor present in the air expressed as a percentage of the amount that would be needed to saturate the air at that temperature and pressure. Knowing the RH helps forecasters to calculate the likelihood of precipitation, but it tells them nothing about the actual quantity of water vapor in the air, because the warmer the air, the more water vapor it can hold before becoming saturated.

Monsoons

On a regional scale, convergence and divergence produce climates markedly different from those determined purely by the Hadley cell regime. It is because of these variations that central and southern India and the mainland of South Asia are not deserts, despite being in the same latitude as the Sahara. The difference is known by the name that reached English from the Dutch *monsoen* and may have reached Dutch from an Arabic word, *mausim*, which means "season." We call it the *monsoon*, although in fact there are two monsoons, both caused by differences in the way land and sea absorb heat (page 52). Parts of West Africa and northeastern Brazil experience monsoon weather, but it is in India and South Asia that the effect is most marked.

Land warms and cools quickly, the sea warms and cools slowly, and India and South Asia are large landmasses that project into the ocean. In winter, the land cools. This reduces the difference in temperature between land and sea, and at the same time the trade winds shift to the south, with the ITCZ . As the land cools, the surface air pressure increases over it. By the middle of winter, high surface air pressure is centered over Siberia and extends almost to the equator, producing an outward flow of air at low level and northeasterly trade winds. These carry air from central Asia and a pattern similar to that illustrated on page 49. This represents the situation in winter, with high surface pressure in the center produced by subsiding, cold air. In winter the weather is extremely

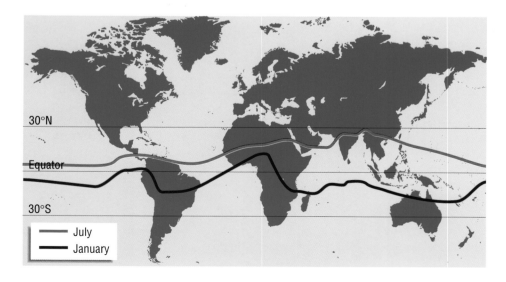

30°N

Equator

30°S

— July
— January

Average positions of the ITCZ in January and July

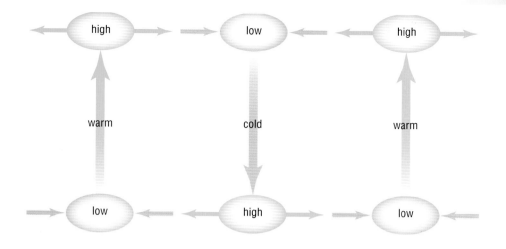

Monsoon circulation

dry. In the 8 months from October through May, Hyderabad in south central India receives an average 7.4 inches (188 mm) of rain and Bombay on the southwestern coast receives 4.1 inches (104 mm). This is the winter, or dry monsoon.

Subsiding air over the land produces high surface pressure and an outward airflow, but at high altitude the pressure is low, because air is moving downward. Its place is taken by air flowing inward, fed by rising air over the oceans to either side of the land. There, surface pressure is low, the air that is rising is warm, and there is high pressure aloft.

In summer, the pattern reverses and the flow depicted in the diagram runs in the opposite direction. Substitute high for low and low for high, cold for warm and warm for cold, and reverse the direction of all the arrows and the diagram will show summer conditions. The land is warmed strongly by the Sun, the air in contact with the surface warms and rises, and air pressure over the land surface is low. This produces high pressure aloft. Air flows outward at high altitude and inward near ground level. Over the ocean the opposite happens. Inward-flowing air aloft causes

air to subside, producing high pressure and outward-flowing air at the surface. This air crosses the ocean, gathering water vapor, and passes over the land, where it rises and loses its moisture.

During autumn the ITCZ moves north and the trade winds change to southeasterlies, because although India and South Asia are in the Northern Hemisphere, they are to the south of the ITCZ, which moves all the way to the southern side of the Himalayas. The mountains form a barrier preventing the incoming air from moving any farther, so the region to their north, in central Asia, remains dry, but south of the ITCZ the winds bring heavy rain. Hyderabad receives 22.2 inches (564 mm) between June and September and Bombay 67.2 inches (1,707 mm). The Asian monsoons make Cherrapunji one of the wettest places in the world. It is in the hills of the northeastern Indian state of Assam, at an elevation of 4,309 feet (1,313 m) and receives an average 425 inches (10,797 mm) of rain a year, of which 316 inches (8,021 mm) falls between June and September. This is the summer, or wet monsoon.

Jet Streams

Where air in a Hadley cell meets air in a Ferrel cell (page 42), in the subtropics, and where air

on the other side of the Ferrel cell meets air in a polar cell, much farther from the equator, there are clearly defined boundaries between warm and cold air. Warm and cold air do not mix very readily and the boundary between them is known as a *front* (page 48). These large-scale fronts are called the *subtropical* and *polar fronts*, respectively.

Above the surface, wind blows parallel to the isobars (lines joining points of equal air pressure) with a speed proportional to the rate at which the pressure changes with horizontal distance. This is called the *pressure gradient* and appears on weather maps as the distance between isobars. Across the subtropical and polar fronts the temperature difference increases the pressure gradient with increasing height. This is because cold, dense air is compressed by the weight of overlying air more than warm, less dense air, so the surface pressure is higher, but pressure decreases more rapidly with height. Consequently, wind speed increases with height, but wind direction remains constant. Winds associated with a temperature gradient are called *thermal winds*.

At the tropopause, above which temperature remains constant with height, the pressure gradient across the fronts is at its most extreme. It produces ribbons of air moving at great speed. These are thermal winds known as the *subtropical* and *polar front jet streams*, and they blow from west to east in both hemispheres. The polar jet stream is the stronger of the two, but less continuous, so the term *jet stream* usually refers to the subtropical jet stream. In winter the jet stream in the Northern Hemisphere lies approximately along the line of the tropic of Cancer and is strongest, with winds sometimes reaching 300 mph (483 km/h). In summer it is at about latitude 50°N and weaker, with speeds seldom exceeding about 50 mph (80 km/h). Local areas of relatively low and high pressure form beneath the jet stream and travel with it. These bring changeable weather to regions in middle latitudes.

Air Masses and Fronts

Warm and cold air do not mix readily. Neither do warm and cold water. Leave a half-filled jar of water in a refrigerator long enough for it to become really cold. Heat a small quantity of water almost to boiling temperature then mix in a few drops of food coloring to make the water easy to see. Take the cold water from the refrigerator. Tilt the jar so you can pour the hot water very carefully and gently into the jar on top of the cold water. Then, slowly and carefully, stand the jar upright. The colored hot water will lie above the cold water and it will stay there until the hot and cold water masses both reach the same temperature. Only then will the color start to spread.

The boundary between the hot and cold water is clearly visible. A similar boundary also forms where cold and warm air meet. Air is invisible, of course, but the position of the boundary can sometimes be seen because of the clouds that form along it. It is not the temperature difference as such that prevents the two bodies of air from mixing, but the difference in their densities.

Where they meet, the denser air sinks beneath the less dense air.

A boundary can exist only if there are two adjoining bodies of air with different characteristics. We take this for granted nowadays but it is not at all obvious. Until this fact was discovered people did not suppose air is exactly the same everywhere, because obviously it is not. Sometimes and in some places it is wet, or dry, or hot, or cold, or clean and fresh, or smoky or stuffy. Air quality can vary in many ways, but these always seemed very local. Leave the smoky city and country air is clean and fresh. Sooner or later dry air will become moist and moist air dry. Changes were gradual from one kind of air to another. As you moved out of the city the air did not improve suddenly, but little by little. It all seemed self-evident, a matter of simple observation and common sense. The challenge to this mental image of the atmosphere began during the latter part of the last century, and it was mounted in Norway.

Vilhelm Bjerknes and the Bergen School

The professor of mathematics of Christiania University in Oslo (now Oslo University) was Carl Anton Bjerknes. On March 14, 1862, a son, Vilhelm Frimann Koren, was born to him. When Vilhelm grew up he helped his father and met some of the leading scientists of his day. Vilhelm became interested in the ways liquids and gases move and circulate on a very large scale. He won backing from the Carnegie Institution, which allowed him to employ talented assistants. He held teaching positions at the universities of Stockholm, Leipzig, and Oslo and in 1917 he founded the Bergen Geophysical Institute and became its director. There, with the help of his

Life cycle of a frontal depression

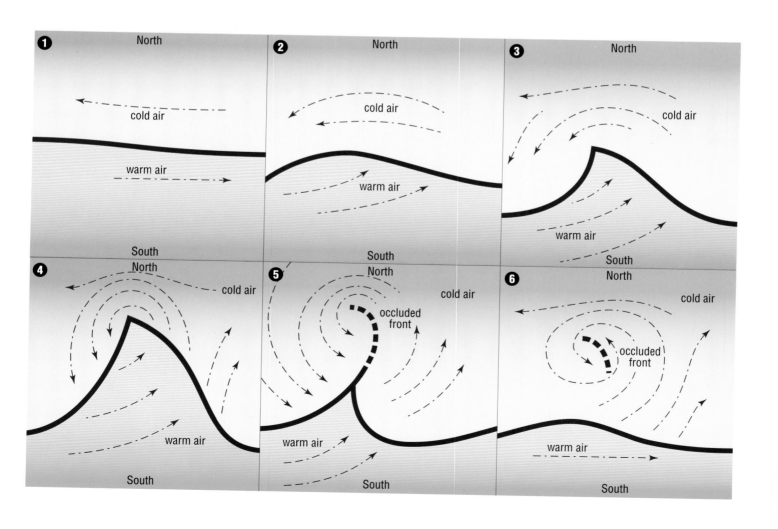

team of collaborators, he established the Bergen School of meteorologists to study the behavior of the atmosphere.

Vilhelm remained there until his death, in 1951. His principal collaborators were his son, Jacob Aall Bonnevie Bjerknes (1897–1975), and Tor Harold Percival Bergeron (1891–1977). They built up a network of weather stations throughout Norway, assembling and analyzing the regular reports they received from them. By 1920 they were able to show that the air is not homogeneous. It comprises immense volumes of "tropical" and "polar" air, distinguished by differences in temperature. They called these volumes *air masses*.

World War I was being fought while much of this work was being done and every day the newspapers were full of stories from the front—the boundary between opposing armies. When they realized that the air exists as air masses, the boundary between two adjacent air masses struck the scientists as resembling the boundary between armies. So they called such a boundary a *front,* the name by which it has been known ever since. Jacob moved to the United States in 1939 and in 1940 obtained a post as a professor at the University of California at Los Angeles. He became an American citizen in 1946.

Frontal Depressions

Polar and tropical air masses meet over the Atlantic at the polar front and the scientists of the Bergen School showed how local areas of low pressure, called *depressions* or *cyclones* (not to be confused with tropical cyclones), develop along it. The diagram shows the sequence of events. At first (*1*) a front lies between polar air to the north and tropical air to the south, with air flowing in opposite directions on either side of the front. A wave develops in the front (*2*). Cold air starts

moving around the warm air. The front is now becoming two fronts. Where the warm air presses against cold air, to the east in the diagram, the front is a warm front. To the west, where cold air is advancing into warm air, it is a cold front. A front is called "warm" or "cold" according to the relative temperature of the air behind it. If the front brings air that is warmer than the air it displaces, it is a warm front; if it brings cooler air it is a cold front. These names refer to the relative temperatures of air on either side of a front, and not to any absolute temperature.

As the wave becomes sharper (*3*) a local region of low pressure forms at the crest. This is the depression, or cyclone, or simply "low." The low intensifies (*4*) and the frontal system now comprises a wedge of warm air surrounded by cold air.

The diagram is very similar to those we see every day in weather maps. Like any map, it depicts a plan view, as seen from above, but this does not give a very clear impression of what is really happening. All the air is moving to the east, but at stage (*4*) the cold air is moving faster than the warm air. Advancing cold air undercuts the warm air, raising it above the ground, and the front slopes. The diagram shows its position at surface level, but it slopes back, away from the warm air, all the way to the tropopause, at an angle of about 2°. The warm front also slopes as it is pushed over the cold air ahead of it. Its slope is much gentler, usually no more than 1/2–1°.

As the cold air continues to advance, some of the warm air is lifted completely clear of the surface (*5*). The two fronts merge and are said to be *occluded*. Finally, a fragment of the occluded front remains (*6*), well clear of the ground, and the original front returns, ready for the cycle to repeat.

When moist air is lifted along a front it cools and cloud may form. Along the gentler slope of the warm front the cloud forms horizontal layers

of the stratus type. From the ground the highest cloud, at the top of the front, is the first to appear. This comprises wispy strands of cirrus and thin, semitransparent sheets of cirrostratus. As the front continues to approach, the cloud thickens with the arrival of altostratus, followed by nimbostratus and stratus, often accompanied by steady rain or snow. The rain stops as the front passes, but the sky often remains cloudy. Then the cold front arrives, its lower edge first. Because it slopes more steeply, warm air is lifted rather more abruptly and some heaped, cumulus cloud forms. Finally, the cold front passes and the sky clears.

Rossby Waves

The polar front marks the high-latitude margin of the Hadley cells and the westerly jet stream is located at its top, near the tropopause. The Swedish-American meteorologist Carl-Gustav Arvid Rossby (1898–1957) is usually credited with having discovered the existence of the jet stream. Another worker from the Bergen School, Rossby moved to the United States in 1926 and it was there that he did his most important work.

In 1940 he showed that undulations form in the high-altitude westerly airflow. At any one time there are usually between three and five of these waves in each hemisphere, with wavelengths (the distance between one wave crest and the next) of up to 1,200 miles (1,930 km). Over cycles lasting a few weeks, these undulations, now known as *Rossby waves,* become more extreme until the airflow breaks down into isolated pockets of air circulating around centers of high and low pressure. It is the development of the Rossby waves that causes the formation of frontal depressions and the eastward movement of the Rossby wave pattern that drags the depressions from west to east.

Oceans and Climates

Winds blowing over the surface of the ocean push the water. This makes waves and it also drives surface currents. Since these are wind-driven, not surprisingly tropical currents flow from east to west, following the direction of the prevailing trade winds. Midlatitude currents flow from west to east, the direction of the prevailing midlatitude westerlies, and inside the Arctic and Antarctic Circles the winds, and therefore currents, travel from east to west.

This makes it sound as though the winds and currents move in parallel belts, as streams flowing in opposite directions, so that a jellyfish, drifting with the surface current, would abruptly change direction if chance should carry it across from one stream into the adjacent one. In the Antarctic the current does flow in this way. It is called the *Antarctic Circumpolar Current,* or *West Wind Drift,* and it flows from west to east all the way around the world, driven by the Southern Hemisphere midlatitude westerlies, forming a broad belt of moving water approximately between latitudes 60° S and 66° 30' S—the Antarctic Circle. It is able to do so because no continental landmass extends south of 60° S to interrupt the flow. Cape Horn, the southernmost point of South America, is at 55°47' S.

Everywhere else, both easterly and westerly currents are deflected by the continents. At the same time, on the very large scale of an ocean, flowing water does not move in straight lines. Because of the rotation of the Earth, it tends to flow in circles, or vortices (page 44). Vorticity deflects the flow of ocean currents to the right in the Northern Hemisphere and to the left in the Southern Hemisphere. The overall result is that in each of the oceans and larger seas there is an approximately circular system of currents, called a *gyre.*

Atlantic and Pacific Gyres

In the tropical North Atlantic, the combined Guinea Current and Atlantic North Equatorial Current, flowing westward, enter the Caribbean and Gulf of Mexico, passing Florida as the Florida Current and then following the coast of the Carolinas before heading across the ocean in a northeasterly direction as the Gulf Stream. It originates in the Tropics and carries warm water. In about the latitude of Boston, part of the current swings farther to the right as it approaches Europe, heading south along the North African coast as the Canary Current. Its water is now cooler than that of the more southerly ocean, but the Canary

Current joins the eastern end of the Atlantic North Equatorial Current and its water warms under the tropical Sun.

Not all of the Gulf Stream turns south. A branch of it continues flowing northeast, as the North Atlantic Drift, passing the western shores of the British Isles, then Norway, where it becomes the Norway Current, which rounds the North Cape and ends in the Barents Sea. Another, smaller branch flows along the western coast of Greenland, as the West Greenland Current. All these branches of the Gulf Stream are warm currents.

There is a similar gyre in the South Atlantic. The warm Brazil Current flows south down the eastern coast of South America, turns easterly and becomes the cold South Atlantic Current, then heads north along the African coast as the cold Benguela Current. In the North Pacific, the Pacific North Equatorial and Kuroshio Currents carry warm water from the Tropics along the eastern coast of Asia and return to the Tropics as the cold California Current, flowing past the western coast of North America. In the South Pacific the Pacific South Equatorial and East Australian Currents carry warm water south, past Australia, and the South Pacific and Peru (or Humboldt) Currents carry cold water north, past the western coast of South America.

Obviously, the Atlantic and Pacific Ocean Gyres transport heat from low to high latitudes, from equatorial regions where in late summer the sea-surface temperature commonly reaches 85°F (29°C) to the very edge of the permanent sea ice. This transport greatly moderates global climates. Without it the polar regions would be much colder than they are and the equatorial regions much warmer.

The Atlantic Conveyor

It is not only the wind that drives the movement of ocean water. There is another "machine" at work on an even bigger scale. It is called the *Atlantic Conveyor.*

As water cools, its molecules move closer together, causing the density of the water to increase. This continues until the density reaches a maximum. In seawater this depends on the salinity, but for water with the average ocean salinity of 34.7 grams of salt per 1000 grams of seawater (34.7 [‰]), the maximal density is reached at 32°F (0°C). Seawater with this salinity freezes at 28.6°F (-1.9°C). As the temperature continues to fall, water molecules start forming

ice crystals. These have an open structure—they form hexagonal shapes with a space at the center—so the density decreases. Ice is less dense than water just above freezing temperature, and that is why ice floats. The water at the edge of the sea ice, therefore at its greatest density as a result of temperature.

It is also very saline. This is because when ice crystals form only water molecules are involved. Substances dissolved in the water are left behind. If you leave some salt water in the freezer until ice forms on its surface and taste the ice you will find the ice is not salty. Salt, "squeezed out" as ice forms, enters the adjacent water, causing its salinity to increase, and because the amount of salt dissolved in the water increases, the density of the water also increases.

Water near the edge of the sea ice is denser than the ice itself and it is also denser than water farther away, which is warmer and on which ice is not forming. The dense water sinks beneath the less dense water and goes on sinking all the way to the bottom of the ocean. It is then called the *North Atlantic Deep Water* and it flows along the bottom as a very slow-moving current all the way to the Antarctic Ocean. Its place at the surface is taken by water flowing north. This is the Atlantic Conveyor. It is the underlying mechanism driving the circulation of all the oceans.

Ocean Currents and the Weather They Bring

As an air mass crosses an ocean its characteristics are modified by the temperature of the water beneath it. This produces marked differences between the eastern and western coasts of continents. The difference affects average temperatures, but it affects precipitation much more dramatically. The rate of evaporation is higher in warm than in cool water, because the water molecules have more energy, so more of them can break free of the hydrogen bonds that hold them to their neighbors. Air warmed by contact with the warm water can hold more water vapor because it is warmer. In the course of its long journey over a warm ocean, air becomes very moist. Less water evaporates from cold water and air chilled by contact with it can hold less water, so an air mass passing over cold water loses much of the water it was carrying and becomes dry. Consequently, the western coasts of midlatitude continents, adjacent to cold currents, usually have drier climates than the eastern coasts. Northwestern Europe is an exception, because the North Atlantic Drift brings warm water to its shores. Farther south, Portuguese shores are washed by the cooler Canary Current.

The difference can be seen by comparing the climates of Brisbane, on the eastern coast of Queensland, Australia, and Antofagasta, Chile, on the western coast of South America. Brisbane experiences the warm East Australian Current, Antofagasta the cold Peru Current. In Brisbane, at 27° S, the average daytime temperature in the four warmest months is 84°F (29°C) and the average nighttime temperature in the four coolest months is 51°F (11°C). The comparable figures for Antofagasta, closer to the equator at 23° S, are 62°F (17°C) and 52°F (11°C). It seldom rains at all in Antofagasta: the annual average is 0.5 inch (13 mm). Brisbane receives an average 45 inches (1,135 mm) a year, with rather more rain in summer than in winter but no month with no rain. Antofagasta is in the Atacama Desert.

The South Atlantic Gyre produces similar contrasts. Rio de Janeiro, Brazil, and Walvis Bay, Namibia, are in almost precisely the same latitude, Rio on the eastern coast of South America and Walvis Bay on the western coast of Africa. At Rio, the average daytime temperature in the four warmest months is 84°F (29°C) and the average nighttime temperature in the four coolest months is 64°F (18°C). The equivalent temperatures in Walvis Bay are 74°F (23°C) and 47°F (8°C). Rio receives 43 inches (1,085 mm) of rain a year, distributed fairly evenly. Walvis Bay has an average 0.8 inch (20 mm) of rain a year. Walvis Bay lies in the Namib Desert.

In the Northern Hemisphere it is the cold California Current that brings dry weather to southern California. San Diego receives only 10 inches (259 mm) of rain a year compared with the 48 inches (1,209 mm) that falls in Charleston, South Carolina, in the same latitude.

Ocean currents, therefore, contribute to the climates of the subtropical deserts.

Desert Weather

Heat Capacity, Conductivity, and Microclimates

Deserts are dry. In particular, their soils are dry. Just how dry depends on the air temperature and winds as well as the amount of precipitation. A desert climate is one in which more water evaporates from the ground than the ground receives as rain or snow.

Obviously, over any extended period the ground cannot lose more water than it receives so instead of "evaporation" what matters is *potential evapotranspiration*. That is the rate at which water would evaporate from the ground surface and be transpired by plants (page 60) if there were an unlimited supply of water. It is close to the rate at which water would evaporate from an open water surface and can be measured by using an evaporation pan. This is a container of a standard size that is placed in the open, exposed to the air, and filled with water. The water depth is measured at the beginning and end of a convenient period such as 1 day or 1 week. The rate of evaporation is calculated from the change in depth, after allowance has been made for the small difference between evaporation from open water and from wet ground, and the amount of any precipitation that fell during the period has been deducted. In the cool, moist climate of northern Europe about 8 inches (203 mm) of water evaporates in a year. In parts of the Sahara the potential evaporation exceeds 90 inches (2,286 mm) a year. This vastly exceeds the annual precipitation there and defines the region as desert. It also has another significance. If the land is to grow crops, the amount of water supplied by irrigation must exceed the potential evaporation during the growing season. Although water evaporates faster the higher the temperature, a cold climate can also be a desert climate if the potential evapotranspiration exceeds precipitation.

Water evaporates readily in hot deserts because the temperature is high and the air very dry. For much of the time the sky is cloudless and by day the Sun beats down mercilessly. Somewhat more than one-third of the incoming radiation is reflected. Dry sand has an albedo (reflectivity) of 35–40 percent (page 20). The reflected radiation does not heat the ground; it goes directly back into space. Once the absorbed heat has raised the surface temperature, the surface itself begins radiating heat back into space.

During the morning the air temperature over the desert rises steadily. Noon passes and the air continues to grow hotter. At In Salah, Algeria, the temperature in July averages 113°F (45°C) and has been known to reach 127°F (53°C). It is not until the middle of the afternoon, between three and four o'clock, that the temperature reaches its maximum, after which it starts falling, slowly at first and more rapidly after sunset. The night is cool, but in summer it is cool only by comparison with the daytime heat. At In Salah, the July average minimum temperature is 83°F (28°C) and it never falls below 70°F (21°C).

Specific Heat Capacity

This is only part of the story, however, because so far as living organisms are concerned what matters is the climate at ground level and in the middle of the day the ground is much hotter than the air. On a hot summer day even in temperate latitudes dry sand can be hot enough to hurt bare feet. In the Sahara it can burn them. Sand and rock can reach 170°F (77°C).

Sand and rock heat up much more rapidly than water and they also lose heat much faster. When a substance is exposed to heat its temperature rises, but different substances warm at different rates. The amount of heat that must be applied to a substance to make its temperature rise by 1° is called the *specific heat capacity* of that substance and with some substances it varies slightly at different temperatures. The specific heat capacity of water at 59°F (15°C) is 4.19 (the units are joules per gram per degree Celsius, but this is not important for the purpose of comparing substances). The specific heat capacity of dry sand and most types of solid rock, at temperatures between 68°F and 212°F (20–100°C), is about 0.8. This means it requires more than five times more heat energy to raise the temperature of water by 1° than to raise the temperature of rock or sand by the same amount. Consequently, as the Sun climbs higher in the sky the dry ground heats much faster than water and much faster than the ground would if it were wet, because then its specific heat capacity would be about 1.48. By the time the Sun passes its zenith and begins to sink, the dry ground has reached a much higher temperature than nearby water has. Then both dry ground and water start to cool.

Just as its specific heat capacity measures the amount of heat needed to raise the temperature of a substance, it also measures the rate at which heat is lost. Sand and rock warm more quickly than water and for precisely the same reason they also cool more quickly. The ground temperature falls sharply, reaching a minimum an hour or two before dawn, but the temperature of water falls much more slowly. Air is heated by the surface beneath it. Over the ocean in subtropical latitudes the difference in day and night air temperatures (the diurnal temperature range) is about 0.4°F (0.2°C). Over the desert in the same latitude the diurnal temperature range is about 72°F (40°C).

Conductivity and Damping Depth

Its low specific heat capacity is only part of the reason why sand heats so fast and reaches such a high temperature. Dry sand consists of irregularly shaped grains loosely stacked together with air filling the spaces between them. Sand is a poor conductor of heat and air is an even poorer one. Radiant heat raises the surface temperature, but the heat is not conducted very far below the surface. The upper, heated layer just goes on getting hotter, but a little way below the surface the temperature hardly changes.

As the surface temperature rises during the morning, heat is conducted below the surface, but it happens slowly and reaches only a certain depth before the daily peak temperature is passed. Beyond this depth, therefore, the temperature does not alter. It is called the *damping depth;* in dry sand it is about 3 inches (7.6 cm) below the surface. Because heat penetrates slowly, the peak temperature is reached at the damping depth several hours later than it is reached at the surface.

Subtropical deserts experience seasons, so there is a seasonal cycle of rising and falling temperature as well as a daily one. The gradual warming during spring and summer also heats the ground, but in many deserts the seasonal temperature range is smaller than the diurnal range, so the effect is not great. The damping depth for the annual cycle is about 0.6 inch (1.5 cm).

This is true only in subtropical deserts, however. Deserts in higher latitudes are found in the interior of continents or in the rain shadow of mountains. In these places the climate is arid either because of moisture loss of the approaching air crossing a mountain range or because of the distance from the nearest ocean. In such continental climates seasonal temperature differences can be extreme, with scorching summers and very cold winters. In Death Valley, California, summer temperatures sometimes exceed 130°F (54°F), but in January they have been known to fall to 15°F (-9°C). The seasonal variation may increase the annual damping depth, but not

beyond 3 inches (7.6 cm), because this depth is determined by a physical property of sand.

Conditions below ground, therefore, are very different from those at the surface. The ground may be blisteringly hot, but just a few inches down the temperature is quite tolerable and remains almost constant throughout the day.

Microclimates

In other words, the climate a few inches below the ground differs markedly from the climate at the surface. A local climate of this kind is called a *microclimate* within the *macroclimate* of the region as a whole. Many living organisms exploit the advantages offered by microclimates.

The subsurface climate is not the only desert microclimate. There are several immediately above the ground surface. Hollows that are shaded most of the time will be cooler than exposed, sun-lit surfaces, for example, and exposure to or shelter from prevailing winds can also create microclimates.

Above ground the air is much cooler than the surface of the sand or bare rock. At a height of 6.5 feet (2 m) the midday temperature may be 55°F (30°C) lower than the temperature at ground level.

Early in the morning the ground above the damping depth is cold. As the Sun rises and its warmth intensifies, heat is absorbed by the ground. During the hottest part of the day energy is transferred from the ground to the air by convection. Air is heated by contact with the very hot ground and rises strongly, creating extremely turbulent conditions. At night, the ground surface is warmed by heat conducted from the layers above the damping depth. As the heat rises to the surface and is radiated away, the ground cools.

Camelthorn acacia in sand dune (Gerry Ellis / ENP Images)

A desert has one macroclimate, but many microclimates that change in the course of the day and in higher latitudes in the course of the year. There is one distinct region below the damping depth. There, about 12 inches (30 cm) below ground level, the temperature hardly changes. It is warm when temperatures above the surface are low and cool when they are high. The ground surface is the place of greatest extremes, but even there conditions are more moderate in the microclimates found in sheltered places. Above ground level, the temperature decreases with height.

Dust Storms, Sandstorms, Dust Devils, and Whirlwinds

Weather systems travel from west to east in middle latitudes. They bring areas of low and high atmospheric pressure, and, associated with the highs and lows, they bring winds. Sometimes they bring very strong winds.

Air flows from an area of high pressure toward an area of low pressure in order to equalize the pressures in the two areas. The difference in pressure between the centers of high and low pressure constitutes a pressure gradient and the movement of air is driven by a *pressure gradient force,* or PGF. The pressure gradient can be depicted on a weather chart in the same way that a hillside can be depicted on a map. A map contour is a line joining points, all of which are at the same elevation, so the distance between contour lines shows the rate at which elevation changes with horizontal distance—in other words, the gradient. On a weather map, a line joining points at which the atmospheric pressure is the same is called an *isobar.* The Greek *isos* means "equal," *baros* means "weight," and so *isobarēs* means "of equal weight."

Why Wind Flows Parallel to Isobars

You would expect the wind to flow at right angles to the isobars, following the most direct route from the center of high pressure to the center of low pressure. That would equalize the pressure very rapidly. Then there would be no winds, because pressure differences would vanish the moment they started to develop.

This is not what happens. There are winds and they can last for hours or days on end, although their speed is still proportional to the pressure gradient and it is still the PGF that drives them. What happens, though, is that instead of blowing across the isobars, well clear of the ground the wind blows parallel to them. Below about 1,500–3,000 feet (460–900 m), depending on the type of surface, friction between the moving air and the surface slows the wind and this causes it to blow at an angle to the isobars, in the direction of the low-pressure center.

Winds are driven by the PGF, but as soon as air begins to move on a large scale across the surface of the Earth it is subject to the Coriolis effect, or CorF (*F* because it was once thought to be a force; see page 44). This acts at right angles to the direction of flow with a magnitude proportional to the speed, deflecting the flow to the right in the Northern Hemisphere and to the left in the Southern. The figure illustrates what happens. The parallel lines in the diagram are isobars. The PGF acts at right angles to the isobars. As the air starts to move, the CorF, acting at right angles to the direction of motion, swings it to the right. Between them, the PGF and CorF produce a resultant force that accelerates the wind, but acceleration increases the CorF, swinging the wind farther to the right until it flows parallel to the isobars. The PGF and CorF are then acting in opposite directions, the PGF at right angles to the isobars, the CorF at right angles to the direction of flow, and the situation is stable. If the PGF increases, it will swing the wind to the left and accelerate it. This will increase the CorF, which

will pull it back. If the wind accelerates, the CorF will swing it farther to the right, but it will encounter increased resistance from the PGF. This will slow it, reducing the CorF and turning it back again.

Dust Storms and Sandstorms

Weather systems and their associated winds take several days to develop and several more days to dissipate, and in middle latitudes they are usually traveling eastward the whole of this time. They bring no rain to the desert, because desert air is very dry. It is possible for the relative humidity to exceed 80 percent near coasts, high enough for some cloud to form if the air also contains a plentiful supply of salt crystals. These are hygroscopic: that is, they readily combine with water vapor to form liquid droplets. More commonly, the relative humidity (RH) must be close to 100 percent before cloud will develop.

The weather seldom brings rain, but it often brings winds blowing at 20 mph (32 km/h) or more. Wind blowing at this speed will raise dust particles and sand grains from the ground. Not all deserts are sandy, of course, but in those that are, sandstorms are common.

The khamsin (page 8) and harmattan are local winds that often produce dust storms and sandstorms—the two differ only in the size of particles they carry. These can be severe and people take shelter from them, sealing all windows and doors and covering exposed parts of their bodies. The hot wind produces huge clouds of swirling dust and sand, dense enough to reduce visibility almost to zero. Storms of this kind are known as *andhis* in India and *simoom* in the Sahara. They cause damage to the eyes. The Egyptians have several proverbs referring to blindness and failing eyesight caused by dust. These problems are distressingly common and dust is a major cause.

There is another way windstorms can develop. When the surface temperature is very high, the rate at which temperature decreases with height—the lapse rate—increases in the lower part of the atmosphere. At night, when the surface has cooled to below the temperature of the air some distance above the ground, the situation is reversed. The figure illustrates the general pattern.

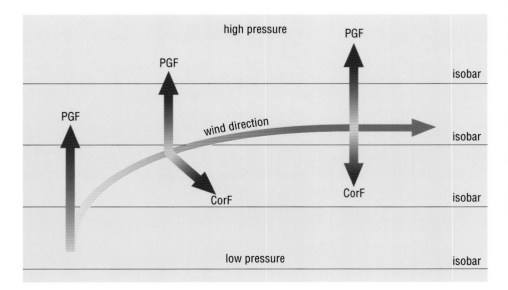

Why wind flows parallel to isobars

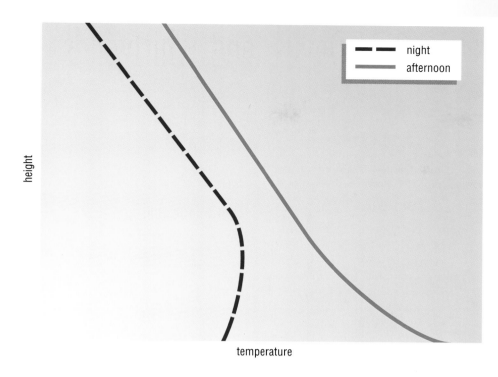

During the day the ground heats strongly and the air temperature decreases rapidly with height. At night the situation is reversed and the ground may even be colder than the air above it.

From the late morning until late in the afternoon, air is being heated strongly from below, expanding, and becoming less dense. Denser air is sinking beneath it, lifting it from the ground. This generates considerable turbulence, with strong low-level winds that raise dust and sand. The resulting storms are most common in the afternoon and can make any outdoor activity difficult.

Dust Devils

Dust storms and sandstorms are big. They darken the sky and their approach can be seen from afar. The desert also has other winds that produce effects that are smaller but no less dramatic.

Surface heating can be very local indeed. Because of its surface texture or composition, or the way it is angled in relation to the rays of the Sun, a patch of sand or rock can become much hotter than its surroundings. Air over the "hot patch" expands, and cooler, denser surrounding air rushes in, lifting the heated air.

As air converges on what has become a very small area of low surface pressure, vorticity sets it rotating, in the Northern Hemisphere, counterclockwise. The air turns around the low-pressure center, but friction with the ground prevents it from moving parallel to the isobars. It flows at an angle across the isobars, spiraling inward, and, to conserve its angular momentum (page 44), the smaller its spiraling radius, the faster the wind blows. Convergence means that the air must also rise, so it spirals inward and upward. It blows fast enough to gather dust and sand, which it carries with it and which make the moving air visible. Small, spiraling columns of dust and sand are called *dust devils* and they are very common, especially in the afternoon.

They are also harmless. Dust devils have enough energy to rise only a short distance from the ground and they last for only a few seconds before the movement of air eliminates the pressure difference that causes them.

Whirlwinds

There are also much larger forms, however, and they are much more alarming. These are the whirlwinds that were very familiar to the authors of the Old Testament: "When your fear cometh as desolation, And your destruction cometh as a whirlwind" (Proverbs 1, 27); "Behold, a whirlwind of the Lord is gone forth in fury, even a grievous whirlwind" (Jeremiah 23, 19).

Whirlwinds are generated in the same way as dust devils, and the names are often used interchangeably, but *whirlwind* in the biblical sense means something much more terrifying than the swirl of air that raises dust, dry leaves, and scraps of paper. A whirlwind funnel can reach a height of more than 6,000 feet (1,830 m), and its winds are strong enough to demolish flimsy buildings—and the tents of desert nomads. They look like tornadoes but never generate wind speeds approaching those of a genuine tornado, and, unlike tornadoes, they grow from the ground up, rather than descending from a cloud. There is no black cloud above a whirlwind.

This makes them more frightening, not less. Predicting tornadoes is very difficult, but at least meteorologists have no trouble identifying tornadic storms—storms capable of producing tornadoes—and these can be seen approaching long before they arrive.

Whirlwinds rise without warning, like screaming wraiths, and very often they occur in families, so several are active at the same time, all wandering about erratically and unpredictably. No individual lasts for more than a few minutes, but as one dies down another arises. It is little wonder that, in ancient times, people familiar with the desert compared them to armies descending with destructive fury on hapless and helpless villages.

Dust devil (Gerry Ellis/ENP Images)

PART 4

Photosynthesis

With the midday Sun beating down mercilessly, there is little sign of life. No animal crawls or scuttles across the ground. No bird crosses the sky or circles slowly, searching for a meal that does not exist. The desert seems dead.

It is not dead. A closer look reveals a few plants. There are not many, they are scattered widely, but they are present and if there are plants, somewhere there will be the animals that feed on plants. If there are herbivorous—plant-eating—animals there will also be carnivores—meat eaters—preying on them. Apart from some species living near volcanic vents on the ocean floor, all animals depend on plants for food, directly or indirectly.

Without plants there can be no animals and there is one substance, chlorophyll, without which there can be no plants. Indeed, without chlorophyll there could be no land-dwelling organism bigger or more complicated than a bacterium.

Chlorophyll is a chemical compound that absorbs photons of light energy. Only photons with a particular amount of energy, corresponding to particular wavelengths of light, can be absorbed. These correspond precisely to the amount of energy needed to raise an electron in the chlorophyll molecule to a higher energy level—from its ground state to its excited state. That electron is then captured by a neighboring molecule, called the *primary electron acceptor,* after which it is passed from molecule to molecule along a chain. As electrons move along the

Damaraland euphorbia

56

chain their energy is used to drive a series of chemical reactions. These reactions convert carbon dioxide, taken from the air, and water, taken from the ground, into sugars. The process is called *photosynthesis* and it can be summarized as follows:

$$6CO_2 + 6H_2O + \text{light energy} \rightarrow$$
$$C_6H_{12}O_6 + 6O_2\uparrow$$

In the products of the equation, $C_6H_{12}O_6$ is glucose, a sugar (though not actually the sugar produced by photosynthesis, which is a more complex substance), and the oxygen is released into the air, as indicated by the arrow pointing upward.

Chlorophyll is the green pigment that gives plants their color, but plants contain two types of chlorophyll and there are other, accessory pigments that contribute to photosynthesis. Chlorophyll *a* is blue-green, chlorophyll *b* is yellow-green, and carotenoids are various shades of yellow and orange. Carotenoids can be oxidized into the brightly colored red, orange, and yellow xanthophylls that produce the colors of fall in temperate forests.

The colors we see around us are those of the light that is reflected from objects. A green plant looks green because it reflects green light. Obviously, light that is reflected cannot be absorbed, so although we think of natural greenery as wholesome, green is the one color for which plants have no use.

Chloroplasts, Reaction Centers, and the Two Photosystems

The photosynthetic pigments are located inside lens-shaped structures called *chloroplasts.* Beneath the outer layer of leaf cells there is a layer of tissue called *mesophyll* and each mesophyll cell contains an average of 30 to 40 chloroplasts. There are pores, called *stomata* (the singular is *stoma*), in the outer layer of the leaf. These can be held open or closed by means of guard cells on either side that can swell or contract. Each chloroplast contains an assembly of a few hundred pigment molecules, including both types of chlorophyll and carotenoids. All but two of these molecules collect light photons and pass them to the central pair of chlorophyll *a* molecules. These are the only ones to trigger the chain of photosynthetic reactions and they are known as the *reaction center.*

The entire assembly composes a *photosystem.* There are two types of photosystem, called *photosystem I* and *photosystem II,* because of the order in which they were discovered. In photosystem I, the chlorophyll *a* molecules at the reaction center respond most strongly to light at the far red end of the spectrum, with a wavelength of 700 nanometers (nm), so they are called *P700*. The reaction center molecules in photosystem II respond most strongly to red light at 680 nm and are called *P680*. Carotenoids also absorb light energy at other wavelengths and pass on their excited electrons to the reaction center.

Light Reactions and Phosphorylation

Photosynthesis proceeds in two stages. In the first, light energy is used to split water into hydrogen and oxygen. The hydrogen is stored temporarily by being attached to nicotinamide-adenine dinucleotide phosphate (NADP), converting it to reduced NADP (NADPH), and the oxygen is released into the air as a by-product. These are the reactions that convert light energy into the chemical energy used in the second chain of reactions, so they are known as the *light reactions* or *light-dependent reactions.*

In the course of the light reactions, some of the excited electrons in photosystem I provide energy to add a phosphate group to adenosine diphosphate (ADP), converting it to adenosine triphosphate (ATP). In doing so, the electrons lose energy and eventually return to their ground state to the chlorophyll. The addition of a phosphate group is called *phosphorylation,* phosphorylation by means of light energy is called *photophosphorylation* and because the electrons are cycled back to the chlorophyll from which they came, this version is known as *cyclic photophosphorylation.*

Other excited electrons are passed along an electron transport chain from photosystem I to photosystem II and are also used to convert ADP to ATP. In this case the electrons are not returned, so the process is called *noncyclic photophosphorylation.*

Phosphorylation is the means by which energy is stored. When ATP loses a phosphate, energy is released. ATP can be transported to wherever it is needed and so it can supply energy to any cell needing it.

ADP consists of adenosine bonded to two phosphate (PO_4) groups and it is synthesized in all living cells. Adenosine consists of adenine, which is one of the components of deoxyribonucleic acid (DNA) and ribonucleic acid (RNA), attached to a ribose sugar, which is a sugar containing five carbon atoms. When energy is supplied to an ADP molecule—in most cells by the oxidation of carbon in the process known as *respiration*—it is able to accept an additional phosphate group. ADP then becomes adenosine triphosphate (ATP). ATP is unstable, however, because each phosphate group carries a negative charge, so they repel each other. If a molecule of water comes into contact with an ATP molecule, the third phosphate group is detached and the remaining two move a little farther apart. The conversion of unstable ATP to the more stable form of ADP plus a phosphate group releases energy (technically, it releases 30.6 kilojoules of energy per mole). This reaction is the source of almost all the energy used by living cells. In a working muscle cell, for example, phosphates released from ATP are transferred to the proteins that cause the muscle to contract and it takes the cell about 1 minute to use up all the ATP it contains. This is regenerated by using energy from respiration. Every second, 10 million molecules of ATP are consumed and the same number are regenerated.

The Calvin Cycle

NADPH and ATP from the light reactions then drive the dark, or light-independent, reactions. These form a cycle in which the starting material is regenerated. It is known as the *Calvin cycle,* because details of its steps were discovered by a team at the University of California at Berkeley led by the American biochemist Melvin Calvin (1911–97), for which he was awarded the 1961 Nobel prize for chemistry.

The Calvin cycle begins by attaching a molecule of carbon dioxide (CO_2) to a molecule of ribulose biphosphate, abbreviated as *RuBP,* by a reaction catalyzed by the enzyme RuBP carboxylase, or rubisco. RuBP is a sugar containing five carbon atoms, so the addition of CO_2 (the reaction is called *carboxylation*) produces a six-carbon sugar. This is unstable and immediately divides into two molecules of 3-phosphoglycerate. Each 3-phosphoglycerate molecule then receives a phosphate group, obtained from ATP, and becomes 1,3-diphosphoglycerate. NADPH then donates two electrons, reducing the 1,3-diphosphoglycerate to glyceraldehyde 3-phosphate, the sugar that is the end product of the cycle.

Three complete turns of the cycle is needed to produce six molecules of glyceraldehyde 3-phosphate. One glyceraldehyde 3-phosphate molecule leaves the cycle and the remaining five are converted into three molecules of RuBP. In synthesizing one molecule of glyceraldehyde 3-phosphate that can be released, the Calvin cycle uses nine molecules of ATP and six of NADPH. These are immediately replaced by the light reactions.

Glyceraldehyde 3-phosphate then enters other metabolic reactions within plant cells. It is used to build other sugars, starches for storage, fats, and proteins.

Photorespiration

Rubisco, the enzyme that catalyzes the carboxylation of RuBP, is also involved in another set of reactions, called *photorespiration*. As well as catalyzing carboxylation it is able to catalyze the oxidation of RuBP (in other words, as well as being a carboxylase it is an oxidase). Carbon dioxide and oxygen compete to attach themselves to the enzyme and if the CO_2 concentration is low, oxygen wins. Unless the air contains more than about 50 parts per million of CO_2 most plants cannot photosynthesize at all and at the average CO_2 concentration of about 350 parts per million a proportion of the energy absorbed by chlorophyll is lost through photorespiration. In many plants this halves the amount of carbon leaving the Calvin cycle.

When the RuBP is oxidized the product splits into one molecule of 3-phosphoglycerate and one of a two-carbon compound, phosphoglycolate. The phosphoglycolate is converted to glycolate, leaves the cycle, and enters a small cell body (organelle) called a *peroxisome* and from there enters a mitochondrion, an organelle in which ATP is synthesized and the reactions of respiration take place. Eventually the glycolate is broken down, releasing CO_2. Because the reactions use oxygen and release CO_2 they are called *respiration,* but they produce neither ATP nor NADPH to supply energy to the plant. So far as scientists know, there is no way in which photorespiration benefits the plant.

It may be that photorespiration evolved at a time when the Earth's atmosphere contained much more CO_2 than it does now. It would not have mattered then, because in the competition for rubisco, CO_2, being more abundant, would always have won.

C3 and C4 Plants

An early step in the Calvin cycle involves 3-phosphoglycerate. This is a molecule with three carbon atoms and so this version of the photosynthetic dark reactions is known as the *C3 pathway.* It is the type of photosynthesis used by most plants, but there is another one, in which the first product is oxaloacetate, a compound with four carbon atoms. This is known as the *C4 pathway* and plants using it are called *C4 plants.* These are mainly tropical and subtropical grasses. Sugarcane and corn (maize) are C4 plants. C4 plants minimize photorespiration by pumping CO_2 into specialized leaf cells and so maintain a concentration high enough to ensure that CO_2 rather than oxygen captures the rubisco.

The C4 pathway begins in the mesophyll cells—the cells just below the leaf surface that contain chlorophyll—with the addition of CO_2 to phosphoenolpyruvate (PEP). This reaction is catalyzed by the enzyme PEP carboxylase and produces the four-carbon compound oxaloacetate. Unlike rubisco, PEP carboxylase has no affinity for oxygen. It cannot behave as an oxidase. Consequently, it is able to seize CO_2 even when concentrations are very low. Oxaloacetate is then converted into another four-carbon compound; in many plants this is malate.

The mesophyll cells are packed together fairly loosely, but there are passageways, called *plasmodesmata,* between them and bundle-sheath cells. These are packed much more tightly around the veins of leaves, with the mesophyll cells outside them. They give the plant a very distinctive anatomic structure, called a *Kranz anatomy. Kranz* is a German word that means "crown" or "garland," and *Kranz anatomy* refers to the way a layer of mesophyll cells surrounds the bundle-sheath cells, which in turn surround the leaf vein. Any plant with leaves of this type is a C4 plant. Fossils have been found of leaves more than 5 million years old with Kranz anatomy, showing the C4 pathway evolved at least that long ago.

Malate, or whatever other four-carbon compound the plant uses, is passed through the plasmodesmata from the mesophyll cells to the bundle-sheath cells. There the malate releases its CO_2 to combine with rubisco and enter the Calvin cycle.

The mesophyll cells are pumping CO_2 into the bundle-sheath cells, so the CO_2 concentration at the start of the Calvin cycle is much higher than it is in the mesophyll cells. An increase in concentration over a distance constitutes a gradient, like a hillside. Pumping CO_2 against a concentration gradient requires energy and the C4 pathway uses more ATP than the C3 pathway. Whereas a C3 plant uses 18 molecules of ATP to synthesize 1 molecule of glyceraldehyde 3-phosphate, a C4 plant uses 30. Nevertheless, C4 plants are able to thrive in conditions under which photorespiration would exceed photosynthesis in C3 plants. They photosynthesize faster than C3 plants and so they grow faster.

In temperate climates C4 plants are often at a disadvantage compared with C3 plants. It is in the tropics, and especially in the dry tropics, that they come into their own.

Photosynthesis requires CO_2 and water. The CO_2 is taken from the air, water from the ground. It enters the plant through the roots and is transported to the mesophyll cells, ready for the photosynthetic light reactions. To obtain the necessary CO_2, the leaf stomata must open. Carbon dioxide enters the leaf and oxygen departs, but water can also escape, evaporating through the open stomata (page 60). This presents no problem so long as water is plentiful. If water is in short supply, the stomata close to prevent its loss. This prevents CO_2 from entering the leaf and oxygen from leaving, so within the mesophyll cells the CO_2 concentration falls and the oxygen concentration rises.

This presents no real difficulty for plants adapted to temperate climates. Most of the time water is plentiful and the plant can afford to lose it through its open stomata. When the ground is dry, the stomata close and for a time photorespiration increases and photosynthesis decreases. A fall of rain replenishes the ground before this can cause harm, but should the drought continue, plants will cease to grow and eventually they will die.

In the arid tropics, and most of all in deserts, the drought is permanent and plants keep their stomata closed for much of the time. These are the conditions under which the C4 pathway is preferable.

CAM

Efficient though the C4 pathway is, plants using it must nevertheless open their stomata to allow the exchange of gases, and while stomata are open some loss of water is inevitable. Cacti, ice plants, pineapples, and a variety of other plants have evolved a strategy to prevent even that loss. The method they use involves incorporating CO_2 into an organic acid, and it was first identified among plants such as stonecrops (*Sedum* species) and houseleeks (*Sempervivum* species). These belong to the family Crassulaceae, of herbs and small shrubs that have thick, succulent leaves in which they store water. The family has given its name to the photosynthetic method, which is called *crassulacean acid metabolism* (CAM) but is not restricted to the Crassulaceae. At least 17 other plant families have it. Not all of those plants are succulents, and not all succulents have CAM.

CAM plants fully open their stomata at night, when other plants keep them closed. When the stomata are open, CO_2 enters mesophyll cells in the leaves and oxygen departs, but because the temperature is relatively low during the cool desert night, very little water is lost by evaporation. During the day, when water would be lost rapidly through open stomata, CAM plants keep their stomata firmly closed.

Photosynthesis is impossible during the hours of darkness, of course, but the CO_2 absorbed at night combines with malic, isocitric, and some other organic acids and is stored in this form in the small spaces (vacuoles) inside mesophyll cells. In the morning the organic acids give up their CO_2, which enters the Calvin cycle.

All plants use the Calvin cycle to synthesize sugar, but C3, C4, and CAM plants differ in the way they capture the CO_2 that is the essential raw material. In C3 plants the entry and fixation of CO_2 both take place at the same time in the same cells. In C4 plants they take place at the same time but in different cells. In CAM plants they take place in the same cells but at different times. The C4 and CAM pathways evolved independently of each other as two solutions to the same environmental problem.

Respiration

Respiration is the chemical opposite of photosynthesis. Photosynthesis is the production of sugar, a carbohydrate, with the release of oxygen. Respiration is the oxidation of carbohydrates with the release of energy and carbon dioxide as a by-product. All plants and animals respire. In vertebrate animals, *respiration* also refers to the act of breathing, which is the mechanism by which respiratory gases are exchanged through lungs or gills.

Green plants are autotrophs, a word from the Greek *autos,* meaning "self," and *trophos,* meaning "feed." They are able to manufacture their own food from simple inorganic compounds. Organisms that must obtain their food by consuming other organisms are *heterotrophs; heteros* means "other."

Factors Limiting Photosynthesis

Carbon dioxide and water are the raw materials for photosynthesis, but by themselves they are insufficient. Each chlorophyll molecule, for example, contains an atom of magnesium. If magnesium is scarce, the plant may be unable to manufacture enough chlorophyll to maintain itself. Proteins contain nitrogen and sulfur, so these are also necessary. A plant needs varying amounts of nitrogen, potassium, phosphorus, calcium, magnesium, manganese, and a variety of other elements. Without them the plant cannot thrive and may die. These essential nutrient elements are obtained from the soil and plant growth will be limited if the supply of any one of them is restricted.

Two of the essential ingredients for photosynthesis are plentiful in the desert—light and warmth. The sunshine is extremely bright and the rate of photosynthesis is directly proportional to the intensity of light. Beyond a certain threshold, however, increasing light intensity starts to cause the oxidation of some of the cell compounds, slowing the rate of photosynthesis. The phenomenon is called *solarization.* In a desert, there may be times when the threshold is crossed and the sunshine is too bright. This slows the metabolism of plants, but not enough to cause them serious harm.

As with most biochemical reactions catalyzed by enzymes, the rate of the reactions involved in photosynthesis approximately doubles with every 18°F (10°C) rise in temperature between 32°F (0°C) and 95°F (35°C). Photosynthesis takes place, but very slowly, at a temperature of 21°F (-6°C). The optimal temperature is about 85°F (29°C). Although increasing the temperature above the optimum increases the rate of photosynthesis, the increase is sustained for only a short time, after which it falls back to the previous level. At temperatures higher than about 105°F (40°C) photosynthesis slows rapidly and most plants die if the temperature remains above 113°F (45°C) for more than a very short time. The temperature affecting photosynthesis is not the air temperature, of course, but the temperature on the surface of the leaves.

During the hottest part of the day, the high light intensity and temperature often combine to inhibit photosynthesis and at all times the scarcity of water—and of mineral nutrients dissolved in it—imposes a further constraint. That is why few plants can tolerate desert conditions and those that do are very tough.

Transpiration and Why Plants Need Water

Centuries ago people wondered how it can be that a small seed grows into a plant the size of a tree. They argued about what substances plants are made of and where they obtain them. Some thought they are made from soil. A Flemish chemist called Jan Baptista van Helmont (1579–1644) disagreed. He believed that plants are made from water and air. To test this experimentally he planted a willow seedling in a container holding 200 pounds (90.9 kg) of soil and grew it there for 5 years, adding only water. At the end of 5 years he weighed both tree and soil. The tree had gained 163 pounds (74 kg), but the weight of soil had decreased by only 2 ounces (60 g). This, he said, proved the plant was made from the water he had added. He was almost right. Water accounts for 80–85 percent of the weight of a nonwoody plant (but less in woody plants, because wood never contains more than about 30 percent water by weight). Organic compounds, made from carbon, hydrogen, and oxygen, account for about 95 percent of the dry weight of a plant, and mineral nutrients, such as nitrogen, sulfur, phosphorus, potassium, calcium, and about 40 other elements, make up the remaining 5 percent.

All plants need water. Even desert plants, growing in soil that is dry as dust, contain water and will die if they lose too much of it. Plants can be grown without soil—the method is called *hydroponics*—but not without water. Water is an essential nutrient, because plants use hydrogen obtained from it in photosynthesis (page 56), although only a tiny fraction of the water absorbed is used in this way and most of the dry weight of a plant is derived from carbon dioxide.

Deprive a plant of water and after a time its leaves and then its stem will become limp and start to droop. This is called *wilting* and it shows that plants use water to give their tissues rigidity—the scientific term is *turgor*. Water the plant and provided it has not been left without water for too long, it will quickly recover its turgor. Inside the plant, water enters and fills cells, making their walls rigid. So plants need water to allow them to hold out their leaves to the sunlight and in the case of nonwoody plants to stand upright.

Roots and Root Hairs

Water enters plants through their roots and never through any of the parts of the plant that are above ground. There are two main types of plant

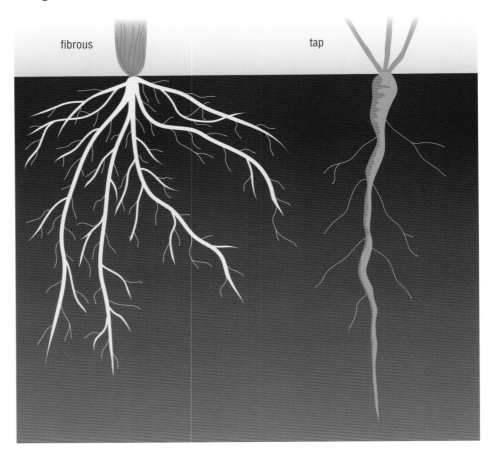

Types of plant roots

roots: fibrous roots, like those of grasses, and taproots, like those of dandelions. Carrots and parsnips are edible taproots. The two types are illustrated in the diagram.

Roots have many branches and near the tip of each branch there are fine hairs. The roots extend these hairs through a large volume of soil and the total surface area of all the hairs is huge. This was measured experimentally for a rye plant (*Secale cereale*) that was grown from seed for 4 months. At the end of that time the total length of all its fibrous roots and root hairs was nearly 7,000 miles (11,260 km) and their total surface area was about 7,000 square feet (650 sq m).

Water enters the plant through its root tips and especially its root hairs and passes from them into cells in the root itself, where it is drawn into a central structure called the *stele*. This comprises one end of a system of tubes, called the *vascular system*, linking every part of the plant. The tubes are of two types, known as *xylem* and *phloem*. Xylem vessels convey water and the mineral nutrients dissolved in it. Phloem cells convey the products of photosynthesis from the leaves to all parts of the plant. Plants need water,

therefore, to deliver the mineral nutrients their cells need.

Xylem

Xylem vessels consist of dead cells. In the evolutionarily more ancient gymnosperms—the group that includes coniferous trees—the individual xylem cells are called *tracheids*. These are cylindrical, are hollow, and have tapered ends, each tracheid overlapping its neighbor to form a continuous tube. Pits on the sides of the tracheid are regions where the cell wall is thin enough to allow molecules to cross and the pits of one tracheid are aligned with those of its neighbor, so the pairs of pits are the route by which water travels. Some pits have extensions of the cell wall rolled around their edges. These are called *bordered* pits. Others, lacking borders, are called *simple* pits, and a pair of pits are said to be *half bordered* if one pit is bordered and the other simple. The illustration shows a tracheid with bordered pits.

In flowering plants (angiosperms) the xylem cells are called *vessel elements,* also illustrated in the figure. Vessel elements are shorter and usually wider than tracheids and they are joined end to end, rather than being overlapped. They have pits, but ordinarily water crosses from one vessel element to the next at the ends. These are perforated or, in some plant groups, open.

Water entering the root passes through the stele, where energy is expended to pump mineral ions (molecules carrying an electrical charge) into the xylem. This increases the concentration of dissolved minerals on one side of the membrane, causing water to follow by osmosis, to equalize the concentration on either side. Consequently, water is being pumped into the xylem by the roots.

Transpiration

It is not pumping from below that pushes water all the way from the roots to the top of the plant, however, but pulling from above. Mesophyll cells in the leaves are surrounded by air spaces in which the humidity is very high. It is from the air in these spaces that the cells absorb the carbon dioxide they need for photosynthesis.

The cells are coated with a film of water, and when the stomata are open to allow gases to enter and leave, water vapor leaves the plant and water evaporates from the film to replace it. This loss of water vapor from plant leaves is called *transpiration,* and although it causes difficulties for plants when the soil is very dry, it does serve a useful purpose. Evaporation absorbs latent heat—the energy water molecules must absorb to allow them to break free. This is taken from the surrounding tissue and so transpiration cools the leaves, in the same way that the evaporation of sweat cools human skin, and it can be enough to prevent the leaf temperature from rising so high that photosynthesis is slowed (page 56).

How Transpiration Pulls Water from the Ground

Evaporation from the walls of the mesophyll cells causes the water that remains to adhere strongly to the hydrophilic (water-attracting) walls of depressions in the cell walls. At the same time hydrogen bonds in the water itself pull the water into the shape with the smallest possible surface area. The combined effect of the two forces is to pull the water into a meniscus—a concave surface in each depression. The pressure inside the cell falls below atmospheric pressure and under this negative pressure water is drawn out of the leaf xylem and into the mesophyll layer.

Tracheids and vessel elements are very narrow and the water inside them forms a continuous column. Water that is drawn out at the top remains in contact with water in the xylem and pulls this behind it. The pressure, starting at the stomata, is felt through the entire column of water molecules and water rises by capillarity, just as it does through pore spaces in the soil (page 38).

It sounds incredible, but the transpiration of water through leaf stomata exerts sufficient pressure to draw up water from the roots to the very top of the tallest tree, against the weight of the water in the column. The pressure is so strong it pulls the sides of the xylem cells inward, and on a hot day, when the transpiration pressure is at its greatest, the trunk of a tree becomes narrower by an amount that can be measured. Water is then flowing quite fast, at up to 130 feet (40 m) per hour or more. On a warm day in summer a fully grown broad-leaved tree may transpire more than 53 gallons (200 l) of water and each of its leaves will replace all its water once every hour.

Beyond the lower end of the xylem, the pressure is felt in the soil if root hairs are in contact with a continuous chain of water molecules outside. Water flows toward the root and then into it under pressure from the top of the plant.

When the rate of transpiration is very low, or at night when most plants close their stomata and transpiration ceases, water continues to enter the

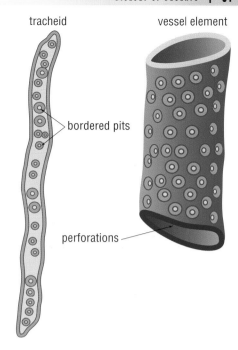

Vessel element and tracheid

plant because of the pressure caused by the pumping of mineral ions into the xylem. This draws in water, pushes it up through the xylem, and the plant may rid itself of the excess by *guttation,* which is the exuding of drops from the tips of its leaves.

It can happen that somewhere along a xylem tube some of the water evaporates. This process is *cavitation,* which breaks the continuous chain of water molecules on which transport depends. A small plant can overcome this. The osmotic pressure that draws water into its roots is sufficient to push the pocket of water vapor to the mesophyll layer and restore the continuous column.

Bigger plants, such as trees, cannot generate enough root pressure to do this. Instead, they allow water to pass through the pits of the blocked xylem tube and into an adjacent tube, in effect constructing a bypass.

Roots, Stems, and Leaves That Conserve Water

When it rains, water drains by gravity through very large spaces between stones and large soil particles such as coarse sand grains. Capillarity (page 38) is what causes it to move through the very small pore spaces. Just as it is capillarity that pulls water upward through the xylem of a plant, so it is capillarity that pulls water downward through the soil and into the groundwater.

Water often sinks gravitationally through the upper layers and by capillarity through the lower layers. If the finely particulate soil lies above a layer of coarser material the water drains only so far, however, leaving moist soil lying above dry soil. Despite capillarity and gravity, the water sinks no farther. This is because there is insufficient soil moisture tension, the force that pulls water through capillaries.

Soil Moisture Tension

Imagine a beaker filled with water. At the bottom of the beaker the water is under a pressure due to the weight of water above it. The pressure decreases with height in the beaker, because the amount of overlying water decreases. At the surface there is no pressure. It is zero. The drawing gives a value of 20 to the pressure at the bottom and 10 to the pressure at the halfway point.

If a tube with a very narrow bore is inserted vertically into the water, water will rise up the tube by capillarity. Level with the surface of the water in the beaker the pressure exerted by the weight of overlying water will be zero. Above that level it will be less than zero. At a level as far above the surface (0) as the +10 level is below it the pressure will be -10, and at a level above the surface equal to the depth of water below the surface it will be -20. Higher up the tube the pressure will be still lower. Water rises up the tube because it is under a negative pressure. Is it pulled or pushed?

The pressure below the surface can be ignored because it is not important and working with negative quantities is inconvenient, so scientists simply eliminate the minus sign. The resulting value, which is now positive, has been changed from a pushing force (pressure) into a pulling force (tension). This is the force known as *soil moisture tension,* or SMT.

The magnitude of SMT is inversely proportional to the size of pore spaces in the soil. The smaller these are, the greater is the SMT. It requires force to draw water through capillary spaces, and if the water reaches a region where

that force is insufficient, it will move no farther. This is what happens when water drains through fine particles to a layer where the particles are larger. Bigger particles have bigger spaces between them, so coarse-grained soil exerts a lower SMT than the soil made from fine particles. A layer of coarse material cannot pull water out of a layer of fine-grained material.

Field Capacity and SMT

Soil from which all the gravitational water has drained out of the large spaces is said to be at *field capacity.* About half its pore spaces will be filled with water and the SMT will be fairly low (about 5 pounds per square inch, or 33 kilopascals [kPa]). Plant roots have no difficulty pulling water toward them against this pressure. In unsaturated soil the water is present as a film coating soil particles. As a root draws in water by osmosis, the film on the soil particles will adjust in a way that causes the water in the vicinity of the root to move slowly toward it.

SMT is higher in soil below field capacity, however, and the drier the soil, the greater the SMT. As SMT increases, the movement of water toward and into the root slows. As the soil dries, SMT increases first in the upper layers and plants absorb more and more of their water from lower layers, where the soil remains moist and SMT is relatively low. There is more oxygen in the upper soil, and as water absorption shifts to lower levels, where there is less oxygen, it becomes less efficient. Oxygen is necessary for cell respiration, and when the supply is curtailed the root works more slowly and the pressure with which it draws water weakens.

When a point is reached at which water enters the root more slowly than it is being lost from the leaves of the plant by transpiration, the plant will start to wilt. In a temperate climate, where transpiration is moderate, wilting may not begin until the SMT reaches about 225 pounds per square inch (1.5 megapascals [MPa]). Under the hot desert Sun and drying wind the transpiration rate is much higher, however, and some plants may start to wilt at an SMT of about 30 pounds per square inch (0.2 MPa).

Roots of Desert Plants

Perennial desert plants—plants that do not die down and disappear completely after one or two seasons—have adapted to soil aridity in various

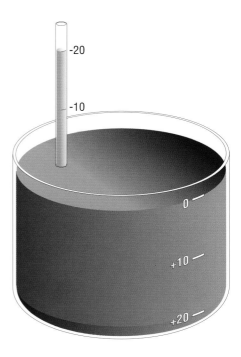

Soil moisture tension

ways. In most, the root xylem is very well developed and strong, ensuring that when water is available it is transported quickly to the rest of the plant. Some plants have roots that can store water, and many have roots with a thick bark that minimizes the loss of water through the root epidermis ("skin"). Many desert grasses achieve the same result in a different way. Their root hairs secrete mucilage to which sand grains adhere, eventually coating the hairs in a *rhizosheath.*

Several groups of plants produce small rootlets on their roots that grow rapidly into full-size roots when there is water for them to absorb. These are known as *proteoid roots* in evergreen trees and shrubs belonging to the family Proteaceae, most of which grow naturally in Australia and South Africa. Retema (*Retama raetum*), the shrub known as "juniper" in the Bible, grows in sand and dry riverbeds (wadis) and has horizontal roots up to 33 feet (10 m) long growing from its ordinary roots. The vessel elements in these roots are shorter and narrower than vessel elements in the ordinary roots and the xylem is able to take up water very efficiently. After a shower, gravitational water drains rapidly through sand. These additional roots are positioned where they can capture water before it is lost.

Reducing Transpiration

Modifications to the roots increase the efficiency with which water is absorbed and transported with the least possible wastage. Another adaptation involves reducing the loss of water by transpiration. CAM plants achieve this by their method of photosynthesis, and because it is more efficient in a desert climate the C4 photosynthetic pathway also conserves water (page 56).

Other plants have leaves that are succulent. They contain large cells that store water. When the photosynthesizing cells are short of water they absorb water by osmosis from the water-storage cells. These then shrink, but they swell rapidly to their former size as soon as water reaches them from the roots. In some plants it is the stem that is succulent.

Most desert plants have leaves with a small surface area in relation to their volume. The needle and scale leaves of coniferous trees are a familiar example of leaf reduction as an adaptation to dry conditions. Conifers grow in high latitudes, where water remains frozen, and therefore unavailable to plants, through a long winter, and also in climates of the Mediterranean type, where little rain falls in summer. It is not simply the overall size of the leaves that is reduced. The internal leaf structures and even the cells are small.

Relatives of the sagebrush (*Artemisia* species) and saltbush (*Atriplex* species) grow ordinary leaves during the rainy season. They shed these at the end of the season and replace them with reduced leaves, which they keep through the dry season. There are also plants that shed their leaves at the start of the dry season, but retain the leaf stalks (petioles). These contain chloroplasts and continue to carry out photosynthesis. In retema and *Calligonum comosum,* a shrub resembling broom, photosynthesis takes place in the young branches, which are green, and in the dry season these branches may be shed.

Reduced leaves often have a thick, waxy cuticle (outer skin) that reduces water loss and many have trichomes—outgrowths from the leaf in the form of hairs or scales. Trichomes are probably adaptations less to aridity than to temperature and light intensity. They reflect light and heat.

Plants must open their stomata, but these can be located where the transpiration rate is lowest, in positions sheltered from the wind and full Sun. Many grasses have leaves rolled almost into tubes, with the stomata on the inside. Oleanders (*Nerium* species) are among the plants that have their stomata sunk in grooves or depressions. Retema has its stomata along the bottom of grooves running the length of the branches where photosynthesis occurs. A few plants of seasonal climates, including the caper shrub (*Capparis spinosa*), close their stomata altogether during the summer dry season.

These extreme adaptations do not reduce transpiration, they stop it altogether, and the leafless plants become dry and brittle. They look dead and yet as soon as it rains they produce new shoots. Most of them survive the drought by storing water inside their stems to supply cells containing chloroplasts. Their stomata are in deep furrows, in permanent shade, and photosynthesis proceeds at a level just sufficient to maintain the plant cells until they are able to end their period of dormancy.

Desert Plants

When the Desert Blooms

Few plants are able to tolerate the desert climate. One that achieves this is the creosote bush (*Larrea divaricata*) of the North and South American deserts. Other plants deal with the effects of drought by avoiding them. These include the plants with roots, stems, and leaves that are modified to maximize the efficiency with which they use water (page 62).

There is another way. It is possible for plants to evade the desert climate entirely. They thrive in the desert, but appear only when water is plentiful. In fact, they are desert plants that grow only during those brief spells when the desert ceases to be a desert.

These are the most spectacular of desert plants. Invisible most of the time, they are the species that emerge after rain, the plants that make the desert bloom with foliage and, especially, with flowers that produce a riot of color. Then, as the ground dries, they are gone, vanished as quickly and mysteriously as they came. Not only are these plants visually spectacular, they are also spectacularly successful. In some of the harshest deserts they are the only plants that can survive.

A few are geophytes—plants that spend periods when conditions are unfavorable underground, as bulbs, tubers, corms, or fleshy rhizomes. As soon as they are moistened they produce shoots. This is a risky strategy, however, because underground storage organs cannot survive indefinitely without dehydrating.

Seed Survival

Most of them are annuals—plants that complete their life cycle, from the germination of seed to production of seed, in a single season. They spend the unfavorable times as seed. This is much more satisfactory. Seeds consist of a plant embryo with a supply of nutrient to sustain the young plant until it can start feeding itself contained within a tough, highly protective coat. Seeds are well equipped for survival and can wait a long time, in some cases many years, for an opportunity to germinate. During their wait their metabolism is slowed almost to a standstill. They can tolerate extremes of temperature and their coat is waterproof, so they face no risk of desiccation that might damage the tissues of the embryo.

Seeds can survive. The challenge comes when the rain arrives and the seeds germinate. The water will soon disappear and when it does, the plants will die. By the time that happens the plants must have produced a new crop of seed, but in order to do that they must grow reproductive structures, eggs must be fertilized, and this growth must be sustained by photosynthesis and the absorption of mineral nutrients from the soil. In other words, the germinating seed must lead to a plant that grows stem and leaves, flowers, and seeds, all in the brief time available to it. Plants that grow rapidly and then vanish are called *ephemerals*.

Most small, nonwoody plants rely on insects to pollinate their flowers and produce brightly colored and often strongly scented flowers to attract pollinators. When the desert plants emerge, so many appear at the same time, all of them in a desperate hurry to be pollinated and set seed before they dry out, that competition for insect pollinators is extreme. It leads to a kind of visual clamor, with plants producing the biggest and brightest flowers possible in an effort to shout down their neighbors.

Response to Moisture

Seed responses are very precise. In the Californian desert, evening primrose (*Oenothera* species) seeds can survive half a century or more, waiting for the particular combination of temperature and moisture that will allow them to grow fast enough to complete their life cycle in the time available. When they receive the signal, the desert is suddenly covered in huge patches of pink, perfumed flowers.

Growth can be very fast indeed. *Boerhavia repens,* a plant related to bougainvillea that grows in the deserts of southern Africa, produces big, bright flowers and sets seed within 8 to 10 days of germinating. This is probably a record, but the pillow cushion plant (*Fredolia aretioides*) of Algeria commences photosynthesis within 10 hours of its seeds' germinating and annual species of *Convolvulus,* which also grow in the northern Sahara, complete their life cycle within 6 weeks and sometimes in as little as 3 weeks.

You can almost see the plants grow. *Blepharis ciliaris,* a herb of the Sahara, keeps its seeds stored in a protective capsule. When rain wets the capsule it bursts violently, scattering its seeds. These are covered with hairs that swell when they are wet and as they swell they position the seed so that when it germinates the radicle—the precursor of the root—enters the soil immediately. The seeds germinate within an hour of escaping from the capsule.

Speedy growth is the secret of the success of such plants, but in itself it is not enough, because the moisture that triggers germination may not last long enough for even the fastest plant to produce a new crop of seed. Desert plants have evolved to avoid germinating at the wrong time.

There are two rainy seasons in the Mojave Desert. One occurs in winter, the other in summer, and the annual plants of the desert are of two kinds: those that germinate in winter and those that germinate in summer. Germination is partly triggered by temperature. Warm temperatures affect the summer germinators and cool temperatures the winter germinators, each seed type responding only when the temperature passes a certain threshold. In order to germinate the seed coats must be wet, so moisture provides the other part of the trigger, but moisture may quickly disappear. One-tenth inch (3 mm) of rain will moisten the soil, but the Mojave annuals fail to germinate unless at least 0.6 inch (15 mm) of rain falls over a short period.

These seeds, and those of many other plants, not all of them confined to deserts, have chemical substances in their coats that inhibit germination. The compounds are soluble in water, however, so if the seeds are made wet enough for long enough, the substances drain from them, allowing the seeds to germinate. There are also plants the seeds of which will germinate only after bacteria have altered their coats. This can happen only after the seeds have been thoroughly soaked long enough to allow the bacteria to multiply. In all these cases, the effect is to prevent germination unless an adequate amount of water is present.

Cassia obtusifolia, an herb that grows in the Sahara, solves the problem differently. It produces two types of seeds. Some germinate as soon as their coats are moistened. This gives them a quick start, so if the rains continue the young plants will appear before their rivals. If the rain does not continue, the young seedlings will die. This does not harm the plant, however, because the second type of seed will germinate only if moisture soaks through the seed coat. This requires the seeds to be in moist soil longer.

Another herb, *Neurada procumbens,* has fruits containing seeds that germinate one at a time. When the fruit and its seeds are wetted, only one of them germinates. The second time it rains another seed germinates, and so on. *Neurada procumbens* grows in deserts from North Africa to India.

Dispersal of Seeds

Even good timing may not guarantee survival. Seeds must also be in the right place and this is not so simple as it may seem. The fact that the parent plant has managed to produce seed apparently proves it has found a place where plants of its species can grow, but if it releases all its seeds there the competition among them may kill them all. On the other hand, scattering seeds may waste them.

In the deserts of the Near East there is a relative of the garden weed plantain, *Plantago cretica,* that keeps its seeds in one place. After it has produced them, the plant dies and as it dries out its flower stalks bend lower and lower until they are pressed against the ground. There they remain until rain wets them. Then they straighten up and the rain washes out the seeds. Once they are wet, the seeds produce mucilage from their coats. This glues them to the ground so heavy rain cannot wash them away.

Some plant species produce different types of fruit on the same plant. One such plant is *Gymnarrhena micrantha,* of the aster family (Asteraceae, formerly known as Compositae), which grows in the Near East. The two types of fruit develop from different types of flower. One grows in clusters just above the ground. Its seeds have long hairs and as they mature they are carried away by the wind. A second type of inflorescence grows below ground. It has only a few flowers, with petals that form a tube opening just above the surface. Its seeds remain buried, and when it rains they germinate where they are.

There is one method of seed dispersal that has made movie stars of the plants using it. They are known as tumbleweeds and there are several species belonging to different families. Pigweed, for example, is any one of three species of *Amaranthus* belonging to the family Amaranthaceae and related to the ornamental plant love lies bleeding (*A. caudatus*). Tumble grass, *Schedonnardus paniculatus,* belongs to the grass family (Poaceae). Once it has produced seed the plant dies, but as it dies its stems and leaves curl into a ball with the seeds held on the inside. The ball is then blown about by the wind, scattering the seeds as it goes. This is the species most often seen in Hollywood westerns. No ghost town would appear adequately windswept and desolate without at least a few balls of tumble grass or one of the other tumbleweeds.

Typical Plants of Old World Deserts

Tumble grass, a plant typical of the North American desert, has its equivalent in the deserts from Morocco to southern Iran in the rose of Jericho or resurrection plant (*Anastatica hierochuntica*)—which is a member of the cabbage family (Brassicaceae) and not a rose. It is an annual that sheds its leaves as its seeds mature. As the bare stem and branches dry they fold inward so the dead plant ends as a ball that is blown about by the desert wind, shedding seeds as it goes. When moistened, the plant uncurls. Dead plants are sometimes sold as curiosities, to be kept as house ornaments that curl and uncurl according to how dry they are.

The rose of Jericho is not the only plant to distribute its seeds in this way. The vine called *colocynth, bitter apple,* or *vine of Sodom* (*Citrullus colocynthis*) produces spherical fruits about the size of oranges (a close relative, *C. lanatus,* is the watermelon) that are blown about until eventually they become buried in the sand or lodged firmly against rocks. Then the fruit rots, leaving the seeds, which remain until rain moistens them and they sprout. The dried pulp of the colocynth is a laxative and the plant has been cultivated for medicinal use for thousands of years.

There are usually some perennial plants to be seen in even the harshest deserts. Only where the sands are perpetually shifting or the desert pavement consists of bare rock, swept clear of sand by the wind, is the landscape utterly devoid of visible life.

Desert Grasses

Some grasses can grow in sand. Indeed, grasses are widely used to stabilize sand dunes along coasts in temperate regions as well as in deserts. The species most often planted on coastal dunes is marram grass (*Ammophila arenaria*), also known as *beach grass* and *mel grass.* Not only does it bind sand together, its tough stems are used to make mats, bags, chair seats, and roof thatch. The equivalent grass in hot deserts is esparto, Algerian, or alfa grass (*Stipa tenacissima*). Its stems are used to make mats, paper, and ropes.

All grasses belong to the family Poaceae (formerly known as Gramineae). Species vary in many ways—wheat, rice, corn (maize), bamboo, and sugarcane are all grasses—but there are important features they all share and it is these that allow perennial grasses to thrive on sand dunes.

Grass roots form a fibrous mat. This binds soil particles together and the root system can be extensive. A grass stem has swellings, called *nodes,* at intervals along it. Nodes that are in contact with the ground often produce roots. These are

Acacia thorn tree (Gerry Ellis/ENP Images)

known as *adventitious* roots because they grow from an unusual position: cells just above each node are the points from which the stem grows. In many species the stem itself is hollow. As well as adventitious roots, a number of stems often arise from the lowest node. They are called *tillers,* and tillering (the production of tillers) causes some grasses to grow as dense clumps.

If the stem is cut, for example, by being grazed, it will simply continue growing from the node below the cut, and since there are nodes all the way down to ground level and often to just below ground level, grazing cannot injure grass. Adventitious roots, nodes, and the stem of a single grass plant are illustrated in the figure.

As the figure also shows, the stem is enclosed by a sheath. This supports and protects the stem. At each node the sheath grows away from the stem to become a leaf, or blade; blades arise on alternate sides of the stem. The stomata are borne on one side of the blade, and in very hot weather many species can roll their blades into tubes, with the stomata on the inside, to minimize the loss of water by transpiration (page 60).

Many perennial grasses have stems that grow horizontally. Some, called *stolons,* lie along the ground, but most grow just beneath the surface. These are called *rhizomes* and are typical of *Ammophila* and *Stipa* species. Both vertical stems and adventitious roots arise from the nodes below ground, so a complete plant can develop from each node and then produce a rhizome of its own. It is the combination of rhizomes and fibrous root mats that binds loose soil.

Grasses are wind-pollinated and so their flowers have no petals, but the fruits often bear stiff hairs, called *awns,* that remain with the seed when it leaves the plant. In many species the awns twist and bend with changes in humidity in such a way as to drag the seed down into the ground. Awns on cram-cram (*Cenchrus biflorus*) seeds stiffen and curl, turning the seeds into burs that cling to the coats of passing animals. Grass seeds remain viable (capable of germinating) for a long time, in some species for 30 years.

Plants That Trap Sand

Sand that is trapped by plants sometimes forms mounds. In the Sahara these mounds are called *nebkas.* Grasses play an important part in building nebkas, but so do other plants, especially certain shrubs and small trees. *Ziziphus lotus* is the shrub or small tree known in ancient Greece as the lotus. As sand accumulates against it the plant produces more lateral branches along the ground. These grow adventitious roots and shoots, causing the plant to spread over a wide area. Its close relative the crown of thorns, or Christ's thorn (*Z. spina-christi*), is another desert shrub that traps sand. As its name suggests, it is believed to be the plant used to make the crown of thorns worn by Christ. Tamarisk shrubs also trap sand and branches that are buried produce adventitious roots. These plants are also of historical interest. *Tamarix mannifera,* which grows from Iran south through Arabia, is the manna tree and the source of manna referred to in the Bible as having miraculously fed the Israelites as they wondered through the wilderness.

Woody plants are dispersed fairly widely, most of them are small, and there is less variety among them than in plants that grow in more favored regions. Not many species can tolerate the severe conditions. Saudi Arabia, for example, contains only about 3,500 native plant species.

The distance between woody shrubs is an indication of the aridity of the ground. Roots spread to gather such moisture as is available (page 60) and the roots of an individual plant occupy a volume of soil, drawing water toward them. Once a shrub is established its roots will command all the moisture within the volume they occupy and for some distance around. No competitor can grow within that radius. The drier the soil, the greater is the size of the area dominated by each plant.

Date Palms

Where moisture is available, however, the land can be made fertile, and the oases of the Sahara and Arabian Deserts are very productive. Their most famous crop plant is the date palm (*Phoenix dactylifera*), a tree that has been cultivated since 4000 B.C.E. Dates are grown commercially from Morocco to India; the most important producers are Iraq and Saudi Arabia.

Date palms are trees 60–80 feet (18–24 m) tall. Where they grow naturally the trees often have several stems, but commercially grown trees have only one, as the others have been removed. Male and female flowers are borne on separate trees; 1 male tree is able to pollinate up to 100 females. Growers usually make certain of pollination by cutting off bunches of male flowers and hanging them among bunches of female flowers. The fruits are produced in bunches at the crown of the tree, a bunch containing 1,000–1,400 dates, each tree bearing several bunches. A well-tended palm yields more than 100 pounds (45 kg) of dates a year.

Ripe dates are yellow. They turn brown as they dry and it is dried dates that are exported. There are three principal types. Soft dates are used in confectionery and are sold pitted and pressed together into blocks. Dessert dates that are sold in boxes, often with the dried fruits still attached to the strands on which they grew, are of the semidry varieties. The most popular semidry variety is Deglet Noor. Dry dates are traded extensively between Arab countries but are rarely seen elsewhere. They keep a long time and are an important item of diet. Dry dates are quite hard and can be ground into flour, although they soften when soaked in water. The food value of dates consists mainly of sugar with some vitamins. Some varieties of dry dates contain up to 70 percent sugar.

Figs, Mulberries, and Almonds

The fig (*Ficus carica*) also originated in the oases of Middle Eastern deserts, although it is now grown in most countries with a warm climate. It was being cultivated in Egypt 6,000 years ago and possibly earlier than that in Jericho. It is the fruit of a small broad-leaved deciduous tree up to about 30 feet (9 m) tall belonging to the mulberry family (Moraceae). Mulberries are also natives of the Middle East. The species cultivated for its fruit is *Morus nigra,* the common, black, or Persian mulberry. It was introduced to southern Europe long ago and was familiar to the ancient Greeks and Romans.

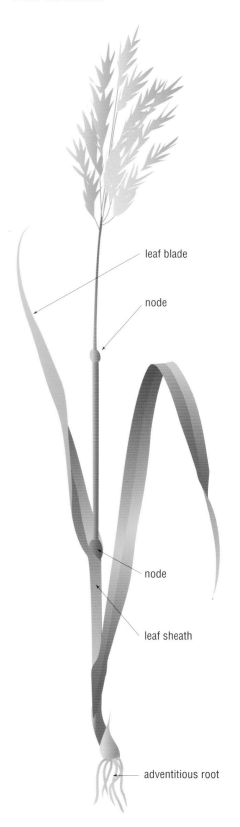

leaf blade

node

node

leaf sheath

adventitious root

Grass

A native of Morocco, the argan tree (*Argania spinosa*) yields an oil similar to olive oil, its leaves are fed to livestock, and its timber is used for fuel. It is now being grown with rows of cereals between the rows of trees in a farming system called *alley cropping* that is particularly well suited to arid climates. The ye'eb or jeheb nut tree (*Cordeauxia edulis*) is an evergreen with foliage that is browsed by camels and goats and nuts resembling the sweet chestnut. It grows naturally in Ethiopia and Somalia and it, too, is now being cultivated.

The almond (*Prunus dulcis*), now grown in many parts of the world, is also a native of the Middle Eastern desert. There are two important varieties, the bitter almond (var. *amara*), from which almond oil is obtained, and the sweet almond (var. *dulcis*), which is the edible nut.

Bitter almonds contain prussic acid (a poison, hydrogen cyanide [HCN]), but this gives them a taste so bitter it would be very difficult for a human to eat enough of them to ingest a lethal dose. Any animal tempted to try them would receive a very unpleasant surprise and would probably feel very unwell for some time. The cyanide protects the plant by ensuring no animal tastes its nuts twice, so the seeds have a chance to germinate. Many plants produce poisons to protect themselves from herbivorous animals. Another is the desert rose (*Adenium obesum*), a shrub that grows naturally in East Africa and southern Arabia and is cultivated in other parts of the world as an ornamental. Its sap is used to make poison arrows. The bitter, poisonous sap of the Sodom apple (*Solanum aculeatissimum*) allows it to thrive where other plants are stripped of their leaves by browsing animals. One species of grasshopper feeds on its leaves, but mammals will not touch it. Even goats and camels leave it strictly alone.

Thorn Trees

Plants need protection in an environment where they are widely scattered and food for animals is scarce. Many of those that are not poisonous have sharp thorns and the most common trees in the deserts of Africa, Asia, and Australia are thorn trees, of the genus *Acacia*. They are known as *wattles* in Australia, where the largest number of species occur, and they have many local names.

They also have many uses. *A. aneura* is mulga, an Australian tree with edible seeds and wood that is used to make boomerangs, and blue or silver wattle (*A. dealbata*) is florists' "mimosa" (it is not true mimosa). Many acacias produce gum, and the tree known on the southern side of the Sahara as *hashab* (*A. senegal*) is one source of true gum arabic, which is used in lozenges and fruit gums as well as in adhesives, inks, and watercolors. Gum arabic is also obtained from the babul or Egyptian thorn (*A. nilotica*) and the tahl gum tree (*A. seyal*). Tannin, used in dyeing, is obtained from *A. catechu*, a tree known as the *cutch, black cutch, black catechu*, or *khair*, found in southern Asia. Its dye is said to be the source of the original khaki color.

Many *Acacia* species, especially among those native to Australia, have no true leaves. Instead, the petioles (leaf stalks) are expanded and flattened and perform as leaves. The modified petioles are called *phyllodes*.

Acacias are legumes (family Fabaceae), on which colonies of bacteria form white or gray nodules attached to their roots. The bacteria convert gaseous nitrogen into soluble nitrogen compounds the roots can absorb.

The thorns that give acacias their common name are long, very sharp, and often swollen at the base. They are usually modified stipules—structures that grow from the base of the petioles. The South African karroo thorn (*A. karroo*) and the cape gum tree (*A. horrida*) of East Africa and India, for example, both have thorns up to 4 inches (10 cm) long. Acacias growing in deserts have more and bigger thorns than those that grow in moister climates surrounded by more abundant vegetation. Those of Australia grow in areas that receive rain occasionally and so are more closely spaced. They are less thorny than those of the Sahara, suggesting the thorns really do serve to protect the plants when these occur as isolated individuals.

Most acacias are broad-leaved evergreen trees or shrubs. Some grow up to 100 feet (30 m) tall, but most are smaller and many have a distinctive flat-topped shape. They are thoroughly adapted to hot, dry conditions. For some, the optimal temperature for photosynthesis is almost 100°F (38°C), a temperature at which the rate of photosynthesis slows markedly in most plants. Over large parts of the dry Indian plain the babul is the only tree to be seen.

Succulents

In all hot deserts there are succulent plants—plants that store water in their tissues to provide a supply for maintaining photosynthesis (page 56). Ice plants, such as *Mesembryanthemum crystallinum*, are succulents and CAM plants, photosynthesizing at night (page 52). Their common name refers to the tiny white "pimples" (papillae) that cover their leaves and give them a frosted appearance. These probably help keep the plant cool by reflecting light.

Ice plants grow in the Kalahari and Namib Deserts, as does another group of about 40 species of plants of the genus *Lithops*, belonging to the same family (Aizoaceae) as ice plants. *Lithops* species are widely cultivated as "living stones" or "pebble plants," plants that resemble the small pebbles among which they grow so closely they are very difficult to see except when they produce their attractive, showy flowers. Their thick, stonelike leaves disguise them as well as storing water.

Euphorbias

Euphorbias are also succulents, some of which are the size of small trees. One of the biggest is the candelabra tree (*Euphorbia candelabrum*) of East Africa. It grows to a height of about 35 feet (11 m) and there are often small groups of candelabra trees growing together. They are curious plants, with multiple trunks that diverge about 10 feet (3 m) above the ground to become branches that are almost vertical. These branch further to give the tree a bushy appearance, but with dense, succulent stems that grow erect, like candles in a candelabra—hence the name. Others, such as *E. aphylla*, which grows in the Canary Islands, are low-growing and form cushions. Their family, Euphorbiaceae or the spurge family, is huge, comprising more than 7,000 species, including the popular house plant poinsettia (*E. pulcherrima*), the rubber tree (*Hevea brasiliensis*), and manioc or tapioca (*Manihot esculenta*), and they are probably the most adaptable of all plants.

What is remarkable about the African euphorbias is their similarity to cacti. Cacti grow naturally only in the American deserts, but desert euphorbias have adapted to the climate by developing succulent stems, many of them with ridges, and spines. *E. canariensis* and *E. echinus* grow as clumps of upright, ridged green stems that look very like some of the smaller *Cereus* species of cacti. This is an example of *convergent evolution*, in which similar environmental challenges produce similar responses among unrelated species.

Despite the similarities, it is not difficult to distinguish cacti and euphorbias. Euphorbia spines occur in pairs, whereas cactus spines occur singly or in bunches. Cut a euphorbia and it yields a milky latex. In most species this is poisonous and forms part of the plant's protection against grazing. The liquid that seeps from a cut cactus is also likely to be poisonous for the same reason, but it is not milky.

There is a further difference between the two types of plant that is not so obvious. Cacti are CAM plants (page 52). Euphorbias are C3 plants, engaging in the most common version of photosynthesis. This means they are rather less suited than cacti to extreme aridity and high temperatures. The C3 photosynthetic pathway requires them to open their stomata during the day, and although in some species the stomata are located in the grooves between ridges, more water is lost through them than is lost by cacti, which keep their stomata closed during the day. They also photosynthesize less efficiently, because the C3 pathway does not inhibit photorespiration. Nevertheless, euphorbias thrive in places where conditions are too harsh for most other plants.

Typical Plants of New World Deserts

Cacti are the most famous of all plants of the American deserts. Indeed, prickly pears and giant saguaro cacti with their strange, upright branches typify deserts. Quite apart from their frequent appearances in illustrations of deserts, most people have seen real cacti. They are grown in most botanic gardens, but our familiarity with them is partly due to their popularity as cultivated ornamental plants, a popularity that began soon after Europeans first saw them. Specimens were sent back to Europe and from there they were taken to most parts of the world. Some reached the desert countries of the Near East, where they were able to grow outdoors, and later they were carried to Australia.

Until the introduction of factory-made dyes during the second half of the 19th century, prickly pears (*Opuntia* species) were grown quite extensively in warm climates to feed cochineal insects, from which a red dye was obtained. The dye was used mainly for coloring the tunics of military uniforms (English soldiers were often called *redcoats*). Prickly pears are still grown on a small scale, mainly in Central America, to feed cochineal insects. Today the dye is used as a non-toxic safe food and pharmaceutical colorant. It was to feed cochineal insects that prickly pears were introduced into the Mediterranean region. Some plants quickly established themselves on uncultivated land, where they were able to grow naturally, and the edible fruits of some species proved popular.

From southern Europe prickly pear plants were taken to various parts of Asia, South Africa, and Australia. They became naturalized—able to grow in the wild with no help from humans—in all these places, but it was only in Australia that they proved harmful.

Prickly Pears and the Cactus Moth

In Australia the prickly pears invaded land used for grazing cattle and became troublesome weeds. Thousands of square miles of good pasture in Queensland and New South Wales became densely infested with them, and useless for farming. At one time the area occupied by prickly pears in Queensland was increasing at a rate of about 1 million acres (405,000 ha) a year.

Eventually they were brought under control by an operation that is still hailed as the greatest success ever achieved by biological pest control—the control of a pest or weed without using pesticides. Two species were causing the trouble, *Opuntia inermis* and *O. stricta,* and these flourished because no native Australian animals would eat them. Prickly pears had no native Australian enemies to keep them in check, so an American enemy was imported.

Cactus moths (*Cactoblastis cactorum*) live in South America, and their caterpillars feed on prickly pear. Moths from South America were released in Australia between 1928 and 1930 and finding themselves amid a vast food supply they multiplied rapidly. By 1932 the area occupied by the cacti was decreasing fast and by 1940 the prickly pears were fully under control. Today

Joshua trees in Mojave Desert (Michael Durham/ ENP Images)

Prickly pear cactus (Gerry Ellis/ENP Images)

both plants and moths live together in fairly small numbers and a stable equilibrium is maintained.

Shapes and Sizes of Cacti

There are cacti of all shapes and sizes. The pear-shaped stems of prickly pears are among the most familiar, but the saguaro (*Carnegiea gigantea*) is probably the cactus most closely identified with the American West. That is the cactus with a main, vertical stem from which branches grow outward, all around the main stem and all at the same level, and then vertically upward, like the arms of a candelabra—although in some individuals the branches grow in all directions or are twisted. The saguaro is also known as the *giant cactus*—it can reach a height of 50 feet (15 m)—and *monument cactus,* because of its tall, straight stem. The stem and branches are all strongly ribbed.

There are climbing cacti, such as *Hylocereus undulatus,* which is one of several species known as *night-blooming cereus.* There are barrel-shaped cacti, including *Ferocactus* and *Echinocactus* species. *E. acanthodes,* the barrel cactus, grows to about 3.5 feet (1 m) tall, but the biggest of these cacti can grow to 6 feet (1.8 m) in height. Others, such as *Mammillaria* species, are quite small. There are also cacti that grow like cushions of many ribbed, but unjointed stems. The six species of *Ariocarpus* from southern Texas and Mexico are of this type.

A few of the approximately 50 species of cacti belonging to the genus *Rhipsalis* are believed to occur naturally in Africa and Sri Lanka, although some botanists think they may have been introduced and then become naturalized there; no record of the introduction has survived. Most *Rhipsalis* species are found in Brazil.

Apart from the possibly African and Sri Lankan species, all cacti are American. They belong to the family Cactaceae and there are more than 2,000 species. Some are trees, but most are succulents. Although they are typical of hot, dry deserts they occur naturally as far north as British Columbia and as far south as Patagonia, and in the Andes they can be found up to 12,000 feet (3,660 m) above sea level.

Scientists find cacti difficult to classify. They are not closely related to any other plant families, despite similarities resulting from convergent evolution, for example, with the succulent euphorbias, and the cacti themselves seem to be actively evolving. This makes it difficult to compare species with the dried herbarium specimens that in most plant families provide standards against which known species are identified and previously undiscovered species recognized as such and classified.

Adaptations to Desert Life

All cacti are CAM plants and they also have shallow roots that take up water rapidly whenever it is available. These features allow some species to live as epiphytes—plants that grow on the surface of other plants. Some *Rhipsalis* species are epiphytes. Although they have no leaves and their green stems have many branches, these are thin and flattened and lack spines, so a *Rhipsalis* growing from the side of a tree is not at all like most cacti. The Christmas cactus (*Schlumbergera bridgesii*), also an epiphyte, is grown as a popular houseplant because it flowers in winter—hence the name. Its succulent stem sections are shaped very much like leaves and are jointed into many long, spreading branches, so the plant does not conform to the usual idea of a cactus.

Succulent plants store water in their tissues (page 62) and cacti use their stems for this purpose. Some species have true leaves, but these are usually small and often shed fairly quickly. Cacti rely on their stems for photosynthesis. Although the swollen structures of prickly pears look like leaves, in fact they are stems—known as *pads.* Like many cacti, prickly pears have stems that grow in sections, each jointed to the next, so one pad grows on the tip of another, but not all are of this type, even among the prickly pears. Chollas have cylindrical stems and some are small trees: *O. fulgida* grows to a height of 10 feet (3 m) or more. Species belonging to the subgenus *Brasiliopuntia* also resemble trees and have unjointed main stems.

As well as storing water, the swollen stems or leaves of succulents have a smaller surface area in relation to their volume than the stems or leaves of other plants. This is a matter of geometry.

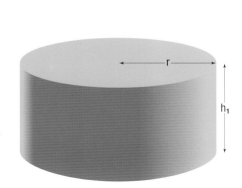

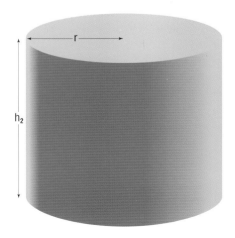

Surface area and volume

Bipinnate leaves

Imagine two leaves, one succulent and one not, both of which (for convenience) are cylindrical in shape, represented by the cylinders in the diagram. Both have a radius r and heights of h_1 and h_2. If $r = 3$, $h_1 = 2$, and $h_2 = 4$, then the ratio of the surface area ($2\pi rh_1 + 2\pi r^2$) to volume ($\pi r^2 h_1$) of the smaller cylinder is 1.67:1 and the ratio for the larger cylinder (height h_2) is 1.17:1.

This helps equip succulent plants to survive, because the amount of moisture they can hold is directly proportional to their volume and the amount of warmth they can absorb, and water they can lose by transpiration is directly proportional to their surface area. Maximizing volume while minimizing surface area increases the amount of moisture they can store while reducing the rate at which it is lost and the extent to which the plant is heated by the Sun.

Like many desert plants, cacti have spines. In *Opuntia* species and other members of the subfamily Opuntioideae to which they belong, these take the form of short, barbed hairs called *glochids* that grow in bunches. In other cacti the spines are modified leaves. Both spines and glochids grow from sunken cushions, called *areoles*. These are modified shoots. In some species they occur singly on raised, wartlike structures called *tubercles,* and in others they grow in rows along raised ridges. Their possession of areoles is one of the features by which cacti can be distinguished from plants of any other kind.

Spines and glochids deter herbivorous animals. They also trap a layer of relatively cool air

next to the plant and dew often condenses on them, also cooling the plant as the water runs down the spines.

Bull Horn Acacia and Its Ants

Desert acacias also have spines, or thorns. Most acacias grow in Africa and Australia, but not all of them, and the thorns of the bull horn acacia (*A. cornigera*), originally from Mexico and Central America, are not as they seem. The thorns are about 1 inch (2.5 cm) long and very swollen near the base. Inside each spine there is a colony of ants (the species is *Pseudomyrmex ferruginea*), and should any animal so much as touch the plant the nearest ants will launch an immediate, and very painful, attack. The acacia's thorns provide a defense that is augmented by the ants, and it is not only hungry animals that are repelled. The ants also bite off the shoots of any other plant that grows into the crown of the acacia.

Obviously, the ants demand payment. At the base of the leaf stalks (petioles) the acacia has nectaries, organs that secrete a sugary liquid called *nectar.* This high-energy food attracts the ants, which feed on it and then drill into the base of the nearest thorn. They hollow out the thorn and establish their nest inside with a convenient nectary just by the door. Each thorn has its own colony of ants.

Payment does not end there, though. At the tip of each of the leaflets that grow on either side of a central stem to form the compound (bipinnate) acacia leaf, like the one shown in the figure, there is a tiny store, shaped like a sausage, containing food rich in oils and proteins. The ants collect this food and take it to the nest. A naturalist named Thomas Belt was the first person to describe these food stores, in a book called *The Naturalist in Nicaragua,* published in 1874, so they are known as *Beltian bodies.* This type of very close and mutually beneficial relationship between a plant and ants is known as *myrmecophily.*

Agaves

Agaves (family Agavaceae) are also plants that grow in or close to deserts but that have been taken to many other parts of the world. Most have short, thick stems and stiff, narrow, pointed leaves that are often crowded around the base of the stem. Many species have succulent leaves. Agave leaves can be up to 10 feet (3 m) long and often have prickles along the edges. Plants with big, succulent leaves and prickles are often called "cacti," but agaves are not cacti. They are monocots—plants with seeds that produce a single seed leaf (cotyledon)—and they are placed with the

lilies (family Liliaceae) and irises (Iridaceae) in the order Liliales.

Not all agaves are American, but two of the best-known species are. *Agave americana* is the century plant, a name that refers to the mistaken belief that it flowers only once in every century. In fact it flowers every 10 to 20 years. Sap, released in copious amounts when its stem is cut, is fermented to make the Mexican drink pulque.

Yuccas and Yucca Moths

Yuccas are also members of the Agavaceae. There are about 30 species. Most are found in the southwestern United States and Mexico, but some occur farther south in Central America. Most species of yucca are pollinated by nocturnal moths belonging to the genus *Tegeticula,* and the relationship between the insects and the plants is as close as that between the bull horn acacia and its ants. It provides a good example of the mutually beneficial relationship between species that is known as *mutualism.*

Each species of yucca has its own species of pollinating moth and can be pollinated by no other, and each species of moth is able to feed on only its own yucca. All these moths are known as *yucca moths.* They work fast, because many yucca flowers last for only one night. The female moth climbs up a stamen and uses her long tongue to scrape up pollen that she rolls it into a ball and holds beneath her head. After she has visited about four stamens she flies to another plant. She inspects the flower to see whether its ovary is at the right stage of development. If it is, and if it contains no moth eggs, she lays a few eggs one at a time in the flower and pushes in her ball of pollen. When the eggs hatch the larvae feed on the seeds, consuming about half of them but leaving enough for the plant to reproduce.

Arrangements of this kind can be exploited by cheats. As well as true yucca moths there are also bogus ones (*Prodoxus* species). They lay their eggs in the ovaries of yucca flowers, but they take no part in pollination.

Tall Yuccas and the Joshua Tree

Some yuccas are the size of small trees. Trecul yucca (*Y. treculeana*) has a thick, straight stem with a crown of leaves at the top. Individuals can grow to a height of 15 feet (4.5 m), although most are smaller, and the Mojave yucca (*Y. schidigera*) reaches between 8 feet and 15 feet (2.4–4.5 m).

The biggest of all the yuccas, and the one most often photographed, is the Joshua tree (*Y. brevifolia*) of the southwestern United States and especially the Mojave Desert. It can reach a height of 35 feet (10.7 m) and it grows at a rate of 4 inches (10 cm) a year. Its single, thick stem divides into a few stout branches and these also divide. The crown of the tree is composed of dense clusters of parallel-sided leaves that last for up to 20 years. Many yuccas yield useful fiber. Fiber from the Joshua tree is sometimes used to make paper.

Creosote Bush

Over large parts of the deserts of the southwestern United States and Mexico as well as in some parts of South American deserts, the most abundant large plant is the creosote bush (*Larrea divaricata* subspecies *tridentata*), also called greasewood. Its small olive-green leaves contain resin and smell of creosote (distilled from coal tar), giving the plant its usual common name. A lotion used as an antiseptic is obtained by steeping the twigs in boiling water.

The creosote bush is a shrub up to about 5 feet (1.5 m) tall, with a tangled mass of branches. It can survive for more than a year without rain. Most of the time the plant looks dead and its branches are dry and brittle, but it recovers rapidly when it does rain. The plant achieves this by losing all its leaves but protecting those leaves that remain in their buds. These become dormant but revive when water reaches them.

Its tolerance for extreme drought allows the creosote bush to grow where few other plants are found. The bushes themselves grow as quite large but scattered clumps, the distance separating them related to the availability of water. When water is present, the roots of each plant draw moisture from the volume of soil around them and there is a region where root growth is inhibited by competition for limited water between the roots of adjacent plants. The moister the soil, the closer together the plants and, conversely, the more arid the ground, the more widely spaced the plants.

Except in very dry years, creosote bushes produce bright yellow flowers in spring followed by seeds in capsules, rather like those of poppies. People who grow creosote bushes in their desert gardens sometimes pick the unopened flower buds and use them in the same way as capers (which are also flower buds, but of an unrelated plant) to flavor food.

This is not the only way the creosote bush reproduces. It also clones itself. Shoots grow at intervals along its horizontal roots. These emerge above the surface as "suckers" and at the same time start growing roots of their own. They are still attached to the root of the original plant, but if that root should die or be severed, the new plant would not be harmed. Even when it is separated from its "parent," however, the new plant is not different from it. It cannot be, because it is part of it, no different from a branch—or a plant grown from a cutting. Genetically, "parent" and "offspring" are identical. They form a clone. (Strictly speaking, a *clone* is a group of genetically identical individuals, each member of which is known as a *ramet,* although people often use *clone,* incorrectly, as a synonym of *ramet.*)

The creosote bush that stands alone in the desert, therefore, is likely to be a clone and its clones often cover an area up to 25 feet (7.6 m) across. Individual plants grow old and die, but clones are different. They can continue to produce new ramets for as long as there are horizontal roots strong enough to produce suckers. Roots die, too, of course, but since each ramet produces new roots of its own, the roots and suckers are constantly being renewed. This means that what appears to be a single plant, but in fact is a clone, can live for a very long time. Some creosote-bush clones in the Mojave Desert are more than 11,500 years old. When they were young the last ice age was just coming to an end.

Plants of Polar Deserts

Tundra is a Lapp or Finnish word used to describe land that is barren. By its very name, then, the tundra is a hostile place, an environment as harsh as any tropical or continental desert, but one of strange contrasts. Although the annual precipitation is very low, for a short time in summer large areas are waterlogged and extensive pools of water lie on the surface.

This is the result of severely impeded drainage. Below the surface the ground is permanently frozen—it is permafrost. Rising temperatures in spring and summer thaw the top layer, known as the *active layer,* which can have a depth of 1–10 feet (0.3–3.0 m) depending on the type of soil it is made up of. The ice it contains melts, but the water cannot drain away because of the thick permafrost layer below the active layer. The surface is uneven, however, so some drainage can take place as water moves from higher to lower ground. This leaves small hillocks, ridges, and mounds extremely dry. The environment therefore consists of very arid islands, called *fell-field* or *fjeldmark,* surrounded by ground that is sodden.

Trees cannot grow there, for the active layer is too thin for their roots—no plant roots can penetrate permafrost—and the climate is too cold and too dry. In some places, and over very large areas, lichens are the only plants that can survive.

Lichens

A lichen is not one organism but a community of organisms living in an intimate relationship. A fungus, called the *mycobiont,* sends its fine network of hyphae—threadlike filaments—into the tinest of cracks in search of mineral nutrients it can absorb. The fungus gives the lichen its shape and structure. Embedded in the fungus there are *phycobionts,* comprising millions of single-celled organisms that conduct photosynthesis. Depending on the type of lichen, these are either green algae, which are very simple plants, or cyanobacteria, which are photosynthesizing bacteria. The phycobionts supply carbohydrates to the fungus.

Lichens are well equipped for life in a cold climate. When the temperature falls below the minimum needed for photosynthesis (see page 56 for a discussion of photosynthesis) they simply become inactive and they can remain in this condition almost indefinitely. As soon as the temperature rises above the minimal threshold, photosynthesis resumes at once.

Dry Valleys and Nunataks

Lichens are the only form of life in the "dry valleys" or "oases" of Antarctica. These are areas where the ground is free of ice, and they cover about 2,200 square miles (5,600 sq km) of the continent. They also grow elsewhere, on exposed rock that emerges above the snow and ice—such an outcrop is called a *nunatak*—as far south as 86°9′ S, where they occur at an elevation of 6,500 feet (1,980 m), and Antarctica supports about 350 species of them. There are also regions near the North Pole where only lichens can survive, though these areas are smaller than their counterparts in the Southern Hemisphere, because the North Pole is surrounded by sea, not land.

Mosses can also grow under harsh conditions and are found in Antarctica at about 84° S and an elevation of 2,490 feet (760 m). The most extensive area of unbroken vegetation in Antarctica is believed to consist of moss growing on top of a layer of peat 3 feet (1 m) thick. This is found on Green Island, off the Antarctic Peninsula, and the vegetation covers nearly 4 acres (1.6 ha).

Sunshine and Flowers

Polar landscapes present scenery on a grand scale, but much of the life they support is tiny. Down near the ice-free surface, lichens and mosses form "forests" and "jungles" within which minute animals graze and hunt. There, where they are sheltered from the drying wind, the plants and animals feeding on them are able to benefit from the one advantage of living in such a high latitude—the long hours of intense sunshine in summer. The importance of sunshine to tundra plants is demonstrated by arctic relatives of the foxgloves (family Scrophulariaceae) that are known as *compass flowers,* because the flowers on the south-facing side of the shoot develop faster than those on the other side, facing away from the Sun.

A hair grass (*Deschampsia antarctica*) and Antarctic pearlwort (*Colobanthus crassifolius*), a member of the carnation family (Caryophyllaceae), grow near sea level along the Antarctic Peninsula as far south as about 68° S. They flower, but reproduce vegetatively and rarely set seed. Antarctic pearlwort produces colorless flowers and the plant grows as a cushion. These two species are the only vascular plants (plants with xylem and phloem tissue) that occur naturally on the mainland of Antarctica, although a few plants have been introduced onto the peninsula, including two species of meadow grass, *Poa pratensis* and *P. annua.*

Plants of polar deserts, like those of hot deserts, must be quick to exploit brief improvements in their generally unfavorable environment, but they have one advantage. In a polar desert that brief episode is predictable, because it occurs in summer, and it allows plants to respond to changes in the length of day. Flowering herbs often start to produce flower buds as the days are shortening. Alpine, or mountain, sorrel (*Oxyria digyna*), for example, forms buds when the day length shortens from 18 hours to 15 hours. The buds remain dormant through the winter, but as soon as the days start lengthening once more, they are ready to flower immediately. Purple saxifrage (*Saxifraga oppositifolia*) and an arctic buttercup, *Ranunculus nivalis,* are in full flower no more than 4 days after the snow has started to melt.

Reproduction

Like the flowering plants of hot deserts, those of polar deserts that rely on insects for pollination compete strongly for attention. They produce big, showy flowers, and some of them go even further by providing warmth for the benefit of visiting insects. Their flowers focus warmth onto their reproductive organs in the same way a parabolic dish for receiving satellite TV focuses radio waves onto its aerial, and, also like some satellite dishes, the whole flower turns as the Sun crosses the sky. It can be up to 18°F (10°C) warmer inside the flower than it is in the air outside.

Despite their bright flowers, however, most of the plants reproduce from shoots that grow from rhizomes (underground stems). Like that of the creosote bush of hot deserts (page 73), this method of reproduction leads to the formation of a clone. Old individuals die, new ones emerge, and they are all part of the same plant, joined below ground.

Reproduction from seed is even more difficult for a plant in a polar desert than it is for one in a hot desert. If its flower is pollinated, and if the temperature remains above freezing long enough for its eggs to be fertilized and seeds to form, then the seeds may survive the winter on the ground. Next spring they will germinate as soon as the temperature rises above a critical threshold. The growing season is very short, so seeds must germinate early in the year if they are to grow into seedlings that are strong enough to withstand their first winter. This means they cannot afford any delay in the coming of the spring thaw. Once the seeds have germinated the young plants must be able to grow steadily through the spring and summer. Anything that interrupts their growth, such as a drought, will kill them. They must also survive the wind and battering by ice crystals and debris the wind throws at them, as well as the needle-sharp ice crystals that can form just below ground and pierce stems and roots. Annual plants are uncommon in cold deserts.

Biennials and Woody Perennials

In the northern tundra there are biennials—plants that live two years, producing seed in the second—such as moss campion (*Silene acaulis*). It forms dense, green cushions and has solitary pink flowers about 0.4 inch (10 mm) across. Apart from having colored flowers, moss campion closely resembles Antarctic pearlwort.

Some of the cushions found on the arctic fell-fields are of shrubs, such as arctic white heather (*Cassiope tetragona*), trailing azalea (*Loiseleuria procumbens*), and bearberry (*Arctostaphylos uva-ursi*), all of which are members of the heath family (Ericaceae). Like plants of hot deserts, they have small, waxy leaves that reduce water loss. The dense mats and cushions they form shelter the ground, reducing evaporation, and also protecting the plants themselves from the drying effect of the wind. Mountain avens (*Dryas octopetala*), widely cultivated as an alpine ornamental plant, is also a low-growing shrub. It belongs to the rose family (Rosaceae) and its roots have nodules containing bacteria that fix nitrogen. All of these are perennial plants—plants that live for more than two years—with woody stems and branches. They grow very slowly in the cold, dry climate. It may take mountain avens 100 years to advance by 3 feet (1 m).

Here and there on moister ground there are also woody plants that in a warmer climate would be trees, but that grow in the Arctic as spreading shrubs, never more than 3 feet (1 m) tall. Dwarf birch (*Betula nana*) is common, as are reticulate willow (*Salix reticulata*) and arctic willow (*S. arctica*). Juniper (*Juniperus communis*) grows as a tree up to 40 feet (12 m) tall in temperate regions, but in the arctic the dwarf variety *J. communis* var. *nana* is only 1 foot (30 cm) tall.

Desert Animals

"Hot-Blooded" and "Cold-Blooded" Animals

Birds and mammals are warm-blooded. Fish, amphibians, reptiles, and all invertebrate animals are cold-blooded. This division of animals into two types, as warm-blooded and cold-blooded, is based upon real physiological differences, but it is nevertheless misleading. Handle a lizard or snake, for example, and you will feel that it is quite warm, despite being "cold-blooded." In fact, its body temperature is not much different from your own and it may be higher. A bird also feels warm, but if you measure the temperature you will find its body is several degrees warmer than your own. So, if mammals are "warm-blooded," perhaps we should think of birds—and possibly lizards—as being "warmer-blooded." Fish, on the other hand, really do feel cold, as do most invertebrates, unless, that is, you take them from surroundings that are warm.

Oddly enough, "cold-blooded" animals originally earned their name not because they were thought to function at a lower temperature than "warm-blooded" animals, but because they were thought to tolerate very high temperatures. Lizards can often be seen basking on rocks that are uncomfortably hot to the touch. Clearly, they would be burned unless they had very cool blood—or so people believed for so many centuries that eventually they came to take the idea for granted. It was only in the 20th century that scientists discovered how and why animals regulate their body temperatures. It is much more complicated than ideas of warm or cold blood suggest.

Exotherms and Homeotherms

A more useful distinction is based not on the body temperature itself, but on how it is regulated. This requires animals to be placed into several categories. The first contains what are called *exotherms* or *poikilotherms*. *Exo-* is from the Greek *exo,* "outside," and *poikilo-* is from *poikilos,* which means "changeable." These are animals in which the body temperature varies with that of their surroundings. Fish and invertebrates are exotherms. Exothermy does not mean their temperatures necessarily fluctuate widely. Fish live in water, and because of its high heat capacity (page 52) the temperature of water changes only slowly and within fairly narrow limits. Most fish die if the temperature of their water changes by more than about 25°F (14°C) over a short space of time, although some can survive such a change if it happens over several hours. Many invertebrates survive times when the weather is too hot or too cold by becoming dormant (page 84).

Animals that maintain a fairly constant body temperature that may be warmer or cooler than their surroundings are called *homeotherms.* The ability to remain warm when the air temperature falls and cool when it rises is essential for most land-dwelling animals. Temperatures fluctuate much more widely on land than they do in water. Changes can be rapid, especially in hot deserts, and the temperature may rise or fall outside the range most animals find tolerable.

In all homeotherms the internal body temperature—sometimes called the *core temperature*—is held within fairly narrow limits. There are two ways in which an animal can achieve this regulation and so homeotherms are of two types.

Ectotherms and Endotherms

Some, such as amphibians and reptiles, use behavioral means. They bask in order to warm their bodies, for example, and seek shade to cool them. These are known as *ectotherms; ecto-* is from the Greek *ekto,* which means "outside."

Others have internal, physiological ways to regulate temperature. When they are cold, for example, blood vessels in the skin contract to restrict the flow of blood and loss of heat to the outside, and they may shiver to generate warmth by moving their muscles rapidly. When they are hot their skin blood vessels dilate and they may sweat; the evaporation of sweat absorbs latent heat from the skin and so cools it. A mammal can make its fur more erect to trap a layer of air that is warmed by its body and provides insulation. Animals of this kind are called *endotherms; endo-* is from the Greek *endon,* which means "within." Only mammals and birds are endotherms.

The distinction is not quite so clear as the definitions make it seem, because most endotherms respond behaviorally to extreme temperatures. Humans are the clearest example. When the weather is cold we turn up the heating and put on warm clothes. When it is hot we wear lighter clothes. Only humans light fires, but many other mammals grow thicker coats in winter and shed them in summer, and they also modify their behavior. They bask in the warm sunshine to warm themselves and lie in the shade when they feel too hot.

Both endothermy and ectothermy allow animals to function in an environment where the temperature is not constant, but a price must be paid for this freedom. An ectotherm living in a hot desert must spend part of every day warming its body and part preventing it from overheating. This reduces the time it has available for other activities, such as feeding. Vertebrate ectotherms cannot live in cold deserts, because the low temperatures make it impossible for them to maintain body temperatures high enough to allow them to

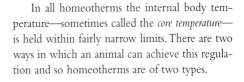

Anchleta's lizard on dune slip (Gerry Ellis/ ENP Images)

be active long enough to feed and reproduce. Invertebrates can inhabit cold deserts by emerging only during favorable periods and because, being much smaller, they can warm themselves more quickly.

Endotherms are not constrained in this way. They can live anywhere there is food for them, but that is where they meet a different constraint. Maintaining a constant core temperature by physiological means involves a considerable expenditure of energy. An endotherm must eat much more food than an ectotherm of similar size.

Metabolic Rate

The energy different animals require can be compared from measurements of their oxygen consumption. Bodies derive the energy they need from the oxidation of carbohydrates, in the process of cellular respiration. This consumes oxygen and oxygen consumption is easy to measure under controlled conditions, using a chamber containing an animal and instruments that compare the amount of oxygen in the air entering the chamber with the amount in the air leaving the chamber. The measurements are then used to calculate energy consumption per day. Every 2.2 pints (1 liter) of oxygen that is consumed by respiration liberates about 4.83 kilocalories (kcal) (20.2 kilojoules) [kJ]) of energy. The result of this calculation is a measure of the rate at which an animal's metabolism functions, often expressed as the *basal metabolic rate* (BMR). This is the metabolic rate of an animal that is lying completely at rest in surroundings where it does not need to warm or cool its body. The BMR for an average human adult male resting at 68°F (20°C) is about 1,600–1,800 kcal (6.7–7.5 megajoules [MJ]), for example, and for an adult female about 1,300–1,500 kcal (5.4–6.3 MJ). The numbers sound large, but this is about as much energy as would power a 100-watt light bulb. When the amount of energy the animal uses is divided by the surface area of its body or by its body mass (conventionally in kilograms) the result is a metabolic rate per unit of surface area or mass per day for that species, sometimes called the *standard metabolic rate* (SMR). Once metabolic rates have been corrected for body size, those of different species can be compared.

Comparisons show a direct relationship between metabolic rate and body size. The smaller an animal, the greater its metabolic rate. This is true for all vertebrates, regardless of whether they are exotherms, ectotherms, or endotherms, and the ratio of metabolic rate to body size is the same for them all.

Food Requirements of Ectotherms and Endotherms

When BMR and body size are plotted on a graph for a number of species that result is a straight line with the smallest animals at the top of the slope and the biggest at the bottom. If the species include both ectotherms and endotherms, however, the graph contains two parallel straight lines, one for each type. The two lines demonstrate that although the BMR to body size relationship is sustained, all endotherms have a higher BMR than all ectotherms. The fact that the relationship holds equally for ectotherms and endotherms also demonstrates that it is not due solely to temperature regulation. Some other factor must partly account for it, but at present scientists have not discovered what that factor is.

Nevertheless, part of the difference between the two arises from the energy that must be expended to maintain a constant temperature by physiological means. Lying on a warm rock in the Sun, or on a cool rock in the shade, consumes much less energy than shivering, sweating, and constricting or dilating blood vessels.

Since metabolic rates can be compared, it is possible to measure the extent of this difference. At 68°F (20°C), the BMR for an adult male human is about 1,800 kcal (7.5 MJ) and that for an American alligator, which is an ectothermic reptile of about the same size, is about 60 kcal (250 kJ).

Energy is released by the oxidation of carbohydrates and animals obtain their carbohydrates from the food they eat. The amount of food an animal must eat, therefore, is proportional to the amount of energy it needs to maintain its metabolism. The higher its BMR, the more food it requires, so endotherms—birds and mammals—are obliged to eat much more than ectotherms—amphibians and reptiles—of similar size.

How Heat Can Kill and How Animals Keep Cool

Animals adapt to the conditions under which they live; these conditions include climate, and animals adapted to different climates tolerate different temperature ranges. A polar bear could not survive for long in the Sahara, any more than a sidewinder rattlesnake could survive in Greenland.

Their tolerance of different climates reflects the way animals regulate their body temperatures. Mammals and birds have a core body temperature of around 97–104°F (36–40°C) regardless of where they live. The body of a wolf, living in the tundra, is at the same temperature as that of a jackal, living in a subtropical desert.

An ability to control its internal body temperature does not mean an animal can remain unaffected by the air temperature outside its body. The regulatory mechanisms can be overwhelmed and extreme heat can kill. In "The Day the Sands Caught Fire," an article in the November 1998 edition of *Scientific American,* Jeffrey C. Wynn and the late Eugene M. Shoemaker described an expedition they led into the Empty Quarter, the Rub' al-Khali, of Saudi Arabia. One day Wynn went out to conduct a geomagnetic survey when the temperature in the shade under a tarpaulin was 142°F (61°C) and the relative humidity was 2 percent. "By the time he returned he was staggering and speaking an incoherent mixture of Arabic and English. Only some time later, after water was poured on his head and cool air was blasted in his face, did his mind clear."

Endothermy evolved as an adaptation to cold climates. It is much more efficient at minimizing and compensating for heat loss than it is at dissipating heat to prevent the body temperature from rising. Many endotherms find it more difficult to hold their body temperature 18°F (10°C) below the air temperature than 180°F (100°C) above it.

Keeping Cool

Mammals cool themselves by dilating blood vessels near the body surface. This increases the blood flow and provided the outside temperature is lower than the core temperature the blood will be cooled. This is an efficient way to transport heat from the interior of the body and then to lose it.

Mammals also allow water to evaporate, deriving the latent heat of vaporization from their bodies. Humans sweat, secreting water onto the skin, from which it evaporates. Other mammals, of which dogs are the most familiar, pant. Panting allows moisture to evaporate from the inside of the mouth and respiratory passages.

Evaporation is an effective way to keep cool, but there is a cost. Water that is lost from the body must be replaced and in a desert that may not be easy. Cooling by evaporation is not satisfactory except as a short-term measure.

Dangers of Overheating

As the body loses water the proportion of plasma (fluid) in the blood decreases. This causes the blood to become more viscous until a point is reached at which the rate of circulation slows. The body is then unable to lose heat by using blood circulation to transport it from the interior of the body to the surface. The core temperature rises rapidly and death follows quickly. Most mammals will die if they lose between 10 percent and 20 percent of the water in their bodies.

Body fluids are not pure water, but solutions of a variety of salts. Evaporation involves only water, however. When water molecules break the hydrogen bonds that link them and escape as vapor, molecules of other substances are not affected. They remain behind. Consequently, when water evaporates from a solution the concentration of that solution increases. Water that is lost through sweating and panting is taken from the aqueous solution in the spaces between cells. As it is lost and the solution outside cells becomes more concentrated than that inside cells, water may start to move across cell walls by osmosis. This increases the concentration of the solution inside the cell.

At first this accelerates the activity of the cell. This is because the metabolism—of a cell or of a body consisting of billions of cells—is a series of chemical reactions catalyzed by enzymes. Enzyme molecules have locations, called *active sites,* at which other molecules, called *substrate molecules,* become attached in the first stage of a chemical reaction. The greater the concentration of substrate molecules, the more often they will collide with the active sites of enzyme molecules and so the faster the reactions will proceed. Eventually, though, all the active sites are occupied and as soon as one is vacated at the completion of the reaction it is filled again. The metabolism can move no faster unless more enzymes are manufactured—as sometimes happens. If dehydration continues, the function of the cell is disrupted and it dies.

There is an optimal temperature above and below which metabolic reactions slow down. This is determined by the optimal working temperature for enzymes, and in vertebrates that tem-

perature is about 104°F (40°C). In turn, this sets the optimal body temperature—in humans 98.6°F (37°C). Should the core temperature exceed this, enzyme-catalyzed reactions start to slow. At temperatures not much higher than 104°F enzymes start to degrade as the bonds holding together the constituent parts of their molecules begin to break. Most mammals suffer brain damage if their body temperature rises above 109°F (43°C) and remains there more than a few minutes.

Living in Burrows

Small mammals avoid exposing themselves to the full rigors of the desert climate. They spend their days below ground, in burrows, where the temperature is much lower than it is at the surface, and emerge to feed at night. If an animal the size of a rat spent the hottest part of the day above ground it would have to evaporate about 13 percent of the water in its body every hour in order to prevent overheating. Rodents do not sweat, but when its body temperature rises a kangaroo rat (*Dipodomys* species) salivates copiously and licks its fur, cooling itself by the evaporation of saliva.

A substantial proportion of the food a bird or mammal eats is used to provide the energy for maintaining a constant body temperature. Some desert rodents, such as the California pocket mouse (*Perognathus californicus*) and cactus mouse (*Peromyscus eremicus*), exploit this fact. They become torpid. Usually they do so in response to a scarcity of food, but sometimes they become torpid when water is scarce. Safe in their burrow, the animals cease to move, their metabolism slows and, with it, the heartbeat and rate of breathing. Their temperature then falls approximately to the air temperature in the burrow. Pocket mice can become torpid for just a few hours and then arouse themselves. Torpor greatly reduces the need for food and water.

The Camel

Large animals cannot shelter in burrows, but because they are large their bodies absorb heat more slowly than do those of smaller animals. This does not prevent them from heating, of course, but desert species have various ways of surviving.

Surprisingly, thick fur can help by shading and insulating the skin. The single-humped camel or dromedary (*Camelus dromedarius*) has fur on its warms their backs, but they lose heat by contact with the ground. During the hottest part of the day, dromedaries sometimes lie close together, their sides touching. This ensures their skins are all at the same 104°F (40°C), rather than being heated further by the Sun.

Antelopes, Gazelles, and Reptiles

Antelopes and gazelles also allow their temperatures to fluctuate. The temperature of a gemsbok (*Oryx gazella*), of the deserts of southern Africa, can rise to 113°F (45°C), and a Grant's gazelle (*Gazella granti*) can tolerate a body temperature of 115°F (46°C) for 6 hours. At these temperatures the animals should suffer brain damage. They avoid this by means of a circulatory system in which the small arteries to the brain lie adjacent to veins returning from the nasal passages and therefore carrying blood that has been cooled. This ensures a supply of cooled blood to the brain.

Reptiles have none of these physiological mechanisms. They avoid excess heat either by seeking shade or by spending much of the day in burrows. This is a method of regulation that permits very fine tuning. Most lizards are fully active within a temperature range of about 7°F (4°C). Other reptiles have a wider range, of up to 18°F (10°C). When its temperature approaches the upper end of the range the animal seeks shade or buries itself, and when it approaches the lower end it seeks sunshine and a warm surface on which to bask.

Dromedary camels (Gerry Ellis/ENP Images)

back. During the middle of the day the top of the fur can be at 160–175°F (71–79°C) and the skin beneath the fur at 104°F (40°C). Dromedaries sweat, but their fur also increases the efficiency of sweating. Their sweat evaporates in the shade, using latent heat absorbed from the skin. If the skin were naked, most of the latent heat would be provided by the solar heat to which it was exposed and it would have very little cooling effect.

At night the temperature of a dromedary's body falls, sometimes to 95°F (35°C). Then, during the day, it rises to about 104°F (40°C). This fluctuation reduces the amount of energy and water the dromedary needs to expend. Its behavior also helps it keep cool. In the early morning, when the ground is cold, dromedaries lie down with their legs folded beneath them. The Sun

Camel (Gerry Ellis/ENP Images)

How Tolerating a Slightly Higher Temperature Pays Dividends

Life is hard in a hot desert and not many plants have been able to adapt to the aridity and high daytime temperatures. Consequently, plants are few and widely scattered, and many are ephemeral, emerging only after rain and spending most of the time as seed (page 64). The fact that each perennial plant is likely to grow in isolation increases its vulnerability to attack from herbivorous animals. An isolated plant is clearly visible, because there are no other plants among which it can be hidden, and the surrounding area offers no alternative food for herbivores.

Everywhere in the world, plants have evolved ways to deter herbivores from eating their leaves, stems, and roots. Many are poisonous and some extremely so. Plant toxins, known as *secondary compounds* because they are formed as by-products of the major metabolic pathways, include strychnine from *Strychnos* species, mescaline from the peyote cactus (*Lophophora williamsii*), and morphine from the poppy *Papaver somniferum*.

Others have spines or thorns, or tough, unpalatable leaves. Desert plants are not unique in being generally difficult or dangerous to eat, but isolation has exposed them to strong natural selection that has intensified these features. Quite simply, the less palatable the plant, the more seeds it is likely to produce, so palatability decreases generation after generation.

Even grasses are less edible than they seem. Most perennial grasses have stems that run along or just beneath the ground surface, out of the reach of most animals. The older leaves can be removed without harming the plant, but they have tough cell walls containing silica—the mineral from which quartz sand is made. This will wear away the teeth of animals seeking to obtain the rather small amount of nutritious material contained inside cells.

Facing Challenges

As though the heat of daytime, nighttime cold, lack of water, and scarcity of food were not sufficient obstacles, the self-protection of plants adds another challenge for desert herbivores to overcome. Herbivores are also under selective pressure, of course, and can evolve ways to render plant toxins harmless and to bypass physical defenses, such as thorns and tough leaves. Rodents have teeth that grow continually, so they remain the

Blue cranes on desert pan (Gerry Ellis/ ENP Images)

same size despite being worn down, and grazing mammals have large, strong teeth that can crush tough material without being damaged. A few animals have even found ways to cooperate with plants, as the ant *Pseudomyrmex ferruginea* has with the bull horn acacia (page 72).

No single herbivore species can evolve ways to counter all the threats presented by all plants, however. The plants cannot achieve total protection, but they can compel herbivores to be selective in their diet. There are only certain parts of certain plants a desert herbivore can eat.

If any animal could eat any plant, an animal could approach the nearest plant of any species. Food would be easy to find. When it arrived, however, the animal would find itself competing with other animals. It would have to assert its claim to a portion of the plant, perhaps by driving away rivals, and this would reduce the time it could spend feeding. Dietary specialization precludes much of the competition, but it means the animal must spend more time searching for a plant it can eat. The time it can spend feeding is still restricted.

Finding More Time for Feeding

Whatever metabolic or behavioral strategy an animal adopts, desert survival depends on maximizing mobility and foraging time. Endotherms are highly mobile. Birds can and do fly long distances and mammals can and do run. Nor do they have diffi-

culty in devoting sufficient time to foraging. Birds fly to where food is available, traveling by air where the temperature is much lower than it is at ground level. Small mammals shelter by day and forage by night—a habit that also affords them some protection from predators. Against these advantages there is a disadvantage. Endotherms need much more food than ectotherms.

Insects cannot fly far in search of food, and reptiles—ectothermic vertebrates—cannot fly at all. Nor can most of them forage at night, because then they are too cold. A reptile will die quite rapidly if it is exposed to a temperature below a certain minimum or above a certain maximum. Within these extremes there is a low temperature at which a reptile can survive but is unable to move or can move only very slowly, and a high temperature at which it is also rendered immobile and will die with continued exposure to the heat. When it is immobile or moves only with difficulty the animal is vulnerable to predators.

Reptilian Strategies

A reptile is fully active only when its body is within a few degrees of 98°F (37°C). There are

Basking and temperature control

two ways for it to maximize its foraging time. The first is to warm rapidly to its active temperature and cool slowly, allowing it to start foraging earlier in the day and continue foraging later into the evening. Alternatively, it can adapt to tolerate higher temperatures, allowing it to continue foraging a little longer in the hottest part of the day. Reptiles have done both.

Although it is true that reptiles must bask to warm their bodies and seek shade to cool them, this is only part of the story. For one thing, basking and seeking shade are more sophisticated activities than they sound. As well as the solar radiation that reaches it directly from the sky, a basking reptile chooses a spot where it is exposed to radiation reflected from nearby surfaces, such as rocks. It lies with its cold body pressed against a warm surface. Later in the day, when the ground is hot, a lizard with long legs (some lizards have short legs or are legless) stands with its legs fully extended to raise its body and tail as far above the ground as it can. Many desert insects also have long legs and hold their bodies as high as they can to minimize contact with the surface. On hot ground, a lizard may raise each foot in turn so it is always standing on three legs with the fourth held clear of the surface. Similarly, some shaded places are cooler than others and ectotherms select the temperature they need.

Physiological Controls

Small reptiles warm quickly, but when a large lizard, snake, or turtle lies basking and its skin begins to warm, blood vessels in its skin dilate. This is an automatic response to rising temperature and it accelerates the blood flow, carrying warmed blood to the interior of the body.

In the early morning, when its body is cold, a reptile basks with its body oriented so its back is fully exposed to the Sun. As its blood vessels dilate the animal warms rapidly. In the late afternoon, as the Sun sinks lower in the sky and the air temperature starts to fall, the mechanism goes into reverse. When the skin temperature falls, the blood vessels cease to be dilated. This slows the circulation and thus reduces the rate at which warm blood from inside the body travels close to the skin and is cooled. The overall effect is that a reptile warms up much more quickly than it cools down. This extends the time it can devote to foraging.

Basking and Changing Color

Reptiles can also control the amount of solar radiation their bodies absorb. When they lie with their backs exposed to the Sun they absorb much more radiation than they do when facing into the Sun. The accompanying figure illustrates this. Lizards and many snakes—but not turtles, of course—are able to increase this effect by spreading their ribs in a way that alters the shape of their bodies. Probably the most extreme example of this ability is found in horned lizards, such as the Texas horned lizard (*Phrynosoma cornutum*). By altering the shape and orientation of its body it can achieve a sixfold difference in the amount of solar radiation to which it is exposed.

Many lizards, including the Texas horned lizard, can also change their body color by spreading the dark pigment melanin throughout specialized skin cells called *melanophores*. Some snakes can also do this, but to a lesser extent. Rattlesnakes can make their bodies lighter and darker. Turtles and crocodilians (crocodiles and alligators) cannot change their color. Darkening the skin increases the amount of radiation the body absorbs and lightening it reduces absorption. Some lizards can alter the amount of radiation their skin absorbs by as much as 75 percent.

All these strategies increase the efficacy of basking and seeking shade as a means of regulating body temperature. They allow ectotherms to remain active for longer and so they increase the time they can spend in search of food. During the hottest part of the day, however, even these mechanisms are insufficient and desert animals must seek shade.

Tolerating a Higher Temperature

That is when a very few of the desert inhabitants have an advantage. They are active at a temperature a little higher than most animals can tolerate. The desert iguana or crested lizard (*Dipsosaurus dorsalis*) of the southwestern United States and Mexico is active when its body temperature is between 104°F and 108°F (40–42°C). When its temperature threatens to rise above the upper threshold, the lizard shelters beneath a creosote bush. Until then, however, it can move around while most other animals are out of sight and inactive.

During this period it has no competitors and can claim for itself all the food it can find. It can claim only plant food, of course. With other animals out of sight there is even less food than usual for carnivores—and most lizards are carnivores. The desert iguana will eat insects and small vertebrates, but it can enjoy its thermal advantage because its diet is mainly vegetarian.

How Freezing Kills and How Animals Avoid It

No one likes to feel cold. The sensation is very uncomfortable and a naked person who is not permitted to move around soon starts feeling cold if the air temperature is below about 84°F (29°C). We are not alone. No animal enjoys the feeling—and for good reason. Cold can kill.

This is not the same thing as saying we do not enjoy living in a cold climate. Many people do enjoy cold weather and the outdoor pursuits it makes possible, such as skiing and skating, and people have been living in the Arctic for thousands of years. When Scandinavians arrived in about 980 C.E. to settle in Greenland they found Inuit people already living. there. We know now that the Inuits had been in Greenland since about 2500 B.C.E. and they had been living for much longer than that in arctic North America. They obtained their food by hunting and fishing, and the game they pursued included bears, moose, caribou, bison, musk oxen, walruses, seals, and whales. All of these are mammals and they also inhabited the Far North. Clearly, low temperatures have never deterred humans or other mammals.

Inuit people are acclimatized to the cold climate in which they live. That is to say, over many generations they have grown accustomed to it and learned how to exploit its opportunities and avoid its dangers. Despite this, the body of an Inuit has a core temperature no different from that of anyone else. Inuits are able to enjoy their environment because they do not feel cold. They keep warm mainly by wearing a thick layer of clothes to provide insulation.

Effects of Falling Temperature

Animal bodies function as a result of countless biochemical reactions catalyzed by enzymes. Most of these proceed at a rate that varies according to the temperature, but their degree of sensitivity to temperature varies. Move far from the optimal temperature and the reactions involved in respiration and digestion start to become uncoordinated. Nervous responses also slow as temperature falls, because they depend on the diffusion of neurotransmitter substances, such as acetylcholine and norepinephrine, across the synaptic junctions between neurons, and the rate of diffusion is directly proportional to temperature. At low temperatures muscles become stiffer and more energy is needed to make them contract.

Suppose a naked person were made to remain immobile while the air temperature slowly fell from a starting point of about 84°F (29°C). This is about 14.6°F (8°C) below the normal body temperature of 98.6°F (37°C). All sweating would cease immediately. Then the individual would start to look pale as blood vessels near the surface were constricted to prevent loss of heat from the interior of the body. Hair would rise, although because humans have little body hair this would be evident mainly as goosebumps caused by contraction of the muscles that would raise hairs were there any to raise. The person would shiver uncontrollably.

As the air temperature fell below about 79°F (26°C) these mechanisms would no longer be sufficient. This is the *low critical temperature* below which the individual's metabolic rate would begin to rise, oxidizing carbon faster to release more heat energy. This increase in the rate of cell respiration would require an increase in the oxygen supply. The metabolic rate would continue to increase as the temperature fell, until the chemical reactions began to fail. The individual would then become confused, feel dizzy, and suffer from cramp and would die if their core temperature fell below about 90°F (32°C). This is the *low lethal temperature*. It varies a little from one person to another, depending on age and physical condition, but it does not vary with nationality or ethnic origin. The diagram shows how these thresholds are related to the basal metabolic rate. It also shows the corresponding high critical temperature, at which the metabolic rate increases, and the high lethal temperature.

Maintaining the Core Temperature

Animals that have adapted to very different climates have different low critical temperatures.

The low critical temperature for a kangaroo rat (*Dipodomys* species) is 88°F (31°C), for example, and that for an arctic fox (*Alopex lagopus*) is -40°F (-40°C). What is more, as the air temperature falls below the low critical temperature the metabolic rate of an arctic fox—or any other arctic mammal—increases more slowly than does the metabolic rate of a tropical species, and its low lethal temperature is much lower.

The core temperature for kangaroo rats, arctic foxes, humans, and indeed all mammals is about 100°F (38°C). It is not difficult to maintain this temperature in a warm climate, where the air temperature is within a few degrees of body temperature, but the situation is very different in a cold climate. Air at -40°F (-40°C) is 140°F (78°C) below core temperature. A mammal living in the Arctic needs to generate 10 times more heat than a mammal of similar size living in the Tropics.

It is not possible for any mammal to generate this much warmth by metabolic means, and the gap is narrow between the low critical temperature and the low lethal temperature. There is a limit to the metabolic rate that can be achieved. The metabolism is "fueled" by food, which must be digested, and that process takes a certain time. Even if the food supply were limitless and an animal could eat incessantly, its digestive system could not process food fast enough. Arctic mammals must have some other way of maintaining their core temperatures, and the clue to the mechanism is provided by the large difference in

Temperature and metabolic rate

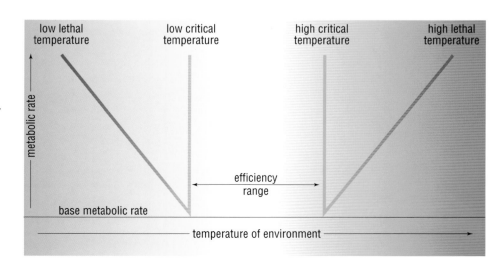

-22°F air temperature

73°F
46°F
41°F
95°F
91°F
99°F
57°F
46°F
32°F

low critical temperatures between the kangaroo rat and the arctic fox. The arctic fox does not increase its metabolic rate until the outside temperature falls to -40°F (-40°C) because it is not until then that the cold penetrates sufficiently to trigger the acceleration. The fox does not feel the cold because a layer of insulation outside protects the inside of its body.

Insulation

Like other arctic mammals, the fox is insulated by its thick coat, although it is only the bigger mammals that have a coat thick enough to keep them warm through the winter. Small rodents, such as lemmings, are not big enough to carry a really thick coat, and they are prone to losing heat rapidly, because of their large surface area in relation to volume (see pages 70 and 76). Consequently, they must spend the coldest part of the winter in hibernation (page 84).

Marine mammals, such as seals, whales, and walrus, have very short fur. Their insulation takes the form of a thick layer of fat, called *blubber*, just below the skin.

The arctic fox's coat cannot be of the same thickness over the whole of its body, however. Its lower legs and paws must be free, the tips of its toes are naked, and its nose and eyes must not be covered. If its feet were at its core temperature they would melt the snow and ice over which the fox walks, and that would be dangerous. Consequently, the bodily extremities are much colder than the internal organs. The drawing shows the temperature on various parts of the body of an arctic fox when the air temperature is -22°F (-30°C).

This difference is even more obvious in a bird. In most species the thin legs and feet have no covering of feathers at all. The extremities contain muscles and nerves, so they receive a blood supply. Warm blood flows from the body to the extremities, where it loses heat to the outside—blood in the fox's paw is 67°F (37°C) below the animal's core temperature. As the cold blood flows back to the heart it will cool the body and before long the core temperature will be falling much faster than the animal can generate warmth.

Countercurrent Exchange and the "Wonderful Net"

This does not happen because of a network of small blood vessels—both arteries and veins—situated close to where each extremity joins the main part of the body. The network is called the *rete mirabile*, or "wonderful net."

Heat is exchanged in the net between warm arterial blood flowing toward the extremity and cold venous blood flowing back into the body. This is called *countercurrent exchange* because heat is exchanged between blood flowing in opposite directions. The outgoing blood is chilled, so the extremity remains cold, and the incoming blood is warmed, so the core temperature is maintained.

Temperature of an arctic fox when the air temperature is -22 degrees

Ectotherms and Exotherms

Exotherms and ectotherms are less able to survive cold, but nevertheless they, too, have established themselves in the Far North and South. Indeed, people working in the tundra in summer must keep every part of their bodies covered, using mosquito netting over their faces, to protect them from clouds of biting insects. Insects—exotherms—emerge and breed during the short summer, but spend most of the year as eggs.

There are even one snake, the viper or common adder (*Vipera berus*), and one lizard, the European common or viviparous lizard (*Lacerta vivipara*), that live inside the Arctic Circle. It would be difficult, and probably impossible, for an ectotherm to incubate eggs in a cold climate, and both species give birth to live young. Even then, reptiles are active only during the brief summer. At low temperatures the metabolism slows and the animal becomes incapable of obtaining food or avoiding predators. If its body temperature falls below about 45°F (7°C) a reptile becomes unable to move at all, and if it falls below freezing the animal dies.

Estivation and Hibernation

Not many mammals inhabit the Mojave Desert, but in one corner of the desert there lives the Mojave ground squirrel (*Citellus mohavensis*), a small, brown-furred animal about 6.5 inches (16.5 cm) long, not counting its tail, and weighing about 5.25 ounces (150 g). It is a calm, relaxed little animal that does not fight others and rarely wanders far from home.

The best place to look for it is around its favorite food plant, the cholla cactus (page 71). Cholla fruit is its main food. Even then, though, the squirrel is seldom seen, because it spends most of its time in its burrow, dug down in the loose sand in the shade of the cactus. It emerges from its burrow in March, when the cholla fruits start to form, and from then until August it feeds and mates. In August it returns to its burrow and remains there until the following March. When the squirrel first emerges in spring it is very thin, but after several months of eating voraciously it grows very fat, adding about 3.5 ounces (100 g) to its weight.

Back inside its burrow in late summer the squirrel goes to sleep. This is no ordinary sleep, however. In the course of about 6 hours its core temperature drops until it is just a degree or two above the temperature of its environment. Then it remains there, rising and falling with the temperature of its surroundings. At the same time, the squirrel's metabolism slows to its basal metabolic rate (page 76). Its heartbeat and breathing slow and for quite long periods it does not breathe at all.

When it is time to awaken, the squirrel can be fully aroused within an hour. The first sign of arousal is an acceleration of its rate of breathing. This increases the supply of oxygen to its tissues, and within 15 to 20 minutes its oxygen consumption reaches the level needed for ordinary activity. Its heartbeat accelerates and the squirrel shivers. Shivering generates body heat. Within about half an hour its core temperature can rise from 68°F (20°C) to 86°F (30°C).

Saving Energy

During the first part of this period of dormancy the outside temperature is high. Dormancy during hot weather is known as *estivation,* from the Latin *aestus,* which means "heat." The latter part of the period covers the Mojave winter, when temperatures sometimes fall below freezing. Dormancy during cold weather is called *hibernation,* from the Latin *hibernus,* "wintry." Many animals engage in one or the other, but for the Mojave

ground squirrel there is no difference. Its physiological changes are the same regardless of the outside temperature.

Both estivation and hibernation allow the squirrel to save energy. Above or below its critical temperature (page 82), its metabolic rate would ordinarily increase, but in its torpid state there is no acceleration.

An animal that is not eating relies for energy mainly on the oxidation of body fat, and oxidizing 1 ounce of fat consumes about 32.4 pints of oxygen (2 liters of oxygen to oxidize 1 gram of fat). When the air temperature is 68°F (20°C), a torpid Mojave ground squirrel consumes one-tenth the oxygen it would consume if it were active.

Measuring an animal's oxygen consumption is not difficult (page 77). In laboratory studies the squirrel has been found to consume 0.12 cubic inch of oxygen per ounce of its body weight per hour (0.08 cu cm per gram per hour). At this rate a fat squirrel, weighing 10.5 ounces (300 g), consumes enough oxygen to oxidize 0.01 ounce (0.29 g) of fat a day. It accumulated about 3.5 ounces (100 g) of fat before it became torpid, so this is enough to sustain it for almost a full year (3.5÷0.01 = 350 days).

Its fat reserve would not really last quite this long, because now and then during its dormant period the squirrel wakes. In laboratory studies it wakes up every 3 to 5 days and will eat and drink during these episodes if food and water are available, although it seems unperturbed if they are not and just goes back to sleep. No one knows whether it stores food in its burrow under natural conditions or how often it wakes, but it very likely consumes more energy than its basal metabolic rate requires.

The Mojave ground squirrel lives economically even when it is active. Most vertebrate animals can tolerate only small variations in core temperature, but the squirrel remains relaxed, even about that. It suffers no obvious harm when its core temperature falls as low as 88°F (31°C) or when it rises to 107°F (42°C). Allowing this wide a fluctuation reduces the animal's energy requirement, because until these limits are exceeded it need not expend food energy responding behaviorally or physiologically.

Tolerance of a wide temperature range in combination with estivation also reduce the amount of water the Mojave ground squirrel needs. Most animals keep themselves cool by allowing water to evaporate and it is no excep-

tion. This uses a considerable amount of water, so reducing the need to cool the body also reduces the water requirement. Like some other desert mammals (page 88), in its natural habitat the Mojave ground squirrel never drinks, obtaining all its water from the food it eats.

Estivation and Diurnation

The Mojave ground squirrel is not the only animal that estivates, and estivation is not confined to desert inhabitants. Many temperate species become torpid in hot or dry weather. Some species of European earthworms, such as *Eisenia foetida,* spend the summer in this state. It is especially common among insects, and many bats estivate to survive periods when insects are not flying, although they do so for only short periods, often for less than a day.

There are also birds that briefly enter a torpid state, with a body temperature close to that of their surroundings. Some hummingbirds (family Trochilidae) do so at night, for example, and the white-throated poorwill (*Phalaenoptilus nuttallii*), a bird of the California desert, enters a torpid state when the air temperature falls below about 64°F (18°C). A temperature of 77°F (25°C) is needed to trigger estivation in most mammals. Becoming torpid overnight, or for a short period during the day, is called *diurnation.* Many species of birds enter diurnation, but it is doubtful whether any bird enters true estivation.

Among desert species estivation is usually a way to conserve water and its effects can be dramatic. Snails are soft-bodied and prone to desiccation, but they have a means of protection. They can retreat into their shells and seal the shell opening with a watertight cover, called an *operculum.* Even so, most snails live in humid climates—but not all of them do. Being exotherms they expend no energy on maintaining a constant body temperature and can survive long periods without food. Some snails live in deserts, where they can remain dormant for years on end, reviving rapidly when it rains.

Estivating Toads

Frogs and toads are amphibians. Like those of all amphibians their eggs have no shells and must be laid in water, and a significant proportion of their respiratory gas exchange takes place through their skins. This is called *cutaneous respiration* and it means the amphibian skin is highly permeable. Its wearer is liable to become desiccated if the skin dries. Nevertheless, Couch's spadefoot toad (*Scaphiopus couchii*) lives in the North American desert. It spends 10 or even 11 months of the year estivating below ground and revives only when the vibration of falling rain arouses it. On emerging it enters the nearest pool of water. It mates and its eggs are laid and fertilized at once and within 9 days they have developed into tiny toadlets.

Its adaptation is an extreme version of the way of life of most spadefoot toads—54 species constituting the family Pelobatidae. There are two genera, *Pelobates* found in Eurasia, and the North American *Scaphiopus,* and their common name refers to a modification of their hind feet, which they use for digging. They breed in the pools that appear after heavy rain, and their young mature rapidly, before their pool vanishes.

Fish That Live in Semideserts

As well as toads that can live in a desert, there are even fish that live in a semiarid environment. African lungfish (several *Protopterus* species) inhabit freshwater, where they grow up to 6.5 feet (2 m) long. While there is water they live as predators, but as drought begins they burrow into the soft mud. Each fish makes a chamber big enough for it to turn around in. When the water level falls below the entrance to the chamber the fish seals this with mud, curls up in its chamber, and secretes mucus that completely surrounds it, leaving only an opening for its mouth. The mucus then sets hard, as a cocoon. As the name *lungfish* indicates, these fish breathe with lungs as well as gills, so they can continue to breathe in the absence of water.

Once inside its cocoon the fish allows its metabolic rate to fall and it enters estivation. In most of the places where they live estivation needs to last for only a few months, but African lungfish have been known to remain in this state for several years. When the rains return the water level rises, soaking and dissolving the cocoon and reviving the fish, no worse for its experience. South American lungfish (*Lepidosiren* species) are very similar, but they do not make cocoons.

Tolerating Freezing Temperatures

Estivation is a response to high temperatures and occurs among some inhabitants of hot deserts. Low temperatures are the problem in cold deserts, and for those unable to migrate to warmer regions the equivalent response is hibernation.

The two are fairly similar physiologically, but hibernation is the more difficult, because of the risk of freezing. In hot weather an animal can fall deeply unconscious and allow its core temperature to fall with no risk that the air temperature will fall below its lethal temperature, but this is not the case in the high-latitude cold deserts. Consequently, a hibernating animal must have some means of preventing its temperature from falling dangerously low.

Some invertebrate animals and a few ectothermic vertebrates such as the wood frog (*Rana sylvatica*) tolerate freezing conditions. There are fish, for example, that have chemicals such as glycerol in their body fluids. These substances act as antifreeze, lowering the freezing point of the fluids and favoring supercooling by preventing the formation of ice crystals even when the temperature falls below freezing. There is a Canadian wasp, *Bracon cephi,* that carries enough glycerol to prevent it from freezing until its body temperature falls below -51°F (-46°C), and there are some butterfly and moth caterpillars that survive being frozen completely solid.

Others have substances in their body fluids that act as ice-nucleating agents. These encourage the formation of ice crystals in the fluid outside cells. This is believed to reduce the risk of ice formation inside cells, which is usually fatal.

Reptiles and amphibians are also immobilized in winter, and even if they were active they would find very little food. They burrow or shelter in rock crevices.

True Hibernation

True hibernation is not common among mammals; it occurs only in those with small bodies, such as bats and some rodents, few of which live in the polar deserts. The arctic ground squirrel (*Citellus undulatus*) hibernates and so does the long-tailed souslik (*Spermophilus undulatus*) of northern Eurasia, a close relative of the ground squirrel.

Marmots (*Marmota* species) weigh an average 11 lb (5 kg) and are the largest mammals to hibernate. The time it takes an animal to enter hibernation and a hibernating mammal to become fully aroused depends on its body size. The bigger the animal, the longer it takes and the more energy arousal requires. This is what imposes the size limit for hibernation.

Entering Hibernation

Hibernation begins with a long period of preparation during which an animal may feed voraciously and its hormonal system causes it to

convert much of its food into a thick layer of body fat. Other hibernators accumulate stores of food inside the nests they have prepared. Most animals do both, accumulating both body fat and food stores. Then, as its normal food supply diminishes, indicating that the time to hibernate is approaching, the animal enters its nest and goes to sleep. It lies in the same body position it adopts for ordinary sleep and its nest resembles its ordinary sleeping quarters, although it is made in a more sheltered location.

As it sleeps, the blood vessels in its skin constrict and its heartbeat slows. Blood pressure remains high internally, but the heart beats only a few times each minute. In ground squirrels the heart beats 200 times a minute when the animal is active and 10 times a minute during hibernation.

Then the body temperature falls. The animal does not abandon endothermy—its physiological control of its core temperature—but resets its temperature control, usually at about 40°F (4.5°C). At this temperature its basal metabolic rate drops to about 1 percent of its active rate and the animal generates around 2 percent of the body heat it produces when active. With the reduced oxygen requirement of its lowered metabolic rate, breathing also slows, in a ground squirrel from about 100 breaths per minute to about 4.

Changes take place in the composition of the blood plasma. This is necessary, because the pumping of the reduced hearbeat is so slow that otherwise blood would start to clot. The brain and nervous system continue to function, because impulses are able to cross synapses even though the temperature falls below the minimum needed for diffusion in other animals. This allows the heart to remain under nervous control and the brain to remain in a state from which it can be aroused by an appropriate stimulus.

Arousal

A body temperature of 40°F (4.5°C) is much higher than the outside temperature during the polar winter, and even inside its nest the hibernating animal may become chilled. When it cools below a certain threshold the nervous system detects the cold and the animal starts shivering. This generates heat, but in doing so it consumes a large amount of energy, which it obtains by oxidizing stored body fat.

It also wakes the animal and that is when it needs the food it hoarded prior to the onset of winter. While it is awake it must eat enough to replenish the fat its body just used. Only if it accumulated enough body fat and hoarded

enough food to replenish it when necessary will the animal survive the winter.

Its reserves must also be sufficient to supply the energy needed to rouse the animal in spring. Then it may have no more than about 4 hours to raise its core temperature from 40°F (4.5°C) to 95°F (35°C).

Arousal begins with a rapid acceleration of the heartbeat, followed by violent shivering in the front part of the body—which warms much faster than the rest of the body. At the same time the breathing rate increases and the blood vessels dilate, first in the front of the body and then in the remainder. The blood flow accelerates and this causes a corresponding increase in the metabolic rate. Only then, when its body has returned to its fully active state, is the animal able to leave its nest and start searching for food.

Spending Winter Beneath the Snow

Hibernation involves such radical changes in the way the body works that it is not surprising so

few mammals have adopted it. The most common small mammals of the Far North are voles and lemmings, composing a subfamily (Microtinae) of the rats and mice (family Muridae). They are tiny rodents, none of them more than about 4.5 inches (11 cm) long with a tail up to 1.6 inches (4 cm) long, and they weigh up to 0.7 ounce (20 g), but despite their diminutive size they do not hibernate. They have an alternative means of surviving the harsh winter. They live beneath the snow.

Snow provides good thermal insulation and, most important in high latitudes, complete shelter from the biting wind. Voles and lemmings make tunnels beneath the snow through which they move around in search of food and in which they build nests. They breed during the winter and by the time they emerge in spring their young are strong enough to look after themselves. The snow also protects them from most predators, although weasels and stoats can follow them through their tunnels. Arctic foxes and other larger animals remain above ground and active throughout the winter.

Polar Bears (Gerry Ellis/ENP Images)

Polar Bears

The polar bear (*Ursus maritimus*) is the biggest animal of the northern cold desert and the biggest of all bears. Males, which are somewhat bigger than females, can measure 10 feet (3 m) from nose to tail and weigh more than 1,400 pounds (635 kg). If an animal of this size were to hibernate, raising its temperature from 50°F (10°C) to 99°F (37°C) would take several days and consume more energy than the animal would use during 3 days of normal activity. It is a demand that could not be met and consequently hibernation is not an option available to polar bears.

Instead, polar bears dig dens, usually in snowdrifts, and spend part of the winter in them, lying dormant. Males remain in their dens for varying periods and are active at other times, by day or night. Pregnant females enter their dens in November or December and remain there until late March or early April. Their cubs are born in the den in December or January.

While they are dormant, polar bears do not eat, obtaining the energy they need by metabolizing body fat. This is not hibernation, but it does cause a small drop in body temperature, of about 9°F (5°C), and a 50 percent slowing of their metabolic rate.

Finding Water and Conserving Water

Off the western coast of southern Africa, the Benguela Current flows northward, carrying cool water from the Antarctic Ocean. Air crossing the current is chilled and its water vapor condenses, producing fog in the Namib Desert.

On nights when the fog rolls in from the sea, large numbers of darkling beetles (family Tenebrionidae) make their way to the crests of the Namib sand dunes. There they stand in rows and stretch their long legs so their wing cases—the technical name is *elytra*—are raised almost vertically and their heads are near the ground. As the fog arrives, water droplets collect on the elytra, trickle down to the insects' mouths, and are swallowed. This is the only water the beetles drink and their food consists entirely of seeds and other scraps of dry plant material.

Extraordinary though this behavior may seem, in fact it is no more than a minor modification of ordinary tenebrionid behavior. All darkling beetles have long legs and many species raise their bodies as a defensive measure, to deter predators. In most species the elytra are fused together, so the beetles cannot fly, and there is an air space between their bodies and elytra that provides insulation and reduces water loss. Most darkling beetles are nocturnal, although some, such as *Adesmia antiqua* of the Sahara, forage by day, sheltering in a burrow only when the heat is extreme. Its long legs hold its body clear of the hot ground.

Advantages of Burrows

Many desert animals retreat into burrows to escape from the heat. This also conserves water, because less body moisture is lost by evaporation into the cooler air below ground. Water vapor exhaled by its occupant makes air in a burrow more humid than the air above ground and this also reduces evaporative losses.

The exhaled moisture does not always soak into the dry sand to be lost. The bannertail kangaroo rat (*Dipodomys spectabilis*), which lives in the Arizona desert and among the sand dunes of Death Valley, California, spends its days in its burrow, emerging to forage only at night. It stores much of the food it finds in its burrow, where the relative humidity is much higher than that of the air above ground. Indeed, it can approach saturation. Under these conditions the very dry food taken into the burrow absorbs moisture from the air. This can increase the water content of the food from 4 percent to 18 percent and the rodent can live indefinitely on a diet of seeds and other

dry plant material without ever drinking. The related but smaller Merriam's kangaroo rat (*D. merriami*) exploits this in another way. It does not store food, but steals from the burrows of bannertail kangaroo rats.

The bannertail kangaroo rat is not the only desert rodent to store food in a humid burrow. Kangaroo rats are members of a genus of pocket mice (family Heteromyidae), found only in North and Central America and the northwest of Colombia. Their equivalents in the deserts of Africa, Arabia, and Asia are the gerbils, a subfamily (Gerbillinae) of the Old World rats and mice (family Muridae). Gerbils are also nocturnal seed eaters. The seeds they collect have often been moistened by dew, but storing them in their burrows increases their moisture content still further. Dry seeds contain 4–7 percent water by weight, but seeds taken from gerbil burrows have been found to contain 30 percent water.

Larger animals, such as antelopes and gazelles, cannot burrow, and so they are unable to store food in this way. This does not prevent them from choosing food items that have been moistened. They obtain water by feeding at night, when dew often collects on leaves and is absorbed by them, in the extreme case of some African desert bushes increasing the moisture content of the leaves from about 1 percent to 40 percent. At their driest the leaves can be crumbled to dust between the fingers.

Water from Plants and Metabolic Water

Wherever there are cacti or other succulents some animals will find ways through their defenses to the water stored in their tissues. In North Africa the fat sand rat (*Psammomys obesus*) feeds on succulent plants that grow in dry riverbeds. These plants are very salty. The rat rids its body of excess salt by excreting urine that is four times saltier than seawater. The Mojave ground squirrel (*Citellus mohavensis*) of the North American desert feeds on cholla fruit (page 84), and some species of pack rats (*Neotoma* species) feed on cholla and other cacti. These plants have a water content of up to 90 percent. Carnivorous animals obtain moisture from the body fluids of their prey.

Even dry food can be made to yield water. This is not water contained inside the food, but water that is produced when the food is metabolized to provide energy. Carbohydrates, fats, and

proteins consist of chemical compounds containing hydrogen. The oxidation of hydrogen yields energy, and the chemical product is water ($2H_2 + O_2 \rightarrow$ energy $+ 2H_2O$). Oxidizing 1 ounce of carbohydrate produces 0.6 ounce of water and an ounce of protein yields 0.3 ounce of water, but oxidizing 1 ounce of fat yields 1.1 ounces of water: the differences are due to the chemical reactions involved. This provides all the water some desert animals need and they can gain weight on a diet of nothing but dry seeds.

They can do so, however, only because they are also able to reduce to a minimum the amount of water leaving their bodies. There are two routes by which water is lost: respiration and the excretion of feces and urine.

Respiratory Countercurrent Exchange

Lungs are made from very delicate tissues that are easily damaged and can not survive prolonged exposure to cool, dry air. Consequently, the respiratory passages through which air passes on its way to the lungs are moist and contact with them saturates the air entering the lungs. Air leaving the lungs is saturated; that means all air-breathing vertebrate animals exhale saturated air. Burrowing rodents collect some of the moisture from this exhaled air, but all mammals, birds, and lizards minimize the loss of water before it leaves the body by means of a system of countercurrent exchange. This is not an adaptation to desert life, but arises inevitably from the way the nasal passages are constructed.

Moisture enters the inhaled air by evaporating from the walls of the respiratory passages. This cools the passages through the loss of latent heat of vaporization, but as the air approaches the lungs the cooling effect decreases. By the time it reaches the lungs the air has been raised to the core body temperature, of about 100°F (38°C), and it has also absorbed more water as its temperature has risen.

Exhaled air is saturated, but moisture from the warm air condenses on the sides of the respiratory passages that were cooled by the inhaled air, at the same time warming them and cooling the outgoing air. A large amount of energy is needed to vaporize water, so using air leaving the lungs to warm the respiratory tissues saves energy.

Despite the fact that the exhaled water is saturated, this countercurrent exchange also saves water. This saving is due to the fact that the amount of water vapor air can hold varies according to its temperature, and air cools as it travels from the lungs to the nostrils. Suppose the inhaled air is at 86°F (30°C) and 80 percent relative humidity. One quart of this air contains 0.00074 ounce of water (24 milligrams per liter). The air is then warmed to 100°F (38°C) and saturated. It then contains 0.0014 ounce per quart (46 mg per liter), so it has absorbed an additional 0.00068 ounce of water per quart of air (22 mg per liter) from the body. As the air is exhaled, suppose it is cooled to 88°F (31°C) by the time it leaves the nostrils. It remains saturated, but at this temperature saturated air contains 0.00095 ounce of water per quart (31 mg per liter). The difference between the water content of inhaled and exhaled air, both saturated but at different temperatures, is 0.00045 ounce per quart (15 mg per liter), and this condenses and remains within the body. At night, when the air is cooler and many of the small desert animals are active, the saving is even greater, because more water evaporates as the air is warmed to core temperature. This greatly cools the nasal passages, increasing the amount of condensation from the exhaled air.

Urine and the Efficiency of Kidneys

Urine is produced by the kidneys of vertebrates and consists of metabolic waste products filtered from the blood carried in water. Minimizing the amount of water that is excreted involves improving the efficiency of the kidneys. Mammalian kidneys are highly efficient, but there is wide variation among them and those of desert animals are the most efficient of all.

Kidney efficiency can be measured by the concentration of the urine excreted—the more concentrated the urine, the less water it contains, and, therefore, the less water the animal needs to drink. If humans have a "kidney efficiency" value of 1 and that of a dromedary (see page 90) is about 1.96, a camel's kidneys are almost twice as efficient as a human's: A pack rat, however, has a kidney efficiency of 2.97, Merriam's kangaroo rat of about 3.25, and a gerbil of 3.85. A kangaroo rat has such efficient kidneys it can drink seawater without coming to any harm. It may be the only mammal that can do this. The Australian hopping mouse (*Notomys alexis*) has what are probably the most efficient kidneys of all. Its urine is about 6.55 times more concentrated than human urine.

The Ship of the Desert

The camel—the "ship of the desert"—is by far the most famous of all desert animals. Part of its fame derives from its economic importance as a beast of burden and also as a source of meat, milk, wool, and hides. Camels are also used for riding and there are clear differences between those animals that have been bred for riding and those bred for carrying loads, just as there are between different types of horses. Because they are so widely used and highly valued, camels exist in large numbers and are a familiar sight in the Sahara, Arabian, Middle Eastern, and Indian deserts and in parts of Afghanistan.

Their uses have not all been peaceful and commercial. Dromedaries—single-humped camels—with two riders, one of them an archer, were used in battle by the Assyrians around 650 B.C.E., and they were also used in wars between the Greeks and Persians. When Alexander the Great sacked the Persian city of Persepolis in 330 B.C.E. he used 5,000 Bactrian camels—two-humped camels—to carry away the loot. The Romans used camels as pack animals and may even have introduced them to northern France. Napoleon used them in his North African campaign of 1798.

Between 1840 and 1907 camels were also taken to Australia, where it was thought they would be as useful as they are in Africa. It was not long before the spread of railroads and road vehicles made the camels redundant, however, and they were released. The Australian desert suited them and they have thrived. Today there are believed to be about 25,000 of them living wild in Australia.

In the 1850s the U.S. Army also experimented with them as beasts of burden in their frontier garrisons in the southwestern United States. That attempt did not succeed and the animals were turned loose. They survived for a time, but none has been seen since about 1900. At various times camels have also been introduced in Spain and Zanzibar.

One Hump or Two

Everyone knows what a camel looks like. There are two species: the Arabian camel or dromedary (*Camelus dromedarius*), which has one hump, and the Asian or Bactrian camel (*C. bactrianus*), which has two. They belong to the family Camelidae, which also includes four South American species: the guanaco (*Lama guanicöe*), llama (*L. glama*), alpaca (*L. pacos*), and vicuna (*Vicugna vicugna*). The camelids evolved in North America during the latter part of the Eocene epoch which ended 35.4 million years ago. Between 2 and 3 million years ago, during the Pliocene epoch, one group expanded into South America and another—*Camelus* species, the ancestors of the dromedary and Bactrian camel—entered Asia. Both groups then died out in North America.

Both of the *Camelus* species were domesticated long ago, although precisely when this happened is uncertain. Camel dung about 4,600 years old has been found at an archaeological site in southern Iran. This is the oldest evidence of

Modern Egyptians riding camels across desert (Gerry Ellis/ENP Images)

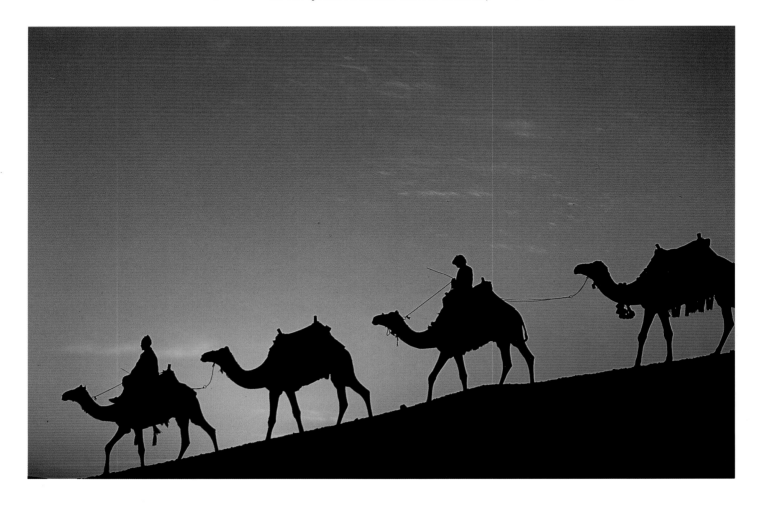

domestication and scientists believe the dung was from a Bactrian camel. What is certain is that the only dromedaries living in the wild today are descended from animals that were domesticated. There is no truly wild dromedary.

Bactrian camels do live wild. There is a small population around Lop Nor, on the eastern edge of the Takla Makan Desert in western China, and a larger one in southwestern Mongolia. Together these two groups are believed to number about 1,000 animals. Some scientists believe them to be truly wild and the species from which the domesticated Bactrian camel was derived. They differ from domesticated camels in a number of small ways and are sometimes known as *C. ferus* to distinguish them. Other scientists believe them to be descended from domesticated camels that returned to living in the wild.

Both camels are about the same size and weight, but the Bactrian camel has shorter legs and a much thicker coat, giving it a shaggy, unkempt appearance, especially in spring when the coat is shed. It lives mainly in cool, rocky regions and on the steppe grasslands of central Asia and is able to withstand the harsh steppe winters. The dromedary is the true desert animal. It can carry heavy loads over long distances, can endure the heat of the Sahara, and has a legendary ability to survive for long periods without water.

Where Does the Camel Store Its Water?

At one time, it was thought that the dromedary carries some kind of reservoir in which water is stored. One group of people speculated that this might be in the form of a bag or bladder linked to the stomach.

Camels are ruminants, related to cattle and sheep, and like them they have a complex stomach that is divided into chambers. In their case there are three chambers rather than the four of cattle and sheep, because two of them (the abomasum and omasum) are united. They lie below the second chamber, the reticulum, and in the drawing are labeled *abomasum*. It was even suggested that sometimes camels were killed for the water they carried.

Other people thought the reservoir might be in the hump. When it was revealed that the hump consists mainly of fat, they suggested the camel might obtain water by oxidizing the hydrogen in the fat. A hump with 50 pounds (22.7 kg) of fat could yield 55 pounds (24.97 kg) of water (page

88). That is about 6.6 gallons (24.97 liters)—a useful amount of water.

That one or the other explanation was true seemed self-evident, because of the time a camel can survive without drinking and because of the rate at which it drinks when water is available. In the space of 10 minutes a camel can drink an amount of water weighing about one-third of its own body weight. This is about 10 times more than a human could drink at one time. A camel has been seen to drink 27 gallons (103 liters) in 10 minutes. This is like an average size man's drinking 6 gallons (23 liters). Anyone who attempted to drink this amount in one session would die of water toxicity, because in excessive amounts water is poisonous to humans. Not surprisingly, people thought an animal drinking that much water that fast must be filling some kind of storage tank.

Both explanations proved incorrect. It is true that in camels the rumen, the first stomach chamber, has pouches (illustration). These are sometimes incorrectly called "water cells," but they contain partly chewed food rather than water, and no more than about 1 gallon (3.8 liters) of that. The main part of the rumen contains digestive juices. A dying person might drink this fluid, but it would be an act of extreme desperation!

Oxidizing fat does yield water (page 104), but there is a problem for the camel. In order to oxidize its hump the animal must supply oxygen, which it obtains from its lungs. As it absorbed the

required amount of oxygen, the camel would lose water in its exhaled breath and calculations show that more water would be lost by that route than could be gained by metabolizing the hump.

Conserving Water

Perhaps, then, a camel economizes by conserving water. A camel excretes urine that is about twice as concentrated as human urine. This makes it appear that although the camel's kidneys are more efficient than those of humans, they are nowhere near so efficient as those of other desert mammals, such as the kangaroo rat. The appearance is misleading, however, because the camel has a digestive system that deals very efficiently with food containing little protein.

In a human, proteins are broken into their constituent amino acids in the stomach and the final waste product of protein metabolism is ammonia, which is converted into urea in the liver. This is a poisonous compound containing nitrogen. It is filtered out by the kidneys and passed continuously to the bladder, from which it is excreted. Ruminant diets are deficient in nitrogen, an essential ingredient of the amino acid "building blocks" of proteins, and so they recycle it. Some of the urea from the liver passes through the bloodstream back to the stomach, where it mixes with cellulose to make new amino acids. The effect is to lower the urea

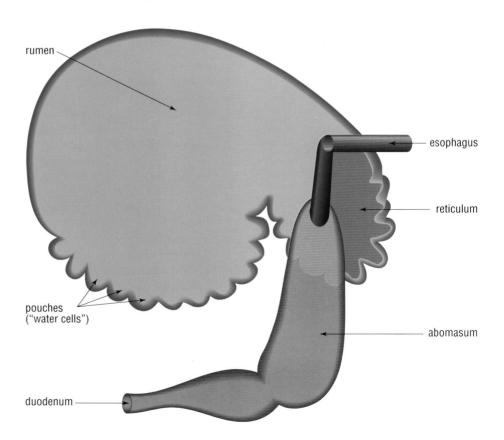

Stomach of a camel

concentration of urine, disguising the true efficiency of the kidneys. In fact, the camel may have kidneys as efficient as those of the kangaroo rat, and it is possible that it could drink seawater without harm. Camels that live near the coast are said to eat seaweed, which is very salty. In summer a camel may excrete as little as 1 quart (1.14 liters) of water a day.

Camels also conserve water by sweating very little until their body temperature exceeds 105°F (40.5°C). At night the camel allows its temperature to fall as low as 93°F (34°C), so it takes several hours for it to heat up sufficiently to trigger perspiration (page 78). Its temperature fluctuates by this amount only when the camel has no access to water in summer. In winter, and in summer if it has water to drink, its temperature varies by only about 4°F (2.2°C).

Insulation

The rate of heating is slowed even more by the animal's insulation. Its thick coat traps a layer of insulated air next to the skin, working in the same way as the many layers of clothing worn by desert peoples. We feel comfortable wearing thin, light-colored clothing in summer, but this is not the best attire for the middle of the day in the Sahara. There, several loose, flowing robes worn on top of each other are much better at keeping the body cool. Like the camel's coat, desert clothing works in two ways. The outer garments absorb heat, preventing it from reaching the skin, and perspiration evaporates into the layer of air between the skin and the inner garment, so it is evaporated by heat from the body, not from the Sun.

The camel's hump is also an insulating device. The hump is a store of food, of course, not water, and it differs only in its location from the fat all mammals store. Instead of being spread over most of the body, it is concentrated on the back. That is the part of the animal exposed to the heat of the Sun, so the hump provides insulation. At the same time, the remainder of the body lacks an outer layer of fat. This means there is no insulating barrier to prevent the escape of heat from the body.

Avoiding Explosive Heat Death

When it loses water, the camel does so from its body fluids such as saliva and moisture in its lungs and not from its blood. This is important. When a human loses body fluid the blood thickens, its rate of flow slows, and the circulatory system becomes unable to carry heat from the inside of the body and lose it from the surface. The body temperature rises and for a person exposed in a hot desert death follows swiftly when the amount

of water lost is equal to about 12 percent of body weight. This is known as *explosive heat death*.

In the camel, the volume of blood remains fairly constant, but the loss of other fluids causes the animal to become thinner and thinner. It can tolerate this, however, and survives a loss of fluid equal to 25 percent of its body weight. Its emaciation is due entirely to fluid loss and the animal continues to eat normally even though it cannot drink.

When it drinks the camel is transformed in a few minutes from an emaciated condition in which its ribs and pelvis are clearly visible into a perfectly healthy animal—although its hump may have been used up and that takes longer to grow back. By drinking it is merely restoring water it has lost and it never drinks more than that. It is not consigning water to a store or "drinking for the thirst to come"—about which obviously it can have no knowledge.

In fact, the camel is not the world's fastest drinker. A donkey can drink water equal to 25 percent of its body weight in about two minutes. These animals are able to restore all the fluid they have lost in one drinking session. Other animals, including humans, are incapable of this. We drink more slowly, but because of that we must drink more often. In the desert a person must drink at least once every day. A donkey can go up to 4 days without drinking.

Endurance

A camel has been known to go 17 days without drinking in summer, and in winter some camels do not drink at all. They have been known to refuse water even though they had drunk nothing for two months. This is not quite so remarkable as it sounds. Desert temperatures are much lower in winter than in summer and although rain is uncommon, it is more likely in winter than in summer. Consequently the body loses less water and there are usually shrubs and succulent plants on which the camels can feed and from which they obtain as much water as they need. Where there is vegetation, camels feed regularly, just as any other animal does.

No one chooses to cross the desert in the scorching heat of summer. It is in winter and spring that the long journeys are undertaken and camels will travel more than 300 miles (480 km) in two to three weeks, drinking nothing along the way. Although they are domesticated, and there is no such thing as a truly "wild" dromedary, desert camels are not tame in the way horses are tame. Their owners leave them to find most of their food for themselves. In winter they must be herded, lest they wander off in search of edible plants and fail to return, but in summer this is

unnecessary. Every few days the camels will visit the human camp or settlement in search of water.

Broad Feet and Loose Limbs

They move well over loose sand. This is another of their adaptations to desert life. Camels are artiodactyls—even-toed ungulates (hoofed mammals) related to deer, cattle, sheep, and goats. All of these animals have hoofs, but those of camels are different from the hoofs of the others. Its two toes are turned forward and covered by a thick pad of skin. The hoofs are present at the tips of the digits, but they have no function and the camel walks on the skin pads. This makes its feet very broad and spreads its weight over a larger area than would be the case if it walked on its hoofs as a cow or sheep does; that means its feet are less likely to sink into soft sand or snow.

The hind limbs of camels are attached only at the top of the thigh, whereas the legs of other artiodactyls are attached to the pelvis by muscles and skin all the way from the knee. This difference gives camels their long-legged appearance and allows them to lie with their hind legs tucked completely beneath their bodies rather than being held to the sides of the body as the legs of a cow are when it lies. It is a small difference, but it reduces the area of the body that is exposed to the Sun when the camel is lying. Camels other than the possibly wild Bactrian camels of Asia, which lack them, have pads of horny skin on their chests and knees that cushion the animals when they kneel and insulate them from hot sand.

Camels run with a characteristically loping gait, called *pacing* that is quite different from the gait of a horse. This is because galloping camels move both legs on the same side of the body together—left-left, right-right, rather than front left-hind right, front right-hind left—causing them to sway from side to side. With this method of walking they cannot travel fast. People do race camels, but only over short distances. A dromedary can carry a rider at up to 10 mph (16 km/h) and maintain that speed long enough to cover more than 100 miles (160 km) in a day. As a pack animal it can carry a load of about 500 pounds (227 kg) and cover 25 miles (40 km) a day walking at about 5 mph (8 km/h).

Bactrian camels are slower. They walk at only about 2.5 mph (4 km/h) but nevertheless they can cover about 30 miles (48 km) a day carrying a load of up to 1,000 pounds (454 kg).

Bad Temper and Laziness

Apart from their feats of endurance, camels are renowned for their bad tempers and supercilious expressions. They seem to regard humans with disdain and are rumored to kick, bite, and spit a noxious fluid with little provocation.

They cannot help their faces and their most familiar expression is much misunderstood. The apparent superciliousness is due partly to their long eyelashes and the height of their heads in relation to those of the people handling them. They look down because they have to, and as they look down their eyelashes partly cover their eyes. The lashes are yet another adaptation to the desert. They keep out windblown sand and for extra protection each row of lashes is double. Their ears are also protected by long hairs.

As though that were not bad enough, camels also seem to sneer. This is because their upper lips are deeply cleft and both upper and lower lips are very mobile. Camels use their lips to manipulate food items. In addition, they are able to close their nostrils and often do so. This keeps out sand and dust, protecting the delicate membranes of their nasal passages, but it makes them look as though they are trying to avoid a disgusting smell.

It is true that camels can be bad tempered, especially during the mating season, although they are usually placid provided they are treated well. They are often reluctant to carry riders or loads. This has given them an undeserved reputation for laziness. It, too, is behavior appropriate to their environment. Where food and water are so scarce, animals cannot afford to waste energy by exerting themselves needlessly.

Convergent Evolution and Parallel Evolution

Ocotilla (*Fouquieria splendens*), which is also known as the *coach whip, Jacob's staff,* and *vine cactus,* is a shrub that grows naturally in the rocky deserts of the southwestern United States and Mexico. It is a curious plant, producing several slender stems, rather like canes, that grow from the base. These are usually 8–20 feet (2.4–6.1 m) tall, furrowed, and have many spines. Fleshy leaves, 0.5–1.0 inch (13–25 mm) long, appear in spring and soon fall, leaving behind their midribs, which harden to become new spines. Between March and July the plant bears branched bunches (panicles) of scarlet, tubular flowers at the tips of its stems. Hedges of ocotilla are grown locally.

Euphorbia splendens is another tall, spiny plant that sheds its leaves and bears bright red flowers. It is known as the *crown of thorns* and grows naturally in Madagascar but is cultivated as a houseplant in other parts of the world. It belongs to the spurge family (Euphorbiaceae). Although they are very similar, the two plants are not related to each other.

Convergent or Parallel?

Such similarities between unrelated species are common, especially in deserts. Some occur because evolution tends to repeat itself, so successful structures appear independently in widely separated evolutionary lines. Eyes are the most obvious example. Since these groups of animals diverged from a shared, and blind, ancestor, eyes have evolved independently many times, in insects, mollusks, other invertebrate animals, and vertebrates. Other similarities evolve because there is a limit to the number of ways in which an organism can adapt to its environment. It is because deserts present stark evolutionary challenges that it is in deserts that the few solutions available have led to so many close resemblances among quite unrelated plants and animals.

Where natural similarities emerge among organisms that are not closely related the process is called *convergent evolution* or simply *convergence.* If the similar plants or animals belong to distinct but closely related species the process is called *parallel evolution.* The distinction is somewhat arbitrary, since all living organisms are related by connections at some point in their ancestry.

Desert Foxes

Similarities between members of the Fouquieriaceae, Euphorbiaceae, and Cactaceae probably result from convergent evolution, because the differences between these plants are considerable and appeared long ago. Widely separated desert foxes have also evolved similar features, but this is an instance of parallel evolution in closely related species, both of which inhabit hot deserts to which they have responded in the same way.

Both the kit fox (*Vulpes velox*) of southwestern North America and northern Mexico and the fennec fox (*V. zerda*) of the Sahara and Arabian Deserts have yellowish coats, small bodies, and very big ears. The fennec is the smallest of all foxes, measuring about 9–16 inches (23–41 cm), not counting the tail, and weighing 1.75–3 pounds (0.8–1.4 kg), but the kit fox is not much bigger. Its head and body measure 15–20 inches (38–51 cm), and it weighs 4–6.5 pounds (1.8–3 kg). Small size is an advantage to a desert carnivore. It enables it to live on smaller prey than a larger animal and to find shade much more easily. Big ears allow an animal to detect the small, rustling movement of its prey, but ears are also effective heat exchangers. They are richly supplied with blood vessels and the blood is cooled as it passes through them. In contrast, the arctic fox (*Alopex lagopus*) has very small ears to conserve warmth (page 108)—and small animals do not make rustling sounds as they move through snow so its hearing does not need to be so sharp.

Today both foxes are classified in the genus *Vulpes,* although the fennec was formerly placed in a genus of its own, *Fennecus. V. velox* and *V. zerda* remain very closely related and have not evolved far from their common ancestor; both foxes have evolved similar adaptations to a similar environment. This represents parallel evolution.

Kangaroo Rats and Jerboas

North American kangaroo rats (*Dipodomys* species) and jerboas (*Jaculus* species) of the Sahara and Arabian Deserts are much less closely related. Not only are they classified in different genera, they are in different families. Kangaroo rats are pocket mice (family Heteromyidae) and jerboas belong to the family Dipodidae. Their evolutionary lines diverged more than 57 million years ago, during the Paleocene epoch. Both have adapted to life on hot ground by developing very long, kangaroolike hind legs and moving about by hopping. This gives them a very similar appearance and probably arises from convergent evolution. Some doubt remains, however, because many other small rodents have long hind legs and hop, so perhaps

Types of evolutionary development

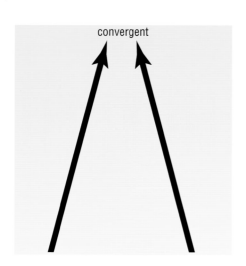

convergent

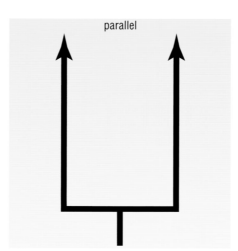

parallel

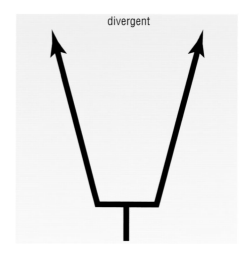

divergent

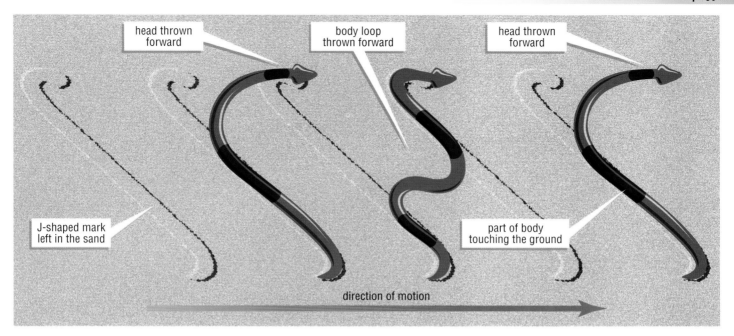

head thrown forward

body loop thrown forward

head thrown forward

J-shaped mark left in the sand

part of body touching the ground

direction of motion

kangaroo rats and jerboas inherited a tendency to do so from their shared ancestor—in which case the long legs result from parallel evolution.

Marsupial "Mice"

There is no such doubt in the case of similarities between marsupial mammals, the group that includes the kangaroos and koala, and the eutherian mammals, such as dogs, cattle, mice, and humans. These two main groups diverged so early in mammalian evolution and are so different that similarities between species living in similar environments must be due to convergent evolution.

Small rodents, such as kangaroo rats, jerboas, and gerbils, have adapted to life in the deserts of America, Africa, and Asia. Similar animals inhabit the Australian deserts, but these are marsupials, raising their young in pouches. The mulgara (*Dasycercus cristicauda*), for example, looks like a short-legged rat with a thick tail. Its head and body measure about 8 inches (20 cm) and its tail about 5 inches (13 cm). It lives in central Australia, sheltering in its burrow for most of the day. It never drinks and has extremely efficient kidneys that allow it to conserve water by excreting highly concentrated urine.

The kowari (*Dasyuroides byrnei*) is even more like a rodent and might pass for a close relation of the kangaroo rats, but it is about half their size. Its head and body are about 7 inches (18 cm) long and its bushy tail adds about 5 inches (13 cm). It has big ears resembling those of mice, and a long muzzle, and its hind legs are longer than its front legs. The most mouselike of them all is the pygmy

planigale (*Planigale maculata*). With a head and body only about 2 inches (5 cm) long and a thin tail about the same length, it is smaller than a house mouse (*Mus musculus*). Like other small animals of hot deserts, both the kowari and pygmy planigale are nocturnal, spending the day in their burrows.

Convergence has produced unrelated animals of startlingly similar appearance, but the similarities are superficial. Desert rodents feed on seeds and other plant material. Mouselike marsupials are carnivores. They belong to the family Dasyuridae, which also includes the quoll or native cat (*Dasyurus viverrinus*) and Tasmanian devil (*Sarcophilus harrisi*), and the small marsupial "mice" feed on insects, lizards, small or very young snakes, and birds. Even the tiny pygmy planigale catches small birds.

Sidewinders and Horned Snakes

Parallel evolution has also affected snakes. They have difficulty moving through loose sand and some have taken to "sidewinding," a method of locomotion in which the snake moves at an angle of about 45° to the line of its body by throwing forward first its head and then a succession of loops of its body. Only two or three parts of its body are in contact with the ground at any time, and because they are placed downward onto the surface the sand does not slide to the sides and cause the animal to lose its traction. The diagram shows how this happens.

Most snakes will sidewind if they need to move through material that slides away when

Sidewinding

they push against it, and sidewinders move in the same way as other snakes across a solid surface. Sidewinding works only for small snakes, but several species have adopted it. The most famous is the sidewinder (*Crotalus cerastes*), a small rattlesnake of the American deserts. It is paralleled in the Sahara and Middle East by the horned viper (*Cerastes cerastes*); from North Africa to India by the carpet, or saw-scaled, viper (*Echis carinatus*); and in South Africa by Peringuey's, or the desert sidewinding, viper (*Bitis peringueyi*). These are small snakes: Peringuey's viper is only about 10 inches (25.5 cm) long and the carpet viper only about 30 inches (76 cm). Despite its small size, its highly toxic venom, excellent camouflage, and bad temper make the carpet viper possibly the most dangerous snake in the world and the cause of most deaths of snakebite in North Africa.

Snakes lack eyelids and those that live in deserts must protect their eyes from dust and sand. Peringuey's viper does so by having its eyes located on top of its head. The sidewinder and horned viper do so by having small "horns" over their eyes. This gives these two species a similar appearance, but it is a feature that has arisen by parallel evolution and is shared by other desert snakes. The Sahara (*Cerastes vipera*) and Persian (*Pseudocerastes persicus*) horned vipers and McMahon's viper (*Eristicophis macmahonii*) have horns. All three are about the same size as the carpet viper and all of them are dangerous to humans.

Desert Invertebrates

Before dressing in the morning, people who live in the desert shake out their shoes. It is a routine action and there is a very good reason for it. A shoe might contain a scorpion.

Scorpions are arachnids (class Arachnida), related to spiders, mites, and harvestmen, and arachnids belong to the phylum Arthropoda, together with insects and crustaceans. Scorpions (order Scorpiones) are the oldest of them all. There were scorpions on Earth in the Silurian period, more than 400 million years ago, although those lived in water. Scorpions began living on land during the Carboniferous period, 362.5 to 290 million years ago. Some of the Carboniferous scorpions were more than 30 inches (76 cm) long. That is much bigger than any scorpion alive today. Today, the biggest scorpion is probably *Pandinus imperator,* which lives in the Sahara. It is 7 inches (18 cm) long. Most are no more than half that size and the smallest is *Microbuthus pusillus,* found in the Middle East, which is only 0.5 inch (1.25 cm) long.

Not all scorpions live in deserts, but many of the 700 or so species do and scorpions are well adapted to desert conditions. They are nocturnal—that is why they find their way into the shoes of people who are sleeping—and many live in burrows. These can be quite deep. *Hadrurus arizonensis* of the Sonoran Desert burrows as much as 3 feet (90 cm) below the surface. Species that do not dig burrows spend the day sheltering beneath stones. When they are on the surface, some species will raise themselves on "tiptoe" from time to time. This is called *stilting* and it allows air to circulate beneath the body.

Scorpions can survive temperatures as high as 115°F (46°C) and lose very little water by evaporation through their exoskeletons, which are rendered almost impervious by a protective layer of wax. The rate at which water passes through the exoskeleton is low; however, it often continues for a long time, but not long enough to kill the animal. A scorpion can lose water equivalent to 40 percent of its body weight without coming to any harm.

Hunting and the Scorpion Sting

Scorpions never drink, obtaining water only from their food. All scorpions are entirely carnivorous. They feed on insects and other invertebrate animals. Scorpions do not hunt by sight and they do not see well. Some cave-dwelling species are blind, but other scorpions have one pair of eyes in the center of the carapace covering the

Desert hairy scorpion (Gerry Ellis / ENP Images)

prosoma—the front part of the body—and between two and five pairs of eyes around the edges of the carapace.

Most detect prey by means of hairs, called *trichobothria,* on their pedipalps—the pair of big "claws" at the front of the body. Others can sense vibrations in the ground. Some desert scorpions can locate a burrowing cockroach 20 inches (50 cm) away and take just a few seconds to dig it out and capture it.

Prey is seized and held by the pedipalps and then killed or subdued by the sting, and it is the sting, borne on the final segment of the postabdomen or "tail," for which scorpions are best known and most feared. All scorpions sting, by raising the postabdomen over the body and injecting venom with a stabbing motion. Scorpion venom will kill most invertebrates, but few species deliver anything worse than a painful sting to humans. Among those, however, there are some that are dangerous. A sting from *Androctonus australis,* of the Sahara, delivers venom as potent as that of a cobra. It is said to kill a dog within about seven minutes and a human in about seven hours. *Centuroides sculpturatus,* which lives in Arizona and New Mexico, can also kill; barefoot children usually are the victims.

Solifugids

Scorpions are not often seen, because most of them lie in wait for prey, emerging only far enough to seize it and then retreating again. They are not the only invertebrate predators living in the desert, however. There are also the solifugids, which are more likely to make an appearance because they hunt by chasing prey rather than ambushing it.

They compose another order (Solifugae) of arachnids and are sometimes known as *sun spiders,* because some species are active by day. They are also called *false spiders* and *jerrymanders,* as well as *camel spiders* and *wind scorpions* because of the speed with which they run in pursuit of prey. What looks like a ball of thistledown blowing over the ground is most likely to be a wind scorpion in hot pursuit of a meal.

They are large animals. *Galeodes arabs,* found in North Africa, is about 2.5 inches (7 cm) long and its legs are about 3 inches (7.5 cm) long. They use only three of their four pairs of legs for running. The legs at the front of the body are smaller than the others and are used as sense organs, to explore objects by touch.

Apart from their size, their main distinguishing feature is the pair of huge chelicerae—pincers—they carry. These are longer than the prosoma and very heavy.

Solifugids do not sting and are harmless to humans. They chase their prey; seize it with their pedipalps, which resemble legs; and pass it to the chelicerae, where it is killed. They are carnivores and feed on any animal they can catch and subdue. They even catch small vertebrates, such as lizards, birds, and mice, and they are voracious. A sun spider will often continue feeding until its body is so swollen it is almost incapable of moving. There are about 800 species, of which more than 100 live in the United States from the Southwest as far north as Colorado.

Wolf Spiders and Tiger Beetles

Wolf spiders also chase their prey, overcoming insects by their speed and strength. Web-spinning spiders lie in wait for prey and do not need good eyesight, but wolf spiders see well. They have fewer eyes than most spiders, but the eyes themselves are better. With two large eyes and four smaller ones below them, they are able to detect small movements and form sharp images. Jumping spiders also have big eyes and good vision. They stalk their prey and jump on it when they are within range.

The desert also harbors predatory insects. Tiger beetles (family Cicindelidae) are active by day. They are about 1 inch (2.5 cm) long, often brightly colored in metallic hues with contrasting stripes or bars, and they have large eyes and mandibles—the section of their mouthparts with which they seize prey. They have long legs and run fast in pursuit of prey. Their larvae are also fierce predators, but their hunting strategy is different, calling for patience rather than stamina.

A tiger beetle larva excavates a vertical hole up to 1 foot (30 cm) deep where it lies in wait. Just its mandibles are visible, wide open at the surface. Only the front part of the body is hard. The rest is soft, but on one of the abdominal segments there are two strong hooks curving forward. When an insect walks within range, the larva grabs and holds it until it is subdued. The two hooks gripping the sides of the hole make it impossible for the prey to drag the larva out and when at last it is exhausted the victim is dragged below ground to be eaten.

Ant-Lions and Worm-Lions

Larvae of some species of ant-lions (family Myrmeleontidae) also lie in wait, but the holes they dig in the sand are pitfall traps, illustrated in the figure. An ant-lion hole is conical in shape, its sides at an angle of about 35°: the steepest angle at which they remain stable (page 34). The larva lies buried at the bottom of the cone with just its mandibles exposed, from time to time moving

Ant falling into an ant-lion trap

around the pit so it is always on the shady side. When an insect—most commonly an ant, hence the name *ant-lion*—tries to explore the hole or cross the top of it, the larva immediately starts throwing sand grains upward. This triggers a minor landslide that carries the prey to the bottom of the pit and into the waiting mandibles. Ant-lions are also carnivorous as adults.

Worm-lion larvae also trap prey in pits they have dug. These insects belong to the genus *Vermileo* of snipe flies (family Rhagionidae), of which most species are carnivorous. Robber flies (family Asilidae) prey on all herbivorous insects. The fact that so many predators can survive indicates that desert insects are plentiful.

Butterflies and moths appear whenever plants flourish and flower after a heavy rain shower. Some butterflies are able to fly from flower to flower inside a bush, completing their entire life cycle without emerging from the shelter this affords.

Darkling Beetles and Scarabs

Beetles are also common; the darkling beetles (family Tenebrionidae) is the most fully adapted to desert life (page 88). They are vegetarian and most species are unable to fly, but they are active during the day and have few enemies. Predators learn to avoid them because of the offensive smell they release, and if this does not work they sham death, behavior that deters the many predators that respond only to live prey.

Some American chafers or dung beetles (family Scarabeidae) have become adapted to feeding on plant material, but most feed on dung. Some work on the dung from below and drag it down into their tunnels. Others make it into balls that they roll along the surface until they find somewhere suitable to bury them. This group includes those known as *tumblebugs* or *scarab beetles*.

One of these is *Scarabaeus sacer*, the scarab that in ancient Egypt was sacred to Khepri, a sun god. The most common type of amulet—a good luck charm—had the form of a scarab, with a representation of the beetle on one side and often the personal seal of its owner on the other. Scarab amulets were in use for many centuries and spread throughout the Mediterranean and Middle East.

Egyptians believed the scarab lays its egg inside its dung ball, and in the way the beetle rolls its ball they saw a metaphor for the cycles of life and in particular for the daily reappearance of the Sun. In a sense they were correct. The scarab contributes to the cycling of nutrients and performs a valuable ecological function. They were wrong about its reproductive habits, however. It does not roll a ball containing its egg but buries the ball on which it then feeds and next to which it lays its eggs, so its larvae also feed on it.

Locusts

There are insects that bite and sting. Some insects transmit serious, often fatal, diseases. Deserts harbor lethally venomous snakes and scorpions. Such animals are treated with respect and avoided, but there is one desert animal that is capable of inspiring the deepest dread. It does not bite or sting and it transmits no disease. Instead, it kills by causing starvation, its attacks are known as *plagues,* and those plagues have occurred throughout history. They were well known to the authors of the Old Testament.

> And the locusts went up over all the land of Egypt, and rested in all the coasts of Egypt: very grievous were they; before them there were no such locusts as they, neither after them shall there be such.
>
> For they covered the face of the whole earth, so that the land was darkened; and they did eat every herb of the land, and all the fruit of the trees which the hail had left: and there remained not any green thing in the trees, or in the herbs of the field, through all the land of Egypt. (Exodus 10, 14–15)

The story goes on to report that the sky over Egypt was darkened for 3 days. Scientists now believe this story of the eighth of the plagues of Egypt describes a real event that took place in about 1470 B.C.E. and affected the Nile Delta. Sadly, the biblical account is wrong in one respect: this was certainly not the first locust plague and there have been many since.

Locust Plagues

There is no discernible pattern to their occurrence. In recent times there were plagues in 1926–34, 1940–48, 1949–63, 1967–69, and 1986–89. During each of these periods there were repeated outbreaks, when swarms of locusts descended on cropland and pasture. During the 1949–63 plague several swarms covered an area of more than 100 square miles (259 sq km) and 50 swarms invaded Kenya early in 1954. One covered an area of about 77 square miles (200 sq km) with a density of about 130 million locusts for every square mile (50 million/sq km), so the entire swarm comprised 10 billion locusts. This was larger than most swarms, which contain between 40 million and 80 million insects, but together the 50 swarms covered about 390 square miles (1,010 sq km) to a height of 3,000–4,500 feet (900–1,400 m).

Although most plagues originate in Africa, they do not always remain there. At various times swarms have crossed the Mediterranean into southern Europe and even as far north as Russia. In July 1999 the newspaper *Izvestiya* reported that swarms had entered southern Russia from Kazakhstan and were moving northward at 31 miles (50 km) a day. Farmers were appealing to the government for financial help and supplies of insecticides. A swarm reached the British Isles in 1954 and in October 1988, during the 1986–89 plague, a swarm crossed the Atlantic. It took 10 days to travel 2,800 miles (4,500 km) from North Africa to the Caribbean, landing from St. Croix and the British Virgin Islands south to the eastern coasts of Surinam and Guyana. During plagues, locusts may visit all or part of 60 countries over an area of about 11 million square miles (28.5 million sq km).

Locusts affect the Middle East, Pakistan and India, and the southern part of Central Asia and China. Australia is sometimes plagued and there was a plague in North America from 1874 to 1877. In that plague there were swarms covering 125,000 square miles (324,000 sq km)—an area bigger than Colorado—to a height of 5,000 feet (1,525 m). The last North American locust plague was in 1938 and affected the midwestern states and Canada.

Two Forms

Historically, the fear locusts inspire arises only partly from the damage they cause. It is also due to the unpredictability of plagues. Swarms appear suddenly, without warning and seemingly from nowhere, as a cloud darkening the horizon that blacks out more and more of the sky as it draws closer. It is composed of insects that are seen only during the plagues. At other, quiet times, called *recessions,* they are not simply hard to find: they are nonexistent.

Locusts are short-horned grasshoppers belonging to the family Acrididae. There are about a dozen species of them. Unlike ordinary grasshoppers, locusts exist in two forms that are quite different in appearance and behavior. They are so different, in fact, that they were once believed to be two separate species. One form, or species, was familiar in certain places and quite harmless. The other was the one that appeared in huge, dreadful swarms. It was not until 1921 that the Russian entomologist Boris P. Uvarov (1889–1970) recognized them as two forms of the same species. He had been studying the

migratory locust (*Locusta migratoria*), which in 1912 had infested the area around Stavropol, in the Caucasus, and at the same time he examined what was thought to be a harmless species about which scientists knew little, *L. danica.* Uvarov discovered that if a *danica* grasshopper came upon other *danica* insects it would move away from them, but if a *migratoria* insect met others like itself it would join them. Further study revealed, however, that *migratoria* grasshoppers sometimes produced *danica* offspring and some insects were intermediate in form between *migratoria* and *danica,* making it difficult to tell which species they belonged to. Then he began to suspect that *L. migratoria,* the cause of the Russian plague, was the same species as the African migratory locust, now known as *L. migratoria migratorioides,* which periodically infested various regions of Africa south of the Sahara. Expanding his study to other species, he finally concluded that *migratoria* and *danica* belonged to the same species, but looked different—and the name *Locusta danica* was abandoned.

Uvarov also discovered how the confusion had arisen. In a paper published in the September 1921 issue of the *Bulletin of Entomological Research* he wrote, "The direct cause of [this] ignorance is that injurious insects, and locusts especially, are studied only in the years of maximum development, and nobody cares about them in the minimum years, when the clue to the whole locust problem is likely to be found."

The Most Serious Pests

Judged by the frequency, severity, and geographic extent of its plagues, the most serious pest is the desert locust (*Schistocerca gregaria*). It lives in the deserts and semiarid regions of Africa, the Near East, and Southwest Asia, wherever the annual rainfall is less than 8 inches (200 mm). In addition to the African migratory locust, there are other, less serious, pests. The oriental migratory locust (*L. migratoria manilensis*) occurs in Southeast Asia, the red locust (*Nomadacris septemfasciata*) in Eastern Africa, the brown locust (*Locustana pardalina*) in southern Africa, the Moroccan locust (*Dociostaurus maroccanus*) from northwest Africa to Asia, the Bombay locust (*Nomadacris succincta*) in southern Asia, and the Australian plague locust (*Chortoicetes terminifera*) in Australia. There are also various tree locusts (*Anacridium* species) found around the Mediterranean. The Rocky Mountain locust (*Melanoplus spretus*) was the cause of American plagues.

The Locust Life Cycle

In its harmless form, when it is said to be *solitarious,* the desert locust is gray, brown, or green in color. An insect about 2 inches (5 cm) long, it is able to fly but does so only occasionally and for short distances. There are usually large numbers wherever food is to be found, but individuals avoid each other, spending their time feeding on the dry, sparse vegetation. They will mate and lay eggs if conditions are suitable. For this they need some moisture 4–6 inches (10–15 cm) below ground in sandy or mixed sand and clay soil, bare ground on which to lay eggs, and some green plants to feed the young. Eggs hatch after an average of 2 weeks. The young, which cannot fly, are known as *hoppers.* They grow for about 30 to 40 days and it takes an average 2 to 4 months for the adults to become sexually mature. Locusts are not found everywhere, and no locusts may be present even where the ground is moist and some of the vegetation green.

This is how the locusts will remain unless there is rain. Then green plants will quickly cover the area and female locusts will lay many more eggs to take advantage of the sudden abundance of food. Numbers will increase and so will the frequency of encounters between individuals.

Then a change comes over the hoppers. Their color turns pink and they may be marked with black, yellow, or orange stripes. They are now in the immature stage of their alternative phase. They are ceasing to be solitarious and are becoming gregarious. They no longer avoid each other; instead, when two hoppers meet they usually stay together, all the time feeding and moving in bands that join each other. In order to grow, the hoppers must molt their exoskeletons. After their fifth molt they are adults, and are now yellow. At night they roost in trees and shrubs, by day they feed, and before long their food supply is exhausted. They have eaten everything and it is time to move on. They are now locusts, moving as a swarm. Solitarious locusts travel by night. Gregarious ones fly by day.

How Swarms Travel

Once airborne, the locusts remain in small groups within the swarm. When a group finds itself at the edge of the swarm it turns toward the center. In this way the swarm is maintained, but inside it the locusts are flying in all directions. The swarm is carried by the wind and does not travel in a direction the locusts have chosen. Depending on the speed of the wind, locust swarms usually travel at 10–12 mph (16–19 km/h) and cover up to 100 miles (160 km) a day, although they can travel farther over sea. Often they enter the Intertropical Convergence Zone (page 46), where they can be carried to great heights on rising air currents. Usually they are carried from east to west. In the Exodus account the locusts come from the east. A swarm that took to the air over Saudi Arabia in 1950 was tracked all the way to the Atlantic coast of Africa, in Mauritania, a journey of 3,100 miles (5,000 km) that took it less than 2 months.

Swarms land when the locusts sight vegetation. A desert locust can eat approximately its own weight in food every day. This is about 0.07 ounce (2 g). One million locusts can eat more than 2 tons, (1.8 tonnes) and 1 ton (900 kg) of locusts—a very small fraction of an average swarm—will eat as much food in 1 day as about 10 elephants, 25 camels, or 2,500 people. When the locusts leave, no green leaf remains.

Reptiles of Old and New World Deserts

Snakes have adapted well to desert life, often evolving similar physiological or behavioral solutions to similar environmental conditions (page 95). Where a particular genus is widespread in a region that includes deserts, some of its species are likely to have colonized the deserts. Cobras, for example, occur throughout the Tropics and subtropics of Africa and Asia, and the Egyptian cobra (*Naja haje*) is found over most of Africa. It prefers the desert, however, where its brown coloration camouflages it well. Like most desert snakes, it shelters in crevices and beneath rocks and feeds mainly on small rodents.

It is a large snake, up to 8 feet (2.5 m) long. When disturbed, a cobra will rear up, extend its hood by spreading the ribs just behind its head, hiss loudly, and lunge repeatedly. This is a threat, meant to intimidate its attacker, and the lunge is often deliberately short and made with the mouth closed. Cobras are not especially aggressive, but sometimes the lunge is genuine and the strike real, and cobra venom is extremely potent.

Coral Snakes

Obviously, the color of the Egyptian cobra camouflages it and camouflage helps the snake to pursue prey unobtrusively and to avoid predators. This is one use of color. In the North American deserts there is another member of the cobra family (Elapidae), which uses color quite differently. The Sonoran coral snake (*Micruroides euryxanthus*) is one of about 40 species of coral snakes distributed over most of the warmer regions of North, Central, and South America. Nearly all coral snakes are marked with brightly colored bands. Those of the Sonoran coral snake are red, black, and yellow.

Coral snakes shelter in tunnels below ground, or beneath rocks, and they feed mainly on other snakes, especially those that tunnel below ground, and on worm-lizards or worm-snakes, members of an order (Amphisbaenidae) of reptiles that live below ground, feed on invertebrates, and are not true lizards or snakes. Coral snakes are not large—the biggest is no more than 3 feet (90 cm) long—but they are extremely venomous and if disturbed they lash out wildly.

There are also harmless snakes with markings very like those of coral snakes. The milk snake (*Lampropeltis triangulum*), for example, also lives in the desert and is easily mistaken for a coral snake. At one time, scientists thought these similarities evolved as a protection. The coral snake is easily seen and dangerous, and predators that learn to

avoid it will not take chances with a snake that mimics it.

Unfortunately, there is a problem with this apparently plausible explanation. No predator that disturbs a coral snake will learn to avoid it in future, for the simple reason that the coral snake will kill it. Consequently, bright bands confer no defense on either coral snakes or their mimics. An alternative explanation, proposed by the German biologist Robert Mertens and called *Mertensian mimicry*, centers on a group of mildly venomous banded snakes, called *false coral snakes*. They cannot kill a predator, but their bite will make it feel very sick. So predators learn to avoid false coral snakes and true coral snakes and their mimics benefit. Even then, though, there is a difficulty. False coral snakes are found only in Central and South America. There is none in the North American deserts and so similarities between North American coral snakes and their mimics cannot be due to Mertensian mimicry.

Yet another explanation, proposed by the British biologist Chris Mattison in his book *Snakes of the World* (Facts On File, 1985), may be the correct one. All of these banded snakes are nocturnal and secretive. Their bright colors do not impede them when hunting, because they do not show up at night. Should a predator dig one from its tunnel during the day, or turn over the rock beneath which it is sheltering, it would confront a brightly colored snake thrashing furiously. This would startle the predator, making it retreat or at least stop moving for a moment, and that moment might give the snake as much time as it needed to escape. In other words, the bright bands are startle, or *deimatic,* coloration.

These are not the only snakes with bright bands. The Californian kingsnake (*Lampropeltis getulus californiae*) lives in the deserts of Utah, Nevada, and Arizona, as well as California. Its bands are white or cream and brown, except in a small area around San Diego, where instead of bands snakes of the same subspecies have stripes running the length of their bodies. They are fairly big snakes, 3–6 feet (0.9–1.8 m) long, and as well as small mammals and lizards they eat other snakes, including rattlesnakes, copperheads, and coral snakes and are immune to their venom.

Pit Vipers

The sidewinder (page 95) is one of several rattlesnakes that live in deserts. These include the Mojave (*Crotalus scutulatus*) and tiger (*C. tigris*) rattlesnakes, as well as one of the biggest rat-

tlesnakes, the western diamondback (*C. atrox*), which can grow to more than 6.5 feet (2 m).

Rattlesnakes are pit vipers (family Crotalidae). The pits are a pair of depressions between the eyes and nostrils, each containing an organ that can detect a temperature change of as little as 0.4°F (0.2°C). Its pit organs allow the snake to locate prey in total darkness by the warmth of its body compared to that of the surroundings. The copperhead (*Agkistrodon contortix*) is also a pit viper. It occasionally grows to about 50 inches (1.25 m) but most copperheads are smaller. They feed on small rodents and are not aggressive.

Not all desert snakes shelter beneath rocks. Some bury themselves in the sand with just their eyes and nostrils exposed. One of these is McMahon's viper (*Eristocophis macmahonii*), which buries itself in loose sand by sweeping its body from side to side. This pushes away the sand beneath its body and it sinks vertically until only its outline in the disturbed sand betrays its position. There it waits to strike at passing lizards and small mammals that are its prey—or at any human who steps on it.

Swimming Through Sand

There are also lizards that bury themselves in sand. Indeed, some skinks move through loose sand with such a smooth swimming motion that one of them is called the *sandfish*. This is *Scincus philbyi,* a lizard about 8 inches (20 cm) long that lives in the Arabian Desert. Skinks are members of the family Scincidae, of which there are more than 1,200 species. Many have very small legs and some are legless, but the sandfish has strong legs and feet, with fringes of scales on its flattened toes that improve its grip on loose sand. It eats small invertebrates, especially millipedes, and because it hunts a little way below ground, swimming like a fish through the sand, it is protected from the heat and can be active during the day.

Other lizards also dig burrows. The Arabian toad-headed agamid (*Phrynocephalus nejdensis*) does so. It has long legs that keep its body clear of the ground when it is on the surface and, like most agamid lizards (family Agamidae), a long tail. It buries itself by wriggling from side to side and feeds mainly on insects, although it also eats some plant material.

Thorny Lizards

Agamid lizards are quite common in the deserts of Africa, Asia, and Australia, and they have few weapons with which to defend themselves. Consequently, some have evolved exotic armor. In the Australian deserts there is a lizard called the *thorny devil* (*Moloch horridus*), whose head, body, tail, and legs are covered with conical scales that look like bristles or thorns and an especially big one over each eye. It needs to terrify its enemies, because it is only about 6 inches (15 cm) long and moves slowly. It feeds mainly on ants and termites. The princely mastigure (*Uromastyx princeps*) lives in the Eastern Sahara. About 9 inches (23 cm) long, it has a thick tail covered with sharp spines that it lashes at any animal threatening it. The armadillo lizard (*Cordylus cataphractus*) is a girdled lizard (family Cordylidae) that lives in southern Africa. It, too, is covered with spiny scales, but it has an additional means of defense. When threatened, it rolls up like an armadillo, holding the tip of its tail in its mouth, so a predator is presented with a solid ball of armor.

Like many lizards, the armadillo lizard can shed its tail voluntarily when threatened and then regrow it. This is called *autotomy*. Often the discarded tail will wriggle for a while, distracting a predator long enough for the lizard to escape.

Iguanas (family Iguanidae) are the American equivalent of the agamid lizards, and convergent evolution (page 94) has given some of them thorny scales. The most spectacular is the Texas horned lizard (*Phrynosoma cornutum*). It has two big horns at the back of its head, with smaller spikes on either side forming a collar, two rows of spines along its back, and spines around its sides. It feeds on ants and is never more than 7 inches (18 cm) long.

The chuckwalla (*Sauromalus obesus*) is also an iguanid. One of the bigger lizards, about 16 inches (40 cm) long, it lives in the arid southwestern United States. Its skin is loose, hanging in folds, and contains glands that can store water. Most lizards are carnivorous, but the chuckwalla is an herbivore, feeding on leaves, flowers, and buds, often of the creosote bush.

Monitors and Venomous Lizards

The biggest of all lizards are the monitors (family Varanidae). They are powerfully built carnivores and some are found in deserts. Gould's monitor (*Varanus gouldi*) of Australia is also known as the *sand monitor.* It is about 5 feet (1.5 m) long and when threatened stands upright on its hind legs, hissing loudly.

There are only two species of venomous lizards, constituting the family Helodermatidae, or beaded lizards—because their scales are surrounded by rows of beadlike granules. They are related to the monitors and both occur in America. The gila monster (*Heloderma suspectum*) occurs in the southwestern United States and Mexico, and the Mexican beaded lizard (*H. horridum*) in western Mexico. They are up to 2 feet (60 cm) long and eat any small animal they can catch, as well as birds' eggs and carrion. Their venomous bite is painful, but rarely fatal to humans.

Mammals of Old and New World Deserts

Lizards are not the only animals that swim through the desert sands. In the Kalahari and Namib Deserts there are golden moles that do the same.

Although they resemble ordinary moles, golden moles (family Chrysochloridae) are only distantly related to them and they live only in southern Africa. Their eyes are covered by skin and their ears by fur, but the bones of their inner ears are large, making the moles very sensitive to vibrations. If disturbed on the surface a golden mole makes quickly and unhesitatingly for the entrance to its tunnel, and for a secure chamber if it is below ground.

These desert swimmers move just below the surface, foraging for food. Their diet consists mainly of invertebrates, but they also catch and eat legless lizards. Grant's golden mole (*Eremitalpa granti*) may swim 3 miles (5 km) in a single night.

There are also hedgehogs in the Sahara and deserts of Asia. They feed mainly on invertebrates, but some will eat prey as large as mice. The desert hedgehog (*Paraechinus aethiopicus*) of the Sahara, and Brandt's hedgehog (*P. hypomelas*) and the long-eared hedgehog (*Hemiechinus auritus*), both of central Asia, have large ears. These act as heat exchangers, helping the animal keep cool.

Big Ears

All hares have big ears, but those of the desert jackrabbits of North and Central America and desert populations of the Cape hares (*Lepus capensis*) of Africa and Asia are even bigger. Jackrabbits are hares (*Lepus* species), not rabbits, and several species inhabit deserts. Most rabbits dig burrows, but few cottontails or hares do so. In summer the black-tailed jackrabbit (*L. californicus*) digs short burrows in which to shelter from the desert heat, but otherwise it lives above ground.

As well as helping animals keep cool, big ears provide an animal with acute hearing. This is essential for desert animals that live above ground. Many predators rely on their hearing to locate prey at night, and prey species need to be able to hear an approaching predator. Golden moles can hide below ground and hedgehogs have spines, but hares and jackrabbits have no defenses or weapons. They escape danger by running, and a black-tailed jackrabbit can run at 45 mph (72 km/h), but even so it can avoid capture only if it has adequate warning.

Carnivorous Mice

Rodents are the most abundant of desert mammals. Most are mainly vegetarian, although they will also eat insects, but the grasshopper mice are carnivores. There are three species (genus *Onychomys*) and they inhabit the deserts and semiarid regions from central Mexico as far as southwestern Canada. Up to 5 inches (13 cm) long with a 2-inch (5-cm) tail, they are bigger than most mice. As their name suggests they feed mainly on grasshoppers, but they also eat any other insect they can catch, as well as scorpions, lizards, and rodents smaller than they.

When one grasshopper mouse detects another nearby it utters a series of high-pitched squeaks, each lasting about 1 second. These cries, uttered more frequently by males than by females, may serve to maintain a minimal distance between individuals or breeding pairs.

Small Desert Cats

There are many predators of small rodents. In the North American deserts snakes (page 100) and birds of prey (page 104) are the principal carnivores, although pumas (*Felis concolor*) sometimes hunt in the desert and will eat rodents and jackrabbits. The puma—also known as the *cougar* and *mountain lion*—is the only cat found in American deserts. Several live in the deserts of Africa and Asia.

The sand cat (*F. margarita*) inhabits deserts from the Sahara to central Asia. Its head and body measure about 20 inches (50 cm) and its tail is about 12 inches (30 cm) long. It is sand colored, as its name indicates, but with dark rings on its tail, and the pads of its paws are covered with fur, presumably as insulation. It is a nocturnal hunter. Pallas's cat (*F. manul*) lives from Iran to western China, on grassland and in mountains as well as in deserts. It is roughly the same size as the sand cat, but stockier, with shorter legs and much longer fur. A secretive animal, rarely seen, it, too, is nocturnal, spending its days in rock crevices, caves, or burrows made by other animals.

Cats are conventionally divided into two groups. The sand and Pallas's cats are both "small" cats, all of which are usually included in the genus *Felis*. Lynxes are the biggest of the *Felis* cats and one of them, the caracal (*F. caracal*), stalks its prey in dry, open country including deserts from Africa to India. The caracal, or caracal lynx, somewhat resembles a small, long-legged puma with

very long, pointed ears that end in tufts of hair. It lives alone, hunting mainly at night but sometimes during the day in cooler weather. Most small cats hunt either by waiting to ambush prey or by stalking and pouncing. The caracal also chases animals and runs them down. It will eat anything it can catch, from mice to small deer, and including birds, reptiles, and domestic sheep and goats.

The Cheetah

Most "big" cats are placed in the genus *Panthera*, except the clouded leopard (*Neofelis nebulosa*) and the cheetah (*Acinonyx jubatus*). The cheetah is also a desert hunter and like the caracal it runs down its prey.

It is famous for being the fastest mammal. Over a short distance it is capable of 64 mph (103 km/h), a speed made possible by the way its body is constructed. Its spine is very flexible and its pectoral (shoulder) and pelvic (hip) girdles are able to move very freely against the spine. The figure shows how this skeletal flexibility gives the cheetah an extremely long stride, allowing it to move in a series of huge bounds. At the same time, its short face—much more like that of a domestic cat than the face of other big cats—means its big eyes look straight ahead, giving it excellent binocular vision with which to judge distances very precisely. Small cats are able to retract their claws. The cheetah is unable to retract its claws completely. This means they are blunt through wear, but it also means they give the cat a firm grip on the ground when it is running.

An average adult cheetah measures about 4 feet (1.25 m) from its head to the base of its tail, and the tail, which it uses for balance, is about 2 feet (60 cm) long. The animal weighs about 130 pounds (59 kg). It hunts gazelles and similar animals but will also take smaller prey, such as hares. Its technique is to select a target and then stalk it slowly and patiently—4 hours if necessary—until it is within about 100 feet (30 m). Then it charges, the prey runs, and the final chase begins. This usually covers about 200 yards (183 m) and lasts less than 1 minute.

Cheetahs probably evolved in Asia. The name is from the Hindi word *chita*, which means "spotted," and they were once used for hunting. Today most cheetahs live on open grassland and desert in Africa and the Middle East, as far as northern India.

Lions

Lions (*Panthera leo*) also hunt in the Sahara and Kalahari Deserts. They are the most social of cats, living in family groups, called *prides*. These consist of up to about 15 related females and their off-spring with up to about six adult males. Depending on the abundance of game and number of lions to be fed, a pride ranges in search of food over anything from about 10 square miles to 160 square miles (26–414 sq km). Ranges overlap, but each pride has a central core area from which other lions are excluded.

Sometimes lions collaborate in hunting. One group of females will circle the prey, using such cover as is available, and then hide. When this group is in position a second group approaches the prey more openly, driving it into the ambush.

Lionesses undertake most of the hunting, but a male lion is quite capable of hunting for itself. Food is shared among the pride, but young cubs can be at a disadvantage. Their small size makes it difficult for them to compete with the adults, and they may go hungry.

Gazelles, the Addax, and Oryxes

Lions, cheetahs, and caracals hunt gazelles. These are hoofed animals related to cattle and sheep, but small, lightly built, and quite at home in the desert. The dorcas gazelle (*Gazella dorcas*), found from the Sahara to India, is typical. It can obtain all the moisture it needs from the plants on which it feeds, so drinking is not essential, although it loses weight on a diet consisting only of dry food.

Male caracal (Gerry Ellis/ENP Images)

It is a small animal, only 2 feet (60 cm) tall at the shoulder, but to escape a cat it can run at 50 mph (80 km/h). The springbok (*Antidorcas marsupialis*) is also a gazelle. It lives in southern Africa. At one time herds numbering tens of thousands used to migrate across the dry plains, but today it is confined mainly to reserves and does not migrate.

The addax (*Addax nasomaculatus*) used to live throughout the Sahara. Today it lives in just some parts of the desert, always a long way from water in territory too barren to support most other herbivores. Its feet are widely splayed, helping it move across loose sand, and it obtains its water from the food it eats.

The addax has long spiral horns. Those of oryxes are also long, but straight. The Arabian oryx (*Oryx leucoryx*), which once ranged over most of the Arabian Peninsula, is now found only in Oman and the Sinai Peninsula. The scimitar, or white, oryx (*O. dammah*) occurs along the Southern Sahara from Mauritania to the Red Sea, and the gemsbok, or common oryx (*O. gazella*), lives in northeastern and southwestern Africa.

Cheetah (Acinonyx jubatus)

Birds of Old and New World Deserts

In some ways birds find it easier than other animals to adapt to the desert environment. They start with a physiological advantage. They are endotherms, of course, and maintain a fairly constant core temperature by physiological means, but the ordinary core body temperature of a bird is about 104°F (40°C), which is higher than that of a mammal. An endotherm needs to activate its regulatory mechanisms—dilating or constricting blood vessels, raising or lowering hair or feathers, shivering or sweating, and so forth—when the difference between its core temperature and the outside air temperature exceeds a certain threshold. The difference of about 3.6°F (2°C) between the core temperature of a bird and that of a mammal is small, but significant. It means that a bird spends a shorter time each day than a mammal having to prevent its body from overheating. Added to this, birds allow their body temperature to fluctuate more than mammals do, and are not harmed if it rises a few degrees.

Moving Through Cool Air

All birds share this feature and there is no difference between desert birds and those that live in other environments. Birds also fly, and while they are flying they are in air that is much cooler than air near the ground surface. Air temperature decreases with height by an average 5.4°F per 1,000 feet (9.8°C/km). During the hottest part of the day the temperature of a sand or rock surface may be about 170°F (77°C). If a small mammal ventures from its burrow, this is the temperature it must brave. At a height of about 6.5 feet (2 m), however, the temperature will be about 115°F

(46°C). This is the temperature of the air around the head of a large mammal such as a dromedary. A bird flying overhead, say at about 200 feet (60 m), moves through air at about 114°F (45.5°C), and the air flowing over its body as a consequence of its forward motion is the equivalent of a wind exerting a chill factor. Many birds fly at around 25 mph (40 km/h), a speed that will have a cooling effect equivalent to a decrease in temperature of a degree or two. The reduction is small, because as the air temperature approaches the body temperature, the chilling effect of a wind decreases. Nevertheless, birds spend a good deal of their time in conditions cooler than those experienced by animals living on the ground, and they are physiologically better equipped for high temperatures.

Despite this advantage, all but a few birds, such as owls and nightjars, are active during the day and they must seek shade during the hottest hours.

Pigeon Milk

It is also easier for birds to find water. All they need do is fly to the nearest river, lake, or waterhole, and they are able to travel a long way. Every morning, mourning doves (*Zenaida macroura*) gather to drink at water holes in the North American desert, some having flown there from 40 miles (64 km) or more away. Then, when they have drunk their fill, they fly off to seek food or return to their young.

Fledglings cannot make such journeys, of course, so a desert bird must have some means of carrying water to its young. Pigeons, including

the mourning dove, do so by producing a liquid called *pigeon milk* or *crop milk*. Pigeon milk looks like cottage cheese, and its production is stimulated by the hormone prolactin, which also stimulates milk production in mammals. It is similar to mammalian milk in composition, consisting of 13–19 percent protein, 7–13 percent fat, 1–2 percent minerals and vitamins (A, B, and B_2), and 65–81 percent water (cow's milk is 50 percent sugars, 35 percent protein, 40 percent fats, and 9 percent minerals). Both males and females produce it, and it provides the only nourishment the fledglings receive for their first few days after hatching. After that it is augmented with solid foods carried by the parents, but the amount of milk the young receive remains fairly constant almost until they are fully fledged.

Obviously, the adults must drink enough water to be able to produce milk in addition to supplying the needs of their own bodies. This imposes a stress on the birds, but one far less severe than the stress imposed on a lactating mammal, which must also use some of the water it drinks or obtains from its food to make milk.

Sand Grouse

Only pigeons and flamingoes produce crop milk. Other desert birds must find different ways to supply water to their young and all but 1 of the 16 species of sand grouse (family Pteroclididae)

Structure of a feather

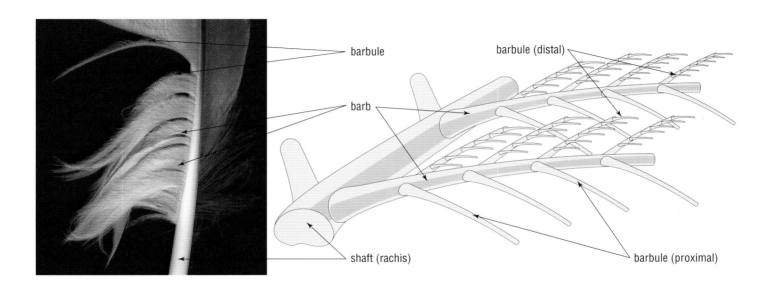

barbule

barbule (distal)

barb

shaft (rachis)

barbule (proximal)

have evolved a novel method. Sand grouse are small ground-nesting birds found throughout the deserts of Africa and Asia. They eat dry seeds, and their grouse chicks can find their own food within a few hours of hatching, but their diet contains very little water and the young birds cannot fly. Their parents give them water by using their breast feathers as a sponge. The exception is the Tibetan sand grouse (*Syrrhaptes tibetanus*), which is never far from melting snow that provides all the water it needs.

Contour feathers, which cover the body of a bird and give it its shape, consist of a central shaft, or *rachis,* from which the barbs grow at an angle of about 45°. The illustration shows this arrangement on part of a feather (left) and much enlarged (right). Each barb is lined on both sides by smaller structures, called *barbules,* that also emerge at about 45°. The feather retains its overall structure because the distal barbules—those farthest from the bird's body—have hooks with which they engage the smooth proximal (nearest the body) barbules adjacent to them.

Sand grouse, especially males, have modified belly feathers. When the feathers are dry the proximal (nearest the body) part of each barbule is twisted into a spiral and is held flat against the barb. When wetted, the barbules untwist and stand approximately at right angles to the barbs. This causes the feathers to form a dense mat, about 0.04 inch (1 mm) thick, that holds water. The belly feathers of male sand grouse hold up to 20 times their own weight of water and those of females about 12 times.

Soon after dawn the sand grouse take off for the water hole, usually a distance of less than about 20 miles (32 km). Females often go first, the males setting off after their mates have returned. When the males arrive they rub their bellies on the dry ground to remove the natural oils in their feathers. Then they drink, after which they soak their belly feathers. Some do this by walking into the water. Others, such as Burchell's, or the variegated, sand grouse (*Pterocles burchelli*) of the Kalahari, float while they drink and then take off from the water.

Some of the water their feathers absorb is lost by evaporation on the flight back to the nest, but after a journey of 20 miles (32 km) the feathers are still wet when the birds arrive. An arriving bird stands erect and the young rush to him and strip the water from his feathers. After that he rubs his belly in the sand to dry it and then all the birds start foraging for seeds.

Desert Falcons

Birds that congregate in large numbers attract predators. In addition to jackals and foxes, birds of prey also keep a watchful eye on water holes. Falcons, especially, hunt small birds.

The lanner falcon (*Falco biarmicus*) lives in the deserts of Africa and Arabia, the saker falcon (*F. cherrug*) in central Asia, and the laggar falcon (*F. jugger*) in India. All of them are fairly small birds, between about 15 inches (40 cm) and 20 inches (51 cm) long. They are fast and maneuver deftly. While flying close to the ground, they sometimes catch birds on the ground or just as they are taking off.

Falcons are powerfully built, with long, pointed wings, and fairly short tails that taper toward the top. The lanner and saker—or sacred—falcons were highly prized in the Middle Ages by aristocrats, who used them for falcony, in which the birds of prey were trained to catch game birds, especially quail, and return to the gloved wrist of their owners. Falcons hunt by diving at great speed—called *stooping*—onto their prey. Small birds are usually killed in the air.

Vultures

Vultures are the birds often associated with deserts, although in fact most vultures avoid deserts. American vultures belong to the family Cathartidae and African and Asian vultures to the family Aegypiinae. The two families are not closely related, although a similar way of life has led to similarities in appearance—another example of parallel evolution (page 94). Both families comprise large birds with the hooked beaks of raptors (birds of prey) and many with bare, unfeathered heads. They feed by scavenging carcasses.

The lappet-faced vulture (*Torgos tracheliotus*) soars over the deserts of Africa, often alone but sometimes in groups of up to four. No other vulture interrupts its feeding, because it is by far the biggest—up to 40 inches (1 m) long and weighing 30 pounds (13.6 kg)—and its huge bill can tear open the hide of an elephant or rhinoceros.

In parts of its range the lappet-faced vulture may be joined by griffon (*Gyps fulvus*), whiteheaded (*Trigonoceps occipitalis*), or hooded (*Necrosyrtes monachus*) vultures. The Egyptian vulture (*Neophron percnopterus*) ranges from Africa to India. Other vultures feed only on dead animals, but the Egyptian vulture will also eat vegetable matter, garbage, and some small animals.

Secretary Bird and Roadrunner

Other carnivorous birds feed mainly on reptiles. The secretary bird (*Sagittarius serpentarius*) is perhaps the species most committed to this diet, although it also eats insects and small rodents. A tall bird, standing about 3.3 feet (1 m) tall, it has long feathers at the back of its head, resembling the quill pens office clerks once used to carry behind their ears. It hunts by walking along and staring at the ground, but its wings span 6.5 feet (2 m) and it can and does fly. It kills snakes by stamping on them.

The North American equivalent of the secretary bird is the roadrunner (*Geococcyx californianus*), a member of the cuckoo family (Cuculidae). It stands about 11 inches (14 cm) tall and has a long tail; it hunts its prey by running swiftly, with its body almost horizontal, then stopping abruptly. It does eat snakes, including venomous species, but its diet consists mainly of lizards, scorpions, small mammals, ground-nesting birds, and insects.

Greater roadrunner (Gerry Ellis/ENP Images)

Desert Ecology

Ecology is the scientific study of relationships among different species of organisms and among organisms and their physical and chemical surroundings. It is a fairly new scientific discipline. The word *ecology* was coined in 1866 in a book called *General Morphology* by the German zoologist Ernst Heinrich Haeckel (1834–1919). He made it out of two Greek words, *oikos* meaning "house," and *logos* meaning "account." Therefore, ecology is an account (or explanation) of house(holds). Just as families keep watch on how money coming into the home is allocated and bills are paid, so ecologists are interested in the ways plants and animals use the resources available to them. It is the study of what has sometimes been called the "economy of nature."

Resources that are important in the economy of nature include shelter, places where young can be raised safely, opportunities for social interaction and mating, a tolerable climate, and most important of all, a source of food. When a plant or animal succeeds in establishing itself in a place where it finds the resources it needs, it is said to occupy an ecological *niche*. The organism defines the niche by occupying it, and the niche does not exist until that happens.

Ecosystem

An area in which organisms occupy niches and interact with each other is called an *ecosystem,* which is short for *ecological system,* and it can be of any size provided the area can be clearly distinguished from surrounding areas. A forest can be distinguished from adjacent farmland, for example; a single tree with mosses, lichens, insects, birds, and squirrels living in its branches can be distinguished from the surrounding forest; and a small pool of water can be distinguished from the dry land around it. A forest, tree, or pool of water—or even a single drop of water with its microscopic inhabitants—can be regarded as an ecosystem. A desert is also an ecosystem.

Food, the most fundamental resource, consists basically of sunlight, water, carbon dioxide, and mineral nutrient compounds present in the soil. Plants require adequate amounts of all these, and it is the scarcity of water that limits the abundance of desert plants. Desert vegetation (pages 80–135) usually comprises widely spaced small shrubs. In the North American deserts, for example, there are sagebrush (*Artemisia tridentata*) with various grasses in parts of Utah and Nevada, and creosote bush (*Larrea divaricata* subspecies *tridentata*) with cacti, including saguaro, and Joshua trees (*Yucca brevifolia*) in the Mojave, Sonoran, and Chihuahuan Deserts.

Feeding Relationships

Green plants form the biological basis of the desert ecosystem, because it is only green plants that can convert the "raw" ingredients of water and carbon dioxide into carbohydrates (see page 56) and simple chemical compounds into proteins. Animals must obtain the nutrients they require by consuming plants either directly or indirectly by eating plant-eating animals. Consequently, green plants are described ecologically as producers and all animals as consumers.

The total quantity of organisms can be measured as their dry weight per unit area. This is known as their *biomass* and it is reported scientifically in grams per square meter (g/m^2 or gm^{-2}). In a desert the total plant biomass is commonly 1000–2000 g/m^2 (42–44 ounces per square yard [oz/yd^2]). This is between 3 percent and 7 percent of the biomass of a temperate broad-leaved forest, and 800–1,600 g/m^2 (33–67 oz/yd^2) of the desert biomass is below ground in the form of roots and rhizomes. There is little vegetable matter for the animals reliant on it and there are spines, thorns, or poisons protecting much of that.

It is not surprising, therefore, that if you cross a desert you will see scattered plants, but you may see no animals at all. The vegetation you see above ground may amount to 200–400 g/m^2 (8–17 oz/yd^2), but this is not the quantity of food available to animals. If they ate all of that, no plants would be left and the animals would starve. Consumers must rely not on the plant biomass, but on the primary, or plant, productivity. This is the amount of material plants add by growth each year.

Plants use up some of the carbohydrate they make in respiration. Deduct this and the result is the net primary productivity (NPP). This is the maximum amount of food available for animals. In deserts the annual NPP above ground is usually 30–100 g/m^2 (1.25–4.2 oz/yd^2) and the below ground NPP adds a further 200–220 g/m^2 (8.4–9.2 oz/yd^2). This is the food supply for animals in the form of leaves, flowers, stems, roots, fruits, and seeds, but some of it is inedible and a proportion falls from the plants and is lost.

Herbivorous animals are known as *primary consumers.* Their biomass can be measured in the same way, and it is very approximately one-tenth of the plant biomass. There are seed eaters, such as pocket mice (*Perognathus* species) and kangaroo rats (*Dipodomys* species), and birds such as the mourning dove (*Zenaida macroura*), but when all the insects, other herbivorous invertebrates, and species that live below ground are included, the biomass of primary consumers cannot be more than about 100–200 g/m^2 (4.2–8.4 oz/yd^2).

Carnivores, which feed on herbivores, are secondary consumers and the same rule applies to them. Herbivores use most of the food they eat to provide them with the energy they need to live. Only about one-tenth of it becomes part of their bodies and available to meat eaters. Consequently, the insectivorous lizards and birds and the snakes and cats that prey on small rodents and larger grazing herds can have a total biomass of no more than about 10–20 g/m^2 (0.42–0.84 oz/yd^2).

Some snakes feed mainly on other snakes. The secretary bird (*Sagittarius serpentarius*) of Africa and roadrunner (*Geococcyx californianus*) of California eat lizards and snakes. These carnivore-eating carnivores are *top predators,* or tertiary consumers, and the rule still applies. There can be no more than about 1–2 g/m^2 (0.04–0.08 oz/yd^2) of them.

Ecological Pyramids

These relationships can be illustrated by a type of diagram known, because of its shape, as an *ecological pyramid,* or sometimes as an *Eltonian pyramid,* after Sir Charles Sutherland Elton (1900–91), the British zoologist and ecologist who invented it. There are three types. The pyramid of numbers shows the number of organisms at each level. This is not very satisfactory, because it takes no account of the size of individuals. If the producers are herbs, for example, there will be many more of them than there would be if they were trees, but the NPP would not necessarily be any greater. The pyramid of biomass solves this by measuring the biomass at each level. This, too, runs into difficulties in some ecosystems, because wide seasonal fluctuations distort it, so it is necessary to know the time of year to which it refers. The most useful version is the pyramid of energy. This converts biomass into the energy it represents (it does this by burning it and measuring the energy released).

All three look very similar and the diagram shows what an ecological pyramid looks like, although it is not practicable to draw the "steps" to scale. Suppose the bottom "step," producers, is 10 inches (25 cm) wide—and a little too big to fit on a page of this book. The second "step," pri-

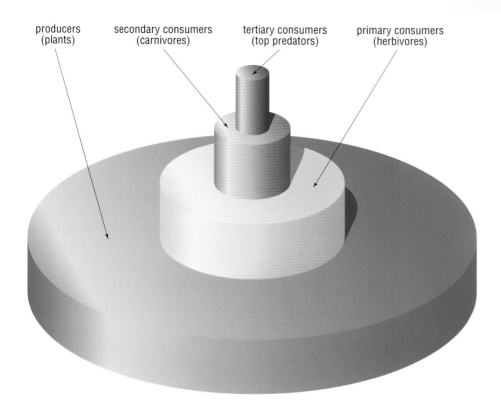

producers
(plants)

secondary consumers
(carnivores)

tertiary consumers
(top predators)

primary consumers
(herbivores)

Ecological pyramid

There is, therefore, a second set of organisms through which food passes, and it can also be illustrated as a pyramid. At each level, the organisms of the second, detrital, group are preyed upon by predators such as centipedes, scorpions, and spiders.

Food Chains and Food Webs

Useful though they are, the pyramids do not show the complexity of feeding relationships among the members of an ecosystem. Indeed, these are so intricate and so flexible that it is almost impossible to illustrate them at all. When they are shown, it is usually as a food chain or food web. A food chain simply shows links between organisms at each level of an ecological pyramid. Grass → gazelle → lion is an example. The difficulty with it is that gazelles are not the only herbivores that eat grass, lions eat animals other than gazelles, and the same applies to the organisms in any such chain.

Link animals by arrows to their sources of food and the result is a food web. It gives an impression of the extent to which the members of an ecosystem are linked to and dependent on each other, but its drawback is that it is static. Most animals eat differently at different times of year, according to the food that is available, and some animals spend only part of their time in the ecosystem. Because they can reflect nothing of this dynamism, food web diagrams can easily mislead.

Ecosystems, even relatively simple ones like the desert ecosystem, are extremely complicated and constantly changing. Ecologists spend their time exploring the relationships among organisms and analyzing the information they discover by direct observation in order to understand how ecosystems function. From this they hope to predict how ecosystems are likely to respond to changes imposed from outside.

mary consumers, would then have to be about 1 inch (2.5 cm) wide; the third "step," secondary consumers, 0.1 inch (2.5 mm) wide; and the fourth "step," tertiary consumers, 0.01 inch (0.25 mm) wide—difficult to print and to see!

Ecological pyramids demonstrate why large predators, such as lions, are uncommon. Depending on how many members it has and the richness—the primary productivity—of the habitat, a pride of lions needs a range of 10–160 square miles (26–414 sq km) in which to find enough game to sustain it.

All plants and animals produce wastes, eventually every individual dies, and wastes and dead material provide food for another pyramid of organisms. Vultures scavenge dead animals, dung beetles utilize animal dung, and ants and other insects feed on leaves. Dead matter lying on the ground is called *detritus* and animals that feed on it are *detritivores*. Scavengers and detritivores break up and scatter detritus, and, of course, they produce detritus of their own. Fungi and bacteria finally break down the remaining organic material, releasing it in the form of simple chemical compounds that dissolve in water and can be absorbed into plant roots.

Life in Cold Climates

Animal Life of the Arctic

It is not true that every so often lemmings commit mass suicide by throwing themselves into the sea. What is true is that from time to time Norway lemmings (*Lemmus lemmus*)—one of the nine species of lemmings—undertake mass migrations in the course of which they may panic and rush into a lake or the sea, where many of them drown. Migrations take place at intervals of 3 to 4 years, and not all migrations lead to such heavy mortality rates—it is largely a matter of luck.

Lemmings are small rodents, closely related to voles in the subfamily Microtinae of the family of rats and mice (Muridae). One species, the wood lemming (*Myopus schisticolor*), inhabits the northern coniferous forest—the taiga. All the others live in the arctic tundra. The arctic, or collared, lemming (*Dicrostonyx torquatus*) grows a white coat in winter, but all the other species remain the same brown color throughout the year.

All lemmings and voles undergo large changes in population size on an approximately three- to four-year cycle, though not all of them do so throughout the whole of their range. Brown lemmings (*Lemmus sibericus*) live in North America; their population density was measured over a 20-year period at Barrow, Alaska. This ranged from less than 4 lemmings per acre (10/ha) to peaks of about 61 per acre (150/ha) and in one year (1960) rose to 91 per acre (225/ha). Brown lemmings share their habitat with arctic lemmings, but these are uncommon, with seldom more than about 1 to every 25 acres (1/10 ha).

Population Fluctuations

No one is quite sure why lemming populations fluctuate so widely. Over large areas of the Arctic the ground surface consists of "islands," averaging 40 feet (12 m) across, surrounded by narrow trenches that form above wedges of ice. Lemmings live mainly in the trenches. They spend the winter beneath the snow, in the grass and sedges on the bottom of their trenches, and it is there that the young are born. Lemmings do not hibernate and through the winter they feed on the leaves and stems of the plants in the trenches. In spring the snow begins to melt and the trenches start to flood. This forces the lemmings above ground. In some years the birthrate is especially high and the animals rapidly deplete their food supply, first in the trenches and then on the surface. They scatter in search of food and predators kill many of them. Members

of several species migrate to new areas. In these years lemming numbers fall drastically during the spring and summer and take several years to recover.

Norway lemmings differ in that they seem to migrate when food is abundant, not when it is scarce. Extremely quarrelsome animals, they are usually solitary, but when their numbers increase—sometimes to more than 121 per acre (300 per hectare)—encounters are unavoidable. Older and stronger lemmings drive away the younger and weaker animals. The outcasts move down from the Scandinavian mountains where they ordinarily live. They wander in all directions, but eventually natural barriers, such as rivers and lakeshores, force them together. This is how they form small groups that merge, eventually into vast crowds, and it is then that the close proximity of so many mutually hostile animals triggers the panic that sends them rushing headlong into forests, onto farms, across glaciers, and sometimes into lakes or the sea. Norway lemmings swim well, but the distance across a lake or the Baltic Sea is too great and they drown. No one witnesses the catastrophe, but millions of bodies are found some time later. An old Scandinavian belief held that lemmings fall from the clouds during storms. Some Inuit peoples also believe lemmings fall from the sky.

With the arctic ground squirrel (*Spermophilus parryi*), lemmings and voles are the only small herbivorous mammals of the Arctic desert, and the squirrel is the only arctic mammal that hibernates. Hibernation is safe only if there are nesting sites where the temperature remains a little above freezing, and there are few such refuges in the Arctic.

Predators of Small Rodents

As the most abundant primary consumers (see illustration page 106) lemmings and voles represent the food supply for a much larger number of carnivorous species. Some carnivores even pursue them below ground. With their short legs and slender bodies no more than 8–9 inches (20–23 cm) long, weasels (*Mustela nivalis*) and ermines or stoats (*M. erminea*) move easily along the narrow tunnels rodents make beneath the snow.

Snowy owls (*Nyctea scandiaca*) also hunt small rodents. These are large birds, up to 26 inches (66 cm) long, white with dark bars or flecks, and long feathers covering their feet. Unlike most owls they hunt mainly by day. When the rodent populations crash, snowy owls move in search of food

as far south as the Great Lakes in the United States and Scotland.

Ptarmigans

Ptarmigans are the only other birds that live in the Arctic year round, and, like snowy owls, even they head south in years when food is scarce. Ptarmigans are ground-nesting birds related to grouse (family Tetraonidae). They occur throughout northern Canada and Eurasia and feed on berries and other plant material. There are three species, the white-tailed (*Lagopus leucurus*), willow (*L. lagopus*), and rock (*L. mutus*) ptarmigans. All three molt their brown plumage in the fall and grow pure white feathers to replace it.

Other birds are summer visitors, but no migrating species can be relied on to be present every year. Ravens (*Corvus corax*) are the most regular, traveling to the coast of Greenland and the whole of the American and Eurasian Arctic.

Cranes and Seabirds

In summer, when the ground above the permafrost thaws, the surface becomes marshy over parts of the tundra and there are birds that nest in the marshes. These include two species of cranes, the sandhill crane (*Grus canadensis*) and the Siberian, or great white, crane (*G. leucogeranus*). Cranes are large, long-legged birds that feed on leaves, seeds, and small animals up to the size of lemmings and voles. The sandhill crane also breeds in parts of western North America. It is brownish-gray in color and, as its alternative name suggests, the Siberian crane is white with black wing tips. It has a patch of bare, red skin on the front of its face, and a red bill and legs.

The Siberian crane is more than 4.5 feet (1.27 m) tall and has a wingspan of 6.5–8 feet (2–2.4 m). It is a handsome bird, and very rare. It breeds in two parts of Siberia, in Yakutia to the west of the Lena River, and beside the Ob River, more than 2,000 miles (3,200 km) to the west. The birds arrive at their breeding grounds toward the end of May, when the ground has started to thaw but is still covered with snow. They build their nests on the ground and the female lays and incubates two eggs, while the male stands guard. A male Siberian crane is more than a match for a hungry Arctic fox. The cranes are wary of humans, however, and will take flight if anyone approaches closer than about 300 yards (275 m), so they are difficult to study. In late September

Arctic Fox (Genny Ellis/ENP Images)

they set off on their journey south. Cranes fly higher than most birds, and people living on the steppes and farmlands of Russia watch as flocks of Siberian cranes pass high overhead uttering their wild calls. They fly all the way to China, and some of the western population fly to India.

Further north, in the icy wastes that lie beyond the tundra, huge, noisy breeding colonies of sea birds congregate in summer on rocky coasts. The Arctic birds include the only completely white gull, the ivory gull (*Pagophila eburnea*). Unlike other gulls, it rarely swims, but it can run fast. Black-legged kittiwakes (*Rissa tridactyla*) are ocean-dwelling gulls that come ashore only to breed. They nest on rocky cliffs throughout the Arctic, gathering in colonies comprising thousands of birds.

As well as gulls, there are auks that come ashore only to breed, spending the remainder of the year far out at sea. These include the little auk, or dovekie (*Alle alle*), which is less than 8 inches (20 cm) long, and the razorbill (*Alca torda*), which is about twice that size. Guillemots are also auks, and there are several species, including the guillemot, or common murre (*Uria aalge*); Brünnich's guillemot, or thick-lipped murre (*U. lomvia*); and black guillemot (*Cepphus grylle*). In the west there is also the Atlantic puffin (*Fratercula arctica*), a bird about 1 foot (30 cm) long with a large head and striped bill that grows larger and more brightly colored during the breeding season. Puffins nest in burrows and feed on fish. Two other puffins breed along the Arctic Pacific coast, the horned puffin (*F. corniculata*) and tufted puffin (*Lunda cir-*

rhata). There are also ducks, such as the eider duck (*Somateria mollisima*).

The large colonies attract predators. The most voracious are the great black-backed gull (*Larus marinus*) and glaucous gull (*L. hyperboreus*). They will kill adults or chicks. There are also thieves. The common gull (*L. canus*) and three species of jaegers, or skuas (*Stercorarius species*), harass birds carrying food to their young, forcing them to drop it then swooping to catch it in midair.

Arctic Fox

Arctic foxes (*Alopex lagopus*) take eggs and hunt birds as well as rodents and are found throughout the tundra and Arctic in North America and Eurasia. They are smaller than red foxes, measuring about 21 inches (53 cm) with a 12-inch (30-cm) tail, but look bigger because of their long fur—in relation to its body size, the longest of any arctic mammal. The fur turns pure white in winter, and in the southern part of its range there is a variant that remains a blue-gray color year round.

White and blue fox fur was very valuable when fur coats were fashionable and the animals have been extensively hunted. Detailed records of the numbers killed have allowed scientists to trace fluctuations in arctic fox populations. These follow those of the lemmings and voles, indicating how dependent the foxes are on the rodents.

Musk Oxen

Musk oxen (*Ovibos moschatus*) are even more superbly adapted than foxes to the harsh Arctic climate. Although they are hoofed animals related to cattle, musk oxen are not true oxen, but goat-

antelopes, a subfamily (Caprinae) of 26 species that have adapted to extreme environments. They are big animals, about 7 feet (2 m) long, protected by a thick, waterproof undercoat covered by an outer coat of long, coarse hairs that reach almost to the ground. This provides such good insulation that snow falling on it does not melt. The very broad feet of a musk ox distribute its weight, making it easier for the animal to move over soft snow—an adaptation that parallels that in the camel (pages 90–95.).

Both sexes have big, very solid horns. These almost meet at the center of the forehead to form a plate about 9 inches (23 cm) thick across the front of the head, from which they curve downward and outward, turning up at the ends, like a pair of sharp hooks. These are formidable weapons with which musk oxen defend themselves against wolves, their principal predators.

Musk oxen move in herds of up to 100 animals, although young bulls driven out by older bulls during the mating season may live alone or in small bachelor herds. When wolves threaten, the musk oxen form a circle, facing outward with their heads down, with the calves inside. The wolves face a circle that is constantly turning to present them with the horns of the biggest and strongest oxen. A wolf that comes within their reach is likely to be impaled and tossed. If it falls inside the circle it will be trampled to death.

Despite their defenses, musk oxen became extinct in Eurasia about 3,000 years ago and by the 20th century they survived only in Canada and Greenland. From there they have now been successfully reintroduced in Alaska, Norway, and Siberia.

Caribou

Caribou, known in Europe as *reindeer* (*Rangifer tarandus*), also have broad, "snowshoe" feet and they, too, are hunted by wolves. They are small deer, males standing about 4 feet (1.2 m) tall at the shoulder and females being somewhat smaller. They are the only deer in which both sexes have antlers. Snow falling on their thick coats does not melt.

There are several populations of caribou, sometimes classified as subspecies, and one of them, the barren ground caribou (*R. t. groenlandicus*), undertakes long seasonal migrations. They live in northern Alaska and Canada and in western Greenland. In spring they assemble in large herds and move northward, always following the same routes and traveling 1,000 miles (1,600 km) or more. Some reach the shores of the Arctic Ocean; others stop inland and spend the summer grazing the tundra vegetation. That is where their young are born in May and June. In September or October they return south, heading for the food and shelter of the pine forests.

In winter, caribou and Eurasian reindeer use their broad feet to shovel away the snow in search of food. The word *caribou* means "shoveler" in the language of the Micmac peoples of northeastern Canada. Their scraping exposes reindeer moss, which is their principal winter food. It is not a moss, but a lichen (*Cladonia rangiferina* and other *Cladonia* species) with shrublike branches about 3 inches (7.5 cm) tall.

Saiga

When scientists first tried to classify the saiga they decided it was a goat. Later they changed their minds and identified it as an antelope. Then it became a gazelle. Today it is considered to be related to both sheep and antelopes. Clearly, its identity is not at all obvious.

The difficulty arises partly from its face and, in particular, its humped, fleshy nose which resembles a short trunk or the nose of a tapir and can be moved about like an elephant's trunk. But inside its structure is much more complicated. It contains intricately arranged bones, hairs, and glands that secrete mucus. During summer, when herds of saiga are migrating and the weather is hot and dusty, the nose filters out the dust before inhaled air enters the respiratory passages. In winter, the air is warmed and moistened as it passes through the long nose, so the animal does not damage its lungs by inhaling bitterly cold, very dry air.

Like many animals that live in strongly seasonal climates, the saiga has a thin summer coat and a long, thick winter coat. Its winter coat adds to its peculiar appearance by making its body look much too bulky for its thin legs. It is adapted to a dry climate and is unable to walk through snow that is more than about 16 inches (40 cm) deep. Its legs can be injured if its feet pierce a layer of ice covering snow. Compacted snow can also deprive a saiga of food, because it is unable to dig through it to the vegetation beneath, even if the layer is quite shallow. It feeds on shrubs, grass, herbs, and lichens.

Saiga live on the treeless steppes and semideserts from the Volga River to central Asia. They are nomads, constantly on the move in search of pasture. In summer they migrate northwards, returning to the south for the winter. During their migrations the herds cover 50–70 miles (80–113 km) a day. In spring the males migrate first, setting off in late April in groups of up to 2,000. The females all give birth, within about a week of one another. Between eight and 10 days later the young are ready to move, and they set off with their mothers in herds of 100,000 or more.

Herds of more than 200,000 have sometimes been seen. Once they reach the summer grazing grounds the big herds disperse into smaller groups of between 30 and 40 individuals. In autumn the big herds assemble once more for the journey south.

The saiga's diet and way of life are similar to those of the caribou and, also like the caribou, it is smaller than most antelopes and even smaller than some sheep. An adult stands 2–2.6 feet (60–80 cm) tall at the shoulder and weighs 46–112 pounds (21–51 kg).

SAVED FROM EXTINCTION

Male saiga have horns. These are 8–10 inches (20–25 cm) long, slightly curved, and have ridged rings along them. It was its horns that brought the saiga close to extinction.

Powdered saiga horn is used in Chinese medicine, and the animals were hunted for their horns. This greatly reduced their numbers, and by 1917 very few saiga remained. In 1920 the saiga was given complete protection from hunting and slowly it recovered. Today there are more than 1 million saiga.

The harsh environment imposes its own dangers and, like most animals that live in cold deserts, from time to time its population decreases sharply. It has responded to the challenge in two ways: behavioral and physiological. Its nomadic way of life allows the saiga to travel long distances in search of food; that is its behavioral response. Its young mature very quickly; that is the physiological response. Females are sexually mature when they are eight months old and males when they are 20 months old. Rapid maturation makes it possible for the population to recover fairly quickly following a period during which many animals die.

Despite its recovery, poaching has intensified in recent years, and the saiga is still not out of danger. The species as a whole is officially classed as "vulnerable," which means its numbers are falling, the area it occupies is decreasing, and there is at least a 10 percent chance that without protection it will become extinct within the next 100 years. The Mongolian saiga, which is one of the two subspecies of saiga (*S. t. mongolica*) is classed as "endangered." This means there is at least a 20 percent chance that it will become extinct within 20 years.

Wolves, Wolverines, and Polar Bears

As the herds of migrating caribou move slowly across the tundra the wolves are never far away. Caribou are an important source of food for North American populations of the tundra wolf (*Canis lupus tundarum*). Those of Asia follow the migrations of the saiga antelope (*Saiga tatarica*) as it migrates across the cold, dry steppe.

The tundra wolf is one of several subspecies of the gray, or timber, wolf (*Canis lupus*). It occurs throughout the Arctic and tundra and is largest of all wolves—up to 5 feet (1.5 m) long with a tail about 20 inches (50 cm) long. Its long coat is pale in color and often white, although tundra wolves can be brown or even black.

All wolves will catch ground-nesting birds, hares, and other small mammals, and they also eat berries. They will eat carrion, scavenge from trash cans, and, given the opportunity, attack domestic animals. Where these foods are available wolves hunt alone, but a single wolf will not attack a caribou. For this the wolves hunt in packs, and if a single hungry wolf comes across caribou it will howl to summon other members of the pack to join in the pursuit—and share the resulting food.

Social Life

Domesticated dogs are descended from wolves and have inherited from them the social behavior that allows them to fit so easily into human society. Wolves often mate for life, and wolf society is based on an adult male and female and their offspring. Cubs are born in early spring and provided they are well fed they are big and strong enough to travel with the pack by the time they are about 4 months old. Some of the young leave the pack during the following winter, but others remain. They help to raise the next litter of their brothers and sisters. The size of a wolf pack depends on the type of prey on which its members depend. A typical pack of tundra wolves numbers about 10 animals.

Living closely together, with a central area in which the cubs are born and to which the pack returns regularly, wolves are constantly interacting with each other. Each individual has a clearly defined status, and there are one dominant male and one dominant female. Usually these are the only animals to mate and fights can occur when other wolves contest their right to do so. Other pack members sometimes seek "promotion" by challenging the wolf immediately dominant to them, young cubs establish their rank among their siblings, but most of the time life is peaceful and the hierarchy maintained by gesture and body language.

A pack occupies a territory of 40–400 square miles (104–1,040 sq km) and the dominant pair mark its boundaries with urine. There is some overlap with the territories of adjacent packs, but a pack will fight any strange individual or pack it meets. From time to time, therefore, a wolf howls and the rest of the pack joins in. This advertises the pack's presence and allows any other pack in the area to avoid it. Sometimes another pack will howl in reply. Wolves do not howl very often, however, for fear of attracting a rival pack that is seeking a fight that will allow it to take over the territory. In general, a pack will move away quietly if it hears howling unless it is feeding at a recent kill or has young cubs traveling with it. These it will defend, especially if the pack is a fairly large one.

Solitary wolves also howl as a way of keeping in touch with other pack members when they are all hunting alone. A wolf that has left the pack into which it was born and is living alone very rarely howls or makes scent marks. It wanders in search of a mate with which it can start its own pack but is wary of drawing attention to itself.

Wolverine

Wolves are not the only large predators of the Arctic. There is also the wolverine (*Gulo gulo*), a member of the weasel family (Mustelidae). Its head and body measure about 3 feet (90 cm), its tail is about 8 inches (20 cm) long, and it is heavily built with a long, dark coat and long muzzle that make it look a little like a small bear. It lives mainly on the ground, but wolverines can and do climb trees. A wolverine is a fierce hunter and would have no difficulty defending itself against a solitary wolf, although grizzly bears and packs of wolves sometimes kill wolverines. In some countries wolverines are hunted for their fur or for sport or because they are regarded as pests that prey on farm animals.

They live in the remotest regions and are generally solitary, although through the summer and fall females are accompanied by their young—called *kits*. Females mark out and defend large territories. Males have smaller territories that overlap those of two or three females with which they mate. Mating takes place in summer, but the fertilized eggs are not implanted until they have undergone a period of dormancy in the womb.

THE "GLUTTON"

For many years the wolverine was seriously misunderstood. It was characterized as a "glutton" because naturalists believed it ate until it could eat no more, then squeezed itself through a narrow space to push the food out of its stomach so it could continue eating until all the food was consumed. This is obviously nonsense, but it is true that the wolverine will eat berries, carcasses of animals killed by other predators, birds, and small mammals, and in winter it hunts caribou. It is quite capable of killing an animal many times its own size.

The wolverine has broad feet, and, like several other mustelids, it walks on the soles of them— this is said to be a *plantigrade gait*. Its feet end in claws, and the plantigrade gait keeps these clear of the ground so they remain strong and sharp. Both wolverines and caribou have broad feet, but the caribou is much the heavier, so the weight pressing on each of its feet is greater and they sink deeper into soft snow than those of a wolverine. On a hard surface the caribou can outrun a wolverine, but the wolverine is faster over soft snow. It kills a much larger animal by jumping on its back and holding on with its claws until the prey tires and falls.

A wolverine cannot eat prey that is much bigger than itself in a single meal, but in the Arctic desert no animal can afford to waste food. Instead, it exploits a climatic advantage: food keeps well in subzero temperatures. Having eaten its fill, the wolverine tears what is left of its kill into fragments—its jaws can break even large bones—and hides each piece in a different place. Perhaps it was this gory activity that gave rise to the myth of gluttony. A female wolverine has been seen to return to one of her stores months later, to feed herself and her kits.

Polar Bear

The wolf and wolverine are powerful and efficient hunters, but the most impressive of all the Arctic predators is the polar bear (*Ursus maritimus*). It is also the largest of all land-dwelling

carnivores. A male can be almost 10 feet (3 m) long and weigh 1,400 pounds (635 kg) or more and females are only slightly smaller.

A polar bear can outrun a caribou over a short distance. Caribou and musk oxen form part of its diet, as well as smaller mammals such as hares and lemmings, birds, and some plant matter, and it will scavenge carcasses of walruses and whales, but it feeds mainly on seals. Sometimes it catches them by waiting beside a breathing hole or a small area of open water for a seal to surface, then seizing it and dragging it onto the ice with tremendous force. At other times it will stalk a seal that is resting on land or an ice floe. Seals can outmaneuver it in the water, so it hunts only on the surface.

Polar bears live throughout the Arctic. In the course of a year an individual will travel more than 600 miles (965 km) in search of food, but most remain within their own geographic region. They are strong swimmers and can spend hours in the water. Their creamy white fur, thicker in winter than in summer, is completely waterproof, and beneath it a thick layer of body fat adds further insulation. Its fur covers the whole of its body except for its nose and the pads of its feet, and its feet are partly webbed. Its small ears also help conserve body warmth.

Most of the time polar bears are solitary, although they sometimes congregate when there is a large source of food or when the melting of the sea ice forces them onto land. At these times encounters are usually peaceful, but during the mating season males will fight rivals.

Mating takes place in early summer, but implantation of the fertilized eggs is delayed, so the gestation period is long—195–265 days. In November and December pregnant females choose where their young will be born and dig out maternity chambers in the deep snow. Cubs are born in December and January and remain with their mothers in the maternity chambers until March or April, being fed on milk that contains 31 percent fat. Their mothers do not eat, relying instead on body fat they accumulated the previous summer. The family stays together until the second summer and occasionally through the second winter.

Animal Life of the Antarctic

Visitors to Antarctica will not encounter lemmings or hares, or the land-dwelling predatory mammals that hunt them. Drake Passage, the stretch of ocean separating the southernmost tip of South America from the northernmost tip of the Antarctic Peninsula, is about 600 miles (965 km) wide at its narrowest point, isolating the continent behind an ocean barrier land animals cannot cross. Were any such animal to survive the crossing it would quickly perish in the harsh Antarctic environment. The mainland climate is much more severe than that of the Arctic (page 20), and there are no plants bigger than mosses, algae, and lichens—and even those can be found in only a few places (page 74).

The only animals are rather more than 100 species of invertebrates, half of which are parasites of birds or seals. Mites are the most abundant, because they are the most tolerant of the extreme conditions. These are arachnids belonging to the order Acarina. Some are parasites found in the nostrils of seals and penguins, but many of them feed on the algae and lichens or on microscopically small soil organisms, and there are also predacious mites that eat other mites or springtails. One mite species, *Nanorchestes antarcticus,* has been found at 85°32' S at an elevation of 7,365 feet (2,245 m). There are also ticks, lice, and one species of flea (*Glaciopsyllus antarcticus*), all of which are parasites. The flea lives in the nests of the southern, or silver-gray, fulmar (*Fulmarus glacialoides*) and snow petrel (*Pagodroma nivea*). When the breeding season ends and the birds depart, the flea hibernates until they return. Where there is soil there are springtails, tiny insects of the order Collembola. These are locally plentiful, but of about 2,000 species that occur in the world as a whole, only about 20 are found in Antarctica.

Sheathbills

An ocean crossing presents no difficulty for sea birds, however, and more than 40 species breed in Antarctica. There is even a land bird, the Antarctic pipit (*Anthus antarcticus*), that breeds in South Georgia and feeds on small invertebrate animals. Sheathbills, composing the family Chionididae, also breed on Antarctic islands.

Sheathbills are thought to be related to both gulls and land-dwelling birds, so they form an evolutionary link between the two groups. There are two species. The black-faced sheathbill (*Chionis minor*) lives all year on some of the offshore islands. The snowy sheathbill (*C. alba*) breeds on

the Antarctic mainland but migrates in winter to the Falklands (Las Malvinas) and Argentina.

Both species live in the same way, running about on the ground and flying only when they must, feeding on anything they can find. They scavenge around the research stations, grow fat on carrion from stillborn seal pups, and harass penguins when they need extra food for their own young. A pair of sheathbills will establish a territory that they defend vigorously. The territory contains a number of penguin nests and their occupants, and the aim is to rob the penguin parents of the food—mainly krill (page 114)—they are taking to their chicks. They will also steal penguin eggs and eat penguin droppings.

Penguins

Penguins are the most famous natives, of course, although they are not confined to Antarctica. There are species, including the little blue, or fairy, penguin (*Eudyptula minor*), that breed around the shores of South Island New Zealand, southern Australia, and South Africa, and along the western coast of South America all the way to the equator, but penguins do not occur in the Northern Hemisphere.

Penguin is the name that was given, in the 16th century, to the great auk (*Pinguinus impennis*), a black and white sea bird of the North Atlantic that is now extinct. On land it had an upright stance and waddling gait, and when European explorers found similar birds in the Southern Hemisphere the name was also applied to them.

There are 18 species of penguins in 6 genera, the only family (Spheniscidae) in the order Sphenisciformes, and they are instantly recognizable. Species vary in size and detailed markings, but all of them are flightless birds that stand erect, walk with a waddling gait on short legs, and as adults have dark blue or more commonly black backs and wings and white fronts. They range in size from the emperor penguin (*Aptenodytes forsteri*), standing about 4 feet (1.2 m) tall and weighing up to 70 pounds (32 kg), which is the biggest, to the little blue penguin, which is barely 16 inches (41 cm) tall.

Staying Warm

They are superbly adapted to life in a cold climate. Although some species live far from Antarctica, the coasts and islands they inhabit are bathed

by cool currents—the Peru Current that flows along the South American coast, the Benguela Current affecting Southern Africa, and the West Wind Drift that passes southern Australia and New Zealand. They do not enter warm tropical waters, and only two species, the Galápagos (*Spheniscus mendiculus*) and Humboldt (*S. humboldti*), breed in tropical latitudes. Most species occur between latitudes 45° S and 60° S.

Penguins are aquatic birds, so in addition to tolerating the low air temperatures of the Antarctic, they must also remain active in water that is close to freezing. The ancestors of penguins were able to fly, but as well as losing this ability, penguins have evolved highly modified feathers. These are small, almost scalelike, and form a dense covering, three layers thick, that is fully waterproof. Beneath the skin, most penguins have a thick layer of fat, and an efficient network of blood vessels where the legs and wings join the body prevents the loss of body warmth to the wings and feet (page 82). The overall body shape of the bird also helps it conserve heat. Its feet, wings, and head are small in relation to its body, giving a penguin a small surface area in relation to its volume. The tropical species have much larger wings and patches of bare skin on their faces to help them lose excess heat.

Emperor Penguin

Some species are better than others at coping with extreme cold. The emperor penguin is probably the best of all. It breeds in the fall (May). Males incubate the eggs, carrying them on their feet, covered by a fold of skin. Incubation lasts 60 days and takes place on the open sea ice, where the average air temperature is -4°F (-20°C) but can fall to -80°F (-62°C) and the wind blows at an average 16 mph (26 km/h) but often much harder. To help keep warm, the emperors huddle together in groups of up to 5,000 birds, with about 11 birds to every square yard of ice surface (10 per sq m). Birds exposed to the wind on the outside of the group are constantly moving forward along the sides and then toward the center, so the whole crowd moves slowly downwind. Once the eggs have hatched, both parents feed them.

King penguins (*A. patagonicus*) are close relatives of emperor penguins and also large—about 3 feet (90 cm) tall. Like emperors, they build no nests and carry their eggs on their feet while incubating them, but they breed in spring and summer. Other species build simple nests of sticks

and stones and Humboldt and jackass (*Spheniscus demersus*) penguins nest in burrows or other sheltered places.

Sociability

On land, penguins move by hopping, waddling, or tobogganing on their fronts. In water they swim fast and are highly maneuverable, using their wings for propulsion and their feet as rudders. They feed on fish, squid, cuttlefish, and krill. Adélie (*Pygoscelis adeliae*), chinstrap (*P. antarctica*), gentoo (*P. papua*), and macaroni (*Eudyptes chrysolophus*) penguins feed mainly on krill and other crustaceans.

Even while they are feeding at sea penguins move in groups, and at breeding time these highly sociable birds form rookeries numbering many thousands of pairs, often of several species but with each species occupying its own area. Parents defend the small area around their nests. They have elaborate courtship rituals and a repertoire of calls and gestures by which birds returning from feeding locate their partners and are recognized by them.

Vast congregations of breeding birds attract predators seeking eggs and chicks, and penguins have enemies. Skuas are also known as *jaegers*,

which is the German word for "hunter." There are three species (genus *Catharacta*) and they feed on fish, krill, and small birds as well as penguin eggs and chicks.

Albatrosses

Skuas have been known to fly from Antarctica to Greenland, but the albatrosses are the most aerial of all Antarctic birds. They occur throughout the Southern Hemisphere and a few of the 13 species are found in the North Pacific, but most live between 45° S and 70° S. Albatrosses go ashore, on remote islands, only to breed. They spend the rest of their time far out at sea, riding the wind over the Antarctic Ocean, sleeping on the sea surface, and drinking sea water. Salt glands in their nostrils accumulate and excrete surplus salt. They feed on plankton, fish, squid, and crustaceans. They also follow ships, a habit that has given rise to the sailors' myth that they are birds of ill omen.

Albatrosses have a flying technique that allows them to remain airborne for hours. A bird glides downwind, gradually losing height as it does so. Its airspeed—the speed at which air flows over its wings—is equal to its forward speed over the sea minus the speed of the wind, because that

Chinstrap penguin colony (Gerry Ellis / ENP Images)

is moving in the same direction as the bird. The wind very close to the sea surface is slowed by friction, and when it is almost touching the wave tops the albatross turns into the wind. The air speed is the equal to the speed of the bird over the water plus the speed of the wind. This accelerates the air flowing over its wings, thus increasing the amount of lift the wings generate, allowing the albatross to climb. It climbs in this way through the layer of relatively slow wind and enters the faster wind that is not slowed by friction, further increasing its airspeed and allowing it to climb still higher. In this way it climbs to about 50 feet (15 m), turns downwind, and once more starts its slow descent.

Albatrosses constitute the family Diomedeidae in the order Procellariiformes, or "tubenoses." The name refers to their nostrils, which are tubular and are located near the base of the bill, rather than on top as in most birds. With a wingspan of about 10 feet (3 m), the wandering albatross (*Diomedea exulans*) has the longest wings of any bird.

Life in Polar Seas

Penguins are harassed by skuas during the breeding season, but a much more terrible enemy awaits them in the sea, and it is fear of that hunter that often halts a party of penguins just before they plunge into the water. Leopard seals (*Hydrurga leptonyx*) eat fish, krill, squid, and other seals, but penguins constitute about one-quarter of their diet.

About 10 feet (3 m) long and weighing about 770 pounds (300 kg), it is the biggest of the Antarctic seals and the only one to prey on birds and mammals. Its body is spotted like that of a leopard and its body is slender, with a long neck. It is built for speed, but dangerous only while it is in the water. Like all seals it moves clumsily on land with no help from its hind flippers—sea lions and walruses pull their hind flippers forward beneath their bodies when on land and use them in walking. Even a penguin has no difficulty escaping from a leopard seal that has hauled itself onto an ice floe, so it does not bother to try catching them and penguins ignore it.

Sometimes a leopard seal will rest peacefully on the ice next to a crabeater seal (*Lobodon carcinophagus*). Crabeaters are smaller than leopard seals and much faster on the ice, where they may be capable of moving at 15 mph (24 km/h). The two species are often found together, in the water as well as out of it, but in the water leopard seals prey on crabeaters, especially on their newly weaned pups. Apart from leopard seals, the main predator of crabeater seals is the killer whale (*Orcinus orca*).

The crabeater seal is believed to be the most numerous of all the seals and possibly the most abundant large mammal on the planet, with the exception of humans. There are believed to be between 15 million and 40 million of them distributed throughout a range of about 8.5 million square miles (22 million sq km) in winter and about 1.6 million square miles (4 million sq km) in summer, when the area of pack ice decreases.

They feed almost exclusively on krill, crustaceans on which penguins, baleen whales, and other Antarctic animals also depend—krill are more important than penguins in the diet of leopard seals. Crabeater seals eat more krill even than the whales, consuming up to an estimated 176 million tons (160 million tonnes) a year, which they strain from the water through their premolar and molar teeth, which are shaped like combs with four (premolars) or five (molars) tines.

Farther south, the Weddell seal (*Leptonychotes weddelli*) breeds on the permanent ice shelves surrounding Antarctica. It feeds on squid and bottom-dwelling fish and invertebrates, which it catches by diving to depths of up to 1,800 feet (550 m). The Ross seal (*Ommatophoca rossi*) also feeds mainly on squid, hunting from remote patches of pack ice.

Krill

The krill on which so many Antarctic birds and mammals depend are related to the shrimps, crayfish, lobsters, and crabs. They look like shrimps, but there are anatomical differences that set them apart, so they form a separate order, the Euphausiaceae, with 85 species. They inhabit most oceans, some species living near the surface, others below it at depths down to 6,500 feet (2,000 m), and some migrate between surface and deep waters. One member of these species, *Euphausia superba*, is about 2 inches (5 cm) long and orange or red in color and transparent, with big black eyes and five pairs of swimming legs. *Euphausia superba* feed mainly on phytoplankton—microscopic green plants that drift in surface waters—and also consume some zooplankton—planktonic animals.

This is the principal species on which many Antarctic animals depend. It lives in surface waters of the Antarctic Ocean, where it forms huge swarms, often more than 15 feet (4.5 m) thick, that color the water over several square miles. A swarm contains up to 1,800 individuals in every cubic foot (63,500 per cu m). They take 2 years to mature and are believed to live for 5–10 years. In all, there are estimated to be at least 550 million tons (500 million tonnes) of krill, or 500 million million (5×10^{14}) individuals, so they may be the most numerous of all animals. A blue whale (*Balaenoptera musculus*) consumes about 4 tons (3.6 tonnes) of them every day.

Krill have been caught commercially since the early 1970s, principally by vessels from Russia, Ukraine, and Japan. The krill fishery is monitored closely by the Scientific Committee established under the terms of the Convention on the Conservation of Antarctic Marine Living Resources, which the member nations of the Antarctic Treaty signed in 1981 to protect the animals dependent on the krill. The first records of commercial catches were made in 1969–70 (the Antarctic fishing season runs from July 1 to June 30). In most seasons from 1979–80 until 1991–92 annual catches exceeded 330,000 tons (300,000 tonnes). The catch peaked in 1985–86, at 468,457 tons (425,870 tonnes). After 1992 the catch decreased to between 88,000–110,000 tons (80,000–100,000 tonnes). According to the Scientific Committee, the decline was due to a reduction in demand for krill rather than overfishing. Biologists suggest it would be possible to catch 65 million tons (59 million tonnes) a year sustainably and no restrictions are placed on the quantity that can be caught.

Salmon fishermen from the northeastern United States and Canada have protested against large-scale krill fishing in the North Atlantic, because salmon also feed on krill.

Arctic Seals

Young ribbon seals (*Phoca fasciata*) also feed on krill, but in the Bering and Okhotsk Seas. As adults they feed on fish and squid. They are small seals, about 5 feet (1.5 m) long. Their common name refers to the distinctive bands in their fur around the neck, rear part of the body, and each flipper.

Hooded seals (*Cystophora cristata*) are bigger—about 8 feet (2.4 m) long. Altogether there are about 325,000 of them. They spend much of their time far out at sea, feeding on fish and squid for which they dive to considerable depths, but in summer they migrate to the Arctic, especially to the ice floes near Greenland, where they all haul themselves out of the water and molt their fur.

The "hood" is an enlargement of the nasal cavity of mature males that forms a sac on the front of the head. The male is able to inflate the sac, which is like a black balloon, and use it to amplify the calls with which he threatens rivals. Alternatively, he can blow the lining of one nostril out through the other nostril and inflate it as a red balloon.

The ringed seal (*Phoca hispida*), the most numerous species in the Canadian Arctic, is an animal about 5 feet (1.5 m) long when adult. It is less common in Eurasia. The total population probably amounts to about 2.5 million. Its name refers to the pale rings that mark the dark gray fur on its sides and back. At sea it feeds on krill and other crustaceans and also eats some fish. Inshore it seeks fish and crustaceans that live on or near the seabed. It rarely goes on land, but hauls itself onto ice shelves or less commonly ice floes, where its young are born, from February to March in the Baltic Sea and March to April in the Canadian Arctic.

In early winter both males and females dig lairs in the snow that accumulates around and then over their breathing holes in the ice. Males haul themselves into their lairs to rest, but females give birth to their pups in the lairs they dig and often make two or three pupping lairs within a short distance of each other, perhaps as alternative refuges to which they can take their young if danger threatens. The lairs provide some protection from polar bears and Arctic foxes, but they are not difficult to find and predators take more than half of all newborn pups.

Bearded seals (*Erignathus barbatus*) have long, bushy whiskers. These are bulky animals, about 7 feet (2.1 m) long, that inhabit shallow waters throughout the Arctic Ocean, with individuals sometimes straying as far south as Japan. No one knows how many of them there are, but their population is estimated to be several hundred thousand. They rest and breed on ice floes and feed on bottom-dwelling fish and invertebrates. Spotted seals (*Phoca largha*) also feed on the seabed and give birth on ice floes. They are a little larger than ringed seals.

Walruses

Bigger and heavier than any seal, the walrus (*Odobenus rosmarus*) is found throughout the Arctic. There are two subspecies, the Atlantic (*O.r. rosmarus*) and Pacific (*O.r. divergens*) walruses. Pacific walruses are bigger than those of the Atlantic. An adult Atlantic male is about 10 feet (3 m) long and weighs about 1.4 tons (1.3 tonnes). Females are rather smaller. Walruses have been hunted extensively, but hunting is now controlled. There are estimated to be about 20,000 Atlantic and at least 200,000 Pacific walruses.

Walruses are highly social. When they haul themselves onto the ice or land they usually do so in such large numbers they are forced to lie on top of each other. Their colonies are generally peaceful if noisy, but walruses will vigorously defend themselves, their young, and each other. Polar bears and killer whales hunt walruses, and their calves are particularly vulnerable.

They feed on invertebrate animals such as worms, sea cucumbers, crustaceans, and especially clams, mussels, and other bivalve mollusks. Occasionally they eat fish and seals. Their food is obtained from the sediment on the sea bottom and a walrus has been observed to dive to a depth of 370 feet (113 m) and remain submerged for almost 25 minutes. They can probably dive deeper. There is little light at such depths, even in summer, and in winter the darkness is total. A walrus uses its strong whiskers to find food and can dig animals from the sediment by rummaging with its snout or spitting a jet of water into their burrows.

Their tusks are used for hauling themselves out of the water, in fighting, and as status symbols. When a dominant animal rears up to display its huge tusks subordinates move out of its way, allowing it to go where it chooses and occupy the best position. The tusks, which can be 3.5 feet (1 m) long and weigh more than 10 pounds (4.5 kg), are enlarged upper canine teeth.

Walruses also have loose skin, lying in folds at every joint, that can be more than 2 inches (5 cm) thick, and males have lumps like warts on the neck and shoulders. They change color. When they are warm, blood vessels in the skin expand to help them lose heat and the animals look pink. When they are cold—as they often are when surfacing from a dive—the blood vessels are constricted and the animals are gray.

When Deserts Grew Crops

Petra is uninhabited today, except by wandering tribes and tourists, but from about 300 B.C.E. to 100 C.E. it was a thriving metropolis and center of caravan trade. After that it began to decline. By then the city lay within the Roman Empire and for a time after its citizens had converted to Christianity it was the seat of a bishopric, but trade routes were shifting. It was captured by Muslims in the seventh century and the Crusaders built a castle there in the 12th century, but then Petra fell into ruin until 1812, when it was rediscovered for Europeans by the Swiss traveler Johann Ludwig Burckhardt (1784–1817).

It is located about 16 miles (26 km) northwest of the town of Ma'an, in Jordan. The map shows its location. Today Petra is in the Jordanian Desert and surrounded by other deserts—the Negev Desert to the west, the Syrian Desert to the north, and the Arabian Desert to the south. People do not build cities in the middle of deserts, so clearly the region was not always so arid and inhospitable. The city the Romans occupied had been standing and prospering for many centuries, and that meant its citizens were supplied with water and with food grown on nearby farms.

When we are shown movies set in the Near East or Egypt in biblical times the landscapes we see are those of today and the moviemakers evidently feel it unnecessary to explain how it is that so many people were able to wrest a living from such barren land. If the scene were to be depicted accurately, however, there would be no mystery. We would see fields growing wheat, barley, and other crops; cattle and sheep grazing; and trees bearing citrus and other fruits. In those days this land was fertile, although the desert was never far away and the biblical writers knew it well.

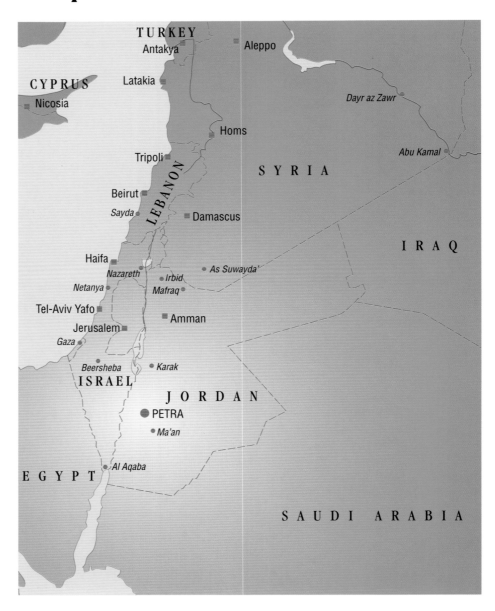

Location of the ancient city of Petra

The Granary of Rome

In those days North Africa was known as "the granary of Rome." Large areas were farmed and the produce exported. The outline of fields can still be seen from the air in parts of what is now the Sahara Desert. Around 120 C.E., Ptolemy (Claudius Ptolemaus), an astronomer, geographer, and mathematician who flourished in the second century C.E., kept a record of the weather in Alexandria, the city where he lived from 127 to

145 C.E. Alexandria is on the coast of Egypt, and Ptolemy recorded that it rained in every month of the year except August and there was thunder in all the summer months. Today, the average annual rainfall in Alexandria, calculated over 45 years, is 7 inches (178 mm), and no rain falls between the end of April and the beginning of October.

People were migrating northward at the time Petra was flourishing. Olives were being grown farther north than had been possible in earlier times and in about 300 C.E. records of wine imports to Britain cease, possibly because that Roman province was self-sufficient in wine.

Farther east there were other towns in regions that are now desert. Silks, spices, and other luxuries from the Orient were carried to Europe by camel caravans traveling along the Great Silk Road. Towns and Buddhist shrines were built at points along the route, presumably at places where the caravans paused to rest and graze their animals. The remains of some of them can still be seen. It was during the first decades of the fourth century C.E. that conditions began to change. The weather became cooler and drier. There were severe droughts and the water level fell drastically in the Caspian Sea. In central Asia the increasingly arid climate caused the grasslands to deteriorate. Nomadic tribes found it increasingly difficult to feed themselves and their horses, and they began migrating westward. Battles with the Asian tribes weakened the Roman Empire to such an extent that it retreated and finally collapsed.

Canoes in the Sahara

This was not the only climate change to affect what are now deserts. Much earlier, around 5,500 years ago, people living in what is now Aounrhet, in central Algeria, depicted their way of life in paintings on cave walls. These show people herding cattle and hunting hippopotamus from canoes. Other, still older paintings show a variety of animals, including crocodiles, rhinoceroses, buffalo, and elephants. Lake Chad was then a large inland sea. Prior to 6000 B.C.E., the annual rainfall in southern Libya was 8–16 inches (200–400 mm) and rivers flowed year round from the Tibesti Mountains. Today it rarely rains at all in this region.

Australia, too, had a much wetter climate prior to about 2500 B.C.E. It was about then that climates throughout the world started to become cooler and drier and deserts everywhere began to expand. This change seems to have marked the peak of the climatic warming that began with the end of the most recent glaciation (page 26). Warm weather is usually wet weather, because evaporation increases as temperatures rise and so, therefore, does precipitation. Falling temperatures reduce the rate of evaporation and produce a drier climate.

The Indus Valley

Between about 2500 and 1700 B.C.E. a civilization flourished in the Indus Valley, centered on the cities of Harappa and Mohenjo-Daro. Farms covering an area much greater than the farmed area of the Nile Valley grew cereal crops, dates, melons, and possibly cotton and raised livestock. At that time the annual rainfall was 16–30 inches (400–760 mm) and occasionally crops were ruined by floods.

By 1700 B.C.E., however, the climate was becoming drier. Crops failed repeatedly and the cities were abandoned. The change happened slowly, but it was relentless. Today the Indus Valley marks the western boundary of the Thar Desert (page 10). The town of Sukkur, in Pakistan, lies close to the ruins of Mohenjo-Daro. It receives an average 3.2 inches (81.5 mm) of rain a year. The increasing aridity also affected all the civilizations of the Middle and Near East, Egypt, and the Mediterranean.

Wetter Middle Ages and the Little Ice Age

More recently, the climate was warmer and wetter in the Middle Ages, from the 11th to 14th centuries. The northern boundary of the Sahara lay then at about 27° N, in the center of Morocco, Algeria, Libya, and Egypt. Most of western Africa lay within the Mali Empire (page 118), the principal city of which was Timbuktu (Tombouctou), on the Niger River.

Climates throughout the world became colder and drier in the 16th and 17th centuries, during the period known as the *Little Ice Age* (page 164). The African summer monsoon did not extend so far north as it had previously. This sometimes resulted in flooding of the Niger, carrying excessive water northward from the Tropics, but it also produced a series of prolonged droughts.

Cahokia

North America has also experienced the effects of changing climate. Six miles (10 km) to the east of St. Louis, Missouri, Cahokia Mounds State Park preserves the remains of the biggest Native American city north of Mexico. It includes Monks Mound, a four-sided pyramid covering 14 acres (5.65 ha) that rises in four terraces to a height of 100 feet (30.5 m), as well as many smaller mounds. In all, the site occupies 6 square miles (5.54 sq km), and at its peak, between 1050 and 1250 C.E., its population is believed to have been as high as 40,000 or even 50,000. Its citizens belonged to the Mississippian culture (page 138), and they were fed from farms in the surrounding countryside. Then the climate became drier until, around 1300, Cahokia was abandoned. When French traders and missionaries arrived there they found only small, scattered settlements. The missionaries founded the present town of Cahokia in 1699, naming it after a tribe of the Illinois people.

Cahokia was the biggest settlement, but it was far from being the only one. Around 1000 C.E. Native American peoples were growing corn extensively in eastern Colorado and western Nebraska and in the east there were large villages along the forested river valleys. By 1150 practically the whole of the Colorado Plateau, in the southwest of the state, and the adjacent parts of Arizona and New Mexico were occupied and being farmed. People grew corn, squashes, and beans, and they hunted game.

As the climate deteriorated, the smaller villages in the driest areas were abandoned first, the others followed one by one, and for a time people congregated in the larger towns until they, too, became uninhabitable because their populations could not be fed. The change is recorded in the pollen held in the soil. Trees became more scattered as forests were replaced by prairie and as the process continued the tall grasses, which require more water, gave way to short grasses.

Today the area around the North Platte and South Platte Rivers, on the border of Colorado and Nebraska, is not desert, but that is because the climate has changed again since Cahokia was abandoned. The present annual rainfall averages 16.9 inches (429.1 mm) at Sterling, Colorado, and 20.9 inches (532.1 mm) at North Platte, Nebraska, but people traveling westward in the gold rush of 1849 found the Middle West was so dry as to be almost a desert.

Desert Civilizations

Sharru-ken, the name by which King Sargon was known in Akkadian, the language he himself spoke, was the first of three rulers of the same name. He came to power in about 2370 B.C.E.. According to an Akkadian legend, his mother gave birth to him in secret then hid the baby in a basket made from rushes and floated it on the river. He was found and raised to be a gardener. Ishtar, daughter of the moon god, fell in love with the gardener and made him a king.

Historically, he had been a vizier at the court of the king of Kish, a city-state in what is now southern Iraq. A vizier was a high official, the equivalent of a modern government minister. Sharru-ken founded a city called *Agade,* and from there he came to rule all the Sumerian city-states to the south as well as the region known as *Akkad* farther north. He was styled king of Sumer and Akkad. His empire lay to the south of the modern city of Baghdad, Iraq.

The First Great Empire

This was not a conquest in a military sense, but more like colonization. Sharru-ken and his followers were Semitic desert people. Little by little they moved into Sumerian cities, their descendants came to hold key positions, and finally they took control. Agade itself grew into a great city, covering more than 200 acres (80 ha). It is said there were splendid buildings, paved streets, and drains to carry away surplus water and prevent flooding. The citizens were fed from fields kept watered from irrigation canals and protected by fortresses.

The empire lived by trade and it expanded rapidly. Akkadian records have been found in Cyprus and its territories may have extended as far as Lebanon. It controlled trade in valuable commodities from as far to the east as Afghanistan and south to the Gulf of Oman.

Agade was a port on the banks of either the Tigris or Euphrates—its precise location is unknown, but Akkad was centered on the region where the two rivers are closest together. Babylon later became the capital of the empire occupying the same area. At its quays there were alleged to be ships from all over the Near and Middle East and possibly from as far away as India.

This mighty empire lasted for a little more than 100 years. The rains became irregular, and despite the irrigation system the crops failed repeatedly. The drought continued for more than a century and little by little the wheat fields were buried beneath windblown sand. Agade and the other cities were abandoned and gradually the first of the great empires of the world collapsed. All traces vanished of its magnificent capital, Agade, founded by desert peoples and destroyed by desert. Its lands now form part of the Syrian Desert.

Civilizations Failing

Akkad fell victim to the general climate change that also destroyed the cities of Harappa and Mohenjo-Daro (page 116) in the Indus Valley and these were not the only victims. Civilizations failed in Crete and Greece at about that time. Towns were abandoned in Palestine. There was a serious decrease in the amount of water carried by the Nile, due to a reduction in rainfall over the mountains of Ethiopia, and the anticipated annual floods did not occur (page 124). Egypt suffered severe famines between about 2180 and 2130 B.C.E., between 2000 and 1950 B.C.E., and again around 1750 B.C.E. People migrated into Egypt from the east at these times, perhaps driven from their own lands by famine. This destabilized and finally caused the collapse of the Old and Middle Kingdoms.

Centuries later greatness returned to what had once been the Empire of Sumer and Akkad, and Baghdad became very powerful, but by the Middle Ages the climate was becoming drier again and Iraqi agriculture was in decline. Baghdad received a final blow in 1258 C.E., from which it has never recovered. In that year Mongol warriors entered the city and massacred its people.

Rise of the Mongol Empire

Ironically, it may have been a period of warmer, wetter weather that started the process leading to the establishment of the Mongol Empire. Pastures flourished on the central Asian steppes, leading to an increase in the populations of the nomadic tribes living there, and in the size of their herds. Then, around 1200 C.E., it may be that the climate turned cooler and drier as the region became dominated by weather systems that drew Arctic air southward. Tribal leaders fought for supremacy in the increasingly crowded, deteriorating grasslands around the Gobi Desert.

In 1206, one of these warlords was elected ruler of the Mongols. His name was *Temujin,* or *Genghis Khan.* He defeated the Tatars, nomadic hunters and horse breeders from the south of Lake Baikal, and forged a federation of tribes. Some were Mongol-speaking people, others Turkish, but together they began to expand their territories. Beijing fell to them in 1215, and by 1227, the year Genghis Khan died, their empire stretched from the Caspian to China Seas. Its first capital was Karakorum, but later, under Kublai Khan (1264–94), it was transferred to Beijing.

After the death of Genghis, further campaigns were launched westward. Kiev, Ukraine, fell in 1240, and advance parties of the Mongol army reached Wrocław, Poland. After soundly defeating a joint force of German and Polish knights, the Mongols headed south into Hungary. Those who settled on the grasslands of southern Russia remained there as the Golden Horde, an empire within the empire.

At its maximum extent, in about 1300, the Mongol Empire extended from the Danube in the west to the China Sea in the east, and from the borders of Lithuania in the north to the Himalayas in the south. In the 16th century a descendant of Genghis Khan, Babur (Zahir ud-Din Mohammed, 1483–1530), conquered part of India and became its first Mogul ruler, putting India under Mongol influence. Kublai Khan, the grandson of Genghis, was possibly the greatest of all emperors of China. The Mongol Empire was probably the largest the world has ever seen, and the last traces of it did not disappear in the West until late in the 18th century.

Mali Empire

No part of Africa fell under Mongol rule, although the Golden Horde traded with Egypt, but West Africa had a medieval empire of its own. The Sarakolé Empire of Ghana, developed from a Ghanaian empire founded by immigrant Berber peoples in the fifth century, occupied the region between the Niger and Senegal Rivers. It flourished from the 8th to the 13th century, when it was conquered by Songhai people from the region around Gao and later absorbed into the Mandingo Empire of Mali. This was centered on the middle and upper reaches of the Niger and gave its name to the modern Republic of Mali.

An empire based on trading, it reached the pinnacle of its influence and prosperity during the reign of Mansa Musa (c. 1312–27). Its two principal cities, Gao and Timbuktu, became centers of Islamic learning, and in 1325 a palace and tower for the mosque were built in Timbuktu. By the 1330s the empire extended over most of West Africa, except for Upper Volta, where several emerging states remained independent. Its merchants opened trade routes to the south, from which they obtained gold, kola nuts, and slaves, bought with salt from the desert.

Then in the 15th century, the Mali Empire began to decline. The Songhai regained their independence, but there were disputes over control of the trade routes, and in 1590–91 a Moroccan expedition crossed the desert and defeated the archers and cavalry of the Songhai sultan Ahmad al-Mansur. The Moroccans were unable to restore the trade routes to the south, however, and managed to occupy only the main cities of Gao, Timbuktu, and Djenne. The empire had effectively disappeared.

In 1352 large herds of wild cattle were recorded in parts of the Sahara, but already the climate was changing. Areas that had once been fertile had turned to desert and people living around the Kufra Oasis, at 25° N 22° E in eastern Libya, where formerly there had been large herds of domesticated cattle, had been compelled to abandon the raising of beef. Pollen records show that numbers of water-demanding plants declined sharply between 1300 and 1500. Even so, the climate seems to have been wetter than it is now, because there were oak woodlands in Mauritania as late as the 17th century.

Too many factors are involved for it to be possible to estimate the extent to which changing climate and the resulting encroachment of the desert contributed to the collapse of the Mali Empire. Nevertheless it seems highly probable that the desert played an important part. There, as in central Asia before and thousands of years earlier throughout the Near and Middle East, decreasing rainfall dramatically changed the course of history.

Anatolia, Mesopotamia, and the Birth of Western Civilization

On the Anatolian Plain, in southern Turkey, a few miles south of the modern town of Konya, there are the sites of some of the oldest cities in the world. In November 1958, the archaeologist James Mellaart discovered one of them and excavated it over the course of four seasons, from 1961 to 1965. It is called *Çatal Hüyük* and consists of rectangular, mud brick houses built so closely together that their occupants entered them through the roofs, presumably by means of wooden ladders, and crossed the roofs when they wanted to walk from one house to another. Each house had a hearth and oven and platforms that may have been for sleeping, sitting, or storing goods. There were no doors or windows.

Çatal Hüyük was occupied from about 6500 to 5800 B.C.E. Its inhabitants had sufficient free time from the tasks involved in finding food to make pottery, wooden dishes, and baskets and to weave cloth. There are archaeological remains of other towns not far away, all of similar date. The map shows their relative locations.

Many of the buildings were shrines containing figures of goddesses and animals modeled in high relief on the walls, frescoes depicting hunting scenes, and statuettes. There were also pictures of vultures devouring headless human corpses, evidently illustrating the method by which these people dealt with their dead.

Early Farmers

Like all ancient sites, those in Turkey comprise several layers of occupation, but in levels dated at about 6200 B.C.E. at Süberde and Can Hassan III, and about 5600 B.C.E. at Erbaba and Çatal Hüyük, there are the remains of plant crops and domesticated animals. By then these communities were feeding themselves partly or mainly by farming. Civilization had begun.

Our words *citizen* and *civilization* are derived from the Latin *civitas,* which means "city," and the origin of civilization is dated from the time when people first built and occupied cities. Villages predate cities, of course. From about 11000 B.C.E. villages were springing up throughout the Near East. Their inhabitants ate cereal grains, which they ground into flour or meal, but they did not cultivate them. The cereals they ate were wild and the meat they ate was game. Their culture was paleolithic, based on hunting and gathering.

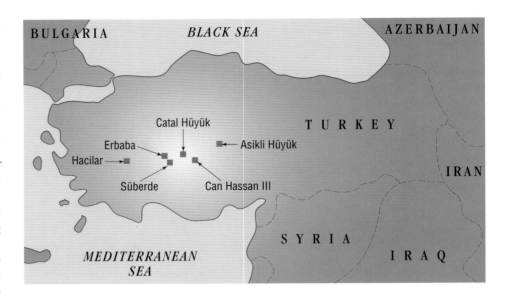

Early agricultural sites in Turkey

Bölling and Allerød Interstadials and the Younger Dryas Stadial

People assembled in these villages during a long period of warm, wet weather that occurred as the ice sheets of the last glaciation (page 26) were disappearing. The evidence for two warm periods—known as *interstadials*—is taken from two sites in Denmark after which they are named. The first, from about 11000 to 10200 B.C.E., is known as the *Bölling Interstadial;* the second, from about 9800 to 9000 B.C.E., as the *Allerød Interstadial.*

Toward the end of the Allerød, the climate was becoming colder and drier as it entered a stadial—cold period—known as the *Younger Dryas.* There were two or perhaps three stadials during the glacial retreat, each of which is identified by pollen from mountain avens (*Dryas octopetala*), a small flowering herb that grows on mountainsides and on low ground in the Far North and that gives these stadials their name. The Younger Dryas, 9000–8000 B.C.E., brought Arctic conditions to northern Eurasia and North America. In southwestern Asia the climate became drier and the cereal grasses—ancestors of modern wheat, barley, oats, and rye—became scarcer.

After the Younger Dryas ended, the climate grew warm again and forests spread into the region. They broke up what had been open range, dividing the landscape into discrete areas and producing within it a complex pattern of natural habitats. The new setting seems to have encouraged people to settle permanently in one

place and to regard the area that they inhabited as territory for their exclusive use. It was around this time that hunting peoples started to herd and corral game animals. Later they started cultivating plant crops, and when the sustained climatic warming allowed cereal grasses to return they began cultivating them. By around 7000 B.C.E. the inhabitants of most of the villages in the Near East were sustaining themselves by farming crops and tending livestock.

Wolf Into Dog

The wolf was the first animal to be tamed and domesticated. Domestic dogs are descended from the Arabian (*Canis lupus arabs*) and Indian (*C.l. pallipes*) wolves, two subspecies that are now extinct. These were smaller animals than the present timber wolf (*Canis lupus*). There are differences in the lower jaw (the mandible) that distinguish the skeleton of a wolf from that of a domesticated dog. A mandible found in a cave at Palegawra, Iraq, and clearly that of a dog, not a wolf, has been dated at about 10000 B.C.E. Wolves are believed to have competed with human hunters for prey and for carcasses left by other predators. People and wolves would have met often, and similarities in social behavior would have allowed them to tolerate each other and then to become friendly. Orphaned cubs would have been kept as pets, and, when they grew up, tame wolves would have hunted alongside humans, sharing the resulting food. Skeletons of "wolf-dogs" are fairly common in Upper Paleolithic sites.

Dogs were also domesticated in North America. A domesticated dog, the bones of which were found in the western United States, lived around 8500 B.C.E.

Farm Livestock

Wolves, wolf-dogs, and dogs were used for hunting and for guarding homes. It was not until around 7000 B.C.E. that sheep and goats were raised. Cattle and pigs were domesticated a few centuries later. Cattle were venerated in shrines at Çatal Hüyük, but these may have been wild animals that were encouraged to remain near the settlement—perhaps by offering them salt, which most cattle crave—and used only for sacrifice or traded with neighboring communities.

It would have been necessary to control their movements, because herds of cattle would have destroyed crops and attracted predators if they had been allowed to roam freely. They were big animals. Wild oxen (*Bos taurus*), the species from which European cattle are descended, stood up to 7 feet (2.1 m) tall at the shoulder. Humped, or zebu, cattle (*B. indicus*) were domesticated around the same time in southern Asia—their remains have been found in Thailand—as were pigs, descended from the wild boar (*Sus scrofa*) that still lives in many parts of Europe and Asia.

By around 8000 B.C.E. farmers were growing cereal crops and pulses—peas and beans of various kinds—in the Near East and the valley of the river Euphrates. The practice of crop growing spread eastward and northward, the herding of livestock was added, and cultures increasingly came to be based on farming, rather than hunting and gathering. The change was not abrupt and scientists are still debating just why it happened. Indeed, it may not be complete, even today. Country people in Europe and North America still collect wild fungi, fruits, and nuts and still fish and hunt game.

Floating papyrus (Gerry Ellis/ENP Images)

The Fertile Crescent

The region into which agriculture spread first includes the Nile Valley (page 128) and then extends from the Dead Sea in the south and southern Turkey in the north in a broad curve southeast to the Persian Gulf. This roughly crescent-shaped stretch of land is often called the *Fertile Crescent,* a name coined by the American orientalist and historian James Henry Breasted (1865–1935). It is where Western civilization began.

It was here that Sargon forged the Empire of Sumer and Akkad (page 118), and where the Assyrians, Babylonians, and Phoenicians flourished. The Assyrian Empire was centered in what is now northern Iraq and was powerful from about 2000 to 612 B.C.E. Ninevah and Nimrud were two of its most important cities.

The earliest Phoenician town was Byblos, a seaport on the coast of Lebanon north of Beirut, known today as *Jubayl.* People have lived there since before 3000 B.C.E., making this possibly the oldest continuously inhabited town in the world. Papyrus paper was exported to the lands of the Aegean through the port of Byblos, and *byblos, byblinos,* is the Ancient Greek for "papyrus." Our word *bible* means "papyrus book"—from Byblos. The Phoenicians were great explorers and traders, traveling by sea. One of their exports was a form of writing in which symbols represented consonants, rather than whole words. It has evolved into the English alphabet we use today.

These civilizations flourished during the warm period that followed the end of the Younger Dryas Stadial. Then, at least at first, the Fertile Crescent really was fertile, with reliable rainfall, warm temperatures, and soils that retained moisture. The region enjoyed weather much like that of the Mediterranean countries and southern California today. There were even permanent settlements in what is now the Arabian Desert.

Already, though, the climate was becoming cooler and drier. As long ago as 5000 B.C.E. farmers in Mesopotamia were starting to irrigate their fields (page 122). Around 2000 B.C.E. farms still occupied a much larger area than they do now and many more people lived between the Euphrates and Tigris than the land could sustain now. Today the Fertile Crescent is mostly desert. The desert has taken over not because of any failing of the ancient civilizations, but simply because of change of climate.

Irrigation, Rivers, Dams

Early farmers soon learned that crops do not thrive in dry ground and that a delay in the arrival of seasonal rains could substantially reduce the harvest. If the rains failed to arrive at all, many people would go hungry. A solution to the problem was to provide water where and when it was needed. This is called *irrigation* and it has been practiced for thousands of years.

In the lands between the Euphrates and Tigris Rivers, where Western civilization began, irrigation was introduced early. The first channels carrying water to the fields may have been constructed as long ago as 4000 B.C.E. Over subsequent centuries the network of channels became very elaborate and strongly influenced the political development of the region.

The First Civil Engineers

Within the great empires that ruled the Fertile Crescent there were many more or less autonomous city-states. Their rulers were concerned with defense, religion, and the security of the food supply, and this emphasis produced strong governments that were willing and able to invest as much money and labor in irrigation systems as was needed. These, like the defense works, were designed and built under the supervision of engineers who were also priests and high government officials. They were the first civil engineers the world had seen, and their example showed later generations and civilizations what could be achieved in the control of natural forces. There was no attempt to coordinate irrigation schemes throughout the entire area, but together the individual schemes of different cities succeeded in irrigating a very large area of cultivable land.

A canal was built in what is now southern Iraq to link Ur, then on the bank of the Euphrates, to the Tigris. The course of the Euphrates has moved over the years, and today the site of Ur is in the desert, about 10 miles (16 km) from the river. It lies 140 miles (225 km) south of Babylon, about halfway between there and the coast of the Persian Gulf. This is the city called *Ur of the Chaldees* in the Bible, and it is reputed to be where Abraham was born. At its height, Ur was the capital of Sumer and immensely wealthy. There was another canal farther north. Its water was carried across a small river by means of an aqueduct.

Water was channeled to the fields around Babylon from an artificial lake held behind a dam on the Euphrates. King Hammurabi (c.

1792–50 B.C.E.) left a written description of canals built from brick with asphalt mortar feeding a system covering 10,000 square miles (25,900 sq km)—an area the size of Vermont. Babylonian farms fed a population of 15–20 million people. The population of modern Iraq is about 22 million.

Babylon is famous for its hanging gardens, built during the reign of Nebuchadnezzar II (604–562 B.C.E.) and known as one of the seven wonders of the world. They comprised a stone structure supporting a series of terraces in the form of platforms, each of which projected over part of the one below. Plants of all kinds, including trees, were grown on each of the terraces, as well as on the flat roof at the top, and the structure was hollow, with galleries on the inside through which people could walk. No one knows how water was raised all the way to the top, but the machinery to do so must have been impressive. The Babylonian irrigation system lasted until the 13th century C.E., when it was destroyed during a Tatar invasion.

Dangerous Floods

In 1929, archaeologists working at the site of Ur found a layer of deposits 8 feet (2.4 m) thick that had been laid down by a major flood in about 3200 B.C.E. There is evidence of other severe floods that occurred between 4000 and 2400 B.C.E. at Kish and Nineveh. The Tigris and Euphrates are still unpredictable. At irregular intervals between April and June they can rise suddenly to produce devastating flash floods that leave behind huge amounts of silt.

The early civil engineers faced a formidable task. Not only did they have to supply water when it was needed, they also had to protect the cities from flooding. Consequently, they devoted a great deal of time and attention to studying the rivers, the weather, and signs—magical as well as physical—that might allow them to predict the amount of water being carried by the rivers. As well as being the first civil engineering, their studies may have been the beginning of science, and the authority that allowed them to recruit and manage a labor force was backed by the first strong, centralized legal system.

The Euphrates and Tigris floods came too late in the year to be of use for crops sown in the winter and too early in the year for crops sown in spring. This meant the floodwaters had to be kept out of the fields. Embankments, called *levees*, were built to contain the rivers as they rose, and large

basins were constructed into which excess water from the rivers could be channeled when necessary. Both the basins and channels had to be kept free of silt. This could be used as fertilizer and the stored water could be directed through other channels to the fields, for use when the ground was dry. Occasionally there were exceptionally high river levels that overwhelmed the defenses, but most of the time the cities were protected and the farms flourished.

Eventually, the irrigation system fell into disrepair. As the climate became drier and the rivers changed their courses, the farms were abandoned. Desert finally claimed the area.

The Kingdom of Sheba

Mesopotamia was not the only part of the world where engineers built irrigation systems. In what is now Yemen, in the south of Arabia, there was once a kingdom called *Saba,* known in the Bible as *Sheba.* Some time around 500 B.C.E., its people, the Sabaeans, built a dam at Ma'rib. Its ruins are still there. The dam, about 50 feet (15.25 m) high and nearly 1,970 feet (601 m) long, controlled the flow of water into the valley below it, allowing the area to be irrigated. The dam broke and was repaired several times, but finally the breach was not mended. Between 542 and 570 C.E. the irrigation system gradually broke down and the kingdom of Saba, or Sheba, disappeared as the desert reclaimed the fields.

In China, the river Gukow was dammed in 240 B.C.E. by a structure 98 feet (30 m) high and 985 feet (300 m) long. Dams for irrigation were also built in Sri Lanka, the earliest from the fifth century B.C.E.

Farming the Negev

Dams were not the only way to capture water. What is now the Negev Desert, in southern Israel, was once farmed. During the Israelite period, about 970–50 B.C.E., the inhabitants built low stone walls to channel rainwater into terraces of fields in a low-lying area. Even then the Negev had a dry climate, but such rain as it received fell mainly as heavy showers.

Water entered the top terrace, soaked the soil until water lay on the surface, then overflowed the low wall and fell into the next terrace, and then the next after that. At the bottom, any remaining water drained into a storage tank below ground, so it could be used later. The system evidently worked well, and it was extended between about 300 B.C.E. and 630 C.E., during the Nabatean and Roman-Byzantine periods.

The Hohokam of Arizona

Irrigation was also used in North America. The most impressive system was developed in Mexico (page 130), but it was not the only one. In central and southern Arizona, mainly along the Gila and Salt Rivers, a group of Native Americans built what eventually became more than 150 miles (240 km) of irrigation channels in the Salt River valley alone, some of them 30 feet (9 m) wide and 10 feet (3 m) deep. Pima and Papago people living in the area later, after the canal diggers had gone, called their predecessors the *Hohokam,* which is believed to mean "those who have vanished" in the Pima language.

The Hohokam arrived in Arizona sometime around 300 B.C.E. They cultivated corn, gathered wild beans and fruits, and hunted game, and they dug a canal 3 miles (5 km) long to carry water from the Gila River to their fields. Little by little more canals were added to the system, and cotton was raised as a crop and later beans and squashes. Water was being lost through evaporation and by soaking into the ground. To reduce losses, by around 700 C.E. the canals were being cut deeper and narrower.

Hohokam people made distinctive pottery, composed epic poems, and learned to make wax molds in which they cast bells made from copper. Their culture lasted for about 1,700 years, but early in the 15th century C.E. it began to disintegrate. No one knows why or what happened to the last of the Hohokam.

Irrigation is more important today than it has ever been. If all the people of the world are to be fed adequately, farming must be made as productive as possible. This means that crops must receive as much water as they need. Irrigation can double or triple crop yields by making it possible to produce two or three crops a year on land that previously produced only one. Such increases have been achieved in many countries.

The Food and Agriculture Organization of the United Nations estimates that in the world as a whole about 520 million acres (211.7 million ha) of farmland is irrigated at present. In 1991–93, 17.02 percent of all the cropland in the world was irrigated, compared with 15.04 percent in 1981–83. The biggest irrigated areas are in China, India, Pakistan, and the United States, but there are more than 130 countries in which some farmland is irrigated.

Aquifer Depletion, Waterlogging, and Salination

Without irrigation there would be no farms in large parts of the southwestern United States. In the Great Basin, the basin-and-range region covering 189,000 square miles (489,500 sq km) in Nevada, western Utah, and parts of California, Oregon, and Idaho, the average annual rainfall ranges from 4–6 inches (100–150 mm) in the south to 10–12 inches (250–300 mm) in the low-lying basins. This is sufficient to sustain natural vegetation, but not to produce farm crops. With irrigation, supplied from the artificial lakes impounded behind the Hoover, Shasta, and other large dams, the Southwest is highly productive. A total of 52.9 million acres (21.4 million ha) of farmland is irrigated in the United States, most of it to the west of longitude 100° W.

Plants use water as mechanical support and as a medium in which to transport dissolved nutrients, but mainly as a source of hydrogen for photosynthesis (page 56). If the ground provides less water than a plant requires, the plant experiences "water stress."

In extreme cases the effects of water stress are obvious. Leaves wilt, stems lose their rigidity, and the plant may collapse. This level of stress occurs where the soil is dry all the way from the surface to below the level of plant roots. If it continues, the top of the plant may wither away and the feeding roots may die. These are the roots through which the plant absorbs nutrients. Loss of its stem, leaves, and feeding roots may not kill the plant, but when its water supply is restored it may not respond quickly. Before it can recover fully it must grow replacements for the parts it has lost.

Less severe stress produces subtler symptoms that are not immediately visible. If the soil contains water below the level of the feeding roots, the deeper roots may absorb enough to sustain transpiration. Its xylem vessels will be full and its turgor pressure maintained (page 56). The plant will not wilt and for some time it will continue to appear healthy, but it is not absorbing nutrients and it is unable to grow.

Crops can experience water stress even in Britain, where the rainfall is moderate and ordinarily falls throughout the growing season. In summer, higher temperatures can increase the rate of evaporation sufficiently to dry soils and there are periods of a few weeks without rain in most years. Irrigation is used on about 267,000 acres (108,000 ha) of farmland, an area that tripled between 1973 and 1998.

Given the advantages, it is not surprising that so many farmers are willing to install irrigation

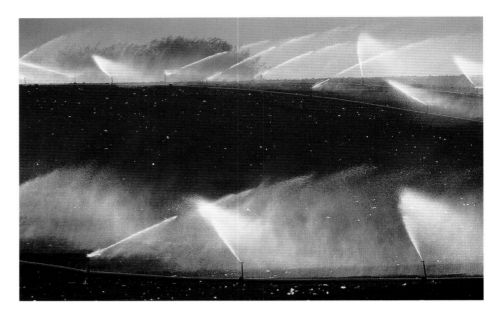

Irrigation sprinklers near Castro, California (Gerry Ellis/ENP Images)

systems. The increased yields more than pay for the cost, and in some countries, including Mexico, Turkey, and parts of the United States, farmers pay a reduced price for electricity that is used to pump water for irrigation.

The Amount of Water Plants Require

Plants need a startling amount of water. Only a minute proportion is used in photosynthesis or held in and between plant cells. Most is lost through transpiration, and to that must be added the amount that evaporates from the ground before it reaches a plant at all. Altogether, it takes about 500 tons of water to grow 1 ton of potatoes, 1,500 tons to grow 1 ton of wheat, and about 10,000 tons to grow 1 ton of cotton. To produce 1 ton of beef from cattle fed on grain requires around 100,000 tons of water. In the United States and Europe, approximately two-thirds of all the water consumed is used to irrigate crops, and in the drier areas, such as California, Egypt, and the Murray-Darling basin in Australia, the proportion rises to more than 90 percent.

In some regions irrigation water is taken from rivers. Elsewhere it is abstracted from the groundwater (page 40). When it is poured on the land, some of it quickly evaporates and some enters plants and is returned to the air by transpiration. A small amount becomes incorporated in plant tissues and is removed when the crop is harvested. Remaining water drains through the soil, enters the groundwater, and flows toward the river at the bottom of the drainage basin, but more water is abstracted than returns. This may reduce the amount of water flowing in rivers. If any polluting substances discharge into the river—and these may originate naturally as well as through human activities—there will be less water to dilute them. Irrigation can make pollution worse.

The Aral Sea

The abstraction of river water has produced spectacularly harmful effects in central Asia. Two rivers, the Syr Darya and Amu Darya, discharge into the Aral Sea and are the main sources of water entering the sea. The Aral Sea is a large, shallow saltwater lake on the border between Kazakhstan and Uzbekistan. In 1960 its surface area was 26,300 square miles (68,000 sq km) and its average depth was 53 feet (16 m), and 226 feet (69 m) on its western side.

In the 1960s the Soviet government embarked on a scheme to put previously uncultivated land in agricultural production. These "virgin" lands, in Kazakhstan, Uzbekistan, and Turkmenistan, were plowed and irrigated with water from the Syr Darya and Amu Darya. As the area of farmland increased, so did the amount of water fed to it. Water levels fell in the two rivers and by the 1980s both sometimes dried up completely in summer. Deprived of replenishment, the Aral Sea started to shrink as water evaporated from it. By about 1990 the volume of water in the sea was half of its 1960 value and its level had fallen by approximately 50 feet (15 m). The sea was reduced to two separate parts, the *Greater* and *Lesser* Aral Seas, with a combined surface area of about 13,000 square miles (33,800 sq km).

Evaporation concentrated the mineral salts in the water. It became unfit for drinking, and most of its fish died. This destroyed a formerly prosperous fishing industry and the livelihoods dependent on it. What had once been ports were now towns far from the sea. There were even fishing boats stranded in what had become a salt desert, and dry salt, blown as a dust by the wind, fell on a large area of surrounding land, rendering it infertile.

The Ogallala Aquifer

Abstraction can also deplete the aquifers from which the water is obtained. Beneath the Great Plains, for example, the huge Ogallala Aquifer holds water that has accumulated from the melting of the snow and ice from several ice ages. The aquifer extends from South Dakota to Texas and underlies parts of Wyoming, Nebraska, Colorado, Kansas, Oklahoma, and New Mexico. It is a sandy formation, about 330 feet (100 m) thick, and its water table is close enough to the surface to be readily accessible to shallow wells. Since the 1940s farmers have been encouraged to irrigate their land with water from the Ogallala Aquifer. The region produces corn and wheat, as well as cotton and grain-fed beef—crops with a particularly large water requirement. It is estimated that about 60 percent of the water held in the aquifer has now been removed. The water table has fallen by about 100 feet (30 m) and pumping has become more costly.

RISING WATER TABLE DUE TO IRRIGATION

Project	Country	Rate of rise (feet per year)
Nubariya	Egypt	6.5–10.0
Beni Amir	Morocco	4.9–10.0
Murray-Darling	Australia	1.6–4.9
Amibara	Ethiopia	3.3
Xinjang Farm 29	China	1.0–1.6
Bhatinda	India	2.0

Source: *The World Environment 1972–1992*, edited by Mostafa K. Tolba and Osama A. El-Kholy (London and New York: UNEP with Chapman and Hall, 1992).

Waterlogging

Water tables can also rise. The table gives examples of the rate at which this can happen.

If a soil is to benefit from irrigation, water should soak through it at a rate of 0.1–3 inches (2.5–75 mm) per hour. Over 24 hours a suitable soil should absorb sufficient water to moisten it to a depth of 2–3 feet (60–90 cm). If the rate of infiltration is slower than this, much of the irrigation water will evaporate before reaching plant roots and some will drain away horizontally, as surface runoff. If water infiltrates faster—through desert gravel or sand, for example—it will descend to the groundwater and be lost that way. Many irrigation systems are so inefficient that less than half the water they deliver reaches the crops for which it is intended.

Where this happens, farmers are sometimes tempted to add more water. What they see is a soil that dries rapidly, and the apparently obvious remedy is to water it more frequently. This will have little effect if the reason the soil dries is that its texture is so coarse it cannot retain water. What may happen, however, is that water drains through the soil faster than it can be removed by the flow of groundwater (page 39). Water accumulates below ground and that is why the water table rises.

Asphyxiation of Crops

At first this process is harmless, or even beneficial if the groundwater is replenishing an aquifer that supplies wells elsewhere. Trouble begins when the water table rises to the level of the plant roots. Depending on the crop this may be far enough below the surface that the soil still appears dry, but plant growth will slow. The yield will be reduced and in extreme cases the plants may die.

The soil is becoming waterlogged and the crop is dying for lack of air. Groundwater occupies soil that is saturated. It is water that can sink no lower because of an underlying layer of rock or other impermeable material it cannot penetrate, so it is held, filling all the spaces between particles. The saturated soil is completely airless. Plant roots must have oxygen, and although some plants of the humid Tropics have evolved adaptations that allow them to grow in waterlogged ground, farm crops have not—and least of all those that are grown in or near deserts. Eventually, the water table may rise all the way to the surface and pools of water will fill every small depression.

Waterlogging is not always caused by excessive irrigation. It often results from cracks in the pipes and channels carrying irrigation water. Water leaks into the ground before reaching the irrigated field, and by the time the leak is noticed the damage has been done. The figure illustrates this by showing a cross section of ground with four irrigation channels carrying water across it. The two channels on the right are sound and the water table lies some distance below them. The two on the left are leaking. They have saturated

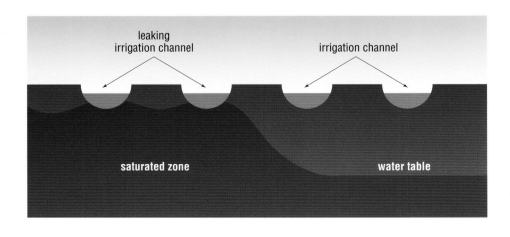

Waterlogging

EXTENT OF SOIL DEGRADATION ON IRRIGATED DRY LAND BY CONTINENT
(thousands of acres; thousands of hectares in line below)

Continent	Slight or None	Moderate	Severe	Very severe	Total of Moderate, Severe, and Very Severe
Africa	21,058	4,396	301	2	4,700
	8,522	1,779	122	1	1,902
Asia	148,774	60,132	14,302	4,176	786,099
	60,208	24,335	5,788	1,690	31,813
Australia	4,003	247	321	49	618
	1,620	100	130	20	250
Europe	24,693	3,311	1,137	259	4,707
	9,993	1,340	460	105	1,905
N. America	37,082	12,182	1,804	494	14,480
	15,007	4,930	730	200	5,860
S. America	17,292	2,587	766	148	37,485
	6,998	1,047	310	60	1,517

Source: *The World Environment 1972–1992*, edited by Mostafa K. Tolba and Osama A. El-Kholy. (London and New York: UNEP with Chapman and Hall, 1992).

the soil beneath them, raising the water table almost, but not quite, to the surface. If the farmer is growing a crop with shallow roots the damage might not yet be evident, but already a deep-rooting crop would fail.

Channels may also overflow. This may also be a problem that develops slowly. River water carries mineral particles. These remain suspended while the water is flowing quickly, but the rate of flow in irrigation channels is slower than that in a river. The amount of material that can remain in suspension is proportional to the energy the water has. As it loses energy by slowing down, it also loses its capacity for transporting particles. These settle on the bottom of the channels as silt, gradually raising the channel bed. If the volume of water being fed into the channels remains constant, sooner or later the accumulation of silt will make them overflow.

Removing Excess Water

Obviously, the remedy is to keep channels open by dredging out the silt and by repairing leaks. Irrigation systems require maintenance, and once the necessary repairs have been made the water table should start to fall. If this does not happen, a more drastic measure is needed. Wells need to be sunk to the desired level of the water table and water above that level pumped out.

The pumped water can be poured back onto the land—although spraying through nozzles is better. This sounds paradoxical, but fields are irrigated only where the climate is dry and, there-fore, the evaporation rate is high. As the water flows from the pump some of it evaporates and if it emerges as a spray of tiny droplets even more will evaporate because the total surface area of water increases. So although water removed from the ground is poured back onto the same ground, a substantial proportion of it is lost. More water is removed than is returned, so little by little the water table falls.

Salination

Waterlogging can be cured fairly simply, if expensively, but it is often accompanied by salination, which is a much more serious problem. Farms are not irrigated with drinking water. They use water of poorer quality, which is water that contains concentrations of mineral salts that render it unacceptable for domestic use. Soil also contains mineral salts derived from the parent material (page 30). These are highly soluble in water.

Slightly salt water is poured onto the land. As it drains downward more salts dissolve into it. Water is also evaporating from the surface. This exerts a pressure drawing water upward by capillarity (page 39) and into the soil around plant roots. Evaporation is the change from the liquid to the gaseous phase, and the molecules escaping into the air are of pure H_2O. Any substances that were dissolved in the liquid are left behind. Gradually, the solution from which plant roots draw water and mineral nutrients becomes more concentrated. Salts may even be precipitated as a white crust on the ground surface.

At first this has no appreciable effect. The point at which crop plants start to suffer varies according to the species. Barley, tomatoes, and sugar beet are fairly salt-tolerant; cotton, wheat, soybeans, and sorghum rather less so; and other beans begin to suffer at quite low salt concentrations. Usually the harm is due not to the toxicity of the salts, although plants can be poisoned, but to their osmotic effect.

Osmosis and Exosmosis

Where a partially permeable membrane, such as a cell wall, separates two solutions of different concentrations, water will pass from the weaker to the stronger solution until the concentration is equal in both. The process is called *osmosis* (page 71), and plants absorb water by maintaining a salt concentration inside their root cells that is higher than the concentration in the soil solution.

The strength of the force drawing water through cell walls is proportional to the difference in concentration of the solutions on either side of the walls. This difference is like a hill—a concentration gradient. The steeper it is, the faster molecules move down it, and consequently the less energy plants need to expend in order to absorb water. Increasing the concentration of the soil solution reduces the concentration gradient, and plants need to work harder to draw in water. Energy they expend doing this cannot be used for other purposes, so their rate of development slows.

Seed germination is delayed or even completely inhibited, and the growth of stems and leaves is affected. For most crops—rice is an exception—there is no immediate reduction in the formation of seeds. With increasing salt concentration, however, the problem becomes much more serious as plants struggle to absorb the water they need. Crop yields are greatly reduced and it can even happen that osmosis starts working in the opposite direction—called *exosmosis*—and instead of water's entering plant roots it is drawn from them. This can happen quite suddenly if a pause in irrigation allows the soil to start drying, with a resulting abrupt increase in salt concentration. Plants cannot survive these conditions.

Salination is widespread, as the table shows. These figures describe the condition on dry lands, which are lands that can be farmed only with irrigation, and in the world as a whole about 0.8 percent of all irrigated dry land is degraded. Salination is the principal cause of this degradation.

Removing Salts

Once land has been degraded by the accumulation of salts, it may remain barren for a long time, because the only way to remove the salts is by washing them away. Water pumped from wells sunk to below the water table can be used to flush the salt from the ground, but care must be taken to ensure the salt water leaving the land does not pollute groundwater or nearby rivers.

As with so many problems, prevention is much better than cure. It is also a great deal easier, although it increases the initial installation cost of irrigation systems. That increased cost is the reason irrigation systems are sometimes incomplete, and waterlogging and salination occur. Water must be allowed to flow. It is not enough simply to pour it onto the land; drains must also be provided to carry it away. A combined irrigation and drainage system parallels the way rain penetrates the ground naturally and then flows from it. Farmers may think it paradoxical to pour water through their land only for it to run away again through drains they have also paid for, but this is the only way to guarantee their fields will become neither waterlogged nor saline. Provided it is planned and installed correctly and subsequently maintained properly, the system will turn a patch of desert into a sustainably productive farm.

Egypt

Despite their strong rulers, strict laws, and advanced technology, life was always uncertain for the peoples of the Fertile Crescent. Their rivers, the Euphrates and Tigris, were unreliable and often dangerous, and eventually their irrigation networks began to fail them. Salination became a serious problem.

Egyptians, on the other hand, enjoyed much greater security, because their river, the Nile, was more dependable.

Prosperity in a Desert

Cairo (Al-Qāhirah), the capital city built on the site of the ancient capital of Memphis, has an average annual rainfall of 1.1 inch (28 mm) and all of that falls between the beginning of November and the end of May. Nevertheless, it is by far the biggest city in Africa or the Near East. It covers 83 square miles (214 sq km) and has a population of about 7 million.

Egypt thrives in its arid climate because its farmers do not rely on direct rainfall to water their crops. They farm the land on each side of the Nile and the river supplies the water (page 186). That water originates as rain, of course, but it is rain that falls far away in Uganda and the mountains of Ethiopia.

Less than 4 percent of the land area of Egypt is habitable. The remainder comprises three deserts: the Western and Southern Desert; the Eastern Desert, which is sometimes considered as part of the Arabian Desert; and the Sinai Desert. Apart from some oases, the deserts are uninhabited. The populated part of Egypt forms two regions that in ancient times were regarded as two countries: Upper and Lower Egypt. Upper Egypt extends from the Sudanese border northward to Cairo, a distance of 750 miles (1,200 km). For the first 200 miles (320 km) the river flows through a narrow gorge, but before it reaches Aswān the land on either side of the Nile widens into a plain about 100 miles (160 km) across. North of Cairo the river enters its delta, and Lower Egypt. The two kingdoms were united during the First Dynasty (c. 3100–2890 B.C.E.), and the kings (pharaohs) began to wear the double crown to symbolize their dominion over both.

Early Farming

The climate was not always as arid as it is now. When the first farmers began tilling the Egyptian

soil, a few centuries before 4000 B.C.E., they did so in savanna grassland, grazed by elephants, giraffes, and rhinoceroses. Farms in Al-Fayyūm, an area of low-lying land southwest of Cairo, grew wheat, barley, cotton, and flax for weaving into linen cloth and raised sheep, goats, and pigs. At about the same time people living farther south at Al-Badari, on the east bank of the Nile near the modern town of Asyūt, were also raising domesticated animals and wrapping dead animals they considered sacred in linen and burying them

King Snefru's pyramid (Gerry Ellis / ENP Images)

near their villages. By about 3600 B.C.E. farming had spread to the delta and along most of the length of the Nile in Upper Egypt.

Already conditions were becoming drier, and as they did so the river on which everyone depended was becoming less reliable. The rains were often lighter over the Ethiopian mountains and in some years they failed completely. This reduced the level of water in the Nile and the dependability of the seasonal floods, resulting in the famines that marked the end of both the Old Kingdom in 2181 B.C.E. and the Middle Kingdom in 1786 B.C.E.

Farming was highly organized. There was a ministry of agriculture, with high officials responsible for such matters as the proper management of the fields and raising of livestock. The land was owned by the pharaoh, temples, or aristocrats and farmed by tenants who paid a rent that was fixed by law. Tenant farmers were lent seed, and oxen for plowing were lent or hired to them. Loans and hire charges were repaid from the harvest.

People ate simply, but usually well. Their diet was based on bread, beans, and onions, but the better off also enjoyed salads of lettuce and papyrus stalks, lentils, peas, and a variety of other vegetables and fruit, and they ate fish, beef, poultry, and game. The Egyptians grew grapes and made wine, were producing olive oil by around 1200 B.C.E., and kept bees. It was they who first used yeast (*Saccharomyces cerevisiae*) to ferment beer—their everyday drink—and leaven bread, and they were also the first people to use bread ovens. They were eating leavened bread by 2600 B.C.E. and were very fond of a wide variety of cakes, including some that were sweetened with honey and fried.

The Annual Flood

Heavy rains fell in Ethiopia in most years and water filled first the Blue Nile and then, when its level started to fall, the White Nile. At Wadi Halfa, where the river enters modern Egypt, the level started to rise in June and reached its maximum in September. During this period the Nile overflowed its banks, flooding the land to either side throughout all of Egypt lying to the north of Aswān. As well as water, the flood brought soil from Ethiopia that had been washed into the river by the torrential rains. When the flood subsided it left the land covered by a layer of fertile silt, called *alluvium*. The annual delivery of alluvium was equivalent to application of fertilizer and made Egyptian farming highly productive.

The annual flood was guided to where it was needed. Fields were low-lying and extended from the riverbank to the edge of the desert. Each field was divided from those on either side by high embankments, forming a series of basins. Short canals led from the river to each basin, but water flowed along them only during the flood. Then the muddy floodwater filled the compartments to a depth of several feet and the fields remained under water for a few weeks during which the mud settled. Salination and waterlogging did not occur, because the land drained well and after soaking the ground the irrigation water joined the groundwater and returned to the river.

Irrigation

The Nile was the only source of water and irrigation was needed from February to July, during the period between floods. It may have been the Egyptians who invented irrigation. They are known to have been practicing it by around 2000 B.C.E.

It worked by baling water, often using a device known in Egypt as a *shaduf* or *shadoof* and in India as a *denkli* or *paecottah*. Used to this day, a shaduf comprises a long, tapering pole mounted on a horizontal crossbeam about 10 feet (3 m) above the ground. A bucket hangs from the thin end, a big rock is fasted as a counterweight to the thick end, and the crossbeam is positioned much closer to the counterweight than to the bucket. At rest the pole is roughly horizontal. To fill the bucket, a worker pulls on a rope to lower the bucket into the river. When the bucket is full he releases the rope and the counterweight raises the bucket to where he can reach and empty it, pouring the water into a channel leading to the field. Where water has to be raised higher than is pos-

Donkey turning irrigation pump wheel along the Nile River (Gerry Ellis/ENP Images)

sible with a single shaduf, two or more can be arranged one above the other. One *shaduf* can irrigate about 2 acres (0.8 ha).

The *sakia*, also spelled *sakieh* and *sāqīyah*, and known in India as the *harat* or *Persian wheel*, was also used and, like the *shaduf*, is still in daily use. This is a vertically mounted wheel that turns continuously. Buckets are attached close together along a loop of rope passing over the wheel, or in some versions of the device to the wheel itself. At the bottom of the loop or wheel the buckets fill with water and at the top of their travel they empty into a channel automatically as they cross the top of the wheel. The wheel is connected by a gear to a horizontal wheel that is turned by oxen yoked to an arm from the center of the wheel and walking in a circle.

Archimedes (c. 287–212 B.C.E.), the Greek inventor and mathematician, invented a third device for lifting water, and it, too, is still used in Egypt. Known as the *screw of Archimedes*, it is a helix, or screw, that turns inside a watertight cylinder, or simply a helix fixed around a central rod. It is mounted at an angle of about 45°, the lower end in water and the upper end supported. When it is turned, originally by means of a handle at the upper end, water is lifted up the helix and falls from it at the top into a gutter leading to an irrigation channel.

Chinampas

Spanish explorers of the 16th century would certainly have heard of the legendary hanging gardens of Babylon, but when they entered Mexico in 1519 the conquistadores came across something no less amazing. What is more, it was still there and working, unlike the hanging gardens, of which no trace remained. When they arrived in the land of the Aztecs they found not hanging gardens, but what were first described as floating gardens.

Mexico was ruled then by the Aztecs, a tribe to whom all the other Mexican peoples paid reluctant tribute. The Aztecs had invaded the region about 200 years earlier after spending centuries leading a seminomadic life as they sought a place where they could settle permanently. After fights with other tribes the Aztecs were confined to two small islands on the western side of Lake Texcoco, which formed part of what they knew as the Lake of the Moon. Their capital began as the city of Tenochtitlán. Later, the conquest of the adjoining city of Tlatelolco by the Aztecs reduced it to the status of a district of the city of Tenochtitlán and the capital became known as *Tenochtitlán-Tlatelolco*. Another tribe, the Xochimilco, who settled farther south in about 1300 C.E., were defeated by the Aztecs in 1352 and 1375 and in the 15th century were absorbed into the Aztec Empire. The Aztecs then adopted, developed, and extended an agricultural system invented by earlier inhabitants.

Archaeologists believe that system was devised by people who lived in Teotihuacán around 100 C.E., making it ancient even when the Aztecs arrived. Teotihuacán, about 33 miles (50 km) northeast of modern Mexico City, was sacked and burned by the Toltecs some time between 650 C.E. and 900 C.E., long before the Aztecs arrived. *Teotihuacán* means "city of the gods" in Nahuatl, the language spoken by the Aztecs.

The Lake of the Moon

The Lake of the Moon lay in the Valley of Mexico, a landlocked basin surrounded by mountains and 7,500 feet (2,288 m) above sea level. Rainfall averages 30 inches (762 mm) a year, of which 27 inches (686 mm) falls between May and October. The valley occupies an area of about 3,000 square miles (7,770 sq km) and during the summer rainy season the lake covered one-quarter of it. In winter, evaporation reduced the lake to five separate lakes: Zumpango and Xaltocán in the north, Texcoco in the center, and Xochim-ilco and Chalco in the south. The lake was about 20 miles (32 km) wide and 40 miles (64 km) from north to south.

It was in the southern town of Xochimilco, in the region known then as Chinampan, that the Spaniards first saw the cultivated plots that came to be called *chinampas*. They were described as floating gardens in a book called *Historia natural y moral de las Indias* (Natural and moral history of the Indies) written by the Jesuit missionary José de Acosta (1539–99) and published in 1590. "Gardens that move on the water have been built by piling earth on sedges and reeds in such a manner that the water does not destroy them, and on these gardens they plant and cultivate, and plants grow and ripen, and they tow these gardens from one place to another." It was not quite as Father Acosta thought, but his mistake was easily made, because the system did involve towing large rafts of vegetation and the cultivated plots were surrounded by water on all sides.

Not much remains today of the Lake of the Moon. Modern Mexico City, on the site of Tenochtitlán, uses so much water that the level has fallen drastically, but in the 16th century the lake formation was complex. The southern part of Lake Xochimilco was swampy, because the soil held freshwater that poured in from a large number of springs. The water table there was higher than the open surface of the lake. Canals were dug that allowed the spring water to flow freely into Lake Xochimilco and from there into Lake Texcoco, which was deeper. There were also freshwater springs around Tenochtitlán, from which water entered the western side of Lake Texcoco, but the supply from them proved insufficient as the Aztec city grew in size. During the reign of Montezuma I (1440–68) a covered aqueduct was built to carry water to the capital from Chapultepec hill in the west. A second aqueduct was built during the reign of Ahuítzotl (1486–1502)—although this was so efficient it caused serious flooding.

Need for Freshwater

Freshwater was essential to prevent salination (page 124). Each summer, heavy rain falling on the volcanic hills washed mineral salts into Lake Texcoco, and each winter, evaporation concentrated them in the deeper, eastern part of the lake. There is no outlet from the Lake of the Moon, and so the salts had been accumulating for thousands of years and it was essential to keep them away from the cultivated land. The injection of freshwater maintained the height of the water table and for a time prevented the intrusion of salt water.

In the 15th century heavy summer rains caused salt water to flow westward with potentially disastrous consequences for the Aztec capital. Nezahualcóyotl, a relative of Montezuma I, assembled a work force of 20,000 men recruited from all the towns in the valley to build a dike of stones and earth enclosed by stockades. The barrier was 10 miles (16 km) long and ran across the Lake of the Moon in a north–south direction from Atzacoalco to Ixtapalapa, separating the western side of Lake Texcoco from the eastern side.

The Chinampas

The "floating gardens," or *chinampas*, were rectangular plots of land reclaimed from the shallow lake. Each plot was 19.7 to 32.8 feet (6–10 m) wide and 328 to 656 feet (100–200 m) long and surrounded by canals. Mud dredged out during the digging of the canals was piled between them. This raised the chinampas a little above the water level and their sides were held in place by fences made from posts interwoven with vines and branches. Willow trees were planted later to replace some of the fences. The people working the plots—the *chinamperos*—reached them in flat-bottomed canoes, but footpaths also intersected chinampa areas.

Before a crop was sown, the chinampero scooped mud from the bottom of the canal and spread it over the plot. Aquatic plants floated on the surface of the canals, and from time to time, a chinampero would cut them and tow them, as a raft of vegetation, to be spread on the plot and then covered with mud. This turned the vegetation into a compost pile and it may have been the sight of vegetation being towed that gave the impression of floating gardens. When the level of the plot rose too high, the surface was lowered and the surplus material was often moved to another plot.

One end of each chinampa was used as a nursery for all the crops except corn, which was sown directly into the chinampa. A layer of vegetation was covered thickly with mud and left to dry. When the mud was firm enough it was cut into rectangular pieces called *chapines*. The chinampero would make a hole in each chapín, drop in a seed, and fill the hole with manure. When the chinampa surface had been leveled and tilled, the chapines were set into the mud.

As well as vegetables, the chinamperos caught the carp and other fish that swam in the canals and axolotls (salamanders) were also eaten. Water birds were netted for food and for their feathers. Flowers were grown, mainly for use in the temples. The name *Xochimilco* means "place of the flower gardens" in Nahuatl.

Land Tenure

In the early 16th century, when the Spaniards arrived and the chinampa system was at the peak of its productivity, the population of the capital and all the towns and villages around the Lake of the Moon was in the region of 400,000. Xochimilco alone had at least 25,000 inhabitants and 100,000 may have lived in Tenochtitlán. Tlatelolco had a market, and on the day of the main market Spanish reports said there were 60,000 people buying and selling. Tenochtitlán was a city of canals green with plants and busy with canoes carrying people and goods.

Under the Aztec administration Tenochtitlán was divided into four wards, called *calpullis,* probably based on occupation by extended families, and each ruled by an aristocrat. The calpullis were divided into 12–15 smaller calpullis. Tlatelcolco contained 10–20 calpullis and Xochimilco contained 18. Each calpulli had its own name.

There were three categories of chinampas. Some belonged to each calpulli. A member of the calpulli could use one of these to support himself and his family for as long as he did not leave the plot uncultivated for 2 years in succession. Some chinampas belonged to the administration—the office occupied by an aristocrat—but not to any person. Finally there were privately owned chinampas, which could be bought and sold.

The chinampa system was highly productive. It is still practiced in the south, around Xochimilco, by chinamperos, who usually harvest two crops of corn and five of other produce every year. They grow beans, chili peppers, tomatoes, onions, and salad vegetables. Plants and flowers—especially dahlia, the national flower of Mexico—from the chinampos of Xochimilco are sold throughout Mexico.

Nomadic Peoples of the Sahara

In the seventh century and again in the 11th the warriors of Islam advanced westward from Arabia into North Africa. Many settled and their descendants still live there. North Africa was not uninhabited at the time of the advance, however, and the descendants of the original, pre-Arab population now live in Morocco, Algeria, Mali, Mauritania, and Niger.

They have had several names. At one time they were known as the *Numidians* and allied themselves with the Phoenicians, who occupied Carthage, the city located where Tunis is today. Later, after the Romans had destroyed Carthage (in 146 B.C.E., at the end of the Third Punic War) and North Africa was under Roman occupation, the coastal area was called *Barbary*, from the Greek word *barbaros*, which means "foreign." The word was applied to anyone speaking a foreign language—the original meaning of *barbarian*. The inhabitants of Barbary were called *Berbers*. This is the name by which they are most widely known, but they find it alien and prefer to be called the *Imazighen*, the "free men" (the singular is *Amazigh*). In the fourth and fifth centuries they had their own kingdoms.

Many became Latin-speaking Christians during Roman times, but there were also Jewish people living inland. They were traders and metal workers and some Berbers converted to Judaism. Many of the North African Jews have now migrated to Israel.

The Berbers

Although they resisted the Arab invasion, most of the Berbers were converted to Islam, but even today they retain religious customs from their pre-Islamic past. Many learned the Arabic language and were absorbed into Arab society, but their own Berber, or Amazigh, languages are still spoken and about one-quarter of the Berber population speaks no Arabic. There are six Amazigh languages, each with several dialects. The languages differ mainly in their pronunciation; the grammar and vocabulary are fairly standard throughout the group. They have their own alphabet, known as *tifinagh,* and although most of the time their languages are written in the Arabic script, *tifinagh* is still used for writing the Tuareg, or Tamashek, language.

About 9 million Berbers live in Morocco. They comprise three groups, each speaking their own Amazigh language. The Riffi, or Riffians, live in the Rif Mountains, which compose the coastal range; the Tamazight in the Middle Atlas range, inland from the Rif; and the Shluh in the High Atlas Mountains farther inland. Almost 5 million Berbers live in Algeria, about two-thirds of them in the mountains.

After a campaign by Algerian Berbers for recognition of their culture, in May 1995 the government established a council to promote the Amazigh language. The Berbers now have two political parties of their own in Algeria. In Morocco, news and radio programs for schools are now broadcast in Amazigh.

Most Berbers are farmers, but some live by farming in the lowlands through the winter and spending the summer in the high meadows with their sheep and goats—this practice is called *transhumance*—and others live as nomads. The nomads are pastoralists—people who live by herding cattle, sheep, and goats. They live in tents made from goatskins. Those Berbers who spend their summers in the high meadows also live in tents but build enclosures surrounded by walls made from pounded earth to provide security for them and their stores.

Tuareg—The Blue People

The Tuareg are the desert people. About 950,000 of them are estimated to live in Niger, about 660,000 in Mali, and significant numbers in the south of Algeria, Libya, and Nigeria. There are also Tuareg living in the Sahel countries of Mauritania, Senegal, Burkina Faso, and Chad. Their ancestors were peasant farmers, living a settled life in North Africa, but they were dispersed by an invasion of Bedouin Arabs (page 134) in the 12th century. Since then they have lived as nomads, dwelling in tents made from animal skins dyed red, or sometimes from plastic.

Tuareg salt caravan (Gerry Ellis/ENP Images)

They are the "blue people" of the desert, a name that refers to the blue color of the traditional robes and turbans worn by the men. At one time men wore a blue veil in the presence of women and strangers, but nowadays the custom is not always observed. Theirs is a matriarchal society—one in which the mother is the head of the family and titles and property are inherited through the female line. Consequently, Tuareg women enjoy much more freedom than Arab women. They are not veiled, their best clothes are colorful, they paint their faces, and they wear much heavy jewelry.

Fiercely proud, the Tuareg were once feared. Bands of blue-clad tribesmen would suddenly appear from nowhere to raid travelers, then disappear as mysteriously as they had come. They rode horses and camels and were heavily armed with double-edged swords, daggers, lances, and shields. The desert was theirs. They also traded, forming caravans to transport merchandise, and they collected taxes from other caravans that crossed "their" desert.

TUAREG SOCIETY

Tuareg tribes are grouped into several federations, some in the north, where they live in true desert; others in the south, living just outside the desert, on savanna grassland. Those in the south breed camels and cattle and sell some of them to the northern Tuareg. They meet in market towns, such as Agadez, at the southern edge of the Aïr Massif in Central Niger. Every August nomads meet to trade livestock, hides, and other goods at I-n-Gall, about 68 miles (110 km) west of Agadez.

Their society is very hierarchical. Nobles enjoy the highest status and the priests and scholars, learned in the Qur'an, are just below them. Laborers belong to the lowest class and are descended from the slaves Tuaregs once owned.

Today their lives are changing. Droughts in the 1970s killed many of their cattle, which are the only form of wealth the Tuareg possess. This forced many of the older people to settle near the cities, and many of the young men joined the army of whichever country they were in. Some Tuareg called for an independent state and in Mali there were clashes with government troops, followed by retaliation and more fighting. Further conflict that erupted in Niger and Mali in the 1990s was resolved by peace accords agreed in 1994 in Mali and in 1995 in Niger. Since then the Tuareg have lived in peace, but a peace that is fragile.

Modernization has also disrupted their way of life. In the 1940s the Tuareg owned and operated some 30,000 caravans. As nomads, they had mobility that made them the natural truckers of the desert and largely controlled the movement of goods. Their camels could not compete with real trucks, however, and their business gradually disappeared. Some have become farmers and others have moved into the cities, but many live in refugee camps near Timbuktu and depend on international relief organizations.

Fulani

Berbers are not the only nomads. The Fulani, also known as the *Peul* and *Fulbe,* are believed to come originally from Lower Senegal. In the 14th century they expanded eastward and by the 16th century were moving into Hausaland, now in northern Nigeria, where many of them adopted a settled way of life and were converted to Islam. In the 19th century a Fulani empire flourished in western Sudan. Their language, called *Fulfulde* or *Fula,* is related to the languages spoken in the Niger and Congo basins, but in northern Nigeria they speak the Hausa language.

Fulani live today in many parts of West Africa, but especially in Nigeria, Niger, Mali, Guinea, Cameroon, and Senegal. Although many have settled in towns or live by farming, the Fulani are typically nomadic. They own cattle and travel from one area of pasture to another, living in temporary camps or huts. Their animals are their only wealth and they are rarely eaten, but the Fulani trade dairy

produce for other foods and goods. They meet the Tuareg at the I-n-Gall August market.

Their society is fairly egalitarian and although most settled Fulani are fervent Muslims, the nomadic people are less strict in their observance and some are pagan. A group of nomadic Fulani usually consists of a man, his wives, and their unmarried children.

Arab Nomads

Nomadic Arab tribes also attend the markets at towns in Morocco and Algeria. There are the Regui-bat, who dress in blue like the Tuareg, as well as the Tekna and Ould Delim tribes, and also the Shluh, who are Berber nomads from the Atlas Mountains. Some of these people have settled in towns, but they retain strong links to the nomadic life. Those who farm nowadays raise sheep rather than camels and practice transhumance, spending the summer with their flocks on meadows in the Atlas Mountains.

People meet and trade camels at Guelmim, in southwestern Morocco, once an important caravan center, and at Tan-Tan to the west of Guelmim. An annual fair, called a *musim,* is held

in Tan-Tan. Around the oasis town of Tindouf, across the border in Algeria, there is a large nomad population, mainly of Reguibat. The map shows the location of these towns.

In the 1980s Tindouf was the most important center for the Polisario Front, most of whose members were Reguibat. They were fighting Morocco, whose troops had annexed what is now called *Western Sahara* (it was then Spanish Sahara). The Polisario Front sought independence for the territory. With the help of the United Nations (UN), a Settlement Plan was agreed on August 30, 1998, calling for the war to end and a referendum on independence to be held. In January 1999, as no referendum had been held, the UN extended its mandate over the territory. The war left parts of Western Sahara heavily mined, especially with antipersonnel mines laid by the Moroccan army close to a wall 497 miles (800 km) long built by the Moroccans to separate the part of the country under their control from that governed by Polisario. The Moroccan army agreed in March 1999 to clear mines from non-military zones.

Nomad market towns

Peoples of the Arabian Desert

When the civilizations of the Fertile Crescent were at the peak of their prosperity and power (page 121), there were also farming settlements in Arabia. Probably it was the people who lived in those settlements who domesticated the dromedary (*Camelus dromedarius*, page 121). When this happened is uncertain, but in the ninth century B.C.E. there are historical records of tribes of people who raised camels. They were called *Aribi* and it seems that in 833 B.C.E. they supplied 1,000 camels to a sheikh called Gindibu who needed them for a battle fought at Qarqar, Syria, against Shalmanser III, an Assyrian king. Samsi, an Arab queen, lost a battle against another Assyrian king, Tiglat-Pileser III, in 733 B.C.E., and his booty included 30,000 of her camels. A bas-relief from the palace of Ashurbanipal of Nineveh, dated at about 645 B.C.E. and now in the British Museum, shows camels being used in battle. People who lived in the Arabian Peninsula probably domesticated camels some time before 1000 B.C.E. These people were pastoralists—making their living mainly by herding animals.

Camels have several uses, but when they were first domesticated their main use was for warfare. Arabian warriors mounted on camels raided outposts of the great empires and the sight of a raiding party could cause panic among the defenders. The Bible describes one such attack by two tribes, the Midianites and Amelektites, that must have taken place prior to about 1050 B.C.E.

> And they encamped against them, and destroyed the increase of the earth, till thou come unto Gaza, and left no sustenance for Israel, neither sheep, nor ox, nor ass.

> For they came up with their cattle and their tents, and they came as grasshoppers for multitude; for both they and their camels were without number; and they entered into the land to destroy it. (Judges 6, 5–6)

Generals soon learned the lesson and Ashurbanipal was just one of many rulers to use them in battle. Camels were especially effective against horse cavalry, because until they grow accustomed to them horses will bolt at the smell and sight of camels. There is a record of this in an account by the Greek historian Herodotus of the battle in which Croesus was defeated by Cyrus II the Great. Croesus, renowned to this day for his immense wealth, ruled the kingdom of Lydia, in the west of what is now Turkey, from about 560 to 546 B.C.E. He conquered the Greeks of Ionia, a neighboring country; formed various alliances; and finally embarked on a

combined Greek and Lydian challenge to the might of Persia. This failed in 550 B.C.E. at a battle against the Persian king Cyrus the Great. According to Herodotus, when the Lydian horses smelled and saw the camels of the Persian army they fled.

In order to secure supplies of camels for military use, the imperial authorities had to enter into alliances with the camel breeders. The Arabian pastoralists thus acquired status and many were recruited into the armies. Over the course of several centuries, Arabs spread throughout the Middle East.

From the earliest times, then, Arabs were closely associated with their camels. The name *Arab* is an Arabic word, 'arab' (singular 'arabī'), meaning "those who speak clearly"—that is, in Arabic. It therefore describes anyone whose first language is Arabic, but the Arabs were originally from Arabia and at first many of them led a settled life as farmers. During the fourth century C.E., however, a series of severe droughts affected the entire Mediterranean region and many farms failed. Southern Arabs, the Yemenites, developed an elaborate irrigation system in the kingdom of Saba (page 122), but after the failure of the Ma'rib dam in the sixth century they abandoned farming and became nomads.

Golden Age of Nomads

The sixth and seventh centuries were a golden age for nomadic Arabs, and although the deteriorating climate forced many to give up farming, others became nomads by choice, convinced of

the superiority of that way of life. This period coincided with the rise of Islam—Mohammed lived from c. 570 to 632 C.E. As Arabs converted to Islam a state grew up comprising the Muslim community and the lands they occupied, led by a *khalifah,* or caliph. Muslims were forbidden to fight and steal from each other, so previously warring tribes united and turned their attention to non-Muslims, forming armies composed mainly of Arab nomads. The caliphate expanded widely and did not end until 1258, when the Mongols destroyed Baghdad (page 118).

Many of the nomads settled in the conquered territories. This reduced the number leading a nomadic life, and today the great majority of Arabs live in cities and small villages, but the ancient tradition has not disappeared entirely. In Arabic, the nomads are known as "desert dwellers," or *badw* (singular *badawi*), a name that is written in English as *bedouin*. Most Bedouin speak Badawi, which is their own dialect of Arabic, and may not understand other Arabic dialects.

Modern Bedouin

The Bedouin live throughout the Near and Middle East and North Africa, constituting about 10 percent of the population of the region but occupying a much larger proportion of the land area. The table shows the estimated Bedouin population by country. These figures include Bedouin who have settled on the edge of the desert and are known as *fellahin*.

Starting in the 1920s, the nomads were increasingly compelled to obey the laws of the

BEDOUIN POPULATION BY COUNTRY	
Country	**Number**
Tunisia	2,030,000
Egypt	1,250,000
Syria	1,000,000
Libya	750,000
Saudi Arabia	700,000
Jordan	326,000
United Arab Emirates	180,000
Israel	60,000
Mali	32,000
Burkina Faso	10,000
TOTAL	6,338,000

Note: *Smaller numbers of Bedouin live in Iraq and Sudan.*

countries through which they traveled. They were forbidden to raid isolated villages or to conduct feuds between tribes. Some enlisted as soldiers or took work in the construction industry, although the Bedouin despise farming and manual labor. Many were forced to settle for political reasons. After the return of the Sinai from Israel to Egypt in 1982, the Egyptian authorities encouraged the Bedouin living there to settle as part of a scheme to develop tourism, earning a living by providing facilities for visitors. In the 1950s both Saudi Arabia and Syria took into public ownership what until then had been Bedouin grazing lands and at about the same time Jordan severely curtailed the grazing of goats. Since that time there have been repeated disputes over land between the *fellahin* and nomadic pastoralists.

Bedouin Life

Nomadic Bedouin spend the dry summer months at the edge of the desert and move into the desert during the winter rainy season, when there is pasture for their animals. They are classed according to the animals they own; the most prestigious are the camel herders, who occupy huge areas in the Sahara, Syrian, and Arabian Deserts. Those herding sheep and goats come next in the social structure. They live close to cultivated land, mainly in Jordan, Syria, and Iraq. Cattle herders are found in Sudan and southern Arabia, where they are known as *baqqarah*.

Bedouin are organized into extended family groups, usually called *clans*. These number several hundred persons and tribes comprise groups of clans. Some tribes are considered "noble" because they trace their ancestry to either the Qaysi or Yamani tribes of northern or southern Arabia, respectively. Other tribes, not descended from these, are considered to be "ancestorless" and their members live by serving members of a noble tribe, for example as entertainers or metal workers. Tribes tend their livestock within well-defined territories.

The head of a Bedouin family is called a *sheikh*. The title is ancient and describes a distinguished, elderly man, "elderly" meaning more than 50 years old, so any senior male is likely to be a sheikh. As well as the head of a family, the heads of the clan and tribe are also sheikhs. Those with authority over clans and tribes govern with the help of informal councils of less senior sheikhs.

The Bedouin are Muslim, and their religion affects their social structure, although they retain some pre-Islamic beliefs and customs. Bedouin women pray to the new moon, for example, and some people still believe in spirits, called *jinni*.

Position of Women

Men may have more than one wife and a family group usually consists of the husband, his wives, and their unmarried children. When Bedouin settle into permanent dwellings each wife lives in her own house. Women wear the veil in public and their husbands are permitted to beat them, at least during the first years of their marriage, provided they do not cause bleeding. Women perform most of the chores around a Bedouin camp, including gathering fuel and water, as well as pitching, striking, and loading the tents. Traditionally, they also spun the goat hair and wove it into the cloth from which the tents were made.

Although women's life is harsh, performing the chores allows them to meet each other with no men present, so they can talk freely. Herding the animals is a task performed by young men as well as young women and allows them to meet secretly. Marriages used to be arranged, but young people nowadays are often able to choose their partners.

Tents, Food, Dress

Nomadic Bedouin live in low, rectangular black tents supported by a line of poles along the center. The length of this line reflects the wealth and importance of the owner of the tent. The sides of the tent can be rolled up to allow air to circulate on calm days, and during bad weather the tent can be sealed firmly. Inside, decorative hangings called *gata* divide the tent into sections. One half of the tent is occupied by the women and children and is used to store goods and provisions. It has a hearth for cooking. The other half of the tent, also with a hearth, is occupied by the men and used for entertaining. Hospitality to visitors is very important in Bedouin culture.

Bedouin diet consists mainly of milk, yogurt, rice, butter, and *ghee* cooking fat, and unleavened bread, with dates and other fruits obtained from visits to oases. Meat is eaten only on festive occasions. The dairy produce is from camel and goat milk.

Dress, for both men and women, is long, flowing robes. These protect against the heat of the day, the cold of the night, and the windblown sand.

Nomadic Peoples of the Gobi

Mongolia—the official name is *Mongol Uls*—is a vast Central Asian country. It covers an area of 604,800 square miles (1,566,500 sq km), but its population is only 2.4 million, of which 627,300 live in the capital, Ulan Bator. This means that outside the capital there are, on average, slightly fewer than three persons for every square mile (1.1/sq km). It is possibly the most sparsely populated country in the world. Saudi Arabia is crowded by comparison, with 22 persons for every square mile (8.5 per sq km). The majority of the Mongolian people are Khalkha Mongols, and Khalkha Mongolian is the official language.

Very little of the land is farmed and most of the settled farmers are descended from Chinese immigrants. Farming is difficult in the arid climate. Cereals can be grown in some places, but the rainfall is so unreliable they cannot be expected to yield a harvest every year. Mongols have always been pastoral nomads and most still lead at least a seminomadic life, despite official encouragement for them to settle in the capital or the second largest city, Darhan. Nomadism has shaped every aspect of Mongolian culture and it is a way of life that makes the best possible use of the natural vegetation. Sparse though the population is, no other system of food production could support any greater density. Mongol nomads manage to survive even in the Gobi Desert.

Horses and the "Manly Sports"

Mongolians are renowned for their skill in horse riding and there are keenly fought contests in the three "manly sports" of horse racing, archery, and wrestling. Children from the age of 4 years take part in the horse races. The main contests take place at the annual Naadam festival, beginning on July 11, the National Day, the most important events being held in Ulan Bator.

Caring for the horses is a task performed only by men, and traditionally Mongolian men considered it demeaning to undertake any work that could not be done on horseback. In the Mongolian version of chess, the most important piece is not the queen, but the horse. The national musical instrument, called a *morin huur*, is stringed, is played with a bow, and has a horse's head carved at one end. Legend has it that the first one was made by a rider from the ribs and hair of his favorite horse and used to express his sorrow at the animal's death. In traditional Mongolian stories the hero is always accompanied by a horse, from which he receives good advice. The national drink, *airag*, is the fermented milk of mares. It is

believed to have special therapeutic and nutritional qualities and special herds of horses are kept to provide a supply of *airag* for factory workers and miners.

Horses are important, but the principal pack animal is the Bactrian (two-humped) camel (*Camelus bactrianus*), and of the 367,000 Bactrian camels in Mongolia, two-thirds are in the Gobi. A camel can carry a heavy load, but it can also produce up to 130 gallons (492 liters) of milk a year and up to 10 pounds (4.5 kg) of wool that is used to make clothes and blankets. Mongolians consider camels to be very beautiful and even hold competitions to choose the most beautiful animal. In the fall and winter, when conditions are especially harsh, the camels are used for riding rather than for carrying loads.

Surviving the Winter

Winter is always the hardest time of year. People move with their livestock to winter campsites. At one time the animals had to feed on the hay made in the summer with nothing more than a stone-walled corral for shelter against the icy wind and blizzards. Severe storms could kill entire herds and flocks. Since the 1950s the authorities have provided better shelter and fodder.

As winter approaches, the animals that are unlikely to survive the winter are slaughtered. This reduces the herd to a size that can be fed. The meat from the slaughtered animals is dried or frozen and people eat it during the winter, when neither horses nor sheep are producing milk. Mongols do not eat horse flesh, but Kazaks do; about 6 percent of the population is Kazak.

Diet

Meat and milk are the staple foods. Not only do Mongols dislike vegetables: they actually despise them and have a proverb, "Meat for men, leaves for animals." Nor do they eat fish, although Mongolian rivers are full of them. Summer, when milk is relatively plentiful, is when the *airag* is made, as well as *arul,* which is dried curd and cheese. Apart from *airag,* the everyday drink is tea, made in a large bowl with added salt and milk.

Although these are the basic foods and people are able to subsist on nothing else, Mongol nomads also eat a certain amount of flour made from wheat, barley, or millet. They obtain this from farmers in exchange for animal products. Tea, from China, is also obtained through barter,

as are metal tools and cooking pots, and silken cloth. Since everything the nomads possess must be regularly packed into bundles and carried by camels, however, there is a strong incentive to travel light.

Dwellings and Camps

The typical nomadic Mongolian dwelling is a *ger,* also called a *yurt* or *yurta.* This is a circular, tent-like structure made from wooden poles covered with skins, woven textiles, but most commonly felt. It is waterproof and strong enough to withstand the weather, but light enough to be dismantled and moved from site to site fairly easily. Inside, there is a hearth near the center, smoke from the fire rises through a chimney hole in the roof, and the furnishings consist of brightly colored rugs. A visitor, even a total stranger, enters a *ger* simply by walking in and sitting down, and will be made welcome.

There is never just one *ger,* but always a group of at least two and as many as six, forming the herding camp that is the basis of Mongolian society. Members of the households living in the different *gers* are often related, but not always, and the arrangement is flexible. Membership of the camps is agreed for 1 year. At the end of the year a household may choose to remain with the others or to leave and join another camp, and if the camp becomes so large as to make the grazing difficult to manage, some of the households will move away and start a new camp elsewhere.

Making Best Use of the Pasture

Like true nomads everywhere, the Mongol pastoralists have a detailed knowledge of the land in which they graze their animals and a concept of territory as a patchwork of particular places they are allowed to enter and use at particular times. A group of nomads moving across a landscape, their camels laden and their animals scattered over a large area, may seem to be wandering aimlessly, but they are not. Every migration is carefully planned and timed to make the best possible use of the natural resources.

As well as camels and horses, the nomads herd sheep, goats, and cattle. Some of the Mongol cattle herds include yaks (*Bos grunniens*), a sturdy, long-haired species native to Tibet. Sheep are by far the most important. They provide milk for making butter and *arul,* as well as meat, wool, hides, and dung. Sheep dung is the fuel used for cooking and heating. A herding camp always has sheep. It has other animals only if there are enough people to tend them and pasture to feed them. Each species is managed separately because their dietary requirements differ, so the families must decide carefully whether the benefit they can expect to derive from a herd of goats, cattle, or horses justifies the full-time work of one or more person for each species.

All the sheep in the camp are managed as a single flock. Every morning they are driven out to the pasture, and every evening they are led back to the camp. Their grazing is controlled and they move out from the camp in a spiral, a little farther each day. When the fresh pasture is too far away for convenience, the camp moves to a new site. The sheep are taken in at night partly to ensure the supply of dung for fuel. Sheep feed all day and defecate in the evening, behavior that has been exploited in many parts of the world. In Britain, for example, sheep were traditionally pastured on the hillsides by day and taken in the evening onto low ground, around the farmstead, where their dung fertilized the fields used for growing crops. Essentially, the method transfers fertility from the hills to the lowlands.

Mongolian sheep are also herded to the camp at night for their protection. Wolves and other large predators attack sheep, especially lambs. To help protect the flocks the Mongolian shepherds have dogs that are notoriously fierce and will attack any animal—or strange person—they perceive as a threat to the sheep. They do not herd the sheep, however.

Mongol people are Tibetan Buddhists—that is, their type of Buddhism came to them from Tibet and centers on *lamas,* who are teachers and spiritual leaders. There are also many beliefs and customs derived from shamanism, the religion that preceded Buddhism. In shamanism, a certain individual called the *shaman,* who may be a man or woman, is believed to be able to communicate directly with the spirits and, as a result of that ability, to heal the sick and foretell the future.

Caravans and the Silk Road

Not only is it difficult to cross a desert, it can be dangerous. People should never attempt it alone. An illness or accident that might be trivial in a city can be fatal in a remote spot in the desert heat. Solitary travelers are also easy targets for robbers. To avoid such dangers as these, people have always crossed deserts as groups. A group of people journeying together is called a *caravan,* and until modern vehicles superseded them camels were the animals most often used to carry travelers and their baggage across deserts.

Sometimes the camels traveled in single file, as a long procession. This is the way they are usually depicted in movies, and there were caravans of this type, especially in China, but more commonly the camels moved across open landscapes as strings, three or four abreast. The strings, of up to 40 camels each, were held together by ropes fastened to the saddle and passed through the nose ring of the camel behind. A caravan could comprise a large number of camels—often hundreds and sometimes thousands, moving in strings three or four abreast. The actual number depended on how many passengers wished to travel, the volume of goods to be conveyed, the availability of animals, and the dangers to be faced along the route—there was always safety in numbers, so the more hazardous the journey, the bigger the caravan.

Caravans did not move at all times of year. Those planning long journeys needed pasture and water for the camels. A camel can last a long time without food or water (page 90), but it cannot survive indefinitely and without nourishment it will weaken. It might also be necessary to time a departure in order to arrive at a particular time. Commercial traffic needed to arrive as quickly as possible, but pilgrims also traveled in this way and those undertaking the *hajj*—the pilgrimage to Mecca—needed to be in Mecca by the seventh day of the month of Dhū al-Hijjah. Consequently, pilgrim caravans would depart for Mecca at certain times from different places.

Each camel was usually loaded with about 350 pounds (160 kg) and passengers did not ride them seated behind the camels' necks. That is the way camel riders ride, but camel passengers were carried in panniers—large bags or baskets—slung one on each side of the animal. In cool weather or over short journeys, the camels might carry heavier loads.

The Caravansary

Each day the caravan would travel at a steady 2–3 miles per hour (3–5 km/h) and stop to rest after 8–14 hours. In very hot weather caravans traveled by night. Wherever possible, the caravan would spend the night at a caravansary.

Because of its size, the caravansary was usually located outside the walls of a town or village. The caravan entered through the only entrance, which was a wide, high, strong door in the tall, thick walls. Inside there was a rectangular paved courtyard, open to the sky, that was big enough to contain up to about 400 camels or mules. In one corner of the courtyard there was a hearth for cooking and water could be obtained from a well in the center. The caravansary was open from dawn until night. Then the door was closed and secured with heavy chains.

A covered walkway, like a cloister, surrounded the central court. Rooms opening off the walkway were used for storing merchandise and stabling animals. Wide stone steps led to another walkway running around the upper story. The travelers slept in rooms off the upper walkway.

The caravansary was publicly owned and open to all travelers, but it provided only accommodation, not food for people, fodder for animals, or bedding. A porter, appointed by the local community, supervised the establishment and had assistants to help him. He had a room beside the door, and it was his job to maintain order and also to guard the building, its occupants, and their property. Travelers seeking food and more luxurious lodgings could go into the town or village in search of an inn, called a *khan.*

Caravan Routes

Caravans traveled certain routes, and, apart from those used by pilgrims, the routes were developed for trading goods, most often with the Mediterranean civilizations. One that existed in Old Testament times, for example, was used to convey gold, silver, and frankincense from South Arabia (Yemen) to Gaza or Damascus. Salt was also a valuable commodity and caravans conveyed it from South Arabia to the Mediterranean. The principal salt routes, however, linked the mines at Taoudenni, in northern Mali, and Bilma, in eastern Niger, to Timbuktu in the south of Mali.

Where possible, routes included stops at oases. A caravan route that was in regular use for many centuries ran from Lake Chad to Bilma, from there across the Fezzan region of Libya, visited the oases at Marzūq and Sabhā, and ended at Tripoli on the Mediterranean coast.

There are few camel caravans nowadays—although some still cater to pilgrims—but the routes have survived. Trucks, four-wheel-drive vehicles, and in some cases buses travel them today, and like the caravans of former times they often travel in convoys for safety.

Wu-Ti, Silk, and the Silk Road

The most famous of all caravan routes was called the *Silk Road.* It was opened around 100 B.C.E. during the reign of the Chinese emperor Wu-ti, also known as *Wudi,* of the Han Dynasty. His real name was *Liu Ch'e. Wu* means "martial" and *Wu-ti* is the name that was conferred on him after his death.

Wu-ti expanded the empire to the south and also to the west, across the Gobi, where his armies tried unsuccessfully to subdue a nomadic people called the *Hsiung-nu.* Autocratic and ruthless, he cared nothing for the dangers and privations faced by his troops, but he made the imperial bureaucracy more efficient, instituted Confucianism as the state religion, and made large areas of central Asia fairly safe for travelers. Routes were established that encouraged trade and this trade eventually linked the two great empires of China in the east and Rome in the west by the most famous route of them all.

The Chinese had been manufacturing silk for many centuries, but the method of production was a closely guarded secret and anyone revealing it to a foreigner was condemned to death by torture. When the first silk cloth reached Europe it was, literally, worth its weight in gold. It was a fabulous material, because no one in the West had the remotest idea how it was made. Spices from the Tropics entered China from the south and they were also exported to Europe. The Roman Empire exported gold, silver, precious stones, and woolen cloth. Few people journeyed the whole length of the Silk Road and caravans would travel particular stages, then return. Passengers and merchandise traveling more than one stage would transfer to the next caravan.

Travelers' Tales and Marco Polo

It was not only goods that traveled the Silk Road. Travelers' tales about China reached the West and Buddhism from India and Nestorian Christianity entered China. The Nestorians are a

Christian sect, founded in Asia Minor and Syria in the fifth century, whose adherents base their beliefs on the teachings of Nestorius. He was patriarch of Constantinople, but was deposed in the year 431 C.E., at the Council of Ephesus, for holding beliefs that were declared heretical. Nestorians believe that the human and divine natures of Christ are independent, so Christ is two persons loosely connected morally. Nestorius died in Egypt in about 451. It is not known when he was born. Today Nestorians live in Iraq, Syria, and Iran.

Even then, Western knowledge of China was very rudimentary. Europeans had to wait until early in the 14th century for a reliable account. That came with the publication of the most famous of all travel books, known in Italian as *Il milione* (The Million) and in English as *Travels of Marco Polo.* Marco traveled to the region of northern China that was known then as *Cathay,* from the *Khitai,* a tribe who had established an independent state there, and for part of the way he traveled the Silk Road.

The Route of the Silk Road

For travelers from China, the Silk Road began at the Han capital, Ch'ang-an'ch'eng, "the walled city of Ch'ang-an," to the northwest of the modern city of Sian, also spelled *Xian.* That is where smaller trade routes converged from all over eastern China. From Ch'ang-an the road ran north, meeting and then following the Great Wall past the Nan Shan Mountains. It skirted the southern edge of the Gobi Desert and passed through Tunhuang, a town built around an oasis in the Kansu-Sinkiang Desert. That is where Marco first entered China. It was then called *Sha-chou.*

West of Tun-huang the Silk Road divided into two branches. One passed the northern edge of the lake of Lop Nor and skirted the Tarim Basin on the northern side. The route Marco followed passed the southern edge of Lop Nor and went to the south of the basin. The Tarim Basin occupies the center of the Takla Makan Desert.

From the Takla Makan the route goes to Soch'e, or Yarkand, then Sufu, or Kashgar—once called *Cascar*—after which it climbs into the Pamir and Karakorum Mountains on the border between the Sinkiang Uighur Autonomous Region of China and Tadzhikistan. The route turned south, along what is now a paved road, the Karakorum Highway leading to Islamabad, then north again to Samarkand, in Uzbekistan. It crossed to the south of the Caspian Sea through northern Iran skirting the Dashte Kavir Desert, crossed Iraq and Syria, passed through Damascus, and reached the coast at the ports of Alexandria, in Egypt, and Antioch, the city in southern Turkey that is now called *Antakya.* Passengers and goods were carried from there by sea to Italy.

With the decline of the Roman Empire and the rise of militant Islam the Silk Route became dangerous and fell into disuse. People still traveled it during periods of political stability, however. When Marco Polo made his journey the Mongol emperor Kublai Khan had established peace in the lands he crossed. There are now plans to restore the Silk Road as the Trans-Asian Highway.

Peoples of the American Desert

Despite its arid climate, Arizona has been inhabited for longer than most parts of North America. There is archaeological evidence of human habitation 25,000 years ago, and for the last 2,000 years people have lived in highly advanced societies. It is in parts of Arizona and across the border in New Mexico that Native American peoples built villages. Those peoples are known by the Spanish word for a village, as *Pueblo* Indians. Oraibi, a pueblo in northeastern Arizona, may be the oldest continuously inhabited settlement in the United States. People have been living there since 1150 C.E., and the present population is more than 600. Located on the Third Mesa (page 36), Oraibi is the unofficial capital of the Hopi Reservation.

The first Pueblo peoples were the Anasazi—their name is the Navajo word for "ancient ones"—who lived in the region where Arizona, New Mexico, Colorado, and Utah meet. After 1100 C.E. one branch of the Anasazi, known as the *Salado* people, started expanding peacefully into the part of southern Arizona, along the Gila and Salt Rivers, occupied by the Hohokam people (page 122).

Nothing is known of their origins, but they are the ancestors of all the later Pueblo peoples. The oldest traces of them date from around 100 C.E., at which time they were skilled at weaving baskets—100–500 and 500–700 C.E. are known, respectively, as their Basket Maker and Modified Basket Maker periods. After the arrival of the Salado, the Hohokam started making baskets. The Anasazi hunted game and gathered wild plants but augmented these by cultivating corn and pumpkins.

No one knows why the Hohokam disappeared, but their name means "those who have disappeared" in the language of the Pima people, who may be descended from them. After their departure, the Pima—the name means "river people" in their own language—occupied the central part of what had been Hohokam territory.

Pima

The Pima were farmers and lived in the river valleys. Cultivating the land and using river water for irrigation as their predecessors had done increased the amount of food available to them and this allowed them to construct villages bigger than those of most of their neighbors. Farming conditions were not reliable, however, and in dry years the crops failed. Hunting and gathering augmented the supply of cultivated food, even in the good years, but in the bad years it was the only means of subsistence. Then, people lived mainly on jackrabbits and mesquite beans.

Their tribal organization was strong. Local chiefs were chosen for their abilities and were aided by councils composed of all the adult men living in the village. The councils were responsible for maintaining the irrigation channels, supervising the farming operations, and protecting the village from attack. Apaches sometimes raided Pima villages. The tribal chief was also chosen, rather than inheriting the position.

Today there are about 10,000 Pima. Most live on reservations in their traditional lands. They share the land with the Maricopo, a group of Yuma. *Yuma Desert* is an alternative name for the Sonoran and Colorado Deserts.

Yuma

The Yuma were also farmers, augmenting their diet by fishing, hunting, and gathering wild fruit and edible seeds. They lived on the flood plains of the Lower Colorado River, downstream from the Pima and at the head of the river delta. Unlike the Hohokam and Pima the Yuma had no need for irrigation. Instead their small, low-lying fields were inundated every spring when the winter snow melted in the mountains of Wyoming, Colorado, and Utah, sending a huge surge of water down the Colorado River and making it overflow its banks. As well as water, between them the Colorado and Gila Rivers deposit an average of 170 million cubic yards (130 million cu m) of silt on the flood plain every year. The silt fertilized their crops and the Yuma grew corn, beans, pumpkins, melons, and various grasses. Later they also grew wheat and cowpeas from seed they obtained from the Spaniards. Food was stored in baskets.

The Yuma lived well. Their village communities consisted of several large families, disputes were settled by a council comprising the male heads of all the families, and one of the family heads was the leader of the village. The fields were privately owned and inherited through the male line.

Papago

Farther upstream, the people living to the south of the Pima were the Papago, a name that means "desert people." They are also known as the *Tohono O'odham* and today their population numbers about 8,300, most of whom live on the Tohono O'odham, Gila Bend, and San Xavier Reservations in southern Arizona.

As their name implies, water was scarce where the Papago lived and they relied on hunting and gathering much more heavily than did their neighbors. Although they farmed they lived a partly nomadic life. Unlike the Pima, the Papago did not irrigate their fields. Instead, they practiced flash-flood farming.

Every year, heavy summer rains would cause sudden, heavy floods—flash floods. After the first rains had moistened the ground, the Papago planted their seeds, usually 4–6 inches (10–15 cm) deep to prevent their being washed away, in alluvial fans (page 36) at the mouths of washes near the limit of the area reached by the flood water. Papago men made some ditches and dikes to guide the flood and reservoirs to impound the water. The ground remained moist for long enough to produce crops of beans, pumpkins, cotton, and fast-growing varieties of corn.

While the crops were growing the Papago lived in villages near the fields. After the harvest the ground dried, and it was not long before both food and water were in short supply. Then, at the end of the summer, the people moved away from their "field" villages to "well" villages in the hills where they spent the winter. There was water on the higher ground and game to hunt.

Papago villages were small, each village consisting of a number of scattered dwellings housing the various branches of several extended families. A village of this type, comprising a loose cluster of houses, is known as a *rancheria*. The oldest man who was still active led the village community and there was a village council to which all the adult men belonged. The council met every evening to discuss matters of common interest. Each village also had its own shaman (page 137), who led the religious ceremonies. A group of related rancherías was the biggest political unit and this became important when the Papago had to defend themselves against the Apache. Then the villages would move closer together, but once the attacks ceased the bonds uniting them loosened.

The Papago and Pima are closely related and both speak dialects of the same language, Piman, which belongs to the Sonoran division of the Uto-Aztecan family of languages. These languages are spoken from the southwestern United States and Mexico to Guatemala. In Chihuahua, northern Mexico, the Tarahumara also speak a Sonoran Uto-Aztecan language.

They live on a high plateau divided by deep canyons and farming is possible only in scattered places where there is good soil. There they grow beans, squash, potatoes, and corn and also raise cattle and goats. The Tarahumara, also known as the *Rarámuri,* live in rancherías and often move from place to place at different seasons of the year.

Hopi

All of these peoples descended from the Anasazi live in pueblos. For centuries they have farmed the land, within the limits imposed by the climate, and led settled, mainly peaceful lives provided they were allowed to do so. In 1680 all the Pueblo Indians rose against the Spanish, who had imposed their own political structures, and drove them from their territory, but this was in response to extreme provocation.

Pueblo peoples fall into eastern and western groups distinguished mainly by the type of farming they practice and their economic organization. They belong to many linguistic and cultural groups, of which the Hopi is one of the best known.

The Hopi speak a language belonging to the Shoshonean division of the Uto-Aztecan language family. About 6,000 Hopi survive today. A member of the western Pueblo group, they live in northeastern Arizona, in a large reservation surrounded by the Navajo Reservation. The Navajo speak an Athapaskan language related to that of the Apache and other languages spoken in California, Oregon, and northwestern Canada. Their ancestors migrated from the north and settled beside the Pueblo peoples. Most Hopi villages are built on mesas, high above the surrounding country. Oraibi, on the Third Mesa, is about 6,500 feet (1,980 m) above sea level. The Hopi raise sheep and grow corn, beans, squash, melons, and other crops.

Their culture is similar to that of other Pueblo peoples. Social life centers on the village and is dominated by religious observances. There is an ancestor cult into which boys and girls are inducted soon after their sixth birthday. Its observances, called *kachinas* (or *katcinas*), involve masked impersonations by men of gods, spirits, ancestors, and clouds. There are also secret societies, each owned by a particular clan, that are responsible for fertility and other rituals. Many of the ceremonies are conducted secretly in underground chambers called *kivas.*

Men can join these societies, some of which demand a rigorous initiation. There are also secret societies for women. The clans and larger family groupings are matrilineal, with descent through the female line. At one time, although no longer, a bride remained in her mother's house. Most of the traditions are eroding as the Hopi, like other Pueblo peoples, adopt more and more of the dominant American culture.

Peoples of the Arctic and Antarctic Deserts

On Monday February 15, 1999, an election was held for the 19 seats that compose the Legislative Assembly of Nunavut, and on April 1 Nunavut came into being as a newly self-governing territory in northern Canada. It is the first territory in North America to be governed by an aboriginal people. The name *Nunavut* means "our land" in Inuktitut, one of the two dialects of the Inuit language spoken in the territory (the other is Inuinnaqtun).

The new territory covers 733,400 square miles (1.9 million sq km), which is 55 percent of the area of the Northwest Territories and 19 percent of the total area of Canada. Nunavut is bigger than Alaska and nearly as big as Greenland. It has a population of about 22,000, about 17,500 of whom are Inuit, giving it a population density of barely 0.03 person per square mile (0.01 per sq km).

Greenland Politics

On February 16, the day after the Nunavut elections, the people of Greenland, or Kalaallit Nunaat, also went to the polls in an election contested by 206 candidates. Kalaallit (Greenland) Inuit constitute about 85 percent of the 59,000 people living in Greenland. The country became a Danish possession in 1380; it was granted home rule in 1979 and full internal self-government in 1981. The Danish government remains responsible for foreign and defense policy.

The Inuit

The Inuit—the name means "the people"—are the desert people of the Far North. They live in the high Arctic and sub-Arctic regions of Siberia, Alaska, Canada, and Greenland. Their close relatives the Aleuts live in the Aleutian Islands and the western part of Alaska, but their numbers have fallen sharply over the past 150 years. There were once about 25,000 Aleuts, but today there are no more than about 2,000 and their traditional way of life has almost disappeared. *Aleut* is a Russian name; the people call themselves the *Unganan* or *Unganas*. Their language has three mutually intelligible dialects and is closely related to the Inuit languages, but Eskimos and Aleuts cannot understand each other. They have been separated for far too long, and the difference between Inuit and Aleut is about as great as that between English and Russian.

It was Inuit from Canada who colonized Greenland. The last immigration took place in the middle of the 19th century when a shaman called *Qillaq*—in Greenland he came to be known as *Qitdlarssuaq*—led a group to northwestern Greenland in search of new lands. His descendants live there still. In Canada and Greenland the people prefer to be called *Inuit*. Those living in Alaska prefer *Eskimo,* a name of uncertain meaning that is probably derived from *aiachkime,* a word in Montagnais, a language spoken by one of the Algonquin peoples of eastern Canada. In modern Montagnais *assimew* means "she laces a snowshoe." In Cree, another Algonquin dialect, the people are the *ashkimew.*

Both the Inuit and Amerindians are descended from Asian people, but that is all they have in common and the two are not closely related. The difference is most apparent in blood types. A substantial proportion of Inuit people have blood type B. This type is common in Asia, especially in northern India, but it is not found at all in Amerindians. Inuit and Aleut languages are also distinctive in not being closely related to any other languages, including any of those spoken by Amerindians.

Kayak and Dogsled

Anorak and *kayak,* the two familiar words that Inuit languages have contributed to English, reflect the Inuit way of life, although the original anoraks—from the Greenland Inuit word *anoraaq*—were hooded pullovers made from caribou skins, not synthetic fibers. *Parka,* the name of the outer coat, is an Aleut word. Kayaks, canoes that carry one person, were made from animal bones covered with skins and used for hunting.

Overland the principal means of long-distance transport was the dogsled, drawn by Eskimo dogs. The *Eskimo* in their name—sometimes in the form of *huskemaw*—became corrupted to *husky* and their feats of strength and endurance became legendary. When sled-dog racing became a popular sport, early in the 20th century, one of the trials followed a course of 1,050 miles (1,700 km).

It seems likely that the Asian migrants who became the Inuit took their dogs with them, indicating that the ancestors of the modern husky left Asia several thousand years ago. Their owners may have allowed them to breed with wolves—or have been unable to prevent them doing so. Huskies possess certain wolflike characteristics and, like wolves, rarely bark.

Natural Resources

Tundra vegetation consists mainly of mosses and lichens, with scattered sedges, grasses, and dwarf shrubs (page 74). Some of the shrubs bear berries and these are about the only edible plant foods to be found in the lands of the Inuit. Farther north, in the true Arctic desert, there are no plants of any kind. Trees grow along the southern edge of the tundra, but elsewhere they are uncommon, so wood is available as a building material only locally and nowhere can it be used as a fuel. Plants are more abundant on the Aleutian Islands than they are elsewhere in the region and Aleut women used to weave baskets and other items from grasses. Generally, though, the Inuit and Aleut peoples depend on animals rather than plants as their primary resource—and animal life is abundant.

Traditional Aleut villages were located on the coast of Alaska. The villagers needed a reliable source of freshwater, a beach where they could haul their boats ashore, and a clear view to give warning of attacks from other tribes. Most villages comprised a number of related families and a chief might rule over several villages. About 4,000 years ago Aleuts migrated from Alaska to the Aleutian Islands, taking with them their traditional way of life.

Aleuts gathered marine mollusks, but obtained most of their food by hunting. They caught birds and freshwater fish, such as salmon, but they were seafaring people and hunted mainly in coastal waters. They caught seals, sea otters, sea lions, whales, and occasionally walruses. Seals and sea otters were pursued in kayaks and killed with harpoons. Whales were hunted in larger boats, called *umiaks,* also by using harpoons. People living on the Alaskan mainland also hunted land mammals, especially caribou and bears.

Many Inuit people hunted in the same way and some still do. They also fished through the sea ice, caught seals when they visited their breathing holes, and stalked seals as they rested on the ice.

These were mainly winter pursuits. In spring communities who had spent the winter together started to disperse. Some fished in lakes or rivers, some pursued seals farther afield, and some set off to hunt the bowhead whale (*Balaena mysticetus*). In summer Inuit families used to move inland, traveling by dogsled, to hunt caribou, bears, and other large animals. They used bows and arrows for hunting on land.

Animals provided all the materials the Inuit needed. Where Amerindian peoples used wood, the Inuit used bone. It provided the skeletal framework for their buildings and boats. Skins provided them with tough, weatherproof clothing, tents, and outer coverings of boats. Blubber, the thick layer of fat that insulates the bodies of whales, walruses, and seals, provided fuel oil as well as food. The Inuit burned it in shallow dishes made from stone or pottery to provide light and heat for cooking.

Diet

The Inuit diet consists of fish, red meat, and blubber. Meat is cooked and eaten soon after the animal has been killed, which is when the Inuit say it tastes best, but they also eat raw frozen meat, for which the Inuit name is *quaq*. In the Arctic climate meat freezes naturally and fairly quickly on exposure to the air. Ice crystals that form in the blood and tissues are said to aid chewing. When meat is cooked it is always boiled and made into a stew or soup. Fish is either boiled or eaten raw and frozen.

The diet seems unbalanced to people brought up to believe it necessary to eat fruit and vegetables, but the Inuit thrive on it. Eventually it was discovered that although the Inuit eat no plant material directly, the animals they hunt do, and the vitamins (including vitamin C) and minerals that animals obtain from plants are stored in their tissues. Cooking destroys some of them, so a diet comprising nothing but cooked meat would be deficient, but the Inuit avoid the problem by eating *quaq,* which is raw.

Tools and Weapons

Animal bones were also used to make arrowheads and the heads of harpoons. The harpoon was attached to a long rope made from skin, and three large, inflated balloons, also made from sealskin and fastened to the rope, made it more difficult for a wounded sea animal to dive. Its struggles to do so helped exhaust it. Some Inuit used rawhide nets to catch seals, but never used them for fishing. Until the Inuit were able to obtain metal tools, knife blades were made of bone or ivory.

Bows were made from wood, bone, or antler and backed with twisted sinew, by a method very similar to that used by the Mongols. As it shrinks the sinew bends the bow into a curve. It is then pulled against the curve, so it bends in the other direction and is held in this position while being strung. This produces a very strong tension. Bones and stones were also carved to make articles of religious significance and more recently tourist souvenirs.

Inuit Society

Inuit society was based on the nuclear family, and the family owned only its dogs—the number of which was limited by the ability of the family to feed them—and what they could make with their own hands or had inherited from others. Kayaks, sleds, bows and arrows, harpoons, tools, tents, and clothing were private possessions, but a dwelling belonged to a family only as long as they occupied it. Once they moved out anyone could move in. The important resources, of hunting territory and fishing waters, belonged to everyone and no one.

There was a clear division of labor. Men built the home and provided the food. Women prepared the food, prepared skins, and made the clothes. This arrangement made men and women so dependent on each other that no one could live alone. Most marriages were monogamous, but occasionally a man might have two or even three wives and women occasionally found a second husband, although such relationships were usually temporary.

Quarrels between families often led to bitter and violent feuds, however. These could continue generation after generation and involve the persecution of the entire family, not only the individual who caused the original offense. Greenland Inuit tried to control feuding by inventing the "song duel." This was a public gathering at which two enemies insulted and ridiculed each other in song.

Arrival of Europeans

The traditional Inuit way of life began to change when European whalers arrived in the 19th century. They established whaling stations and traded with the Inuit, who found they could obtain manufactured goods in exchange for skins, furs, and ivory from walrus tusks. This improved the living standard for the Inuit, but contact with the Europeans also exposed them to diseases to which they had no immunity and there were many deaths.

Missionaries accompanied the whalers and traders. They opened missions and schools, and in 1970 the government of the Northwest Territories assumed responsibility for education. The Inuit were encouraged to settle and many abandoned their nomadic lives. Then, from the 1950s, mines and oil fields were established by industrial interests. These provided employment for local people, who then settled in the towns built to accommodate them.

Greenland Economy

Greenlanders have also settled in permanent houses. They live mainly by fishing, especially for shrimp, and sheep farming. More recently mining companies have conducted explorations for minerals. These certainly exist, but the climate and ice sheet make conditions extremely difficult for mining and it will be some years before the industry produces significant quantities or provides much employment. Until then the principal industries are fish processing, mainly of shrimps; handicrafts; fur preparation, and some small shipbuilding. Seal hunting has declined greatly, but Greenlanders are allowed to hunt whales for their own use.

Those Inuit who continue to live by hunting and fishing use modern methods. Nowadays animals are shot with rifles rather than harpoons. Dogsleds have been abandoned in favor of much faster, if noisier, snowmobiles. Seal hunters work from boats with outboard motors. Everyone wears clothing made in factories and bought in stores.

Inuit life may be less colorful than it once was, but in many ways living conditions have greatly improved. There are schools for the children and medical services for everyone, and the necessities of life are more easily obtained. Yet life has not improved for everyone and the Inuit have experienced the difficulties faced by other Native Americans in trying to adapt to, and be accepted by, the majority culture.

Antarctica

Antarctica has no native population. For centuries people believed there was a large continent in the Southern Hemisphere, but that belief arose from a love of symmetry. Southern lands were "needed" to balance those in the north. Belief led to rumor and legend, but it was not until the age of the Portuguese explorers that Europeans penetrated deeply into the Southern Hemisphere. Exploration intensified during the 19th century, but the first permanent stations for scientific research were not established until the 1940s.

Today there are about 40 stations that are occupied through the year (see illustration, page 21), together with a variable number of summer stations. In summer the population is about 4,200, falling to about 1,000 in winter.

Antarctica also attracts tourists. Each year about 10,000 visitors arrive by sea. They live on board their cruise ships and spend only a short time ashore, most landing on the Antarctic Peninsula. About 100 tourists arrive each year by air and others visit the continent on commercial flights that do not land.

Because Antarctica has no indigenous population it has been possible to regulate activities there, through the Antarctic Treaty. This allows scientific research but prohibits industrial or commercial development.

Desert Buildings

People build their homes from whatever materials are easily obtainable. If they live surrounded by big rocks, they build stone houses. Elsewhere they use mud or timber.

In the Far North the most plentiful material is snow, so that is what the Inuit use. Their word for house is *igdlu* from which we derive our word *igloo*.

It is a Canadian invention. The Eskimos of Alaska and Inuit of Greenland do not make igloos, but in what is now Nunavut it is the home in which families traditionally spend the winter. Building an igloo takes an experienced man no more than two hours.

Building an Igloo

First the builder selects a level site close to a deep drift of fine, compacted snow. From this he cuts rectangular blocks using a long-bladed knife, resembling a sword. Traditionally the blade was of bone, but today it is usually metal. Each block measures about 48 by 24 by 8 inches (120 by 60 by 20 cm). The first layer of blocks is laid in a circle and their tops are trimmed so they slope inward. A second layer is laid on top of the first, trimmed in the same way, and as further layers are added the structure curves inward to make a dome. Finally, room remains for one block on top, at the center. This will be the window and it is made from a piece of transparent seal intestine or a block of clear ice.

Entry to the igloo is by a semicylindrical passageway with recesses on either side for use as cupboards. A flap of sealskin hangs over the outer end of the entry tunnel and a low wall made from snow blocks may be built outside, a few feet away from the entrance. Between them these keep out the drafts. Inside there is a low platform covered with twigs and furs on which everyone sleeps.

Inuit who do not build in this style make their homes partly below ground, with upper walls and a roof made from stone, or from a frame of wood or whalebone covered with turf. In summer, when they may travel widely in pursuit of game, families often live in tents made from animal skins.

Covered Pits

At one time semiunderground homes were also built in the deserts farther south. During their Pioneer period, approximately from 300 B.C.E. to 500 C.E. the Hohokam people (pages 122 and 140) lived in shallow pits covered with a wooden or brushwood framework sealed with clay.

The Anasazi (page 162) stored food in covered pits of this kind, but they did not live in them. Their homes were either in caves or made from a wooden framework covered with mud that baked hard in the Sun—what modern builders would describe as a *timber-frame* method of construction—and they installed storage pits, often with roofs, in both their caves and outdoor dwellings.

Adobe

Blocks of baked mud are still used as a building material and both the blocks and the material they are made from are called *adobe*. Adobe is used where timber is hard to find and so buildings cannot be constructed by fitting cladding over a wooden frame. Instead, the walls must be solid and made from either masonry or clay, and of the two, clay is easier and quicker to use. Adobe walls provide excellent insulation against both heat and cold. This makes them especially suitable for desert climates.

Adobe was a traditional building material in North Africa, the Middle East, and Arabia by the time Spain came under Moorish rule in the eighth century. The word *adobe* is the Spanish version of *atob,* the Arabic name for a sun-dried brick. When Spaniards arrived in North America, taking in their knowledge of adobe construction with them, they found an identical technique being used by Native Americans.

Adobe soil is a mixture of sand, silt, and clay. When mixed with water it becomes sufficiently plastic to be easily shaped and it dries into a hard mass. Soil with these properties is common. Work begins with sorting or sieving the soil to remove stones bigger than about 1 inch (2.5 cm) across. Then the soil is mixed with enough water to turn it into a plastic mass of about the same consistency as the clay a potter would use. Once it has been well mixed it is left to stand for a day or two. This allows time for water to penetrate and soften all the small lumps. If straw or any other fibrous material is available it is then added. This strengthens the bricks and straw has been used in this way for thousands of years.

Clay Bricks

When the captive Israelites, forced to make bricks for the Egyptians, asked pharaoh for time off so they could go into the desert to make sacrifices, he punished them by refusing to continue supplying them with straw to make bricks, but without reducing the quota of bricks they were required to produce. Henceforth they had to find their own straw in their own time: "So the people were scattered abroad throughout all the land of Egypt to gather stubble instead of straw" (Exodus 5, 12).

The straw is mixed into the clay and the whole mass is trampled by bare feet. After that building can begin. Walls are built on a stone foundation—or nowadays a concrete base. The foundation must be impermeable to prevent water from being drawn into the adobe by capillarity (page 38). This would cause the clay to swell and the lower blocks to crumble, making the wall collapse.

North and Central American peoples used to shape the clay by hand into lumps roughly the size and shape of loaves of bread. These were laid one course at a time and each course was allowed to dry thoroughly before the next was added. The Spanish introduced molds for shaping the adobe into bricks. Nowadays the molds usually make bricks 3–5 by 10–12 by 14–20 inches (8–13 by 25–30 by 35–50 cm). The shaped bricks are dried completely before being used, and they are then used as ordinary house bricks are, with wet adobe clay as mortar. Finally, the finished walls are coated with plaster or, nowadays, cement.

Pueblo Apartment Buildings

Adobe construction was widely used in the Native American pueblos, but stone was also used. Between 1050 and 1300 C.E., known to archaeologists as the *Classic Pueblo period,* dressed stone came into use. That is stone that is shaped to improve the fit of one stone against another. Walls became thicker and stronger, and buildings were made bigger.

The builders constructed apartment buildings up to four stories high and with up to 1,000 rooms. In effect, each block of rooms was a village in itself. Rooms on the ground floor often had only one opening, in the roof, and the upper rooms had small windows and doors, but each story was set back from the one below. This gave every room a terrace made on the roof of the room below. The roofs were strengthened to take the weight by laying a layer of adobe 6–8 inches (15–20 cm) thick over a layer of rush matting supported on massive timber beams.

Pueblos also had underground rooms, called *kivas,* in which important religious ceremonies were performed. Some of these were 80 feet (25 m) across. Many Hopi pueblos are of this terraced type.

Cliff Dwellings

Some pueblos were built on ledges and in sheltered alcoves on the walls of canyons and mesas. These are usually known as *cliff dwellings.* Mesa Verde National Park, in southwestern Colorado, contains cliff dwellings built in the 13th century. Some are multistory structures built under overhanging cliffs, the largest of which, known as *Cliff Palace,* contains hundreds of rooms and several kivas.

Examples from the peak of pueblo construction can also be seen at Chaco Culture National Historical Park, in San Juan County, northwestern New Mexico. The site covers 53 square miles (137 sq km) and contains 13 ruins dating from pre-Columbian times as well as more than 300 smaller archaeological sites. Pueblo Bonito is a multistory settlement built in the 10th century, with about 800 rooms and 32 kivas.

African Homes

African houses are usually built as a number of separate buildings standing apart, each of which is one room. The rooms may be linked to each other—by walls, not passageways—and a fence or wall often encloses the group. All the rooms look identical. One is used for sleeping, one is the kitchen, another is for food storage, and the largest is likely to accommodate cattle. Adobe and clay mixed with stones are common building materials.

Some houses have more than one story. Those built by the Somolo people of Burkina Faso, for example, comprise six or seven circular buildings that are merged together, some with two stories and others with three. A single house contains up to 20 rooms. Each wife has her own room, there are rooms for the children, and some rooms are used to store food.

The Dogon people of Mali and Burkina Faso live in villages comprising dwellings clustered on the sides of escarpments. Their houses are made from adobe and roofed with thatch. Each dwelling accommodates a family, and the senior members of the community live in bigger houses.

In the Sahara and Middle Eastern deserts most ordinary houses are made from adobe, but stone is often used for more important buildings. Most desert buildings are square or rectangular, although in Ethiopia some Tigre farmhouses are circular, made from stone, and multistoried. When the Tuareg build permanent houses they are usually square and made of stone. Roofs are often flat, because there is no need for them to divert rainwater away from the walls or to shed snow and a flat roof is more economical in its use of materials.

Explorers of the Polar Deserts

In 1882, as the Norwegian sealing ship *Viking* sailed within sight of Greenland, a young member of the crew caught his first glimpse of the ice cap. As he was pondering what he had seen, it struck him that it might be possible to cross the ice cap—to cross Greenland. Over the next few years he developed an audacious plan. The inhabited towns and villages lie along the western coast. His plan was to start from the uninhabited eastern coast so there was no town to which the party could return and it would be compelled to continue. On August 15, 1888, the party of six explorers arrived at the eastern coast and their journey began. Their leader, then aged 26, was Fridtjof Nansen (1861–1930).

Nansen was a keen outdoor sportsman and expert skater and skier, and all the members of his team were in peak condition. They needed to be, because the crossing was arduous. On September 5 they reached the highest point, 8,921 feet (2,719 m) above sea level, and on September 26 they reached the west coast. It was then too late in the year to return to Norway, because of the sea ice, so the explorers spent the winter at Godthåb (now Nuuk). Nansen made use of his time there to study the Inuit and their way of life.

In 1909 the Belgian explorer Adrien de Gerlache (discussed later) crossed Greenland in the opposite direction, from west to east, at 77° N.

Drifting with the Ice–the *Fram*

Soon after his return from Greenland, Nansen was planning his next expedition, to study the movement of sea ice, which he calculated would carry a ship from Siberia to Spitzbergen. He designed a ship, the *Fram* (Forward), that would be lifted by the ice as the sea froze around it, instead of being crushed, and with a crew of 13 the *Fram* sailed from Kristiania (now Oslo) on June 24, 1893. It reached 78°50' N 133°37' E, northeast of the Novosibirskye Ostrova (New Siberian Islands), on September 22, where it became locked in the ice. The ship was not damaged and drifted with the ice, just as Nansen had predicted. The following March, Nansen and one companion, F. H. Johansen, left the *Fram* to journey north by dogsled and kayak. On April 8 they reached 86°14' N, the highest latitude anyone had reached at that time. They spent the winter in the Far North, in a hut of stone covered with a roof of walrus skin, and returned to Norway on August 13, 1896.

Nansen's *Fram* was the first ship to drift with the sea ice, but it was not the last. In 1937 a Soviet

icebreaker, the *Georgy Sedov,* was trapped by ice in the Laptev Sea and spent 27 months drifting across the Arctic Ocean. Airplanes were able to land on the sea ice and in 1937 a Soviet airplane based at Zemlya Frantsa-Iosifa (Franz Josef Land) landed four men at the North Pole. There they established a scientific research station, called *North Pole 1,* on a large ice floe. This drifted for 9 months. By the time the ice floe reached the Greenland Sea it was melting and the station and its crew were removed.

Arctic Aviators

Other Arctic explorers flew. The American aviator Richard Evelyn Byrd (1888–1957) claimed to be the first person to fly across the North Pole, on May 9, 1926, as the navigator with Floyd Bennett as pilot, although there was doubt over whether the claim was valid. Byrd's diary of the time, discovered in 1996, suggested that an oil leak from the starboard engine of his three-engined Fokker airplane had caused them to turn back. If that is so, the first flight over the Pole was made later in 1926 by an airship, the *Norge.* That expedition was financed and led by the American explorer and scientist Lincoln (originally William Linn) Ellsworth (1880–1951). The other members of the crew were the Italian aeronautical engineer Umberto Nobile (1885–1978) and Roald Amundsen (discussed later).

It was not the first time Ellsworth and Amundsen had flown together. In 1925 they made an attempt at the North Pole flying in two amphibian airplanes, each carrying three men. They reached 87°44' N before making an emergency landing. They were marooned for 30 days, which they spent carving a runway on the rough surface of the pack ice. Then one of the planes took off, heavily overloaded with all six members of the team, and managed to return to Spitzbergen. Nor was it Ellsworth's last emergency. In 1935, with the Canadian pilot Herbert Hollick-Kenyon, he flew from the Antarctic Peninsula to the Little America base, but they ran out of fuel and had to complete the journey on foot. Ellsworth later flew over Zemlya Frantsa-Iosifa and Novaya Zemlya for the American Geographical Society.

The first to cross the Arctic Ocean by air was the Australian-born British explorer Sir George Hubert Wilkins (1888–1958), who was knighted for the achievement. On April 16, 1928, Wilkins and Carl Ben Eielson took off from Point Barrow, Alaska, and landed, 20.5 hours later and 2,100 miles (3,400 km) away, at the Svalbard archipelago, north of Norway. Wilkins was not

only an aviator. He also pioneered the scientific use of submarines. In 1931 he navigated the U.S. submarine *Nautilus* beneath the Arctic Ocean as far as latitude 82°15' N.

Shackleton

Wilkins served as naturalist on the last Antarctic expedition made by Sir Ernest Henry Shackleton (1874–1922). This was the Shackleton–Rowett Expedition that began in 1921. Shackleton himself never completed it. He died at Grytviken, South Georgia, on January 5, 1922.

Shackleton began his Antarctic career in 1901, when he joined the British National Antarctic Expedition as third lieutenant. Sailing in the *Discovery* and led by Captain Robert Scott, the team reached the Ross Ice Shelf and Shackleton, Edward Wilson, and Scott traveled south by dogsled to 82°16'33" S, but Shackleton was unable to complete the expedition because of ill health. In 1908 he returned as leader of the British Antarctic Expedition, sailing in the *Nimrod.* They failed to reach their intended base and spent the winter on Ross Island, in McMurdo Sound. Shackleton led a party that came within 97 miles (156 km) of the South Pole.

In 1914, Shackleton led the British Imperial Trans-Antarctic Expedition. The plan was to cross the continent from the Weddell Sea to McMurdo Sound, via the South Pole. Their ship, the *Endurance,* became trapped in ice, drifted for 10 months, and was finally crushed. Six of the explorers spent the following five months drifting on ice floes before escaping to Elephant Island, one of the South Shetland Islands. This involved them in an 800-mile (1,287-km) journey in an open whale boat, followed by a crossing of the island to seek help.

Overwintering in Antarctica–the *Belgica* and *Southern Cross*

By the time of the Scott and Shackleton expeditions the feasibility of overwintering in Antarctica had been established. The first ship to spend the winter there was the *Belgica,* a Belgian vessel commanded by Adrien-Victor Joseph, baron de Gerlache de Gomery (1866–1934). The mate on the *Belgica* was a Norwegian, Roald Amundsen. De Gerlache explored the region north of the peninsula then sailed into pack ice, where the *Belgica* remained trapped for 13 months, from March 1898 to March 1899.

During the same winter, an expedition from London led by Carsten Egeberg Borchgrevink, sailing on the *Southern Cross,* camped at Cape Adare, on the northern tip of Victoria Land, the region on the western side of the Ross Sea.

Bellingshausen

Earlier explorers had approached the Antarctic coast, so those intending to land already had an idea of what to expect. The first crossing of the Antarctic Circle was by Sir James Cook in 1772. Nearly half a century passed before anyone else attempted this voyage. In July 1819, the *Vostok* and *Mirnyi* sailed from Kronstadt, Russia, on an expedition authorized by Czar Alexander I and led by Fabian Gottlieb von Bellingshausen (1778–1852). They crossed the Circle on January 26, 1820, and crossed it several more times before returning to Russia. At one point they were within 20 miles (32 km) of the coast.

Dumont d'Urville and Wilkes

In 1837, a French expedition led by Captain Jules-Sébastien-César Dumont d'Urville (1790–1842) sailed from Toulon in two ships, the *Astrolabe* and *Zélée.* They managed to map the coast of the northern part of the Antarctic Peninsula and chart the waters offshore, but the exploration had to be abandoned when scurvy broke out among the crew of both ships. They returned later and named part of the continent *Terre Adélie,* after Dumont d'Urville's wife. The famous Adélie penguins are also named after her, and the principal French research station, on the coast near the Magnetic South Pole, is called the *Dumont d'Urville Station.*

One day in January 1840, the two French ships saw an American ship approaching. This was the *Porpoise,* commanded by Charles Wilkes (1798–1877), leader of the United States Exploring Expedition that lasted from 1838 until 1842. The two commanders ignored each other, Dumont d'Urville sailing north, Wilkes maintaining his westerly course, each believing the other had insulted him. Wilkes sailed along the edge of the ice pack for about 1,500 miles (2,400 km), spotting land several times. This was the first proof that an Antarctic continent existed. The part of the continent he saw is now known as *Wilkes Land.*

Ross and Weddell

James Clark Ross (1800–62) was also in the area at the time. He was a British naval officer leading an expedition with two ships, the *Erebus* and *Terror.*

Sailing from Hobart, Tasmania, in November 1840, they headed first for the Auckland Islands. There they found two boards bearing notices. One said Charles Wilkes had stopped there on March 10, 1840. Beside it, the other announced that Dumont d'Urville had been there on March 11.

Ross found the way south blocked by a smooth, perpendicular cliff of ice, 150–200 feet (46–61 m) high and flat at the top. He called it the *Victoria Barrier.* In fact it was the edge of what was later renamed the *Ross Ice Shelf.* Ross also named an active Antarctic volcano after one of his ships, as Mount Erebus, and an extinct volcano nearby after the other, as Mount Terror. Both are located on Ross Island, where the United States McMurdo base and the British Scott base are presently located, on the western side of the Ross Sea.

Ross sailed around the ice of the Weddell Sea. That sea was discovered in 1823 by a British sealer, James Weddell (1787–1834), who named it *King George IV's Sea.* In his search for seals, Weddell claimed to have sailed about 214 miles (344 km) farther south than James Cook.

Byrd, Ellsworth, and Palmer

Other regions of Antarctica are also named for explorers or their wives. Whatever the truth about his Arctic flight, Richard E. Byrd led three highly successful expeditions to Antarctica, in 1928–30, 1933–35, and 1939–41. During the first expedition he established a supply base called *Little America* on the Ross Ice Shelf close to the Bay of Whales. From there he flew as navigator over a large area of the continent. He discovered the Rockefeller Mountains, which he named after one of his sponsors, and the territory behind them, which he called *Marie Byrd Land,* after his wife. He made his last flight over the South Pole on January 8, 1956.

Lincoln Ellsworth, a member of what was possibly the first team to fly over the North Pole, also explored much of Antarctica from the air. The Ellsworth Mountains and Ellsworth Land are named after him.

The southern part of the Antarctic Peninsula with its adjacent islands is called *Palmer Land.* It is named after an American sea captain and explorer, Nathaniel Brown Palmer (1799–1877). He went to sea at 14 and later became a sealer. In 1818 he was made captain of the schooner *Galina* and began his explorations in 1819, mainly as part of a search for seal rookeries.

Scott

The most famous Antarctic expeditions both began in 1910. The British naval officer Robert

Falcon Scott (1868–1912) led one, and the Norwegian explorer Roald Engelbregt Gravning Amundsen (1872–1928) led the other. Scott's first expedition lasted from 1901 to 1904. He was the first person to survey the surrounding area from a tethered balloon, in 1902. The 1902 expedition used dogsleds to penetrate deep into the interior of the continent. The second expedition aimed to study the Ross Sea and reach the South Pole.

In 1908, Shackleton had used an automobile in his exploration of Ross Island and had pioneered a route up the Beardmore Glacier using Manchurian ponies. These achievements persuaded Scott to attempt the journey to the Pole with motorized sledges, ponies, and dogs. His party of 12 men set out from Cape Evans, Ross Island, on October 24, 1911. It was not long before the motorized sledges broke down and had to be abandoned. Then the ponies failed and had to be shot. Finally, when they reached 83°30' S, the dogs could not continue and had to be sent back. On December 10 the party commenced the ascent of the Beardmore Glacier by hauling the sledges manually. By the end of the month seven men had dropped out. The remaining five—Scott, E. A. Wilson, H. R. Bowers, L. E. G. Oates, and Edgar Evans—reached the Pole on January 18, only to discover that Amundsen had arrived there about a month earlier.

On the return journey the weather was very severe and supplies of food and fuel were low. Evans died on February 17, at Beardmore; Oates walked away into a blizzard on March 17. Scott, Wilson, and Bowers continued for a further 10 miles (16 km) but were then confined to their tent by a blizzard that continued for 9 days. That is where they died, of cold and exhaustion, only 11 miles from the depot where they had left stores that would have saved them.

Amundsen

Amundsen had sailed on the *Belgica.* For his southern expedition he took Nansen's ship, the *Fram.*

The *Fram* anchored in the Bay of Whales, on the eastern side of the Ross Sea close to the edge of the ice shelf, 60 miles (96.5 km) farther south than the Scott camp at Cape Evans. Amundsen then led a party to deposit supplies at several points along the first part of the route south.

His team of five men, 52 dogs, and four sledges set out on October 19, 1911, and reached the South Pole on December 14. They left the Pole on December 17 and reached their base on January 25, 1912.

Explorers in Africa, Arabia, and Asia

It was not until the 15th century that European explorers began to travel to Africa. One of the first was a Venetian, Alvise Ca' da Mosto (or Cadamosto, 1432–88), who sailed on March 22, 1455. He stopped at Madeira, the Canary Islands, and passed the mouth of the Senegal River. On another voyage in 1456 he reached the Cape Verde Islands—and may have been the first European to do so. He sailed some distance up the Gambia River and explored part of the coast.

At the same time as Ca' da Mosto was exploring West Africa, so was Diogo Gomes (1440–84), a Portuguese explorer. He also sailed up the Gambia River, and at the town of Kuntaur (then called Cantor) in central Gambia he met men who came from the remote city of Timbuktu. Illness among his crew prevented him from traveling farther inland, but the name of Timbuktu became a magnet to later European adventurers.

Laing, Caillé, and Timbuktu

Serious European exploration began in the 19th century. It was part of the colonialist expansion into Africa and much of it centered on the river systems, as routes into the interior of the continent. Timbuktu had not lost its appeal, however, and on August 18, 1826, the Scottish explorer Alexander Gordon Laing (1793–1826) became the first European to reach it.

Starting from Tripoli, Libya, he crossed the desert to Ghudāmis in northern Fezzan, where he entered Tuareg territory and was badly wounded in a fight. He stayed in Timbuktu until September 24, but two days after leaving he was murdered by his guide.

Two years later, the French explorer René-Auguste Caillé (1799–1838) became the first European to visit Timbuktu and return alive. He left the West African coast in April 1827, posing as an Arab traveling to Egypt. He fell sick on the way and was delayed for 5 months, but reached Timbuktu on April 20, 1828. After spending 2 weeks there he headed north for Morocco and then back to France.

Clapperton and Barth

Another Scot was the first European to visit and describe northern Nigeria and Lake Chad. Hugh Clapperton (1788–1827), a naval captain, accompanied by Major Dixon Denham, an English officer, and an Edinburgh physician, Walter Oudney, traveled south from Tripoli and reached Lake Chad early in 1823. From Lake Chad the party continued to Kano, Katsina, and Sokoto, in what was then the kingdom of Bornu and is now northern Nigeria.

One of the most comprehensive studies of North and Central Africa was made between 1850 and 1855 by the Prussian geographer Heinrich Barth (1821–65). He spoke Arabic fluently—as well as French, Spanish, Italian, and English—and had already explored the North African coast before embarking on a journey across the Sahara. The expedition left Tripoli in 1850, led by the English explorer James Richardson (1806–51), who had earned his reputation traveling in India, and including the German geologist and astronomer Adolf Overweg (1822–52)—the first European to travel all the way around Lake Chad and sail on its waters.

They went southwest, into what is now northern Nigeria. Richardson died there in 1851 and Barth took command. He and Overweg traveled south and around the southern shore of Lake Chad. Overweg died in September 1852, and although his own health was by then poor, Barth continued alone, eventually to Timbuktu. He stayed there for 6 months before heading back to Tripoli and from there to London.

By the time his journey ended Barth had traveled about 10,000 miles (16,000 km). He was able to describe the middle section of the Niger River and had recorded the routes he had followed.

Duveyrier, Rohlfs, and Nachtigal

Henri Duveyrier (1840–92), the French explorer, met Barth and was inspired by him. Like Barth, Duveyrier learned to speak Arabic, and in 1859, when he was 19, he set off on a 3-year journey through the Northern Sahara. In the course of that and later travels, Duveyrier spent a great deal of time living with the Tuareg, studying their dialect and way of life.

Gerhard Friedrich Rohlfs (1831–96) was much more of an adventurer. Born near Bremen, in northern Germany, in 1855 he joined the French Foreign Legion. He learned Arabic, and in 1862, disguised as an Arab, he explored Morocco and the Atlas Mountains and traveled as far south as the Fezzan region of Libya, where he arrived in 1864. In 1865 he embarked on a journey no other European had attempted, from Tripoli across the desert to northeastern Nigeria, then down the Niger River to the Gulf of Guinea, near Lagos. In 1874 he undertook another journey, this time from Tripoli to Egypt. In 1885 Rohlfs was made German consul in Zanzibar, in East Africa.

Gustav Nachtigal (1834–85) also became a consul, in Tunis. He was a doctor, first in the German army and later as physician to the ruler—called the *bey*—of Tunisia. While in Tunis he made several journeys into the desert, and in 1869 King William I of Prussia sent him to Bornu, the kingdom in what is today northern Nigeria. He crossed the desert and the Tibesti Mountains to enter Borkou (or Borku) a region that was then controlled by Ouaddaï, a Muslim sultanate, and inhabited by nomadic and seminomadic tribes. Nachtigal crossed Chad and the Sudan and continued to Cairo, where he arrived in November 1875.

Exploring the Kalahari and Namib

Exploration was less intensive in southern Africa. The Scottish explorer and missionary David Livingstone (1813–73) crossed the Kalahari Desert in 1849.

The Namib Desert remained largely unknown until the 19th century. In the 1890s South West Africa became a German territory. German military expeditions then began detailed surveys and the compilation of maps of the desert.

Arabia

If exploring the Sahara and Kalahari was difficult for Europeans, traveling in Arabia was even more so. Until the 18th century almost nothing was known in Europe about the interior.

King Frederick V of Denmark was the first European ruler to send a scientific expedition to Arabia. It was led by a German surveyor, Carsten Niebuhr (1733–1815), and it set out in 1762. The team of five visited the Nile, crossed it into Sinai, then sailed south along the Arabian coast as far as Jidda. From there they traveled overland to Mocha (al-Mukhā) in the far southwest.

An important travel book appeared in 1888. *Travels in Arabia Deserta* was written by the English traveler Charles Montagu Doughty (1843–1926). In 1876 he set out from Damascus, traveling with pilgrims bound for Mecca. He did not reach Mecca, but visited towns in the mountainous region of Jabal Shammar, deep inside Arabia, as well as the port of Jidda.

Philby and Ibn Sa'ūd

During World War I, Turkey fought on the side of Germany. This made the entire region to the south of Turkey militarily important to the British and French and this meant winning allies among the Arab rulers. In 1917, the British government sent Harry Saint John Bridger Philby (1885–1960) to meet 'Abd al-'Azīz ibn Sa'ūd.

After the meeting, Philby traveled from Al-'Uqayr, on the eastern coast just south of the island of Bahrain and opposite Qatar, to Jidda on the western coast. This journey took him across the northern part of the Rub' al-Khali, the Empty Quarter. In the 1920s he set up his own business in Arabia, and in 1930 he became a convert to Islam. He became a friend and adviser to Ibn Sa'ūd, who had gained control of most of Arabia and who formed the Kingdom of Saudi Arabia in 1932. Philby helped to map Arabia and contributed to the study of its archaeology and the languages of its peoples.

Lawrence of Arabia

From 1920 to 1924 Philby represented the British government in Jordan—then called *Transjordan*. He took over the position from the most famous of all the explorers and adventurers ever to travel in Arabia, T. E. Lawrence—Lawrence of Arabia. No one has done more to popularize and romanticize Arab culture.

Thomas Edward Lawrence (1888–1935), known later in his life as John Hume Ross and T. E. Shaw, began his career as a student of military architecture. It was this interest that took him to Syria and Palestine and then, from 1911 to 1914, to the banks of the Euphrates as a member of an archaeological expedition. He spent his free time exploring, learning Arabic, and getting to know local people. He helped to map the region between Gaza (*Ghazzah* in Arabic, '*Azza* in Hebrew), now in southern Israel, and Al-Aqabah (Aqaba) in southern Jordan. This led to a job preparing a militarily useful map of Sinai in the Map Department of the War Office in London. He soon returned to the region, first to Cairo and then to Arabia.

Ḥusayn ibn 'Alī, the amīr (commander) of the territory around Mecca, was in revolt against the Turks. After consultations with Abdullah, one of his sons, Lawrence went to see another son, Fayṣal, who was leading troops near Medina. Lawrence returned to Cairo and persuaded the British authorities to supply money and weapons to the local rulers opposing Turkey and unite them in a resistance that served British purposes.

That is how Lawrence came to lead a small guerrilla force operating behind Turkish lines, destroying trains and bridges. His other aim was to forge the quarrelsome tribal leaders into a coherent Arab nation, using bribes, promises of booty, and his own example of stamina and courage. His force captured Al-Aqabah in July 1917 and reached Damascus in 1918, but in the course of his campaign Lawrence was captured, tortured, and wounded several times.

Out of these experiences Lawrence wrote *The Seven Pillars of Wisdom*. This is an account of the desert campaign, but it also describes the Bedouin beside whom Lawrence fought and for whom he had a genuine and deep affection. After the war he argued strongly for Arab independence.

Wilfred Thesiger

The British soldier, traveler, photographer, and travel writer Sir Wilfred Thesiger (born in 1910) has kept the romance of the desert alive in more recent times. He was born in Addis Ababa and lived there until he was 9 years old, so could claim that northern Africa was his home.

He made several crossings of the Rub' al-Khali, but his main interest was the Ma'dan, or Marsh Arabs. They live in southern Iraq in a region of marshland between the Euphrates and Tigris. Thesiger described them in his book *The Marsh Arabs*, published in 1964.

Rediscovering the Silk Road

European exploration of the deserts of central Asia began in the late 19th century. The Silk Road (page 138) had fallen into disuse as sea routes grew safer and more reliable. Its rediscovery began with the work of the Prussian geographer and geologist Ferdinand Paul Wilhelm, Freiherr von Richthofen (1833–1905). He traveled throughout China and described the country in his five-volume work *China, Ergebnisse eigener Reisen und darauf gegründeter Studien* (China, results of my own travels and studies based on them), published between 1877 and 1912. It was von Richthofen who named the travel route the *Silk Road*.

In 1893 the Swedish explorer Sven Anders Hedin (1865–1952) began a 5-year journey across the Ural and Pamir Mountains, past Lop Nor, and to Beijing, along the old Silk Road. Later he discovered the way the Lop Nor lake had formed, from shifts in the course of the Tamir River. When he was there the area had no inhabitants. The groups of Uighur people who once lived there left around 1920, because of a plague that killed many of them. The lake itself, which covered about 770 square miles (2,000 sq km) in 1950, ceased to exist in 1970 when dams held back the water of the Tamir that used to feed into it. Between 1899 and 1902 Hedin explored the Gobi Desert and from 1927 to 1933 he led a Sino-Swedish expedition that discovered evidence of Stone Age cultures in what is now desert.

Sir Aurel Stein and the Cave of a Thousand Buddhas

The name most closely associated with the rediscovery of the Silk Road, however, is that of Hungarian-born Mark Aurel Stein (1862–1943). Stein became a British citizen in 1904 and was knighted in 1912. He died in Kabul.

Sir Aurel Stein conducted three expeditions, in 1900, 1906, and 1913, into what are now Xinjiang and the Uighur Autonomous Region of China. These lasted a total of seven years and followed the old caravan routes between China and the West for about 25,000 miles (40,200 km). Stein traced the Silk Road across Lop Nor and found the Jade Gate that had once stood at the border between China and the Western Kingdoms and the walls built to prevent nomads from entering China. As he went, he excavated ancient sites carefully, discovering long-lost cities and, near the city of Tun-Huang (page 138), the Cave of the Thousand Buddhas.

This is a temple that was carved into a cliff in 366 C.E., at the start of a period, lasting to the early 13th century, when the city was a major Buddhist center. Eventually there were nearly 500 temple caves, now known as the *Mogao Caves*. Many are now open to the public, and in 1987 the area was declared a World Heritage Site. In one of the caves Stein discovered a hoard of about 60,000 paper manuscripts and other documents, dating from the fifth to 11th centuries, that had been walled up in 1015. They included Buddhist, Taoist, Zoroastrian, and Nestorian scriptures, stories, and ballads and were written in Chinese, Sanskrit, Tibetan, Uighur, and other languages. There were also paintings and temple banners. Stein removed many of them and the French scholar Paul Pelliot later removed more. These returned to London and Paris, where they were properly stored, cataloged, and published, but news of their removal reached the Chinese authorities in Beijing. They bought what material remained in Tun-huang and dispatched it to Beijing, but the money sent to pay for it was stolen en route and most of the material was stolen before it reached Beijing. Much of it has now been lost.

Oil and the Economies of Modern Desert Countries

In 1859, Colonel Edwin L. Drake (1819–80) was trying to recruit workers to drill for oil just outside the city of Titusville, Pennsylvania. The story goes that the reply they gave him was "Drill for oil? You mean drill into the ground to try and find oil? You're crazy!"

Perhaps their attitude is not surprising. Drake was not a colonel at all, but an impoverished former streetcar conductor who wore a top hat spattered with mud. In any case, oil seeped from the ground not far from Titusville. There was no need to go looking for it. All the same, "Colonel" Drake succeeded in persuading

workers to join him and they sank a well to a depth of 70 feet (21 m). Oil gushed from the ground and for the people of Titusville prosperity followed. Oil City was founded in 1860, not far from Titusville, and millions of barrels of oil traveled from there by river to Pittsburgh between 1860 and 1870.

It was said to be the first oil well in the world. In fact, though, the Chinese struck oil while drilling for salt—the two often occur together—in the third century C.E., and the Greek historian Herodotus, writing in the fifth century B.C.E., described how salt, oil, and bitu-

Petroleum refineries on the Nile

men—a more viscous kind of petroleum—were obtained.

The Birth of the Oil Industry

People have been using oil for at least 5,000 years, but the uses were limited. The oil was obtained from places where it seeped from the ground and the most liquid part of it was used for lighting. In

PER CAPITA GDP IN DESERT COUNTRIES, 1997
(U.S. $)

Country	GDP	Category
Algeria	1,600	OPEC
Bahrain	7,840	oil producer
Burkina Faso	230	
Chad	180	
Djibouti	835	
Egypt	790	
Ethiopia	100	
Iran	1,000	OPEC
Iraq	540	OPEC
Israel	15,920	
Jordan	1,510	
Kuwait	17,390	OPEC
Lebanon	2,660	
Libya	6,510	OPEC
Mali	250	
Mauritania	460	
Mexico	3,320	Oil producer
Mongolia	310	
Morocco	1,110	
Namibia	2,000	
Niger	220	
Nigeria	260	OPEC
Oman	4,820	Oil producer
Qatar	11,600	OPEC
Saudi Arabia	7,040	OPEC
Somalia	150	
Sudan	300	
Syria	1,120	Oil producer
Tunisia	1,820	
United Arab Emirates	17,400	OPEC
Yemen	260	Oil producer

Note: *OPEC: member of the Organization of Petroleum Exporting Countries; oil producer: non-OPEC country that exports petroleum.*

both Arabic and Persian this oil was called *naft,* from which we derive our word *naphtha.* Bitumen was used as mortar, for setting of jewels, as a cement for laying mosaics, and as an adhesive for attaching the handles of tools and weapons to their blades. Lighter oil was used as a solvent for cleaning fabrics as well as for lighting. Various medicines and ointments contained petroleum.

Surfaced Roads

Asphalt was being used to surface roads as long ago as the fifth century B.C.E. Herodotus, the Greek historian who lived at that time and who was a great traveler, described walking the length of one of them, known as the Royal Road. It ran between Susa, which was the capital of Elam, a country in what is now southwestern Iran, and the Aegean coast in what is now Turkey, for a distance of 1,500 miles (2,413 km). Herodotus said he walked the whole of it.

The need for good roads became evident when knowledge of horseback riding spread to the Middle East from the region of what is now Ukraine where it began. Domesticated horses were used as draft animals as well as for riding. This included using them to draw two- and four-wheeled war chariots. These were rather heavy, clumsy vehicles and probably used to carry soldiers into battle rather than as weapons in their own right—in modern terms they were personnel carriers rather than armored cars. The design was improved over the years. Originally they had solid wheels. These were replaced by much lighter wheels with spokes, and the new, fast chariots were usually drawn by four horses running abreast.

Chariots were used in warfare, for hunting, and for racing. Civilian versions were the fast sports cars of their day, but, like modern cars, they were not designed to travel over rough ground or through mud or loose sand. A poor surface delayed them and a rough surface could damage them. That is why the Assyrians and Persians covered their roads with asphalt to make a smooth, hard surface. One ancient inscription included the claim by a king that he had found his kingdom in mud and left it "laced with roads glistening with asphalt." Asphalt is still used in road building.

Asphalt is a sticky black or brown substance that is a thick liquid when hot but that sets hard. It was known in India as "earth butter" and its earliest use may have been to seal the brick walls of a reservoir in Mohenjo-Daro soon after 4000 B.C.E.

Rock Oil and Rockefeller

Oil was not "invented" at Titusville, but the sinking of its well did mark an important development, because for the first time petroleum—at first known as "rock oil"—was available in large amounts all in one place. This made it an industrial commodity. It could be processed—refined—and new uses for it could be found.

One of the first businessmen to appreciate the significance of the increasing output in Pennsylvania was John Davison Rockefeller (1839–1937). He built an oil refinery near Cleveland, Ohio, in 1863 and used oil as the fuel in its furnaces. Rockefeller founded Standard Oil. Eventually the company he established was declared illegal and disbanded, but the successors of Standard Oil include such familiar names as Exxon, Mobil, Amoco, and Chevron. By 1890, petroleum was also being obtained from wells and refined in Russia.

Still the market was fairly small—and likely to shrink as gas lighting replaced oil lamps. Lighting was the main use for oil, but some was used as a source of cleaning fluids and lubricants. Its expansion began with the mass production of automobiles, which demanded highly refined gasoline. In the 1930s the rapid expansion of air travel and aircraft manufacture increased the demand still more, and for fuel of even higher quality. When jet engines were introduced, demand increased again. With the increasing demand for fuel oils there was also a demand for lubricating oils. More oil was needed and oil companies began searching for it outside America. The use of oil for heating buildings began in the 1920s.

Oil from the Middle East

In 1901, the Iranian government granted an oil field concession to an English investor, William Knox D'Arcy. In 1909 D'Arcy formed the Anglo-Persian Oil Company. Wells were drilled, crude oil was piped to a refinery at the port of Ābādān on the Persian Gulf, and the first oil was exported from there in March 1912. More wells were drilled, more refineries built, and by the late 1930s Iran was a major oil producer. By 1914 the British government had become a major stockholder in the Anglo-Persian Oil Company. Eventually it was the biggest single stockholder, and in 1955 the company's name was changed and it became British Petroleum (BP). The government sold its stock in the late 1970s and 1980s, BP became Britoil, and Britoil acquired Standard Oil (Ohio).

Farther south, Ibn Sa'ūd—or to give him his full name 'Abd al-'Azīz Ibn 'Abd Ar-Raḥmān Ibn Fayṣal Ibn Turkī 'Abd Allāh Ibn Muḥammad Āl Sa'ūd—ruled Saudi Arabia, but both he and his country were very poor. In May 1933 he granted a concession to an American oil company, but five years passed before they struck oil. That was in the Dammam field, south of the port of Ad-Dammam on the Persian Gulf and close to the modern town of Az Zahrān (or Dhahran).

Then World War II began and operations were halted, so the king was no better off. The oil company resumed work after the war and it was then that the king started to receive substantial payments. By 1953 these amounted to $2.5 million *a week*. He had no idea what to do with all his money. Such wealth offended his austere religious convictions and swindlers and criminals of all kinds were moving into his country. He hated all of it.

In the 1950s oil was discovered in Libya. Until then that country had had few natural resources and relied on foreign aid to pay for the import of many of the commodities it needed. Once the oil was flowing the economy of the country was transformed and Libya became one of the wealthiest countries in Africa. It used its wealth to develop agriculture and manufacturing industries, and it established health and educational services for its people. In 1956 oil was discovered in Syria, but production did not commence until 1968. Petroleum and products made from it now account for more than half Syria's exports, but Syrian oil fields are much smaller than those of the major Middle Eastern producers.

Oil fields discovered in Algeria in the 1960s proved to be among the biggest in the world. They are also rich in natural gas, of which Algeria is now one of the world's most important producers.

The Al-Burmah (or El-Borma) oil field in southern Tunisia opened in 1964. Tunisian reserves are smaller than those of Libya and most Middle Eastern oil-producing countries, but they are economically important nevertheless. Oil production also began in Oman in 1964. Nigeria

OIL RESERVES BY REGION
(BILLIONS OF BARRELS)

Region	Reserves	Undiscovered Reserves	Total
North America	106	121	227
South America	93	44	137
Western Europe	19	28	47
Eastern Europe and Russia	104	64	168
Central Asia	24	39	63
Middle East	666	122	788
Africa	62	48	110
Oceania and Asia	45	81	126
WORLD TOTAL	1,119	547	1,666

MANUFACTURING AS A PROPORTION OF GDP AND EMPLOYMENT

Country	Percentage of Total Value	Percentage of Labor Force
Algeria	9.3	11.3
Bahrain	19.5	11.8
Burkina Faso	20.0*	1.1
Chad	12.7	1.5
Djibouti	5.0	n.a.
Egypt	26.9*	12.7
Ethiopia	7.6*	1.6*
Iran	13.9	13.7
Iraq	9.5	8.2
Israel	21.5*	18.8*
Jordan	16.2	10.6*
Kuwait	11.2	6.8
Lebanon	13.0	n.a.
Libya	8.4	n.a.
Mali	6.4	5.5
Mauritania	10.7	1.0
Mexico	18.7	14.5
Mongolia	27.0*	11.7*
Morocco	18.6	n.a.
Namibia	8.9	4.6
Niger	6.6	2.8
Nigeria	5.4	4.1
Oman	4.3	8.6
Qatar	11.4	3.6
Saudi Arabia	9.4	6.5
Somalia	4.4	n.a.
Sudan	8.0	4.2
Syria	5.7	13.1
Tunisia	18.2	19.6
United Arab Emirates	8.6	9.2
Yemen	10.2	4.6

* Includes mining.
n.a.: not available.

became an oil-producing country in the late 1960s. In the late 1980s oil was discovered in Yemen and now accounts for more than 95 percent of that country's exports.

VITAL STATISTICS FOR DESERT COUNTRIES

Country	Birth Rate per 1,000	Death Rate per 1,000	Life Expectancy at Birth (Years) Male	Female
World average	25.0	9.3		
Algeria	28.5	5.9	67.2	69.5
Bahrain	27.4	5.4	69.0	72.4
Burkina Faso	47.0	20.0	43.5	42.9
Chad	44.6	17.7	44.9	49.6
Djibouti	42.0	15.0	48.6	52.6
Egypt	28.0	9.0	65.4	69.5
Ethiopia	48.2	16.2	48.4	51.6
Iran	33.7	6.6	66.1	68.7
Iraq	34.1	9.8	57.3	60.4
Israel	20.0	6.0	76.3	80.2
Jordan	34.3	3.0	64.4	69.9
Kuwait	24.3	2.2	74.4	79.0
Lebanon	26.9	7.1	66.6	70.5
Libya	44.4	7.7	62.1	66.6
Mali	50.0	20.0	44.7	48.1
Mauritania	46.9	15.2	46.1	52.1
Mexico	30.4	4.8	66.5	73.1
Mongolia	25.0	8.0	64.0	67.0
Morocco	27.9	6.0	67.0	71.0
Namibia	37.5	11.9	57.5	60.0
Niger	54.5	24.6	41.1	40.2
Nigeria	45.4	15.4	53.5	55.9
Qatar	19.9	3.4	68.8	74.2
Saudi Arabia	35.1	4.7	68.4	71.4
Somalia	44.3	18.2	44.6	47.8
Sudan	41.1	11.5	54.2	56.1
Syria	40.0	6.0	68.4	71.3
Tunisia	23.9	5.9	68.4	70.7
United Arab Emirates	25.0	3.4	69.2	75.2
Yemen	45.1	11.8	55.9	59.1
United States	14.9	9.2	73.4/67.5	79.6/75.8

Note: *Figures for life expectancy in the United States are given first for white and then for black and other persons.*

Oil and National Wealth

Deserts are hard places to live and in material terms their populations are poor. The discovery and exploitation of oil clearly make an important difference to them, although this difference is not so obvious as it might seem. The table compares the per capita gross domestic products of most of the desert countries of the world.

The gross domestic product (GDP) is the combined value of all the goods and services produced within a country in a year, but not including income from overseas investments and not allowing for depreciation or the use of capital in the process of production. The per capita GDP is the GDP divided by the size of the population. It does not represent the amount individual citizens are actually paid. For comparison, the per capita GDP in the United States in 1997 was $28,495.

The table indicates those countries that produce oil. Those labeled *OPEC* are members of the Organization of Petroleum Exporting Countries (OPEC). As the table shows, the smallest oil-producing countries are also the richest. This is because their smaller populations means there are fewer people among whom the GDP is shared and it demonstrates that oil wealth is based on the exploitation of a natural resource, rather than on manufacturing. In economic terms, oil is a primary product and although a country may process the petroleum into oil products, thus adding value to it, the economic activity remains wholly dependent on the oil itself, which is the primary product.

OPEC

OPEC was established in September 1960 and its headquarters are now in Vienna. Its original members were Iran, Iraq, Kuwait, Saudi Arabia, and Venezuela. Since then Qatar, Indonesia, Libya, United Arab Emirates, Algeria, Nigeria, Ecuador, and Gabon have joined. The aim of OPEC is to regulate the oil market by coordinating production and export among its members. If world prices fall, production is reduced, and if prices rise, production increases, but without individual OPEC members' competing with each other.

The effectiveness of OPEC was first demonstrated at its meetings in September and October 1973, when it increased oil prices by 70 percent, and in December 1973, when it raised them a further 13 percent. There were additional price rises in subsequent years. Today OPEC is less influential. This is partly because oil production is taking place outside the OPEC area, in Alaska, the Gulf of Mexico, and the North Sea, for example, and partly because oil consumers have turned to alternative sources of energy—mainly nuclear power and coal—and have increased the efficiency with which energy is used.

Running Out of Oil

For years there have been fears that a day will come when the oil fields have been drained and the world runs out of petroleum. It is true that the world has only a limited supply of petroleum and each gallon that is used is lost—the resource is finite. It is also true that so far the world has used a total of about 724 billion barrels. This is roughly two-thirds of the amount of proven reserves that are known, have been measured, and can be extracted economically using present technology. There are also reserves that remain undiscovered, but are calculated to exist on the basis of studies of rock formations.

The second table gives approximate figures for proven reserves and undiscovered reserves, and the total of the two, distributed among geographical regions. At present the world is using about 22 billion barrels of oil a year and the rate of use is not increasing.

The figures are given in billions of barrels. The barrel (abbreviation *bbl*) is the unit by which oil is commonly measured: 1 bbl = 42 gallons = 159 liters. As the table shows, the reserves are not distributed evenly. Almost 60 percent of them are located in the Middle East.

It is unlikely that the world will ever run out of oil in a literal sense. As demand increases, so does the intensity of exploration, which reveals new sources. Should oil become scarce, consumers would switch to alternative fuels and oil would cease to be used long before the last of it was gone. Before that happens, there are vast reserves of tar sands and shale oils that could be exploited. Obtaining oil from these is much more expensive than taking it from conventional oil fields, and it might be difficult to exploit them in ways that are environmentally acceptable, but they exist. Natural gas is even more abundant, locked in marine sediments in compounds called *natural gas* (or methane) hydrates. Estimates suggest that the reserves of these are approximately double those of all other fossil fuels (coal, oil, and natural gas) combined.

Methane Hydrates

The first oil wells were drilled in Pennsylvania, but today the mention of "oil" and even more of "oil wealth" conjures images of Arabia, North Africa, and the Middle East—of derricks rising above the sand dunes. There is a major oil field in Alaska, of course, but oil and the natural gas that occurs with it are closely linked in most people's minds to hot deserts.

Methane hydrates could change this. In years to come we may associate natural gas with the cold deserts of the North. We may heat our homes and cook our food on fuel obtained from beneath the Arctic permafrost and from offshore fields in high latitudes—although gas will also be mined at many other offshore sites, not only in high latitudes.

Natural gas consists principally of methane (CH_4). In the reservoirs from which oil and gas are removed, these fuels are mixed with water and held in the pore spaces between the grains of a rock such as sandstone. The gas reaches the surface mixed with water and other impurities that have to be removed before the methane can be used.

It was Russian oil engineers, working in the Far North, who first encountered problems with the transport of gas. They found that pipes frequently became clogged and had to be cleared. The pipes carried gas and water at close to freezing temperatures and under high pressure, and the material clogging them turned out to consist of ice crystals arranged as cages that enclosed methane. This is methane hydrate. It looks very much like ordinary ice, but when held in the hand it feels more like Styrofoam.

Methane hydrate forms naturally as methane percolates upwards through the sediments that cover the seabed. At a particular level the gas is at a temperature and pressure that allow ice to enclose it. A team of scientists from the Lawrence Livermore Laboratory in California and the United States Geological Survey found that when a mixture of very cold ice and methane were mixed and then slowly warmed, they began to react. At a pressure of about 25 megapascals, which is 250 times ordinary sea-level surface atmospheric pressure, the two substances start reacting at about the melting point of the ice. At this pressure, ice melts at 28°F (-2°C). The hydrate formed slowly, over several hours, and when all the ice had been used, the hydrate was stable. It did not melt even when its temperature rose far above the melting temperature for ice. The team found that the hydrate survived warming, provided it was held under pressure. It decomposed if the pressure was reduced slowly, but after rapid depressurization at temperatures

between -27°F (-33°C) and 27°F (-3°C) it took up to 25 hours for the ice to melt.

Methane hydrate remains stable in seabed sediments that lie beneath more than 1,000 feet (300 m) of water. It also occurs beneath permafrost in some areas, though on a much smaller scale. No one knows precisely how much methane exists as hydrate. The U.S. Geological Survey estimates that the total amount of carbon in the methane is equal to at least twice the amount of carbon contained in all the other known reserves of fossil fuels (coal, oil, and gas) on Earth. Most other geologists who have studied the matter agree with this estimate.

This is a huge amount of fuel. Because of the crystalline structure of the ice enclosing them, methane molecules are packed together more closely in a hydrate than they are in other types of reservoir. Volume for volume, therefore, methane hydrates contain more natural gas than conventional fields. The hydrates also cement rock particles together, forming impermeable seals that cap any free gas trapped below them.

So far no one has found a way to mine methane hydrates safely and economically. No doubt a way will be devised, because the potential is so great. Meanwhile, research into the hydrates continues for other reasons. Hydrates present problems and risks, as well as opportunities.

Occasionally, an oil drill penetrating the cap covering a conventional oil well encounters a layer of hydrate. When this happens, friction from the drill can cause the hydrate to decompose, releasing free gas that then explodes without warning. An oil platform resting on an undetected layer of hydrate may collapse as the hydrate shifts under the weight. Decomposing hydrate might trigger a submarine landslide that could release gas and produce a shock wave that reached the nearest coast as a tsunami. Submarine landslides are not uncommon.

A slide that released the stored methane could have climatic consequences. Methane is a greenhouse gas 10 times more effective than carbon dioxide. There is evidence that some rapid climate changes in the distant past were due to sudden large releases of methane into the air, and decomposing hydrates are the likely culprits.

Economic Development

A challenge nevertheless remains for the oil-rich desert countries. This is to use their wealth to develop economies that will continue to sustain them when oil production declines. It is what most of them are doing.

Commodities such as agricultural produce, timber, coal, and petroleum are said to be *primary*. When they are processed into some other form, they become *secondary*. Wheat grain is a primary product, for example, and bread is a secondary product. Processing a primary commodity into a secondary one adds value to it because of the labor that must be expended in the processing, and, obviously, the processing provides employment. If the processed commodity can be exported, the national economy benefits.

This transition, from an economy based principally on primary production to one based principally on secondary production, occurred first in the countries of Western Europe and in the United States. In these countries part of the wealth produced by the primary sector of the economy was saved. Some was invested in building factories to process the primary produce and some was used to improve public services, especially in education. Attempts to extend industrialization to other parts of the world have proved difficult. There is no single, simple reason for this. The difficulties arise from the combined effects of shortages of capital for investment, defining of industrialization in terms only of manufacturing using expensive modern technologies, and lack of an adequately educated and trained labor force.

Today the economies of the less industrialized countries are growing, but the desert countries still lag behind. In Thailand, for example, manufacturing accounts for about 28 percent of the GDP and provides more than 15 percent of all employment. In Zambia the corresponding figures are 36 percent and 2 percent. As the third table shows, however, manufacturing contributes no more to the economies of the oil-producing countries than it does to those of countries without oil.

Manufacturing is the process by which primary commodities are converted into secondary goods. As economies develop, the first primary commodities to be utilized are those that are available locally. In the case of the oil-producing countries the primary product is petroleum—called *crude* because it is in the state in which it emerges from the well. Crude petroleum is chemically very complex. When it is heated its constituents separate. One by one they vaporize as the temperature reaches their boiling point. Each vapor in turn is then collected and cooled to condense it. In this way petroleum is "cracked" to break it into its "fractions" and the overall operation is called *refining*. Other constituents are removed by using solvents.

The lighter fractions are used as fuel, but all the chemical compounds obtained from petroleum have uses as the raw material for the chemical industries based on petroleum—the petrochemical industries. Plastics, paints, synthetic fibers, and adhesives are just a few of the groups of substances obtained from petrochemicals.

Many of the plastics have familiar names. Polyvinyl chloride is PVC, foamed polystyrene is called *Styrofoam*, polymethyl methacrylate is *Plexiglas* and *Perspex*, polyamide is nylon, and polytetrafluoroethylene is Teflon. These are the materials from which goods are made and they are the secondary commodities an oil-producing country would be expected to make as it sought to build an industrial economic base. In fact, very few do so. Chemicals and chemical products account for about 10 percent of the value of all exports from Qatar and refined oil, as fuel and lubricants, for 81 percent. Of the total value of all Saudi Arabian exports, refined petroleum contributes 82 percent and petrochemicals 5 percent. Refined petroleum contributes nearly 20 percent of Algerian export earnings, and chemicals nearly 5 percent of those of Mexico. Other oil-producing countries produce some petrochemicals, but not sufficient for them to be of major economic importance.

Vital Statistics

There is another way the level of economic development is reflected in national statistics. Vital statistics include those describing the birth and death rates and life expectancy at birth. The birth rate is the number of babies born each year for every 1,000 of the population, and the death rate is the number of deaths each year for every 1,000 of the population. The average life expectancy at birth is the average number of years a newborn child can expect to live and it is calculated separately for males and females. A high birth rate is characteristic of a less-developed economy and a comparatively low standard of living. It indicates a traditional society in which children are valued for their labor in family enterprises, usually subsistence farming, and for the economic support they provide for their parents in later years. It also indicates a society in which many infants die, so a large number of babies are born to ensure that enough will survive.

A high death rate indicates a society in which people die young, usually of infectious diseases and illnesses linked to poor nutrition. As health care improves, the death rate falls, and so a higher proportion of the babies survive. This is what causes a population to increase in size. The fourth table gives these vital statistics for all the desert countries, and for the United States as a comparison. Taken together, they provide a measure of the level of economic development in each country. They show that the people of oil-producing countries do not all enjoy a high standard of living, but that those living in desert countries that have no oil are extremely poor.

Quality of Life

Nevertheless, standards of living are improving in ways that can be measured. The rate of infant mortality is a good indicator of the quality and extent of health services. It is reflected in life expectancy, but this indicator also reflects the adequacy of the national diet. Access to health care can also be measured by the number of doctors and hospital beds in relation to the size of the population.

In the United States, for example, there is one physician for every 629 persons and one hospital bed for every 205 persons. This is typical for a developed country, although some countries do even better: France has one physician for every 343 persons and one hospital bed for every 86 persons; the comparable figures for Germany are one physician for every 290 persons and one hospital bed for every 138 persons.

In Kuwait there is one physician for every 619 persons and one hospital bed for every 456 persons. United Arab Emirates, with a per capita GDP similar to that of Kuwait, has one physician for every 545 persons and one hospital bed for every 360 persons. These figures are slightly lower than those for developed countries, but without the income and economic opportunities provided by the possession of oil reserves they would be very much worse. Mauritania is a poor desert country, though not the poorest. It has one physician for every 11,085 persons and one hospital bed for every 1,217 persons.

The literacy rate and figures for school attendance are also useful indicators of well-being. In the United States all children receive primary education and the adult literacy rate is virtually 100 percent. In Kuwait only 8.6 percent of children receive primary education, and 44.8 percent have no formal education at all. The adult literacy rate is 79.3 percent, but it is markedly higher for males (82.3 percent) than for females (76.0 percent).

Kuwait is the richest of the desert countries. The second richest is Qatar, a tiny state bordering the Persian Gulf which has a population of only 589,000 and, as the table shows, a per capita GDP of $11,600. In Qatar, there is one physician for every 793 persons and one hospital bed for every 509 persons. At 79.4 percent, the adult literacy rate is similar to that in Kuwait, but there is little difference between figures for male and female illiteracy. Only 9.8 percent of children receive primary education and 53.3 percent receive no formal education.

These figures illustrate clearly that there is more to economic and social development than can be read from the per capita GDP.

Minerals, Metals, and Textiles

Not all desert landscapes conceal reserves of oil or natural gas, but in some places they contain other riches that can be exploited. The landscapes consist of vast areas of bare rock and sand, exposed by the lack of vegetation.

Rock is made from minerals, which are inorganic compounds each with its own distinct and often complicated chemical composition. Every rock comprises a suite of minerals and some minerals are economically valuable.

Industrial Minerals

Jewels and semiprecious stones are obviously valuable because they are pretty and also rare. Other minerals have industrial uses. Almost all the metals we use are obtained from minerals extracted from rocks. A mineral that contains a high enough concentration of a useful metal for this to be extracted economically is called an *ore mineral*.

Certain rocks can be processed for the chemicals they contain. Phosphate rock can be crushed and processed to obtain phosphorus, which has several industrial uses, or phosphate fertilizer. Gypsum is precipitated when sea water evaporates and it has many industrial uses.

Mining

Unfortunately, both the geological and the economic characteristics of minerals are a little more complicated. Commercially useful minerals are not distributed evenly. Even where reserves are known to exist it may not be possible to exploit them. That requires capital investment in machinery and the means to transport the recovered minerals to factories for processing or ports for shipping overseas. Poor countries may be unable to finance such a costly operation and the remoteness of the prospective mines, difficulties in recruiting local labor, political uncertainty, or any one of dozens of other factors may make it impossible for the government to attract foreign investors.

Bahrain, Burkina Faso, Chad, Djibouti, Egypt, Ethiopia, Kuwait, Lebanon, Oman, Qatar, Somalia, Sudan, and United Arab Emirates are all desert countries with no valuable mineral reserves. Some of these countries are very small. Bahrain covers only 268 square miles (694.2 sq km) including its offshore islands. Lebanon occupies 4,016 square miles (10,400 sq km), Qatar 4,416 square miles (11,437 sq km), and Djibouti 8,950 square miles (23,200 sq km). Perhaps it is not surprising that they have no important mineral resources: where the resources are distributed randomly, these small areas are missed. Sudan, on the other hand, is the largest country in Africa, with an area of 966,757 square miles (2,503,890 sq km)—more than 3½ times the size of Texas.

North Africa

North African countries, other than Egypt, do possess minerals. Libya, to the west of Egypt, has reserves of manganese, gypsum, iron ore, and lignite, also called *brown coal,* which is a poor-quality coal.

Tunisia, Libya's neighbor to the northwest, has some of the largest reserves of phosphate rock in Africa. The reserves are mined and most of the rock is used domestically to manufacture industrial chemicals and fertilizers, which are exported.

Algeria has high-grade iron ore and phosphate rock. It also produces sand, gravel, and crushed stone used in the construction industries.

Morocco's mineral resources provide 10 percent of the total value of Moroccan exports. The country has iron ore, zinc, lead, manganese, and copper, as well as rock salt and coal.

Southern Sahara and Sahel

Mauritania exports substantial amounts of iron ore, accounting for about 43 percent of its export earnings. The country also has reserves of copper, titanium, gypsum, and phosphate rock.

Its neighbor Mali also has reserves of iron ore, as well as nickel, copper, manganese, and bauxite—the ore from which aluminum is obtained. These remain largely undeveloped. Gold is the one metal that is exported, accounting for nearly 15 percent of export earnings. Gold is used to make jewelry, of course, and nowadays it has important uses in electronics. Although gold has only 71 percent of the electrical conductivity of copper, unlike copper it is chemically inert. This makes it an ideal metal for printed circuits and for plating of terminals and other contacts.

Its softness and ductility mean gold can also be made into a very thin film and this is also a useful attribute. One ounce (28 g) of gold can be made into a sheet of gold leaf with an area of 187 square feet (17.4 sq m) and an even thinner film will reflect 98 percent of the light falling on it, yet allow someone on the dark side to see through it clearly. Gold film is used to cover the face visors on space suits, on satellites to prevent overheat-ing, and on the windows of some large buildings to enhance their appearance and to reduce air-conditioning cost.

Niger is one of the world's most important producers of uranium. This accounts for about 53 percent of the country's export earnings. It also has very high-grade iron ore—the ore is about 50 percent iron—as well as phosphate rock and coal. Nigeria has iron ore and tin, as well as limestone that can be used for building.

Arabian Peninsula and the Middle East

There is also high-grade iron ore in Saudi Arabia, as well as gold, bauxite, ores of copper and lead, gypsum, salt, limestone, and marble. In the south of the Arabian Peninsula, Oman has no significant mineral reserves and Yemen has iron ore. Yemen also produces salt.

Syria produces significant amounts of phosphate rock and also has reserves of iron ore. Iron and steel account for nearly 2 percent of Iran's export earnings. The country also has reserves of copper and coal, which are largely undeveloped. Iraq has deposits of sulfur, phosphate rock, gypsum, and salt, but these are of little economic importance.

Jordan exports phosphate and potassium (potash) fertilizer made from its own deposits; together they constitute about one-fifth of the total exports. Jordan also has reserves of uranium, copper, gypsum, kaolin—the source of china clay, used in making fine ceramics and as an inert filler in many products, including paper—and sand of glass-making quality.

Israel is one of the world's principal producers of potash fertilizer—mainly potassium chloride (KCl) and potassium sulfate (K_2SO_7)—and also has deposits of phosphate rock, gypsum, and glass-quality sand. Other minerals, including compounds of bromine and magnesium, are extracted from the water of the Dead Sea.

Namibia and Mongolia

In southern Africa, Namibia is richly endowed with minerals. There are reserves of uranium, tin, tungsten, and copper, as well as smaller amounts of lead, zinc, cadmium, lithium, and silver. Gold and diamonds are mined. Minerals make up half the value of Namibian exports, of which diamonds account for more than 30 percent.

Mongolia is also rich in minerals. It has ores of iron, tin, copper, zinc, molybdenum, and tungsten, as well as gold, a variety of semiprecious stones, a phosphate rock called *phosphorite,* and fluorite. Minerals account for almost 60 percent of the value of Mongolia's exports.

Mexico

Mexico has the richest mineral reserves of all the desert countries and is the world's biggest producer of silver, bismuth, and celestite. Celestite ($SrSO_4$) is the most important ore mineral for strontium (Sr). In addition to these, Mexico is a major producer of arsenic, fluorite, antimony, cadmium, lead, mercury, zinc, sulfur, and gypsum and possesses deposits of graphite, iron ore, and copper. It also has gold.

Its minerals are not exported directly, but in the form of manufactured goods. Mining contributes only 1.3 percent of the Mexican gross domestic product and provides 0.4 percent of the employment, whereas manufacturing contributes nearly 19 percent and provides 14.5 percent of the jobs. Metal goods are economically the most important manufactures, followed by chemicals.

Cashmere

Minerals are not the only resources capable of economic exploitation, however. Although desert countries support little agriculture, their peoples do raise sheep and goats, which produce wool or hair that can be spun, dyed, and woven.

Hair from the Kashmir breed of goats is soft and fine, with fibers 1–3.5 inches (2.5–9 cm) long. Like that of wild goats and sheep and some other domesticated breeds, the coat of a Kashmir goat has two layers. The outer layer is of long, coarse, water-repellent hairs and the inner layer of soft hairs that provide thermal insulation. In spring the animals molt their thick winter coats, and it is then that the cashmere wool is obtained by plucking or combing it from the goats, although in Iran the goats are sheared as sheep are. The coarse hair is used to make ropes, bags, and tent curtains.

Cashmere is the finest of all types of wool and was first used to make shawls. Today it is also made into sweaters, suits, dresses, and overcoats. A goat yields from a few ounces to about 1 pound (0.5 kg) of cashmere each year. It takes the wool from 4 to 6 goats to make a sweater and an overcoat requires wool from 30 to 40 animals.

European factories started making imitation Kashmir shawls early in the 20th century, but these are a poor substitute for the real thing. Only a small amount of cashmere wool is produced, the demand for it is very large, and consequently it is expensive. It comes mainly from China, Mongolia, and Iran, with smaller amounts from Afghanistan and Turkey.

Carpets and Rugs

Asian nomadic peoples have always woven woolen carpets. More durable than pottery and lighter than metal articles, a decorated carpet is a form of ornamentation especially suited to the nomadic way of life. Carpets are also the only medium of artistic expression available to their makers. The designs are traditional, but very elaborate, and the carpets and rugs have always been made to very high standards. Although at first made for tents, they were soon ornamenting the interiors of mosques and palaces.

The export of carpets and rugs to Europe from the desert countries of the Middle East and central Asia began in the 16th century. At that time they were much too expensive to be used on the floor. Their wealthy owners hung them on walls or over balconies or laid them over chests and tables. They were displayed where they could be seen and admired without being harmed.

Persian Carpets

Carpet making reached a peak in Persia (Iran) in the 15th and 16th centuries. At that time the finest carpets and rugs were made in royal workshops attached to palaces. Sheep were bred specially to produce suitable wool, gardens were sown with dye plants and carefully tended, and skilled spinners, dyers, and weavers were well rewarded. Most of the carpets were made from wool, but the very finest were made from silk. Persian carpets became famous throughout Europe and have remained so ever since.

Two techniques are used. Flat carpets, called *kilim,* are woven. The weft (cross-threads) is made from dyed wool or silk and the warp (longitudinal threads) from cotton, linen, or hemp. These carpets resemble woven tapestries. Pile carpets are made by individually knotting colored threads around the warp threads. Several types of knot are used and some Indian carpets have about 2,500 knots to every square inch (388 per sq cm).

Spread of Persian Techniques

Persian carpet making influenced the designs and techniques used in neighboring countries. Egyptian rulers of the Mamlūk dynasty (1250–1517) sponsored carpet manufacture in their country. Mamlūk carpets were knotted, using a knot that originated in Persia, and many were exported.

Persian techniques also spread into the Caucasus, where carpets were made for local aristocrats. Carpets are still being made by Kazakh, Sarūq, and other nomadic peoples living near the Caspian Sea and on the borders of Iran and Iraq.

Early Turkish carpets also followed Persian designs and used Persian techniques. They were made mainly in Anatolia, in central Turkey, by nomadic peoples, including the Kurds. By the 18th century Turkish carpets were so popular abroad that in the western port of Izmir (formerly Smyrna), where people came into direct contact with traders, carpets were being made specifically for export. This association between carpets and the port remains to this day. Carpets are still among the goods exported through Izmir.

Bokhara

Bukhara, or *Bokhoro* in the Uzbek language, is the principal city in the province of Bokhoro, in Uzbekistan. Set at the center of the Bukhara oasis, it has a long history. The Arabs captured it in 709; Genghis Khan in 1220; Timur, also called *Tamurlane,* in 1370; in 1506 it was taken by Uzbek people and became the capital of the khanate of Bukhara. Today it has a population of about 250,000 and has grown substantially since natural gas was discovered nearby in the 1950s, stimulating the establishment of light industries that provided jobs and attracted workers from outside the city.

Its name is associated with "Bokhara" carpets, but these are made not in Bukhara, but over a large area of western Turkistan. Turkistan is not a single country, but the name that is used to describe an area of more than 1 million square miles (2.6 million sq km) in central Asia bounded by Siberia, Tibet, Afghanistan, India, and Iran and inhabited by nomadic Turkic peoples.

"Bokhara" carpets are made by members of nomadic Turkmen tribes, mainly the Tekke, Yomut, Afghan, Sarūq, Ersar, Beshir, and Baluchi, most of whom live in Turkmenistan and adjacent parts of Uzbekistan and Tadzhikistan. Turkmen carpets are made entirely from wool and are knotted. Not all are meant as floor coverings. Nearly square rugs that are laid on floors are made mainly for trading. Others are used as flaps to cover the entrances to tents or to be hung inside as decoration, and some are made into saddlebags.

Textile exports earn desert countries useful amounts of foreign exchange, but they are much more important indirectly. Their fame attracts visitors seeking to buy them close to where they are made and in some cases to see them being made. These visitors are tourists and usually wealthy.

Tourism

Today there are new travelers on the Silk Road. Most do no more than visit a few of the towns along the route, but there are some who journey along parts of one of the old roads. The more adventurous arrange their own itineraries using local transport services or even bicycle part of the way. For the less confident there are tour operators who will make all the necessary bookings and advise about the visas foreigners require. Many visitors travel in organized parties by train, bus, or hired car.

Tourism is now of major economic importance to most countries, not least to those occupying desert lands. In 1997, a total of 595 million tourists traveled abroad—a 5 percent increase on 1996—and spent $425 billion—7 percent more than in the previous year.

Legendary Cities

Visits to the more remote parts of the world are becoming easier and less expensive. For about $1,600, for example, it is possible to travel from London to spend 8 nights along the Silk Road, with stops at Tashkent, Samarkand, and Bukhara. The romance of the names exerts an obvious attraction. Samarkand has existed since the fourth century B.C.E. Then it was known as *Maracanda* and was the capital of a kingdom called *Sogdiana*. Alexander the Great captured it in 329 B.C.E. In the centuries that followed the city was occupied by the Turks, Arabs, and Persians. It was destroyed by the Mongol leader Genghis Khan in 1220 C.E. and later rebuilt, and its citizens revolted against their Mongol rulers in 1365.

After that Samarkand became the capital of the empire established by Timur (1336–1405), also known as *Tamerlane* or *Tamburlane,* who was born not far from the city. He was the last of the great Mongol conquerors and probably the most violent. His empire extended from Delhi, which he destroyed, to Moscow. His troops burned many cities and killed all their inhabitants. Timur lived as a nomad and never had a permanent home, but he tried to make Samarkand the finest of all cities, although he never spent more than a few days there. He was buried in the ornate Gūr-e Amīr mausoleum. This still stands and is one of the many places visited by tourists. After a series of attacks by Persian forces and nomadic tribes, Samarkand suffered a severe economic decline and was completely abandoned from about 1720 until 1770.

TOURISM IN DESERT COUNTRIES (MILLIONS OF U.S.$)		
Country	Income From Visitors	Expenditure by Nationals Who Travel Abroad
Algeria	27	135
Bahrain	228	163
Burkina Faso	22	23
Chad	36	26
Djibouti	13	15
Egypt	2,800	1,278
Ethiopia	36	25
Iran	67	241
Iraq	12	n.a.
Israel	2,784	3,148
Jordan	696	420
Kuwait	107	2,322
Lebanon	710	n.a.
Libya	7	210
Mali	17	56
Mauritania	2	14
Mexico	6,164	3,153
Morocco	1,163	302
Namibia	263	82
Niger	15	21
Nigeria	54	144
Oman	92	47
Saudi Arabia	2,050	2,000
Somalia	8	13
Sudan	3	30
Syria	1,325	398
Tunisia	1,325	251
Yemen	38	76

n.a.: not available.

Mongolia and Different Lifestyles

Samarkand, Tashkent, Bukhara, and the Silk Road are names that resonate through the cultures of Europe and Asia, but cities, buildings, and ancient monuments are not the only attractions that draw visitors. So do lifestyles that are radically different from our own. Mongolia also welcomes tourists, who travel there to meet the descendants of the ancient Mongol warriors; explore their capital, Ulan Bator; join in their festivities; and visit their homes, the traditional *ger.*

The name *Ulan Bator* means "red hero" and dates from 1924, when Mongolia became a people's republic. Before that it was known as *Niislel Khureheh,* "Capital of Mongolia," a name it was given in 1911 when what was then Outer Mongolia declared its independence. Before that it was called *Da Khure,* which is the name of the Tibetan Buddhist monastery built in 1639 that provided the focus for a permanent settlement.

Greenland

Thousands of miles away, Greenland has become a tourist destination, where people can visit what claims to be the biggest national park in the world, established in 1974 and covering 289,500 square miles (750,000 sq km) in the northeast of the country. Greenland offers splendid scenery—

with glaciers and the ice sheet—and a thriving culture in the coastal towns and villages.

The number of tourists allowed into the country is controlled at a level that can be accommodated but has risen over recent years. There were 16,000 visitors in 1995 and it is hoped to increase the number to 60,000 a year by 2005.

North Africa and the Middle East

Figures are not available for the income Greenland, Mongolia, and some other countries derive from tourism, but, as the table shows, for many desert countries it is large enough to be economically important. North African beaches attract European tourists; Tunisia and Morocco are the countries that have most vigorously developed and promoted this resource.

Both earn more than $1 billion a year from tourism—and not only from visitors who wish only to soak up the Sun. The site of the ancient city of Carthage is now a suburb of Tunis, the Tunisian capital, and the Carthaginians established a series of trading ports along the Moroccan coast. The city of Larache was founded in the 12th century B.C.E. by Phoenicians from Tyre. Syria also earns more than $1 billion a year, though not mainly from its beaches, since it has only a short stretch of coastline. Its attractions are the reminders of its ancient history.

Egypt earns $2.8 billion a year from tourism. Visitors to Egypt travel there primarily to see the Pyramids, the Sphinx, and the ancient temples. It is also history that draws people to the other countries of North Africa and the Middle East. These are regions containing archaeological remains dating from Roman times and, in the lands bordering the Euphrates and Tigris Rivers, from the oldest of all Western civilizations.

Three of the world's major religions also arose in the Near and Middle East, and some of the visitors to the region are pilgrims. They are especially important in Saudi Arabia and Israel.

Possibilities for Expansion

For political or religious reasons not all desert countries encourage tourism, but most benefit to some extent. For many years the Libyan government thought tourism unimportant, but in 1997 it changed its mind. In keeping with the national ethos that strongly emphasizes the Bedouin way of life, it offers the desert itself as a destination and experience. Libya has been politically isolated for some time and is difficult to reach, but as its isolation ends, its annual tourist income of $7 million will certainly rise.

There is a potential for economic expansion in many desert countries. Oman, for example, earns only $92 million a year, yet it has been inhabited for at least 10,000 years, and in ancient times its people exported frankincense to markets throughout the Mediterranean and Middle East. Frankincense is a plant resin used in incense and once believed (wrongly) to have medicinal value. An Omani empire once extended through part of East Africa and Zanzibar was the capital of Oman. Yemen also produced frankincense, and in the fourth century B.C.E. the Ma'īn kingdom was exporting it to Egypt, as well as spices and other goods. Saba was the kingdom of Sheba (page 142). Al-Baydā', a city of about 500,000 people, was the capital of a sultanate that ruled a large area of southern Arabia in the seventh to 16th centuries.

Fossils of *Australopithecus* species—ancestors of humans—up to 4 million years old have been found in Ethiopia, making that part of Africa the oldest of all in terms of human habitation. In the second millennium B.C.E. the kingdom of Da'amat was established and grew wealthy through trade. Soon after 300 B.C.E. it was superseded by the kingdom of Aksum, ruled, according to legend, by descendants of Solomon and the queen of Sheba. During the fourth century C.E. the kings became Christian and linked to the Coptic Christians in Egypt. Their power also spread into

Arabia and in the sixth century extended as far as Yemen.

Need for Investment and Peace

In desert countries there is no shortage of history, tradition, and ancient culture that might fascinate tourists, but there are difficulties to be overcome before thriving tourist industries can emerge. Extremely poor countries, such as Ethiopia, Chad, Somalia, and Sudan, lack the infrastructure and facilities tourist operators demand. Before vacationers start to arrive and enjoy the country, airports, good roads, reliable buses and trains, restaurants, and comfortable hotels must be provided. Of course, building, maintaining, and operating such facilities provide employment, but adequate capital must be available for investment before work can begin.

Even then, tourists must feel safe as well as comfortable, and political instability in some desert countries makes this difficult. Egypt, Yemen, and Turkey are among the countries where foreigners have been attacked, kidnapped, or threatened, and Libya, Iraq, Somalia, and Sudan are among those placed off-limits by political strife.

Just as tourists can visit a country, so citizens of that country can travel abroad, becoming tourists themselves. Tourists take foreign currency into the lands they visit, but it is currency they have removed from their own country. Foreign currency is valuable, but the economics of tourism need to balance and the table shows the amount spent by nationals traveling abroad against the amount taken in by foreigners. In some countries, such as Kuwait, Iran, and Nigeria, the two are distinctly unbalanced.

Proximity to a source of wealthy tourists also helps. Namibia does well by attracting South Africans. The most successful country of all, however, is Mexico, where Americans spend more than $6 billion a year.

Solar Energy

Picture a chimney, like a very tall factory chimney, that stands by itself on the flat desert plateau. Around its base the desert surface is covered by a glass roof supported about 6.5 feet (2 m) above the ground. Close to the chimney the roof is double-glazed.

Because of its size the structure is visible from afar. The glass roof covers an approximately circular area about 4.25 miles (6.8 km) in diameter, and the chimney at its center rises to a height of about 4,900 feet (1.5 km). At present the tallest structure in the world is the CN Tower in Toronto, with a height of 1,815 feet (553 m). This mighty chimney is nearly three times taller.

Its purpose is power generation—it is a "solar chimney"—and it produces about one-fifth the output of a big modern nuclear or coal-fired power plant. So far it exists only as a plan, but a smaller experimental prototype was built in 1983, at Manzanares, 93 miles (150 km) south of Madrid, in Spain. It was 640 feet (195 m) tall, had a glass roof 787 feet (240 m) across, and generated 50 kilowatts (66 horse power) of power. It ran for 7 years and proved that the idea works. Two more demonstration plants were then built in Sri Lanka. Preparations to build a much bigger one in the Thar Desert, in India, reached an advanced stage before they had to be abandoned for political reasons in 1998. That plant would have had a solar chimney 2,000–3,000 feet (600–950 m) tall with a glass-covered area of 38.6 square miles (100 sq km). Jörg Schlaich, the German civil engineer and professor of engineering at the University of Stuttgart who first developed the concept, built the Spanish one and planned the Indian one, wants to build one this size as a demonstration model to attract investors.

The 4,900-foot (1.5-km) chimney is planned for the southern Kalahari Desert, in South Africa. It has been designed by a team led by a German physicist, Wolf-Walter Stinnes, as part of a study for the government of Northern Cape Province.

How the Solar Chimney Works

The diagram shows how the chimney works. Sunshine passes through the glass and heats the ground beneath. Air in contact with the ground is heated but cannot rise because it is trapped below the glass. The double-glazing near the center reduces the amount of heat lost by conduction through the glass.

Hot air rises up the chimney, drawing cooler air beneath the glass cover and creating a constant flow. As it rises it turns one or more turbines set

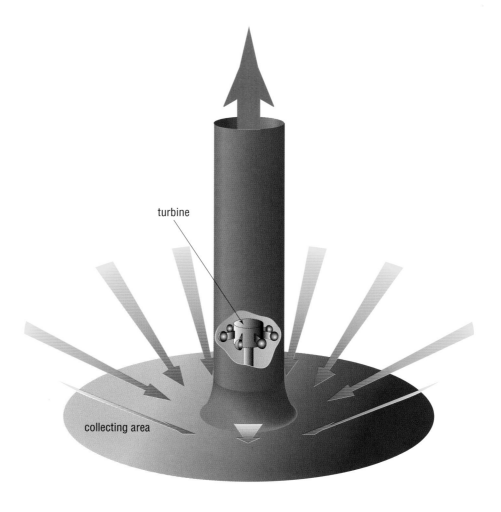

turbine

collecting area

Solar chimney

inside the chimney and linked to the generating plant. The amount of power that can be generated is proportional to the difference in air pressure at the bottom and top of the chimney. Because air pressure decreases with height, the taller the chimney, the lower the pressure will be at its top, so increasing the height of the chimney also increases its power output. At the same time, the air beneath the glass will try to expand as its temperature rises, but because it is trapped its pressure will increase.

Efficiency can be increased both by building higher to reduce pressure at the top and by increasing the covered area to increase pressure at the bottom. The glass cover is the most expensive part of the structure to build, so the designs opt for taller chimneys and smaller collecting areas.

Costs

Deserts lack many resources, but they possess in abundance those that a scheme of this kind needs.

They have large areas of land that cannot be farmed or used for housing and they have ample sunshine. The Kalahari plant itself would be built mainly from concrete and glass, both of which can be made from desert rocks and sand.

It would be expensive to build. The full-scale South African plant would cost about $400 million. This is a great deal of money and the electricity the plant generated would cost much more than electricity from a conventional plant, especially in South Africa, where coal is cheap and plentiful, but it would also last longer. The chimney should go on working for 100 years and the turbines would also last well, because they would spin in an airflow moving at constant speed—it is stopping, starting, and changing speed that cause wear on moving parts. Experiments have found that the airflow continues even at night. During the day, sunshine warms the ground and the flow of air carries heat away, but the rate of heating exceeds the rate of cooling, so the ground grows continually hotter until the hottest part of the day. At night the warm ground continues to heat the air above it and maintain the airflow. It might be possible to increase this effect, for example, by a system of pipes that carried water heated by day into an insulated reservoir and returned it at night to warm the air.

Wind Power

No one can be sure that a full-scale solar chimney would work—or even that a structure of that size could be built. There are other, more established ways of harnessing solar energy, however.

Wind generators are the most familiar—and count as solar-energy devices because the weather systems that produce the wind are driven by solar energy. They can be erected for much less than a solar chimney, but they suffer from a major disadvantage. Although a desert is a very windy place, wind energy is very diffuse even there.

A modern wind generator consists of an aerodynamically efficient rotor, very like an airplane propeller. Depending on the design it has two or three blades and it is mounted on a tower high enough to expose the rotor to winds that are not slowed by friction with the ground. The power it produces is proportional to the square of the diameter of the circle swept by its rotor and the cube of the wind speed. This means the structure must be as big as possible. In a wind blowing at 20 mph (32 km/h), a wind generator with a rotor diameter of 50 feet (15 m) on a tower about 80 feet (24 m) tall can capture wind energy equivalent to about 48 kilowatts (kW) (64 horsepower). Gearing connects it to a generator. If the mechanism is 50 percent efficient, the output will be about 24 kW (32 horsepower). This huge machine produces no more power than will operate 24 one-bar electric heaters—and only that for as long as the wind is blowing.

Wind generators are not new. Some were designed in the 1930s, although they were not built. The first very large one to be built, with a rotor diameter of 87 feet (26. 5 m) and a tower 117 feet (36 m) tall, was erected in 1940, on a hill in Vermont called *Grandpa's Knob*. Its generating capacity was rated at 1.25 million watts (MW) (1.68 million horsepower). After it had run for several years metal fatigue weakened one of its blades and destroyed it.

Solar Cells

Photoelectric cells convert light into electricity. Arrays of cells are used to power spacecraft and satellites. All they need is sunlight, they have no moving parts, and the technology on which they are based is well understood, mainly because of its development by the space industry.

The cells exploit the fact that an electric field exists at the junction where two layers of different materials are in close contact. A photoelectric or solar cell has an upper layer of dark material that absorbs sunlight. Beneath that there is a *top-junction* layer, comprising a metal grid. This forms one of the two electrical contacts that are needed for a current to flow. Light passes through the grid to the *absorber layer,* where two dissimilar materials in close contact produce an electric field. Below that there is a metal layer covering the entire base of the cell. This is the *back-junction layer,* from which the current flows out.

The absorption of light falling on the device passes energy to electrons in the three layers. These move in the direction imposed by the electric field at the absorber layer and are carried away by a wire connected to the back-junction layer. To complete the circuit, the external wiring must rejoin the cell. Flowing electrons—the electric current—lose the energy imparted by the absorbed sunlight by doing useful work, such as producing light or heat or powering machines, and return to the cell to absorb more.

Although photoelectric cells generate power reliably, they do not generate it cheaply. They are made from fairly costly materials and, because their efficiency is somewhat low, a large number is needed if a useful amount of power is to be generated. Under standard testing conditions, of light falling at 1,000 watts per square meter (3.7 Btu per square foot) and a temperature of 77°F (25°C), the most efficient convert no more than about 24 percent of light into electricity.

Solar Ponds

Solar ponds also have no moving parts. They exploit the property that salt water is denser than freshwater, so a layer of freshwater can be used to insulate a layer of salt water.

For example, a pond, usually several feet deep and with a large surface area, is lined with black plastic to absorb radiant heat. A layer of water saturated with salt covers the lower part of the pond and freshwater is carefully poured above it. Fresh and salt water do not mix readily, because of their different densities, so the freshwater forms a layer above the denser salt water. Solar heat passes through the freshwater and is absorbed by the black lining. This warms, and it warms the salt water in contact with it. Convection currents warm the rest of the saltwater layer, but they do not affect the overlying freshwater. The salt water grows hotter, but the freshwater remains at the same temperature as the air—any heat it does absorb is lost to the air in contact with the surface.

The salt water can reach a temperature approaching 212°F (100°C). It is piped away to a heat exchanger, where pipes containing hot salt water pass through a tank containing cool freshwater—much like a domestic hot water tank—and back to the solar pond. From time to time more freshwater must be added to the upper layer to replace the water that evaporates, although evaporation losses can be eliminated by covering the entire pond with transparent plastic.

A Place for Solar Energy

Those desert countries with reserves of oil, gas, or coal have the fuel they need for energy for their industries and for commercial and domestic use. For countries without fuel reserves of their own, however, the cost of energy is a major constraint on development.

In most of the poor desert countries the power supply is erratic and does not serve every community. In most modern factories and offices, using computers, printers, fax machines, and other electronic devices as well as machines powered by electricity, a power failure means work has to stop.

In desert regions it should be possible to fit office buildings, factories engaged in light industry, and apartment buildings with their own means of solar power generation. The amount of energy that each building could produce would be small, but adequate for running electronic equipment, cooking, and heating water.

There would also be an environmental benefit, because solar devices burn no fuel and therefore emit no greenhouse gases, ash, or other combustion products. There are also environmental disadvantages, however. The concentrated brine used in solar ponds is extremely corrosive and causes serious pollution if it spills, and extremely poisonous substances are used in the industrial process by which photoelectric cells are made. They, too, can cause severe pollution. Wind farms occupy very large areas and one with a power output comparable to that of a conventional generating plant might remove so much energy from the wind as to affect the climate in ways that cannot be predicted.

Solar power provides a means of exploiting space and sunshine, the two resources that are available in every desert. Technologies that may be inappropriate in an industrial country, especially one in a temperate region, may have much to offer in an industrializing country in a low latitude.

PART 7

Climate Change and the Future for Deserts

In the summer of 1934 a dust cloud 3 miles (4.8 km) high covered an area of 1.35 million square miles (3.5 million sq km) from Canada to Texas and from Montana to Ohio. Birds, choked by the dust, fell dead from the sky and as fast as the dust was cleared from the desk of President Franklin D. Roosevelt in the White House more settled. Dust fell on ships in the Atlantic Ocean, more than 300 miles (480 km) away from the American coast.

This was the worst of the Dust Bowl years, when drought reduced exposed soil to a fine powder and the wind carried it away from farms in Kansas, Colorado, Oklahoma, and Texas. A number of factors combined to make that drought unusually severe, but it was neither the first nor the last. Droughts ruined crops again in the 1950s, 1970s, and 1990s. They occur at intervals of 22 or 23 years.

Drought afflicting countries along the southern border of the Sahara, in the Sahel region, caught the world's attention in the 1970s. That drought began in the 1960s and lasted until the 1980s, but it was in the 1970s that its tragic effects became evident. It was not the first time the Sahel had experienced severe and prolonged drought. Several had occurred in the 17th century and caused severe famines.

Those earlier droughts coincided with the coldest part of the Little Ice Age (page 9). Between 1690 and 1699 the average temperature in England was 2.7°F (1.5°C) lower than the temperature between 1920 and 1960. Still further back in time, the Middle Ages was a warm period, and from about 7,000 to 5,000 years ago, in the period known as the *postglacial climatic optimum,* temperatures in Antarctica and Europe were 3.6–5.4°F (2–3°C) warmer than they are today. About 10,000 years ago the most recent full-scale ice age came to an end.

Constantly Changing Climate

Until the 1950s, most scientists assumed the climates of the world changed little from one century to another. The ice ages were known, of course, but during them the climate remained steadfastly cold all the time and during interglacials, such as the one in which we are living now, conditions were warmer and equally unchanging. There were relatively warm years and cool years, of course, as well as periods of dry weather that caused droughts and excessive rains that caused flooding, but these extremes canceled each other. Plot average temperatures and rainfall for a particular place over several centuries on a graph and the lines will rise and fall as a series of spikes. Fit a trend to them and the resulting line will be level, indicating no overall change.

No one believes that now. Climates are changing constantly and always have been, but at rates that are slow compared to a human lifetime. This makes significant changes difficult to detect against the natural variation of warm, cool, wet, and dry years. Over about the last century there was a warming from about 1880 to 1940. This was most pronounced in the Arctic and in Siberia, but in the Southern Hemisphere south of about 30° S there may have been a cooling. From about 1940 to some time between 1975 and 1985 temperatures fell. Then, from the late 1980s, they began to rise again and are believed still to be rising.

Detecting this rise calls for powerful statistical methods to interpret data recorded by extremely sensitive instruments. If the global climate is warming, it is doing so by less than 1.8°F (1°C) every 10 years, which is a smaller amount than the ordinary variation from year to year. Sea level is also believed to be rising, but at no more than 0.08 inch (2 mm) a year and then not everywhere, because some coastal areas are rising as they continue to rebound from the removal of ice sheets, the weight of which once depressed them.

The Sahel Drought and the Intertropical Convergence

The Sahel drought was caused by a change in the seasonal migration of the Intertropical Convergence. This is the belt along which the trade winds of the two hemispheres meet. Their convergence produces a region of low surface pressure and rain.

The position of the low-pressure zone changes with the seasons. During the Southern Hemisphere summer its northern boundary is at about latitude 5° N but most of the zone lies south of the equator. In the Northern Hemisphere summer the zone shifts northward. In August its northern boundary lies along the southern border of the Sahara, runs through Yemen and Oman, and crosses the Indian subcontinent along the southern foothills of the Himalayas, in latitudes between about 15° N and 25° N.

Its northward migration carries summer rains to the Sahel. During the drought years the zone remained well to the south of its usual location and the rains failed to arrive.

Trade Winds and ENSO

Weather extremes are also associated with the El Niño phenomenon or, to give it its proper name, an El Niño–Southern Oscillation (ENSO) event. These occur at intervals of 2–7 years, but are sometimes especially severe. ENSO events have been occurring at least since the 16th century. In the 20th century they were severe in 1925–26, 1941–42, 1957–58, 1965–66, 1972–73, 1976–77, 1982–83, 1986–87, 1991–94 (this event was continuous over several years), and 1997–98.

Ordinarily, the trade winds just south of the equator blow from the southeast and drive a current of warm water across the South Pacific in a westerly direction, from South America toward Indonesia. The surface water is strongly warmed by the Sun and as water is carried across the Pacific a deep pool of warm water accumulates near Indonesia. At the same time the layer of warm surface water near South America is fairly shallow. This allows the cool water of the Peru Current, flowing northward from Antarctica, parallel to the coast, to rise in a series of upwellings.

Walker Circulation and the Southern Oscillation

Air rises over Indonesia and flows from west to east at a high altitude. This return flow of air is called the *Walker circulation,* after Sir Gilbert Walker (1868–1958), the British mathematician and meteorologist who first described it in 1904. It produces a region of low surface pressure around Indonesia, where air is rising, and one of high pressure off South America, where air is sinking.

From time to time this pattern reverses. This was first observed in 1897 as a change in pressure distribution and a number of scientists studied it. The phenomenon was described fully by Walker in his presidential address to the Royal Meteorological Society in 1928. During a reversal, pressure is low off South America and high near Indonesia. This is a Southern Oscillation (because it occurs only in the Southern Hemisphere). It causes upper air to flow from east to west, and the surface winds either to weaken or to reverse direction. The wind-driven surface current also reverses direction, causing a thinning of the warm water pool near Indonesia and a deepening of the warm water off South America. The consequences of this usually appear in December, which is why it is called *El Niño,* "the boy child."

La Niña

At other times the usual pattern intensifies. Pressure rises in the already high-pressure region in the east and falls in the low-pressure region in the west, and the southeasterly trade winds blow more strongly. This accelerates the east-to-west surface current, deepening the Asian warm water pool, and produces a very thin layer of warm surface water off South America. This intensification, the opposite of El Niño, is known as *La Niña.* Together, a complete cycle of a Southern Oscillation, El Niño, and La Niña constitute an ENSO event.

ENSO events affect the weather over a large area. In particular, El Niño causes heavy rain in the usually arid belt along the western coast of South America, and drought in Australia. La Niña makes the aridity even more extreme in South America but produces heavy rain in Australia.

Interdecadal ENSO

ENSO events vary in strength, however, and scientists have now discovered their strength is influenced by another cycle, called the *interdecadal ENSO.* This is a slow increase then decrease in the surface temperature of the eastern Pacific that has been traced back as far as 1860.

A similar cyclical temperature change—so far without a name—affects part of the Central Pacific, and there are two temperature cycles in the North Pacific. These cycles have periods measured in decades, and when they coincide with the temperature changes produced by an ENSO event they intensify it. The event is then a severe one. When the cycles are out of phase with ENSO, so that El Niño warming coincides with cool water in the eastern Pacific, the ENSO event is weak.

North Atlantic Oscillation

There is also a climatic cycle in the North Atlantic, called the *North Atlantic Oscillation* (NAO). This consists of a change in the distribution of surface pressure, but between north and south rather than east and west as in the Southern Oscillation. An area of low pressure is located more or less permanently near Iceland and an area of high pressure near the Azores. The difference in pressure between them drives weather systems across the Atlantic from west to east, but their effect varies with changes in relative pressure. When pressure is lower than usual in the Iceland low, it is higher than usual in the Azores high, and when pressure is higher in the Iceland low, it is lower in the Azores high.

When the pressure contrast is large, European winters are mild, winters in the northwest Atlantic are cold, and the Mediterranean region—including North Africa—is dry. This was the situation from around 1975 until 1995. Then the contrast sharply decreased. If it remains low, European winters may become colder and the Mediterranean region wetter. Climate changes such as ENSO and the NAO are linked, in the sense that they affect each other.

The Greenhouse Effect

Today, the change that worries many scientists arises from the possibility of an enhanced greenhouse effect. Nitrogen, oxygen, and the other gases that the atmosphere comprises are transparent to solar radiation. It passes through them unimpeded and warms the surface of land and sea. Once warmed, these surfaces then begin radiating heat at wavelengths inversely proportional to the temperature to which they have been raised. The hotter the body, the shorter the wavelength at which it radiates. Consequently, the land and sea emit radiation at much longer wavelengths than those of the radiation they receive from the Sun.

Some atmospheric gases are partially opaque to these wavelengths. Their molecules absorb the radiation. This warms the air, but there are some long wavelengths that are not absorbed. These are called *windows* and radiation escaping through them allows the overall balance to be maintained. By day, the amount of incoming solar energy exceeds the amount of outgoing radiation, and the air warms, but at night there is no incoming radiation and the air cools, although its temperature never falls so low as it would if there were no gases absorbing radiation. In that case the average temperature at the surface of the Earth would be -0.4°F (-18°C) rather than 59°F (15°C), which is the actual average.

This is the *greenhouse effect*—although in a real greenhouse the warming is due mainly to the inability of warm air to escape and mix with the air outside. It is entirely natural and without it life on Earth would be extremely uncomfortable. The gases that cause it, the so-called greenhouse gases, are mainly water vapor, carbon dioxide, methane, nitrous oxide, and ozone. Recently humans have added chlorofluorocarbons (CFCs), which do not occur naturally.

Global Warming

Millions of years ago, and over millions of years, carbon dioxide was removed from the air by photosynthesis (page 56) and then stored in the form of organic material that did not decompose completely—complete decomposition would have oxidized its carbon, returning it to the air. This organic material is now coal, oil, and natural gas. The possibility of enhancing the greenhouse effect arises because by burning these fuels we complete the oxidation of their carbon and return the carbon dioxide to the air. There is then more of it to absorb radiation. We also release carbon dioxide when forests are cleared and burned, our farming methods release methane from the digestive systems of cattle and sheep and from bacteria in flooded rice fields, and our cars and factories release nitrous oxide and unburned fuel that react to produce ozone.

Many scientists fear that by releasing into the air gases that absorb long-wave radiation—so-called greenhouse gases—we may enhance the natural greenhouse effect. This would cause a general rise in the global average temperature. Computer models have been used to calculate the magnitude of the effect. If the concentration of greenhouses gases were to double, the models warn that the average temperature would increase by between 2.7°F and 8.1°F (1.5°C and 4.5°C), but most probably by about 4.5°F (2.5°C). This higher temperature might be reached by the end of the 21st century, so the rate of warming would be about 0.45°F (0.25°C) every decade. The warming would be most marked in the Arctic and Antarctic, somewhat less so in temperate latitudes, and there would be least change in the tropics.

Would the Deserts Bloom?

The most obvious effect would be to shift the climate belts away from the equator. The humid Tropics would extend farther north and south and rainfall would increase in the tropical and subtropical deserts. At the same time, however, climates might become drier in what are now temperate regions, in southern Europe and the central United States.

It would not necessarily mean that what are now deserts would become fertile. Warmer temperatures would cause more water to evaporate from the oceans. This would produce a general increase in precipitation, but when the temperature rises, so does the rate of evaporation, and a rise of around 4.5°F (2.5°C) in a climate that is already warm would increase the rate of evaporation enough to exceed the additional rainfall. Despite receiving more rain, desert soils might become even drier. In higher latitudes, where climates are cooler, this is not what would happen. Those regions would become generally moister.

Uncertainties

The prospect is worrying and scientists and environmentalists have urged governments to impose curbs on the emission of greenhouse gases—and especially of carbon dioxide from the burning of fuel. The governments of most nations have signed the United Nations Framework Convention on Climate Change, and in 1997 they met in Kyoto, Japan, to discuss the Kyoto Protocol on Climate Change, which set targets for reducing greenhouse-gas emissions. Several meetings of the signatories of the Kyoto Protocol were held in 1998 and 1999. It is possible, therefore, that in years to come emissions of greenhouse gases will be stabilized and even reduced.

Despite the apparent certainty and the understandable concern, the scientific picture is very far from clear. Since 1881, the global average temperature has increased by about 1.1°F (0.6°C). It does seem the climate is warming, and there was a series of relatively warm years in the 1990s. Appearances may be deceptive, however, because of the 1.1°F (0.6°C) warming, 0.7°F (0.37°C) occurred prior to 1940 and the main increase in greenhouse-gas concentrations took place after 1950. In any case, 1881 was an unusually cold year.

It is not certain that the average temperature is increasing at all. There are three independent sets of temperature records. The longest set is from measurements made at surface weather stations, on weather ships, and by ships at sea. According to figures from the British Meteorological Office, these show a steady warming of 0.27°F (0.15°C) per decade, which is the lower value of the warming calculated by the climate models. There are doubts about the measurements, however. Many weather stations are sited at airports that were once in the open countryside but during the period covered by the records the cities some of them serve have expanded to surround them. The buildings produce a "heat island" effect that raises the temperature. Scientists try to correct for this effect, but doing so is extremely difficult.

Instruments carried beneath weather balloons also provide temperature records. These show that the average temperature has fallen by 0.1°F (0.07°C) per decade according to one set of measurements (by the National Aeronautics and Space Administration [NASA]) or by 0.04°F (0.02°C) according to another (by the Meteorological Office). Eight satellites operated by NASA also measure air temperature, each satellite making about 30,000 measurements every day. These show the average temperature is falling by 0.02°F (0.01°C) per decade.

Of the three sets of measurements, one shows a slight warming and the other two suggest a very slight cooling. None of the sets of data is entirely satisfactory, however, and most scientists believe the temperature is rising, but more slowly than the models predict.

If the climate is growing warmer it may well be due to the fact that the amount of energy radiating from the Sun is not constant. In recent years the solar output has been increasing and it is now close to a maximum. The amount of change is very small, but its climatic effect on Earth is complex and some scientists believe it is sufficient to account for a slight warming. This would also explain the recent sequence of warm years.

It would also account for the rising concentration of carbon dioxide in the atmosphere. The

solubility in water of gases, including carbon dioxide, decreases as the temperature of the water increases. So as the sea warms, carbon dioxide dissolved in it is released into the air. In addition, warmer water stimulates the activity of bacteria and bacterial respiration also releases carbon dioxide. The rate at which the carbon dioxide concentration has increased corresponds much better to the rate at which the solar output has increased than it does to emissions from burning fuel. Of all the carbon dioxide released from factories, power plants, and cars, about half vanishes and cannot be accounted for.

Also, if warming is taking place it appears to be because the nights are a little milder, not because the days are warmer. This means precipitation may increase, but the rate of evaporation will not, so the climate of continental interiors will become wetter, not drier, and deserts may shrink. In this case, global warming could be beneficial rather than harmful agriculturally, although the problem of rising sea levels would remain. Sea levels are rising slowly, probably because of expansion due to warming.

At present it is impossible to say whether global warming has commenced or, indeed, whether it is a serious threat at all. It is extremely difficult to measure a worldwide change that averages less than half of 1 degree every 10 years. Climates change constantly, and runs of 10 or even 20 warm (or cool) years are not significant. Most scientists studying the climate believe we must wait many more years, and perhaps until late in the 21st century, before a long-term trend becomes apparent.

By then, of course, it will be too late to remedy the effect. So perhaps we should take precautionary measures now, just in case.

Shutting Down the Atlantic Conveyor

There is another concern. As the last ice age was drawing to its close the Laurentide ice sheet covering much of North America began to retreat, releasing icebergs into the North Atlantic. Together with meltwater, these formed a layer of freshwater that lay on top of the ocean. This altered the formation of North Atlantic Deep Water, and, because of that, it shut down the Atlantic Conveyor (page 50). It was this change that triggered the cooling, almost back to ice-age climates, of the Older and Younger Dryas (page 120).

This time there is no huge North American ice sheet to melt, but some calculations suggest that a substantial increase in rainfall would also deposit a layer of freshwater over the North

Atlantic and might have a similar effect on the Atlantic Conveyor. If that happened, global warming would, paradoxically, produce near-ice-age conditions over much of Northwest Europe.

Melting Ice Sheets and Sea Levels

There is no large North American ice sheet, but Greenland still lies beneath ice and so does the much bigger area of Antarctica. If these were to melt, they would release into the oceans water that at present is lying on land. The volume of the oceans would increase and sea levels would rise accordingly. The complete melting of the Greenland ice sheet would raise sea levels by 20–23 feet (6–7 m), and if the entire Antarctic ice sheet melted, sea levels would rise by 164–330 feet (50–100 m). This would inundate many low-lying islands and coastal regions. Much of the eastern United States would disappear under water.

At present, sea levels are rising, probably by 0.04–0.08 inch (1–2 mm) a year. This is caused mainly by the expansion of seawater due to slight warming. There is no evidence that the ice sheets are melting. Studies of the southern—most vulnerable—part of the Greenland ice sheet have found it to be thinning, especially in the east, in places by as much as 3 feet (1 m) a year. The thinning is occurring at elevations up to 5,000 feet (1,500 m) above sea level. The cause is unknown, but it is not due to melting or a decrease in snowfall. At higher levels, the ice sheet is growing thicker, in some places by up to 10 inches (25 cm) a year. Overall, the southern ice sheet is thinning, but not greatly.

Two ice sheets cover Antarctica, separated by the Transarctic Mountains. The East Antarctic ice sheet, which is much the larger of the two, covers a high plateau. The West Antarctic ice sheet covers an archipelago of mountainous islands. Scientists are confident that the East Antarctic ice sheet is stable. It is neither thickening nor thinning and its base is firmly grounded on the underlying rock. There is no likelihood that it will melt. The West Antarctic ice sheet is not so securely grounded, but its thickness is not changing and it is not likely to thin, far less disappear. The line marking the edge of the ice that is grounded on rock is retreating, but at a slow rate that has remained constant for the last 7,500 years. This change is not linked to climate, but to complex movements of the ice itself.

Sunspot Cycles

People have always been fascinated by the stars and planets, and for as long as astronomers have had telescopes with which to observe them, part of that fascination has centered on sunspots. These are dark patches—"spots"—that appear on the face of the otherwise featureless Sun, and what is interesting about them is that they come and go. To early scientists the sunspots looked like imperfections in the Sun.

*It is important to remember that you must **never** look directly at the Sun unless you have equipment that is specifically designed to allow you to do so safely. Ordinary sunglasses are not sufficient protection. Looking directly at the Sun can cause serious and permanent damage to your eyes.*

Asian astronomers were counting and recording them many centuries before European observers began studying them. In about 1611, when the first telescopes were becoming available, Galileo and several other scientists became interested in them. It was in 1843 that the German astronomer Samuel Heinrich Schwabe (1789–1875) discovered the sunspot cycle.

Heinrich Schwabe was trained as a pharmacist and at the age of 17 took over his mother's business in Berlin, preparing and dispensing medicines. Astronomy was his passion, however, and he devoted many hours to the search for a planet inside the orbit of Mercury. To do this he projected the image from his 2-inch (5-cm) telescope onto a screen, hoping to see the silhouette of the supposed planet as it crossed the Sun. What he found, after watching the Sun closely since 1826, was that the number of sunspots increased and decreased over a cycle of 10 years. The Swiss astronomer Rudolf Wolf (1816–93) confirmed this and refined the cycle to 11.2 years. Wolf also confirmed that the sunspot cycle had been running at least since 1700, which he believed to be the limit of reliable records.

What Are Sunspots?

Sunspots are dark because they are regions where the temperature is markedly lower than that of the visible surface of the Sun—called the *photosphere*—surrounding them. They consist of a dark center, called the *umbra,* surrounded by what look like dark filaments, forming the *penumbra.* Some appear by themselves, but most occur in pairs, the first to appear called the *leader* and the second the *follower.* Each cycle begins from a sunspot minimum, when there are at most a few sunspots near the solar equator. New spots appear farther from

the equator and their number increases to reach a maximum after two or three years. After some years the number starts decreasing, returning to a minimum about 11 years from the time the cycle began.

They are magnetic phenomena. Each sunspot is a magnetic pole, which is why they occur in pairs—one spot of each pair is a north pole, the other a south pole. A sunspot that appears isolated does have a partner, but the two may be a very long way apart. Pairs of sunspots tend to form groups. Groups also occur as pairs, and lines of magnetic flux link both pairs and groups. During a very active maximum there might be 10 groups with up to 200 spots each, as well as more than 100 pairs that are not in groups.

The Solar Wind and Cosmic Radiation

As well as radiation, the Sun emits a stream of electrically charged particles. These compose what is known as the *solar wind.* They are deflected by the Earth's magnetic field, but some become trapped in it, flowing along the flux lines between the magnetic poles. Where the magnetic lines descend at the poles, the particles lose energy. This is emitted as light and produces the Aurora Borealis and Aurora Australis. The strength of the solar wind—and the frequency and brightness of the aurorae—is related to the number of sunspots. The more sunspots there are, the stronger the solar wind "blows."

The Earth is also bathed in radiation from every other part of the sky. This is *cosmic radiation,* which does not come from the Sun. Cosmic radiation is deflected by the solar wind, so the stronger the solar wind, the less intense is the cosmic radiation experienced on Earth—or, more to the point, in the Earth's atmosphere. The more intense the cosmic radiation, the more clouds that form in the atmosphere, and, therefore, the more incoming solar radiation that is reflected back into space. Intense cosmic radiation produces cool temperatures, and when cosmic radiation is weak, with fewer clouds, temperatures rise.

The Spörer Minimum and the Maunder Minimum

In 1889, the German solar astronomer Gustav Spörer (1822–95) published an article describing

his discovery of a sunspot minimum that lasted an unusually long time in the late 16th century. The article was largely ignored, but it caught the attention of Edward Walter Maunder (1851–1928), a photographic and spectrographic assistant at the Royal Greenwich Observatory, in England. Searching through old records at the observatory, he discovered another, even longer period of minimum sunspot activity, lasting about 70 years from 1645 until 1715. During that time hardly any sunspots had been observed. It included several periods of 10 years during which no sunspots at all were reported and one period of 32 years during which no spots appeared north of the solar equator.

He knew his discovery was important for two reasons. The first was that it challenged the prevailing idea that the Sun never changed. Clearly it did change, and quite dramatically. The second arose from a paper published in the *Philosophical Transactions of the Royal Society* in 1801. It was by the eminent German-British astronomer Sir Frederick William Herschel (1738–1822). He had noted a link between sunspot activity and wheat prices. These fluctuate according to the size of the harvest, which in turn is determined by the weather. It suggested a connection between sunspots and climate.

Maunder wrote an article on the subject in 1890. In 1894 he wrote another, called "A Prolonged Sunspot Minimum," and in 1922 he published a third, longer article with the same title. No one took his idea seriously, but it was again considered half a century later by the American solar astronomer John A. Eddy. He checked Maunder's findings against records from other parts of the world and found them correct. He also checked the climatological implication, working in collaboration with the British climatologist and historian of climate Hubert H. Lamb.

Cosmic Radiation and Carbon-14

This was possible because cosmic radiation produces carbon-14 (^{14}C), a radioactive isotope of carbon. As cosmic particles—mainly protons and alpha particles (comprising two protons and two neutrons) traveling at 186–435 miles per second (300–700 km/s)—strike atoms in the atmosphere they liberate free neutrons. When a free neutron strikes a nitrogen atom it is absorbed and a proton is released. A nitrogen atom has a total of 14 protons and neutrons, and is written as ^{14}N. Absorbing one neutron and losing one proton leave the number of particles unchanged, but the loss of one proton alters the chemical characteristics of the atom, changing it from nitrogen to carbon: $^{14}N + n \rightarrow {}^{14}C + p$.

Carbon-14 is unstable. It decays with a half-life of 5,715 years, but it behaves chemically identically to the most common carbon isotope, ^{12}C. It oxidizes to $^{14}CO_2$ and is absorbed by photosynthesizing plants. When the plants die, the ^{14}C continues decaying and no more is absorbed, so the proportion of ^{14}C in the plant tissues decreases at a steady rate.

This process provides the basis of radiocarbon dating, but variations in the intensity of cosmic radiation create large anomalies in the proportion of ^{14}C in organic material. Instead of a steady decrease over time, there are sudden increases or decreases that can be measured. This ability to detect variations in the intensity of cosmic radiation in wood that had been independently dated by counting tree rings allowed Eddy to place dates on the changes in cosmic radiation and, from that, sunspot maxima and minima.

Sunspot Minima and the Little Ice Age

The period with so few sunspots that Maunder had found is now known as the *Maunder minimum* and the earlier one is known as the *Spörer minimum*. They both coincide with especially cold parts of the Little Ice Age. This was a period that lasted altogether from about 1420 to the latter half of the 19th century during which the climate over the Northern Hemisphere was generally cooler than it is now or was earlier. There were relatively warmer and cooler episodes within the overall period, but every warmer period was followed by a return to cold, wet years. During the Spörer minimum, between 1560 and 1599, mean winter temperatures in central Europe were about 2.3°F (1.3°C) lower and in Denmark from 1582 to 1597 they were 2.7°F (1.5°C) lower than the 1880–1930 average. It was during the Maunder minimum that temperatures reached their lowest.

Eddy found that over the last 5,000 years there were at least 12 sunspot minima as big as the Maunder minimum. Each of them coincided with a period of cold weather and glacial advance.

Global Warming and a Sunspot Maximum

Some scientists believe the warming observed in modern times is caused by increased solar activity and consequent reduction in the intensity of cosmic radiation. Warming the seas reduces their capacity to hold dissolved carbon dioxide, so as sea temperatures rise carbon dioxide comes out of solution and into the air. This is called the *warm champagne effect*. Biochemical reactions also proceed faster as the water warms—this is the *warm beer effect*. These include the oxidation of carbon in decomposition. Both effects release carbon dioxide into the air, so the increase in the amount of carbon dioxide in the air is a consequence of warming, not the cause of it, and it has nothing to do with the burning of fuel or any other human activity.

Milankovich Cycles

Edward Maunder was not the only scientist to investigate astronomical causes of climatic changes on Earth. Maunder concentrated on variations in the amount of energy Earth receives from the Sun and discovered the sunspot minimum associated with the coldest part of the Little Ice Age (page 166). In Belgrade, meanwhile, a Serbian mathematician and physicist was also looking for astronomical influences, but in this case influences that could be traced over a much longer period. The British astronomer Sir John Herschel (1792–1871) was the first of a number of scientists to suggest there might be a link between climatic changes and variations in the amount of solar radiation received at the surface of the Earth (Herschel's father, Sir William Herschel [1738-1822], had discovered infrared radiation in 1800.) In 1864, the Scottish climatologist James Croll (1821–90) suggested that changes in solar radiation might trigger ice ages. It was a fairly vague proposal, and Milutin Milankovich, the Serbian scientist, made up his mind to test it.

Milutin Milankovich (1879–1958) was educated in Vienna but moved to the University of Belgrade in 1904 and remained there for the rest of his life. He spent 30 years studying the relationship between the Earth and Sun and its climatic consequences over the last 650,000 years and published his findings in 1930. He was interested not in variations in the amount of energy radiated by the Sun, but in variations in the rotation of the Earth on its axis and in its orbit about the Sun. These affect the amount of radiation the Earth receives.

Sunspots are generated inside the Sun by processes that are still not fully understood and that so far remain unpredictable. Milankovich was studying the movements of astronomical bodies. These are well known. Not only can they be predicted with great accuracy, their past behavior can also be calculated precisely.

Milankovich discovered three variations that affect climate. Two relate to the Earth's rotation, and the third to its orbit.

Axial Tilt

The diagram labeled (A), *axial tilt,* shows that the Earth's axis of rotation is not vertical—it is said to be oblique. If you imagine the orbit of the Earth about the Sun follows the edge of a disk that has the Sun at its center—this is called the *plane of the ecliptic*—the Earth's rotational axis is not at right angles to it. Instead of being at 90° to the plane of the ecliptic, it is at 66.5°, a difference of 23.5°.

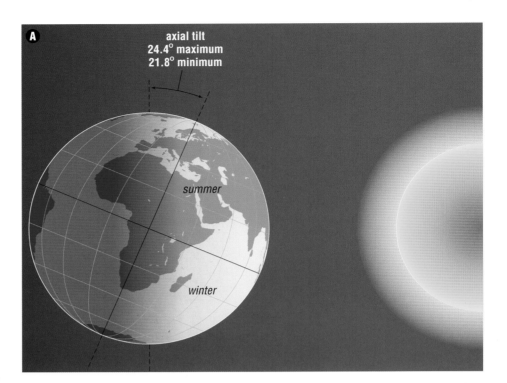

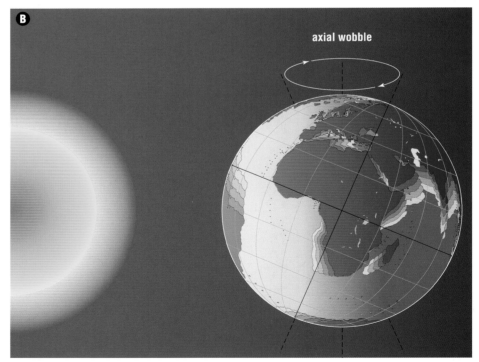

Milankovich cycles

So the rotational axis is tilted at 23.5° to a line perpendicular to the plane of the ecliptic.

This is the angle at present, but it varies between a maximum of 24.4° and a minimum of 21.8° over a period of about 41,000 years. As the diagram shows, it is the tilt, or *obliquity,* of the Earth's axis that produces our seasons. If the axis were perpendicular to the plane of the ecliptic,

the Sun would be directly overhead at the equator at noon on every day of the year, day and night would always be of equal length everywhere, and there would be no summer and winter. In diagram (A), one hemisphere is tilted toward the Sun and is enjoying summer, and the other is tilted away from the Sun and is having winter. The bigger the angle of tilt, the more extreme the seasons are, because the more each hemisphere in turn is tilted toward and then away from the Sun. This is one of the cycles Milankovich found to have a climatic influence.

Precession of the Equinoxes

The Earth is a spinning object with its mass concentrated around the rim. In other words, it is a gyroscope and in one important respect it behaves as one. It is subject to precession. If a force is applied to the rotational axis of a gyroscope, precession causes the gyroscope to move at 90° to the force in the direction of rotation. This makes precession sound complicated, but there is a familiar example of it in action. Remember what happens when you spin a child's spinning top. The axis around which it spins is hardly ever vertical. Because it is tilted, gravity pulls at it on the side that is leaning. Instead of falling over, however, the spinning top wobbles. The top of its axis describes a circle around the vertical. This is because precession causes the force to act at 90° in the direction of rotation. Instead of falling over in the direction it is leaning, the force is directed 90° away from that direction. This makes the top lean in the new direction, but as soon as it starts to do so, the force is deflected through a further 90°. The top tries to lean in all directions at once, and that is why it wobbles. As the top slows down it ceases to be a gyroscope, and so eventually it falls.

The Earth behaves in the same way, as shown in diagram (B), labeled *axial wobble*. It takes the rotational axis about 21,000 years to complete one turn. This wobble alters the dates of the spring and autumn equinoxes and summer and winter solstices—the dates at which the Sun is directly overhead at the equator at noon (the equinoxes) and the dates when the noonday Sun is overhead at the Tropics (the solstices). This gradual change is called the *precession of the equinoxes*. At present, in the Northern Hemisphere, the spring or vernal equinox is on March 20–21, the summer solstice on June 21–22, the autumnal equinox on September 22–23, and the winter solstice on December 22–23. About 11,000 years from now spring will be in September, summer in December, autumn in March, and midwinter in June. In other words, the hemispheres will have exchanged the months in which each season occurs.

When this happens, the Northern Hemisphere will receive more solar radiation than it does now in midsummer and less in midwinter. Consequently, summers will be warmer and winters cooler.

Orbital Eccentricity

This would make no difference at all if the Earth moved in a perfectly circular orbit, but it does not. The orbit is elliptical. An ellipse has a center and two foci. In the case of the Earth's orbit, the Sun is at one focus and the other is unoccupied. This means that although the Earth orbits the Sun, the Sun is not at the center of its orbit. The orbit is eccentric and the extent of its eccentricity can be calculated. The figure on the next page shows the orbital ellipse, with the Sun at one focus, F_1, the other focus, F_2, unoccupied, and the center, C. The distance between F_1 and C is the linear eccentricity, *le*, and the distance between C and the orbital path is α. The eccentricity (*e*) is then calculated as $e = le/\alpha$. All the planets of the solar system move in elliptical orbits, but the degree of their eccentricity varies. Venus and Neptune have almost circular orbits (*e* = 0.0068 and 0.0097 respectively). Pluto and Mercury have the most eccentric orbits (*e* = 0.2482 and 0.2056 respectively). Mars (*e* = 0.0934) has a more eccentric orbit than Earth (*e* = 0.017).

Perihelion and Aphelion

Clearly, at one time in the year the Earth is closer to the Sun than it is at other times. When it is at its closest approach the Earth is said to be at *perihelion* and when it is farthest away it is at *aphelion*. At present, the Earth is at perihelion on January 3 and at aphelion on July 4. This means that we are closest to the Sun in the middle of the Northern Hemisphere winter and our proximity makes the winter somewhat milder than it would otherwise be. We receive about 7 percent more radiation at perihelion than we do at aphelion.

This would make northern winters warmer than southern winters and southern summers warmer than northern summers if land and sea were distributed equally in both hemispheres, but they are not. The difference, with much more land in the north and much more ocean

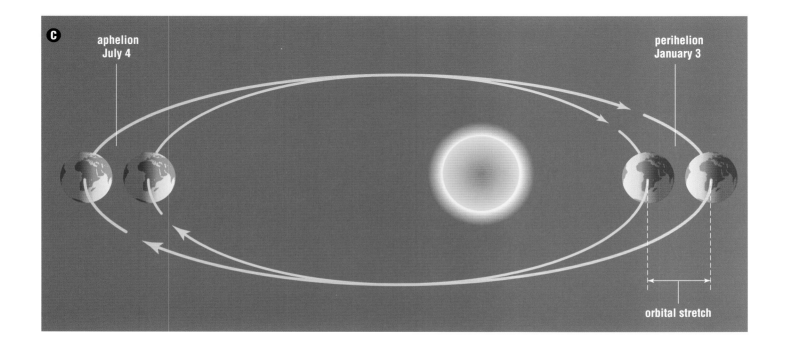

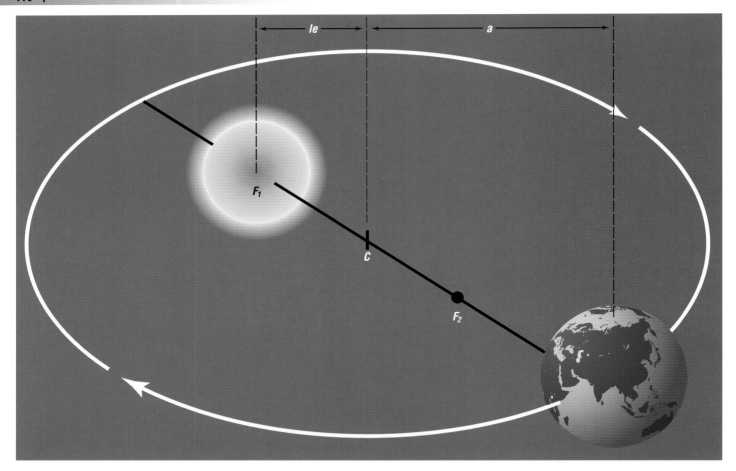

in the south, actually reverses the effect, because land warms and cools quickly and water warms and cools slowly, with the consequence that continental climates experience much more extreme temperatures than do maritime climates. In fact, therefore, northern winters are the cooler and northern summers the warmer.

Eventually, though, the precession of the equinoxes will bring the Earth to perihelion in the middle of the northern summer and to aphelion in the middle of the northern winter. This will reverse the effect. Winters will then be much colder in the more continental climates of the Northern Hemisphere and summers will be much warmer, although the effect will be less marked in more maritime climates of the Southern Hemisphere.

Orbital Stretch

The orbit is elliptical, but the shape of the ellipse changes. (See diagram on preceding page.) Sometimes it is almost circular and at other times it is stretched. At present, the orbital eccentricity, e, is 0.017, but it varies from $e = 0.001$, which is almost circular ($e = 0$), to $e = 0.054$. Like the other changes, the orbital stretch increases and

decreases in a cycle, in this case with a period of about 95,000 years. At maximal stretch the Earth is farther from the Sun at both perihelion and aphelion than it is at other times. This alters the amount of solar radiation reaching the Earth and it also affects the dates of the solstices and equinoxes.

By itself, each of these three cycles has only a small but nevertheless significant effect. Sometimes they coincide, however. When this happens the effects are added together. They account for the fact that from 12,000 to 9,000 years ago the Northern Hemisphere received 8 percent more solar radiation in summer than it does now. That was enough to trigger the melting of the ice sheets that brought the last ice age to an end. Increased warmth in summer was accompanied by a reduction in solar radiation in winter, but this affected the Southern Hemisphere subtropics, so it did not halt the glacial melting. For a time all the heat was absorbed as latent heat in the melting of the ice, so climates did not begin to grow warmer until most of the ice had gone. Much earlier, the Milankovich cycles coincided to produce the reduction in solar radiation that caused the ice sheets to start advancing. Milankovich suggested that the cycles coincided with nine ice ages.

Orbital eccentricity

For many years, climatologists doubted that the Milankovich cycles could affect the climate strongly enough to alter it. As more has been learned about the way feedback mechanisms can enhance climatic influences—for example, when pale colors of sand or snow reflect sunlight or dark colors of forests absorb it—and about past climates, the evidence has tended to support the Milankovich theory. In 1976, studies of sediments taken from the seabed found that the climate had changed at the times predicted by the Milankovich theory. This was regarded as confirmation of the theory. Most scientists now believe the astronomical cycles he described exert a strong influence on the initiation of ice ages and interglacials.

Snowblitz

The influence is strong, but the astronomical variations Milankovich described are not enough in themselves to trigger the onset of an ice age or the ending of one. An additional factor is needed, and this is provided by changes in the area covered by snow and ice. Snow- and ice-covered surfaces reflect up to 90 percent of the sunshine that falls on them. Sunshine comprises heat as well as light and, obviously, the radiation that is reflected cannot be absorbed. Consequently, air in contact with ground that is covered by snow or ice remains cold.

In its most extreme form this influence has been called the "snowblitz theory." This idea became popular in the 1970s, when evidence suggested that the global climate was growing cooler. There were fears of a return to the cold conditions of the Little Ice Age, or even of the start of a full-scale ice age.

According to the snowblitz theory the climate can change from the way it is at present to a full ice age in a matter of a few decades. The change begins with the release of a large amount of freshwater into the North Atlantic. This could happen if rainfall increased substantially—because rain is freshwater or if the Greenland ice sheet were to melt—although this is very unlikely in the foreseeable future. The freshwater would float above the denser salt water, eventually accumulating as a deep layer. This would alter the circulation of ocean currents by preventing cold, very salty water from sinking at the edge of the sea ice to form the North Atlantic Deep Water that drives the Atlantic Conveyor. The Atlantic Conveyor carries cold water towards the equator, allowing water to flow away from the equator to replace it.

The northern North Atlantic would then cool rapidly, and in winter it would freeze, partly because it would be colder than in previous years and partly because freshwater freezes at a higher temperature than salt water. The area of sea ice would expand so that more solar radiation would be reflected, causing further cooling.

Air crossing the northern Atlantic in winter would not be warmed by contact with the sea because the sea would be frozen. European winters would become much colder. In summer the sea ice would melt, but the North Atlantic Drift would have ceased to carry warm water beyond the latitude of Spain, so the ocean would remain cold and European summers would be cool. More winter precipitation would fall as snow, the snow would melt later in the year, and the cooler conditions would be spread throughout the Northern Hemisphere by the normal west-to-east movement of air in middle latitudes.

Eventually there would be a year when not all of the winter snow melted in summer. It would remain lying until the first snow of the following winter fell to join it. The surface would continue to reflect incoming radiation throughout the summer, chilling the air. Year by year the snow-covered area would expand and the summer period when temperatures rose above freezing would become shorter. As the weight of accumulating snow increased, the lower layers would be compressed into ice and ice sheets would form in Europe and Canada. The ice sheets would then expand southward, a little each year. The ice age would then be established. According to the snowblitz theory, the entire process could happen very rapidly.

Snowball Earth

The snowblitz scenario is based on the change that occurred as the most recent ice age was coming to an end. Suddenly, the Northern Hemisphere was plunged back into ice-age conditions, and the snowblitz describes how it probably happened. Few climatologists believe the scenario could occur today, however, because there is no source for the large amount of freshwater that would be needed. The cooling at the end of the last ice age, leading to the episodes known as the Older and Younger Dryas, was triggered by the vast amounts of water that flowed into the Atlantic from the melting of the Laurentide ice sheet, covering much of North America. The cold episodes are called "Dryas" because they are recognized by the presence in the soil of pollen from *Dryas octopetala* (mountain avens), an alpine and subarctic plant.

There is evidence to suggest there have been times in the much more remote past when ice covered the entire Earth. There were glaciers even at the equator, and only the tops of the highest mountains protruded above the ice sheets that covered the continents.

This condition is believed to have occurred four times between 750 million and 580 million years ago. Mean temperatures were about -58°F (-50°C), and all of the oceans were frozen to a depth of more than 0.6 mile (1 km). It happened because the breakup of large supercontinents produced much smaller landmasses. Everywhere on land was closer to the sea than the centers of the supercontinents had been, and rainfall increased over the land. Rain washed carbon dioxide from the air, the carbon dioxide reacted with minerals on the land and was carried into the ocean, and so the atmospheric concentration of carbon dioxide fell.

This caused temperatures to fall by reducing the greenhouse effect. Sea ice froze in high latitudes. The ice reflected sunshine and caused further cooling, triggering a snowblitz effect. Snow and ice covered the land, and the sea ice expanded until it covered all the oceans. The ice then sealed the surface, isolating the land and sea from the atmosphere.

The condition is called *snowball Earth* and it lasted for about 10 million years. It ended because volcanoes continued to erupt, releasing carbon dioxide into the air. The carbon dioxide accumulated until there was enough to produce a huge greenhouse effect. Temperature rose and within a few centuries all the ice had melted.

The warming did not end with the disappearance of the ice. The greenhouse effect continued until air temperatures reached more than 120°F (50°C). As the air temperature rose, the rate of evaporation increased. Clouds formed and rain fell. The rain washed the carbon dioxide from the air, checking the greenhouse warming, until the climate stabilized.

Rainmaking

Think just how many of the world's problems we might solve if only we could control the weather. We would be able to prevent droughts, like those that in the last few decades have devastated Ethiopia and the countries along the southern border of the Sahara, and that earlier in the 20th century caused the Dust Bowl tragedy in the Great Plains. Hurricanes would no longer be allowed to wreck homes and destroy crops, or tornadoes to cause destruction, death, and terror. And we would abolish deserts—although that might not please everyone, especially the people who live in them.

One day all these things may become possible, but not by using brute force to "manufacture" the weather we would prefer. We do not have the power to achieve that. An average summer thunderstorm releases energy equivalent to burning 7,000 tons (6,356 tonnes) of coal. An average hurricane releases double that amount and an average tornado, lasting no more than a few minutes, releases about as much energy as is used to keep all the streetlights in New York City shining for one night. Even if we could spare that much power and could afford to generate it, we can be fairly certain that producing and releasing it would cause more environmental problems than they would solve. If we are to alter the weather we will need a more subtle approach.

Fortunately, a few exist. They do not allow us to control every aspect of the weather, but only to manipulate it a little under certain conditions, but sometimes they can help.

Protecting Fruit from Frost

Fruit orchards are often planted in places sheltered from winds that can dry and chill the growing tips of branches and damage blossoms. The trees thrive in such places, but they face another danger, from frosts. These can occur where cold air sinks into valleys and hollows and accumulates there. In the 19th century, Florida citrus growers found a way to protect their trees. They use wind machines. These are huge propellers mounted on tall columns and driven by motors. As the propellers turn they generate a wind and this mixes the air, preventing the cold air from settling into a layer close to ground level.

This technique is simple, but ingenious, and it manipulates the weather on a very local scale. Sometimes the wind machines were not enough. Then the growers used "smudge pots." These are no longer used because of the pollution they cause. They were heaters that burned oil set out on the ground at a density of up to 70 to the acre (173 per hectare). The protection they afforded arose not from the heat they produced, but from the smoke. If the pots were lit in the early evening when a frost was predicted, the smoke would form a layer that prevented the cold air from accumulating. Wind machines and smudge pots were often used together.

Fog Dispersal

Kerosene burners were used in the 1940s to disperse fog from airfields. The method went under the unwieldy name of *fog investigation dispersal operations,* but the happier acronym of *FIDO.* The burners were positioned along both sides of a runway and the heat they produced decreased the relative humidity of the air, causing the fog droplets to evaporate. FIDO was effective, but very costly in terms of the amount of fuel it used.

The Bergeron–Findeisen Process

Research into weather manipulation on a much bigger scale also began in 1946 and is still continuing. It is based on the Bergeron–Findeisen process. This is an explanation of the way certain clouds form that was proposed in 1935 by the Swedish meteorologist Tor Bergeron and the German meteorologist Walter Findeisen.

It occurs only in mixed clouds that contain both ice crystals and water droplets. The air temperature in a cloud of this type is between 32°F (0°C) and -40°F (-40°C). Warmer clouds contain only water droplets and colder ones only ice crystals. Water molecules are constantly escaping into the air from the surface of water or ice. In the layer of air next to the surface, water molecules are pressing against the surface and condensing into it. If the number of molecules condensing onto the surface is equal to the number escaping from it the vapor next to the surface is saturated. The pressure exerted on the surface by molecules in a layer of saturated water vapor is known as the *saturated vapor pressure.* Molecules can escape from an ice surface without the ice's melting first, but with more difficulty, because they are bound together more tightly in the solid than in the liquid. Consequently, the saturation vapor pressure over an ice surface such as an ice crystal or snowflake is lower than that over a liquid water surface such as a closed droplet.

Inside a cloud ice crystals and water droplets are constantly moving. If the air next to the liquid droplets is saturated, then it will be supersaturated with respect to ice crystals because of the lower saturation vapor pressure. Molecules will attach themselves to ice crystals, which will grow bigger. The molecules that are removed from the air and added to the ice crystals lower the air to below saturation with respect to the liquid droplets. Water evaporates from them, making them smaller. The overall effect is that the ice crystals grow rapidly at the expense of the water droplets.

When ice crystals collide they stick to one another and form snowflakes. The type and shape of the snowflakes depend on the temperatures they encounter as they move about in the cloud. As they move, now and then they come into contact with liquid droplets. These are supercooled—their temperature is below freezing—and they freeze instantly on contact with any solid surface. In clouds where the temperature is below freezing at high level, but above freezing at low level, droplets repeatedly freeze onto crystals, fall to a lower level where their surfaces melt, and are then carried aloft, where they freeze again and gain more ice by collision with supercooled droplets. This is how hailstones form.

Cloud Seeding

This is the Bergeron–Findeisen process, and the research that began in 1946 aims to exploit it. If crystals of a suitable size and shape are fed into a mixed cloud they will stimulate the formation of ice crystals. In early attempts aircraft dropped sodium chloride (common salt) and calcium chloride crystals and sprayed freshwater or salt water into clouds. Powdered salt was also blown upward from the ground.

These had little effect, but silver iodide and dry ice—solid carbon dioxide—proved more successful. Silver iodide crystals are very small—0.01–0.1 µm across (1 µm is one-millionth of a meter, or about 0.00004 inch). They are similar in shape to ice crystals, so water condenses onto them as it would onto ice. The usual way to apply silver iodide is to dissolve it in acetone to make a 1–10 percent solution. This is burned at about 2,000°F (1,100°C) in small devices suspended beneath aircraft. The Russians have also tried using 70-mm artillery to fire projectiles that explode inside clouds, each projectile releasing 3.5–7 ounces (100–200 grs) of lead iodide or silver iodide. Rockets have also been used. Silver iodide can be generated at ground level. The crystals are carried upward in the rising hot air and then swept into the cloud by air currents.

Dry ice has a temperature of about -108°F (-78°C) and chills the air. This saturates it and causes water vapor to condense. The dry ice is usually made into crushed pellets and dropped into a cloud from aircraft. Carbon dioxide is little used nowadays because it soon vaporizes and loses its effectiveness.

These methods are called *cloud seeding;* their aim is to stimulate the production of ice crystals by an amount that is sufficient to cause precipitation to fall from a cloud that might otherwise have yielded none. It is hard to tell whether a cloud would have delivered precipitation if left undisturbed, but experiments suggest that cloud seeding works about 10–20 percent of the time.

Taming Storms

Causing precipitation is only one of the potential uses of cloud seeding. If seeding material is injected into a cumulonimbus (storm) cloud at the right moment it can cause the formation of large numbers of small hailstones that fall from the cloud, rather than a smaller number of much bigger hailstones that could damage crops.

Some years ago attempts were also made to use cloud seeding to reduce the intensity and alter the track of hurricanes. In Project Stormfury, carried out between 1962 and 1983, clouds forming the eyewall of a hurricane were seeded with silver iodide. The idea was that seeding would increase production of ice crystals. Their formation would release latent heat, and this would intensify convection in the cloud. The original eyewall would weaken and a new one would form outside it, at a larger radius. This would reduce the force of the winds around the eye, because their intensity is due to the conservation of angular momentum. As the rotational radius of the storm increases, its wind speed decreases.

At first the experiments seemed promising. Wind speeds apparently decreased by 10–30 percent in four of the eight attempts made. Later, however, scientists began to question the results. Today it is thought the wind reduction was entirely natural and that cloud seeding is unlikely to alter hurricane behavior.

Seeding can have other effects. If more than a certain amount of material is used, a cloud is *overseeded*. This rapidly produces a very large number of very small ice crystals. Their formation removes water vapor from the air, reducing it to well below saturation, and the crystals evaporate into it, dispersing the cloud.

At present, large-scale weather modification seems beyond our capability. Cloud seeding has some effect, but there is no evidence that severe storms can be dissipated in this way. Research continues, however, and in years to come it may prove possible to intervene to reduce the ferocity of storms.

Halting the Spread of Deserts and New Crops for Dry Climates

In the early 1970s, as the continuing drought in the Sahel region drove starving people south in search of pasture for their animals and food for themselves, there were fears that the desert itself was spreading. More than 100,000 people died, as well as up to 4 million head of livestock. In 1973, the drought in Ethiopia is believed to have claimed up to 250,000 lives and drought returned again in 1984–85. People became familiar with the word *desertification* through newspaper and magazine articles and television programs.

In 1977 the United Nations (UN) held a Conference on Desertification in Nairobi. The UN claimed to have coined the term *desertification,* but they were mistaken, because it was first used in 1949, admittedly in French, in the book *Climats, Fôrets et Desertification de l'Afrique Tropicale* by A. Aubreville. The word was not new and neither was knowledge of the process it described. Fears of the southward encroachment of the Sahara were being expressed as long ago as the 1930s.

UN Convention to Combat Desertification

The subject was also debated at the Rio Summit (the United Nations Conference on Environment and Development) held in June 1992 in Rio de Janeiro, where it was agreed that a treaty should be prepared as a guide to nations in halting land degradation. This led to the UN Convention to Combat Desertification (CCD). Unlike many international agreements, the CCD aims to involve local people and make use of their special knowledge and expertise. Information about programs that are devised and succeed in one place will be passed to groups in similar situations in other parts of the world.

The program to achieve the aims of the CCD is based on national plans that are coordinated internationally through what has been called the *Global Mechanism* (GM). The GM will be administered by the International Fund for Agricultural Development in collaboration with the UN Development Program and the World Bank. The industrialized countries are funding the CCD, and individual countries are working closely with particular projects. The Netherlands, for example, is working with Burkina Faso, Spain with Latin American countries, and Germany with Mali. A desert studies program has been instituted at the University of Kuwait, and Kuwait has also started collecting data on the movement of sand dunes. Senegal has opened a center to monitor the environment. Argentina, Bolivia, and Paraguay are

Date palm oasis being inundated by sand

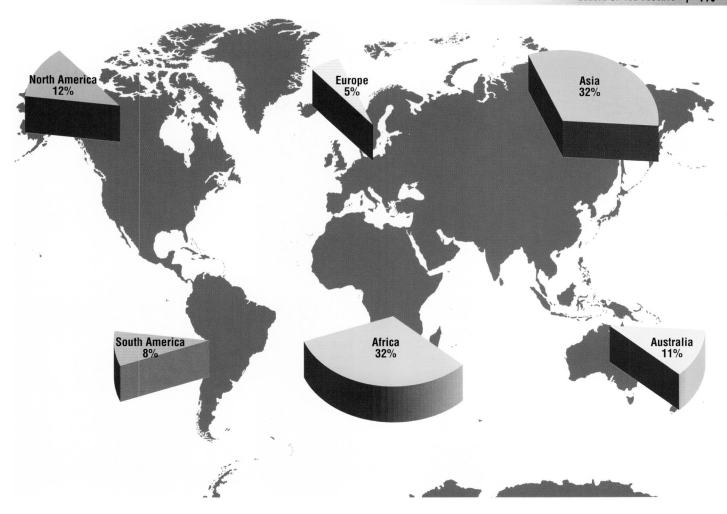

North America
12%

Europe
5%

Asia
32%

South America
8%

Africa
32%

Australia
11%

collaborating in the development of methods to manage dry lands.

How Deserts Are Made

Desertification results from the effect of drought on bare, exposed soil. Removal of trees for wood or fuel and overgrazing of grass and herbs (page 184) destroy the root systems that bind soil particles together. As the surface soil dries to powder, it is blown away by the wind. The wind, carrying the topsoil, blows over adjacent land where plants are still growing. Friction with the plants slows the wind, causing it to lose energy. As the wind loses energy the soil settles. It buries the plants, clogging their stomata and shielding them from the sunlight, so they are unable to photosynthesize (page 56) and die. Their roots then decay and cease to bind the soil, which also blows away. In this way the desert spreads into the semiarid land along its borders.

People living in these semiarid lands see their crop yields fall and harvests fail. There is less pasture for their livestock. They have to walk farther to find firewood, because the nearby trees have

gone. Eventually their lives may become unsustainable, forcing them to move.

Some or all of a number of physical changes accompany this process. The water table falls, so wells dry up and plants wilt because their roots can no longer reach moist soil. Where there is water it may be brackish or salty, making it undrinkable. Soils may be poisoned by excessive amounts of salts (page 124). Soil erosion may increase.

Despite the dramatic description and the familiarity of the word, there is no agreed definition of desertification and it is by no means certain that the Sahara is spreading. The UN Environment Program defines desertification as "land degradation in arid, semiarid, and dry subhumid areas resulting mainly from adverse human impacts." Most scientists would qualify this statement. The deterioration must affect both vegetation and soil, it must be caused at least partly (but not necessarily mainly) by human management, and, most importantly, it must be sustained for at least 10 years. Deterioration for a shorter period than this may be part of a cycle from which the land will recover naturally (page 180).

Arid lands

Although "desertification" conjures a picture of land turning into a desert resembling the Sahara, this is the most severe condition. Most deteriorating land is in a better state than this and not all of it is located along the edges of deserts. It can occur anywhere on land with an annual rainfall of less than about 31.5 inches (800 mm). As the map shows, although Africa and Asia together comprise almost two-thirds of the world's 23.5 million square miles (61 million sq km) of vulnerable arid lands, every continent has some.

Improving Land Management

At present there is nothing we can do to modify the climate on a large scale (page 172), but it should be possible to improve land management. The first aim of any improvement of land use must be to maintain a vegetation cover at all times. This serves two purposes. Plants increase the roughness of the ground surface, which increases friction with moving air and slows the wind, and plant roots bind soil particles. Together, these effects greatly reduce soil erosion and can often prevent it almost entirely.

In the 1970s there were schemes to halt what was then believed to be the southward spread of the Sahara by planting a belt of trees across Africa from the Atlantic to the Red Sea. This was over-ambitious and the tree belt was never completed, but the CCD is starting to take effect at a more modest level—and it begins by acknowledging that desertification can be combated successfully.

Security of Tenure

An important first step is to make people feel secure in their access to the resources that sustain them. Traditionally, many of the inhabitants of deserts and the lands bordering them have lived as nomads. They did not own or even rent the land, but their way of life was based on a detailed knowledge of the seasonal distribution of pasture and water and each group had certain places it visited and to which it enjoyed unchallenged rights. That way of life was disrupted in the course of the 20th century and many of the nomads now live in settled communities (page 184). Wars and the famines often caused by them generate waves of refugees seeking food and sanctuary. Unable to cope with the scale of the need, countries sometimes close their borders. This also affects the nomads, who can no longer be sure they will be able to lead their herds and flocks to the traditional pastures.

Settled farmers also need security of tenure. Providing it is an essential first step in recruiting local people to cooperate with programs for reducing and preventing erosion. This is because they are being asked to do extra work in order to improve the land. Unless they can be confident that they and their children will enjoy the bene-fit of that improvement it may be impossible to persuade them to invest the necessary labor. If the land is improved, it may well be the landowner who benefits, not the farmer. This is because improving the land will increase crop yields, mak-ing it more valuable, and the landowner may evict a poor farming family in order to install a more prosperous one, who can pay a higher rent. With-out that assurance the farmers are being entirely rational when they refuse to undertake extra work. Work consumes energy that must be pro-vided by food. Where food is scarce and the work guarantees no long-term benefit, the price is not worth paying.

Once farmers and nomadic pastoralists feel secure, they can be helped to improve their agri-cultural methods. This is not a matter of sending teams of foreign experts to dictate to them, and far less does it mean trying to impose European or American techniques in parts of the world where the climate and soils make these inappro-priate. It means discussing with the farmers and nomads the type of modifications that might reduce erosion and then making sure they have access to the finance and materials needed to make those modifications.

Farming and nomadic communities living on the borders of the desert are invariably composed of the very poorest people. They have no means of raising the money to buy materials and banks are reluctant to give them credit. Alternative sources of employment, in small-scale light indus-try or tourism, for example, can provide income. Those who leave farming for other employment will spend part of their earnings on buying food from the farmers, so some of that income may be invested.

Spraying sand dunes with a mixture of oil and synthetic rubber stabilizes the surface by binding sand grains. Tree seedlings, especially of eucalyptus and acacia species that can grow with only 6 inches (150 mm) of rain a year, are then planted through the surface coating.

Heavy rains are the main cause of erosion on hillsides. They wash away the topsoil. This can be checked by building low dry-stone walls from the abundant rocks that litter the desert surface. Walls across each of the gullies slow the water, so soil it is carrying is precipitated.

Corridor Farming

Trees can be planted to shelter cultivated land, not on the grandiose scale of a tree belt the width of a continent, but locally. Crops can be grown between rows of trees. This is called *corridor farm-ing* or *alley cropping* and has been practiced suc-cessfully in several semiarid regions, using acacia trees. These are legumes, with bacteria attached to their roots that fix atmospheric nitrogen (page 70), so they need very little fertilizer.

Apple-ring acacia, also called *winter thorn* and *camel thorn* (*Acacia albida*), has the unusual habit of bearing leaves through the dry season and shed-ding them at the start of the wet season. This means the tree provides food livestock can eat at a time of year when there is little other food available. Animals that feed on its shoots and leaves remain healthy and its branches can be cut and stored without losing their nutritional value.

The trees are planted as seedlings at the same time as the farm crop. The crop is harvested as soon as it is ripe and the trees are left to continue growing, and they do so through the dry season. In the following year a new crop is planted and the trees are cut down almost to ground level. Their leaves are fed to livestock and the wood is used as fuel. This is similar to coppicing, a Euro-pean management system that produces a regular crop of small poles and firewood. Far from killing the tree, cutting it in this way usually extends its life. The tree becomes smaller and bushier, but it continues to produce fodder and fuelwood for many years.

Dry Farming

Dry farming methods were devised in North America after the Dust Bowl years (page 194) to allow cultivation in semiarid climates. One method is to grow a crop, harvest it, and then leave the land fallow for 3 years. During those years plants are allowed to grow naturally, but controlled by light plowing at regular intervals. The plants accumulate moisture in their tissues and the plowing prevents them from losing an excessive amount of it by transpiration (page 60). After three years the buried and partly decom-posed "weeds" will have moistened and fertilized the soil sufficiently for the next crop to be grown. On a farm using this method, one-quar-ter of the area is under cultivation at any one time and the cropped area changes each year, accord-ing to a regular four-year rotation.

Finding New Crop Plants

Farming has developed over thousands of years by exploiting a very small proportion of the plants that exist on Earth. There are about 9,000 species of grasses, for example, of which we have domesticated a little more than 20 for human consumption—wheat (four species), oats, barley (two species), rye, oats, rice, maize (corn), sugar cane, millets (about 10 species), and sorghum. Of the 18,000 species of legumes we make use of six (peas, beans, soybeans, peanuts, alfalfa, and clover). These crops may not be the best choices for all soil and climatic conditions.

Increasingly, scientists are hoping to halt ero-sion in dry climates by using entirely new crops or traditional crops that have been modified to make them suitable. The development of new crops means the domestication of wild plants. The modification of traditional crops uses modern biotechnology—genetic modification—to make the plants more tolerant of dry climates or salt-laden soils. The search is proving very successful.

Vetiver

A few years ago staff employed by the World Bank in India came across an obscure grass called *vetiver* (*Vetivera zizanioides*). Looking rather like pampas grass, it grows naturally in rain forest, in the Himalaya Mountains, and in the deserts of Rajasthan. It thrives in shade, on sun-drenched sand, in snow, and even lives for up to 40 days under water. Despite its toughness it is unlikely to become a weed because it propagates itself mainly vegetatively and very slowly, rather than by seed. Its roots grow almost vertically downward, to a considerable depth.

Rows of it can be planted on hillsides, parallel to the contours, where the plants merge to form a screen that is strong enough to hold back soil and other material moving down the slope. This prevents erosion on hillsides that were once forested.

Grasses and Amaranths

Vetiver is not edible, but another grass, *Echinochloa turnerana,* produces a highly nutritious grain. It grows wild in Australia and grows well with just one watering. Amaranths (*Amaranthus* species) also produce edible grain. They are natives of Central and South America, where they were cultivated for their grain until they were displaced by corn and by cereals introduced by European colonists. *A. hypochondriacus* has edible leaves as well as seeds and the seeds contain about 15 percent protein and 63 percent starch. The Spanish church forbade the growing of it because it was used in Aztec ceremonies the Christians were determined to suppress. *A. caudatus* is the garden plant love-lies-bleeding and is also known as *Inca wheat.*

The value of amaranths is that they are rich in the amino acid lysine. This is an essential ingredient in the human diet, but very few plants contain it (soybean is one that does) and we fill most of our requirement from animal products, which do.

Quinoa and Buffalo Gourd

Quinoa (*Chenopodium quinoa*) is another South American plant. Little known outside the Andes of Bolivia, Chile, Ecuador, and Peru, where it grows naturally, quinoa is one of the best sources of protein of all plants. The outer layer of its seeds contain saponins and other substances that make them unpleasantly bitter. This may deter insect and bird pests, making the plant easier to grow, and the bitterness can be removed by washing the seeds in cold water.

From the desert and wasteland of Mexico and the southwestern United States, buffalo gourd (*Cucurbita foetidissima*)—also known as *chilicote* and *mock orange*—produces abundant fruits containing seeds that are rich in oil and protein. One plant, growing in very dry conditions, can produce an average of 60 fruits with 2.5 pounds (1.15 kg) of seeds. One acre sown to them could produce more than 1 ton (2.3 tonnes per hectare) of seeds that are 34 percent polyunsaturated oil and 30–35 percent protein. The fruits can be harvested mechanically, and they dry out so completely that the seeds can be threshed from them. The dried pulp is fed to cattle.

Below ground, the buffalo gourd grows a tuber in which it stores water. After two growing seasons the tuber weighs around 70 pounds (32 kg), of which 70 percent is water, and it is filled with starch. One buffalo gourd grown in very dry conditions produces as much starch as 20 potato plants grown in moist, well-drained soil.

Jojoba, Apple-Ring Acacia, and Ramón

One plant from the arid regions of Central America and the southwestern United States that has been domesticated is the jojoba (*Simmondsia chinensis*), which yields a liquid wax with many industrial uses. Jojoba wax has largely replaced oil from sperm whales as a high-quality lubricant. The wax can also be hydrogenated to make a solid white wax that can be used for polishing.

As well as shoots and leaves for feeding livestock, especially cattle, the apple-ring acacia produces seeds, carried in pods like peas and beans. These contain up to 27 percent protein. They can be eaten by humans but are more commonly fed to cattle. The acacias can be grown beside peanuts (groundnuts). Both crops yield approximately similar amounts of protein, the acacia producing its crop at the start of the wet season and the groundnuts producing theirs at the start of the dry season.

Ramón, also called *breadnut* and *capomo* (*Brosimum alicastrum*), also bears leaves throughout the year. It occurs naturally in much of Central America as far north as southern Mexico and, less commonly, in Jamaica and Cuba. The tree grows in humid forests, but its roots descend so deeply it can always find water, and so it is very tolerant of drought. Cattle relish its leaves and shoots, pigs enjoy its fruits, and people can eat its seeds raw, boiled, or roasted—they taste rather like potatoes. The dried seeds can also be ground into a meal and mixed with maize meal to make tortillas. The tree itself can be tapped for its sap, which can be drunk like milk. A close relative from Venezuela, *B. utile,* is known as the *cow-tree.*

Genetic Engineering

Today scientists are also working to make conventional plants more tolerant of drought and soils contaminated with salt. This has always been possible, but slow. It was achieved by identifying varieties of crop plants, or species related to them, that possessed desirable qualities of drought resistance or salt tolerance. These were then crossbred with varieties that produced dependable high yields. The most promising individuals from the resulting progeny were selected and bred with each other, and after many generations a new variety emerged with the desired characteristics. This was traditional plant breeding. Until recently it was the method of genetic manipulation by which all our cultivated plants were developed.

It is now possible to achieve the same result much more quickly. Plants with the desired characteristics are examined genetically to locate and identify the genes that confer those characteristics. The relevant genes are isolated and transported into the cell nuclei of the target crop plant. They become incorporated into the genetic structure of the crop, which then acquires the characteristics they confer.

This is genetic engineering. It is difficult in practice and not always successful, but the techniques involved are advancing very rapidly. Environmentalists, especially in Britain, strongly oppose genetic engineering for ideological reasons and have campaigned vigorously—and sometimes violently—against it. There is no evidence that it has harmed or is likely to harm human health or the environment, however, and most scientists consider it a vital component of the measures needed to halt soil erosion, increase food output, and reduce the use of agricultural chemicals. Already, and increasingly in years to come, dry and semiarid marginal lands will be reclaimed and become productive through the use of crops genetically engineered for the purpose.

Improved Irrigation

Deserts are barren for lack of water. Where water is available a wide variety of crops can be grown quite easily. A supply of water is all that is needed to make the desert productive. Obviously, that is what has been tried repeatedly for thousands of years.

Unfortunately, it is not so simple as it seems—even if water for irrigation can be found. A desert climate is defined as one in which more water can evaporate in a year than falls as rain or snow. In other words, the air is very dry. Consequently, liquid water exposed to the air will evaporate rapidly. Pouring water onto the ground is extremely wasteful, because most of the water will evaporate and never reach the crop roots.

Compensate for this by adding more water and as the cost rises, so may the water table until the ground becomes waterlogged (page 124). Then evaporation from the surface may leave a deposit of salts that accumulates and eventually poisons the soil. If irrigation is to prove effective and safe, it must be applied with care.

First, though, a source of water must be found. This may be a well, but there is always a risk of depleting the groundwater and lowering the water table until the well runs dry. Water can be taken directly from rivers, but that can also cause problems (page 186). The third alternative is to find some means of holding water that would otherwise be lost.

Capturing the Monsoon Rains

In the monsoon climate of the Indian subcontinent the average annual rainfall is often more than would qualify the area as desert. Some places on the border between India and Pakistan, for example, receive up to 10 inches (250 mm) of rain a year. The trouble is that all of the rain falls in the space of about one week during the summer monsoon. The rain then is so intense there is no time for it to soak into the ground. Instead, the huge, heavy raindrops batter the soil surface into an impermeable covering—called a *cap*—and the water flows across the ground and is lost. Indeed, it flows so fast, it carries much of the topsoil with it.

Local people have found a way to capture and hold water from the monsoon rains. On the lower ground they have built dams made from earth across the valleys. Each dam has a sluice gate that can be opened if necessary to allow excess water to escape, but mostly it remains shut.

The rains flow off the hillsides and into the valleys as countless torrential streams. There their progress is checked and the water accumulates.

For about a week after the rains have ended there is an artificial lake behind each dam, but its level falls quickly as the water soaks into the ground. Then, when no more water lies on the surface, the farmers move in to plant their crops of wheat and chick-peas in the damp soil.

Even after the water has apparently vanished, it has not been lost. It drains downward and becomes groundwater that can be reached by wells. So once the fields have dried, irrigation is possible to extend the growing season.

Their method does more than conserve water. It also captures the topsoil eroded from the hillsides. This is deposited on the fields as a rich, fertile silt. This system for trapping and holding water long enough for it to soak into the ground is very similar—and the principle is identical—to that devised long ago in the Negev Desert (page 122).

Drip Irrigation

Drip or trickle irrigation greatly reduces waste. Water is carried to the crop along plastic pipes, 0.5–1.0 inch (1.3–2.5 cm) in diameter, that have small openings, called *emitters,* at intervals along them. The spacing of the emitters can be varied to meet the requirements of particular crops. A fruit tree might have up to eight emitters spaced around it, for example, or there might be one or two to supply water to a grapevine.

Water trickles from the emitters very slowly. No more than 1 gallon (3.7 liters) of water may flow from each emitter in an hour. The water moves through the soil mainly by capillarity (page 38) and only the soil near the plant is moistened.

Drip irrigation works especially well in hot, dry climates and it has been used extensively in Israel. There, the pipes are buried below ground so the water is delivered directly to the roots of the crop plants and the ground surface remains dry. This practice almost eliminates losses by evaporation.

This irrigation method is simple to install and requires little maintenance, although the emitters readily become clogged; therefore the irrigation water must be filtered carefully before it enters the system. Crops watered in this way produce shallow roots concentrated close to the emitters. If a pipe fails or a few emitters clog, the plants they serve are likely to show signs of stress very soon and may be lost unless repairs are carried out quickly. Soil cultivation and crop harvesting methods may need to be modified because of the presence of the irrigation pipes.

Adding Fertilizer

These are disadvantages to drip irrigation, but the advantages greatly outweigh them. Because the rate of flow is so low, fertilizer can be added to the irrigation water. This nourishes the growing plants very efficiently. Fertilizer amounts can be precisely controlled and adjusted when necessary and none of the fertilizer drains out of the soil and is lost.

Water used for irrigation is not pure enough for domestic use. It is not fit for drinking, but there is no need to purify it to such a high standard. In fact, irrigation water can be quite salty. The salts it contains are deposited in the soil, but do not harm the plants. The soil around the plant roots is kept permanently moist, so the salts accumulate around the outer edges of the wet area.

Salt-Tolerant Plants

Most of the water on Earth is salty. Land-dwelling animals cannot drink it and it will kill most plants—but not all species. In mangrove forests and salt marshes there are plants that tolerate high salt levels, for example. If the physiological features that allow them to grow in a saline environment could be transferred to other, intolerant species, these plants could also be grown in salt water.

This is an aim of scientists working to engineer genetic changes in crop plants. So far success has been limited, because although some ordinary crop plants are more tolerant of salt than others, none is very tolerant. Transferring relevant genes from slightly salt-tolerant to even less salt-tolerant species represents only a small gain. The date palm (*Phoenix dactylifera,* see page 66) is one of the most tolerant, but it can grow in soils containing no more than 5 parts per thousand, or per mille ($\%_0$) of salt. Seawater contains an average of 35 parts per thousand salt, and in places where an arm of the sea is almost land-locked and the evaporation rate is high the salinity rises to 40 parts per thousand. It reaches this level in the northern part of the Gulf of California, for example, between Baja California and Sonora, and in parts of the Persian Gulf.

Cultivating Halophytes

The alternative is to exploit the salt tolerance of *halophytes*—plants adapted to saline conditions that are found along coasts. At present it is impossible to transfer genes conferring salt tolerance from halophytes to halophobes (salt haters), however, and it may always remain impossible. This is because the salt tolerance of a halophyte is based not upon one or even a small set of characteristics, but on the entire physiological system of the plant. It can include roots with an outer layer of cells through which salt cannot pass. Layers of waxy material may separate cells inside the plant, forcing water to pass through the cells, where salt is removed and excreted. There may be specialized salt-storage organs, or salt bladders, on the leaves. These accumulate salt and burst when they are full, releasing it. All of these features are determined genetically, but transferring them to a halophobic species would involve completely restructuring the plant.

Another approach is possible, however. Some natural halophytes can be domesticated. This is the idea being explored by a team of scientists led by Professor Edward P. Glenn, of the University of Arizona at Tucson.

Domesticating the Salt Lovers

Domestication begins with the collection of hundreds of halophytic plants. These are screened to determine the extent of their salt tolerance, their edibility, and, of those that are edible, the nutritional value. After one has been selected, the second step involves learning how to grow, harvest, and utilize it.

Several species show promise. Palmer's grass (*Distichlis palmeri*) yields seeds that were once eaten by some Native Americans. Livestock can eat glassworts (*Salicornia* species) and glasswort seeds are edible, with a nutty flavor, and contain an oil that can be used for cooking. Grown experimentally in Mexico, the United Arab Emirates, Saudi Arabia, and India, glassworts have yielded an average 7.5 tons per acre (17 tonnes per hectare) of the whole plant, from which 1,780 pounds per acre (2 tonnes per hectare) of oil was obtained. Saltbushes (*Atriplex* species) are also edible for farm animals.

Care must be taken to make sure salt does not accumulate in the soil while the crop is being grown. Since salt water is being used for irrigation, the only way to prevent its accumulation is to irrigate copiously and almost continuously, in some cases by flooding the fields.

The plants still require domestication. One important feature of domesticating any plant grown for grain is to prevent it from scattering its seeds before harvest—as wild plants do. Early farmers had to solve the same problem with wheat and barley and did so by growing crops from seed saved only from those plants that retained their seed when ripe. This suggests the problem is soluble.

There is also a problem that may not be soluble. Halophytes contain salt in their tissues. The salt has no nutritional value, but it occupies space, making the plant relatively bulky in relation to its nutrient content. The bulk limits the amount an animal can consume at a time, but volume for volume the food is less nutritious than that from other, halophobic, plants.

Seawater Is Plentiful

Despite the difficulties, halophytic crops could be very useful. Seawater is abundant. In some places the groundwater is too salt for agricultural use and there are large areas suffering from salination, caused by poor irrigation in the past. Halophytes might be grown in such places and certain plants might also be able to tolerate and absorb levels of elements that would poison other species.

Most of the salt water is in the sea, of course, and can be used only on land near the coast. Even so, this limitation still leaves large areas of coastal deserts that might be cultivated. It remains to be seen whether farms growing halophytes and irrigated by salt water will prove both biologically and economically feasible. Research into their viability began as long ago as 1949 and there are still no commercial halophyte farms. If, one day, they do start to appear, land that is now barren will be brought to life.

PART 8

Desert Advances and Retreats

Deserts seem eternal. It is hard to see how such vast expanses of barren wilderness might ever change. Yet they do change. They change with the arrival of the rains, with droughts that can last for years, and with longer-term climatic changes.

People who live in or on the edge of a desert must adapt to those changes. This is never easy, but where people depend on desert resources the difficulty increases in proportion to their degree of dependence. There are mining towns in many deserts, for example, populated by miners and other workers and their families. Their necessities are supplied by shops stocked with food and other goods imported from outside the desert. The people are not at all dependent on the desert. Whether the rains arrive or fail is of no concern to them.

Farmers, growing crops or husbanding livestock, are much more vulnerable. Adequate rain means good harvests and luxuriant pasture, with adequate food supplies to last until the next season. Drought means hardship, but hardship that can be postponed at least for a time, because there are food stores to fall back on, and livestock can be killed for food before they starve.

Most vulnerable of all, though, are the people who rely on the desert itself for all their needs. These are the hunters and gatherers, the people whose diet comprises wild plants, game, small animals, honey, eggs, and insects, and whose few possessions are made from the materials that occur naturally in their environment. They have no reserves and their only response to hard times is to move elsewhere. Some people romanticize the apparently simple way of life such people follow, but in truth it is harsh in the extreme.

Australian Aborigines

When the first humans arrived in Australia, perhaps as long as 60,000 years ago, they found a land very different from the forests and lush pastures of southern Asia, the region from which

they had come. There were tropical forest and grassland in the northern part of their new homeland, but much of the interior was desert.

They were not farmers—at the time they arrived in Australia farming had not been invented anywhere in the world. In any case, Australia had no animals that could be organized into herds. Kangaroos, the biggest mammals, cannot be corralled and driven as cattle or sheep can. They are a source of meat, however, and the new colonists lived by gathering wild plants and hunting game.

As their numbers increased, the local groups would divide. These groups occupied a particular area and shared a common language. The subgroups would then depart in search of a new territory that would supply their needs—and in the Australian deserts those needs were defined in terms of water.

Eventually there were about 500 language-based groups. Each group comprised a number of smaller groups, all of them living permanently in an area centered on a source of water around which their ancestors originally settled and where their spirits were believed to have remained. By the time European settlers arrived in the 18th century some estimates gave the size of the existing population as about 300,000. Others said there were more than 1 million. The Europeans called the people *aborigines* or *aboriginals,* a name that simply means "the people who were already there when we arrived."

Aboriginal Society

All the members of a group were related to each other, but relationships were not confined to men and women. Various nonhuman species were also classed as relatives. The components of their natural surroundings and natural phenomena, such as rain, were part of their social order and there were rituals for communicating with them.

Aboriginal people learned to exploit the meager resources available to them, but their life

was always hard and precarious. They built no permanent dwellings, had very few material possessions, and did not wear clothes. They would construct a simple windbreak for shelter, but a small campfire and the dogs that slept beside them provided their only warmth on cold nights when the temperature can fall to 50°F (10°C). Their life was primitive and much of their time was spent searching for water and food, but the conditions were made endurable by their rich mental and spiritual life. They developed very complex social arrangements and religious rituals, with a culture based on the concept of the *Dreamtime,* through which past and present merge and spatial distances vanish.

Aborigines are now Australian citizens. They are emerging from a long period of oppression by white Australians that has left them impoverished and dispossessed. There are few groups who still live by hunting and gathering. Most live in towns and have jobs.

Dwellers in the Kalahari

It is not possible for people to live a settled life if the desert must provide all their food, drink, and raw materials. The resources are too thinly spread and undependable. When it rains, plants flourish, animals arrive to feed on them, and times are good (see page 64). Between rains, when the land is parched, food is hard to find. The interval between rains is unpredictable, but it is sometimes measured in years.

In the Kalahari Desert of southern Africa there are people who live by hunting and gathering, but their traditional way of life is not so wholly dependent on the desert as that of the Australian Aborigines. The San, also known in some places as the *Basarwa,* are a group of peoples some of whom were once farmers. They were driven into the desert long ago by incoming Bantu-speaking peoples and had to adapt to foraging for plants and hunting game.

Many traded with the Bantu peoples and for a time they lived quite well by trading. At first they traded cattle, then ostrich feathers, which were fashionable dress ornaments, strongly in demand in the cities of Europe and America. They also traded ivory. These goods were exchanged for agricultural produce and the guns with which they shot elephants. Eventually the elephants disappeared, the cattle died of a serious disease called *rinderpest,* and the market for ostrich feathers collapsed when the fashion changed, as fashion does. The San people were driven into increasingly abject poverty until hunting and gathering were the only means of subsistence available to them.

Myths of Abundance Among the !Kung

There are several groups, of which the most closely studied are the !Kung, !xong, and G/wi—! and / represent a click sound. A famous study of the !Kung, made in the early 1970s, found them living well. They were healthy and needed to devote only two or three hours each day to the search for food, and their diet was rich, nutritious, and very varied.

On the basis of this report, some Europeans and Americans came to see the !Kung as the protectors of a peaceful, leisured way of life in tune with their natural surroundings, from which they effortlessly obtained everything they required. It was learned later, however, that this study had lasted only three weeks and by chance had coincided with a brief period of abundance following heavy rains. Usually, their lives are harsh. Their life expectancy at birth is 30 years, many babies and infants die, and when food is scarce, the adults lose so much weight they are close to starvation.

Life of the G/wi

Among the G/wi, who live a similar life to the !Kung, in most years there is enough food between November and about July for a band to live together as a single community. Water holes are full for up to 8 weeks during that period.

The group cannot remain in one place, of course. Every 3 or 4 weeks, when the edible plants have been depleted in the area around the camp, the people move to a new location. In early winter, when frosts damage the plants, reducing the food supply, the community divides into its constituent households. There are up to about 16 households in a band and among them they forage in an area of 300–400 square miles (780–1,040 sq km).

Their diet is based on about eight species of plants. These provide the staple food; different plants are available at different seasons—they are not all eaten at the same time of year. Meat is provided by hunting grazing mammals and by collecting reptiles, birds, and insects. Eggs are also eaten. Antelope skins provide clothing, blankets, and bags for carrying small items.

Changing Times and the End of a Way of Life

In 1971 a diamond mine opened at Orapa, in Botswana. Other mines appeared in succeeding years in various parts of the Kalahari. The mines provided jobs and attracted people from outside the desert. Cattle ranches were established on the edge of the desert. Local crafts became popular among visitors. A tourist industry began. Little by little, the San came to work for the ranchers or found other employment. The Botswana government persuaded many to leave their traditional lands in the Central Kalahari Game Reserve and resettled them in villages outside the reserve. Few still practice the old hunting-and-gathering way of life.

No doubt there are those who regret the change and feel disoriented by it. In time, though, an improved diet and health care will lead to improvements in health and longevity. Children can now attend schools, so their lives will be enriched by education. Most importantly of all, the people have at last escaped from their dependence on the ever-changing desert.

Pastoralism

Along the southern edge of the Sahara, in the Sahel region, climate cycles produce successive years when the rains make farming possible, but from time to time they also cause prolonged drought. Some years ago SOS Sahel, a British-based voluntary agency, sponsored the Sahel Oral History Project, in which individuals living in Mauritania, Senegal, Mali, Burkina Faso, Niger, Chad, Sudan, and Ethiopia were interviewed in order to obtain firsthand accounts of the traditional way of life in their countries.

Farming is widely practiced across the Sahel, but in the drier regions, closer to the desert itself, there live the pastoralists. These are people who grow no plant crops, but live by tending their livestock. It is a nomadic way of life, but rather different, perhaps, from the image the word *nomad* conjures.

Fatimetou's Story

The parents of Fatimetou Mint Mohamed el Mokhtar, a 70-year-old Mauritanian woman, owned cattle, camels, goats, and donkeys and spent their time traveling in search of pasture. The family knew the location of all the wells. Where possible, the livestock and humans used separate wells to prevent contamination of the water the people drank and used for cooking.

"While we lived as nomads," Fatimetou said, "I never worked. We didn't farm and I didn't even sew, because I was lazy and had many slaves to do all the menial work." The slaves tended the animals and Fatimetou cooked the meal of rice with meat, peanuts, butter, and milk. They drank camels' milk. The animals supplied all their food and material for making their tents, which were erected over a frame made of wood gathered from the acacia trees. "Our men brought us anything else we needed."

The drought of the 1970s was not the first Fatimetou had endured. There was an earlier one when she was in her twenties and recently married—possibly linked to the 1925–26 ENSO event. Their animals began dying and they made a long, difficult journey to a place where they heard there had been rain. Hardly had they arrived before the locusts joined them, eating all the vegetation and even starting to eat the tents. Eventually they were reduced to killing and eating their camels, one at a time.

After the 1970s drought, the land was very slow to recover. Fatimetou and her family moved from place to place, but eventually were forced to admit defeat. They sold what remained of their livestock and moved to the Mauritanian capital, Nouakchott, a city of about 600,000 inhabitants not far from the coast. There her husband set up a small shop. It prospered and after a time he was able to move into the market, a more central location.

Fatimetou was one of the formerly nomadic women allocated some land by SONADER, a government agency. The women were taught how to cultivate vegetables and were provided with free seed and water for the first three years. They grow cucumbers, tomatoes, carrots, turnips, potatoes, beetroot, aubergines, salads, and mint. The children go to school and help with light work. Because the government gave her the land, with the documentation to confirm her ownership of it, her children will inherit it.

Slaves were not paid, but the head of the family was responsible for feeding and clothing them. There are no slaves in Mauritania nowadays, and everyone who works is paid—in theory at least. Indeed, some of the men complain that modern women are marrying former slaves now that they are no longer expected to marry within their tribe. It is believed that slavery continues to be practiced in Sudan, although the Sudanese government denies it.

Surviving the Drought

Not all the pastoralists settled in the city after the 1970s drought. One man described a life spent wandering from place to place, living in tents that the women made from wool. Often they dug wells to find water for the animals, sometimes spending all night digging.

Many of the animals died during the drought, but when the rains returned people starting rebuilding their herds. "The bush is our home," the man told the interviewer; "we feel lost in the city. As we sit here, we live in the hope that the vegetation will recover enough for us all to resume our nomadic life."

Life Among the Tuareg

Fauré Maussa is a Tuareg. She was 90 years old when she was interviewed in Niger and gave fascinating insights into traditional nomadic life before it began to disappear as a result of modern changes. Her father owned one of the biggest herds in the area, she said. He had between 200 and 400 cattle, goats, sheep, and camels. They also kept chickens and guinea fowl. All the animals were marked, so they could be identified if they wandered away or were stolen, and the species were managed separately, each tended by its own specialist.

Ordinarily, the entire family accompanied the father as he traveled from one pasture to the next, but when he embarked on very long journeys some of the family stayed behind. Despite being nomads, they had a base where they spent much of their time. Among the Tuareg, the animals belong to the head of the family. When he dies his wife inherits them. Then she decides how to distribute them among her children. If the man had more than one wife, a teacher and prayer leader, called a *marabout,* decides how the cattle should be apportioned between them. Each child is entitled to inherit something, but males receive twice as much as females.

Many years ago, when Fauré was young, the desert was even more dangerous than it is today. Journeys were made on foot and bandits laid in wait to rob travelers. As protection against them, the marabouts accompanying the party used their magical powers to render everyone invisible, so the bandits passed without seeing them. According to Fauré, this worked! Journeys also took a long time. She and her husband made the pilgrimage to Mecca. This is a long way from Niger and after they had returned she calculated they had been away for 7 years.

Fauré gave birth to four children while she was in Mecca. She told the interviewer that her eldest son was still living there. He was married with a family of his own and refused to return to Niger, but had said he would come looking for his parents and take them back to Saudi Arabia to live with him. Fauré was waiting for him and seemed content to retire from the nomadic life.

Difficulty of Settling

There are strong pressures to persuade nomads to settle, but it is difficult for the older people to make such a radical change. Sheikh Ahmed el Sigaydi, then 70 years old, was living in El Meseiktab, a settlement near Shendi, north of Khartoum, in Sudan, but longed to resume his nomadic life. He was head of his tribe and had spent most of his life moving around the desert with his herds of cattle, sheep, and camels. He lost many of his animals during the drought of 1983–85 and had been forced to sell some of the survivors to pay taxes and buy essential supplies. He had tried to keep as many female animals as possible, to give him a chance of rebuilding his herds, though his son doubted whether this would ever be possible. The old man could see the advantages of a settled life, starting with education for the children. "The younger generation sees a future in the new settlement, with chances for education and a better life." But he had reservations: "The children are not so healthy as before. Perhaps this is because they no longer tend animals, which gave them fresh air and plenty of milk."

Meanwhile, life was hard. The 57 households composing the settlement—a total of about 450 individuals—had no means of saving, and their only way to earn enough money to feed themselves was by doing small unskilled jobs for the villagers.

"We are nomads, and I fear we do not know enough to start up settled farms. We used to practice rain-fed farming in such valleys as Hawada in the Butana plains, and those with pack animals still go there in the rainy season. Last year, my sons and I couldn't go, because we no longer had such animals. We have problems with our valley wells becoming covered with sand and earth and we have no animals to help dig new ones. The last drought affected the water table, so that wells are now too deep to dig."

Slow Death for a Way of Life

Drought and famine are themes that recur in the accounts of life in and near the desert. Newspapers and television reported the suffering this brought in the 1970s, so the world paid attention—and grew alarmed at what some maintained was a consequence of climate change brought about by emissions of so-called greenhouse gases from factories, trucks, and cars (see page 164). This was one drought among many, however. Elderly men and women who have spent their entire lives in the region have experienced up to five severe droughts and have endured the famines associated with them.

Until now, nomadic pastoralists had few choices. Tending animals was the only way of life open to them. Unskilled and poorly educated, they were not equipped to take up other occupations, even if jobs had existed. So after each drought and famine their suffering continued for as long as it took to rebuild their herds and flocks. The most recent droughts, of the 1970s and 1980s, are different in having befallen the region at a time when alternative ways of life were being offered to the nomads. For the first time people are able to choose whether or not to resume their former lives. The choice is hard for the older members of the communities, but much simpler for the young. Most of them opt for education, lifestyle choices, and the settled life these imply. Gradually, nomadism is dying.

Overgrazing and Desertification

Cattle prefer grass that is long enough for them to seize a clump of it. They bite off the clump and chew it. Sheep are different. They nibble the grass and prefer it to be short. Goats are famous for being able to eat almost anything. They will eat leaves from shrubs and the low branches of trees—and they will climb trees in search of tender leaves when food is scarce. Camels will eat grass that is so dry and brown other animals refuse it and they will also nibble the twigs and tough leaves of even the thorniest shrubs. Donkeys can also survive on very poor vegetation.

Each species feeds differently and so among them they utilize pasture very efficiently without competing. Traditionally, a party of nomads would arrive at an area of pasture, set up their camp, and stay there for several weeks. Their animals fed on the natural vegetation, but in doing so they trampled the ground, urinated, and defecated on it, until such plants as remained were unfit to eat. When the pasture was becoming seriously degraded one or more of the men would ride out in search of a new site. Once this had been identified the group packed up their tents and moved. That is how the pastoral way of life functioned. The pasture they left behind was useless. Every last bit of nutritional value had been wrested from it. At the same time the feces and urine deposited by the livestock fertilized it. Left undisturbed, the plants soon recovered and the pasture was restored to its original condition.

Veterinary Care

This was a highly sensible, sustainable way to manage the sparse vegetation of the deserts and their semiarid margins, but animals were often sick. Their owners did their best to cure them and had considerable understanding both of their stock and of the uses of medicinal herbs, but most livestock illnesses were incurable. The animals died.

Today that has changed. There are centers to which pastoralists can take sick animals to be examined and treated by trained veterinarians. Modern veterinary medicines and techniques are available. Consequently, animals that fall ill have a better chance of surviving than they did a few decades ago. A result of this is that livestock numbers have increased.

Markets for Meat

Demand for livestock has also grown. Traditionally, the nomads would sell no more animals than necessary in order to buy materials they could not produce themselves. They needed to buy grain, for example, and metal tools and implements. They might also sell sick animals they knew would not recover. Occasionally they would kill an animal for their own use, most commonly to celebrate some important event in their lives, but not often. They were very attached to their livestock and did not like to eat them.

Economic development has led to the emergence of a new class of city dwellers who are much wealthier than most people used to be in

Fence separating overgrazed pasture from native desert grassland (Gerry Ellis/ENP Images)

the past. Traders, entrepreneurs, administrators, and members of professions, they enjoy a relatively high standard of living. The visible evidence of a high living standard is a diet that includes meat as a regular item. There is now a market for meat and the meat can be obtained fairly cheaply from the pastoralists. They have an even greater incentive to increase the size of their herds and also to change their composition. Camels are rather less in demand now that motor vehicles are used to transport goods and people. Cattle, sheep, and goats are in demand for their meat, but many herds came to consist mainly of cattle.

Cowboys Versus Farmers

Although the pastoralists make good use of the land, they have always faced competition for it from farmers. This is a conflict as ancient as the invention of farming itself. It is the theme underlying the biblical story of Cain and Abel, and of many stories about fights between cowboys and farmers in the "Wild West." In Africa the conflict continues still.

It grew worse during the droughts of the 1980s. These affected everyone, but in different ways. The pastoralists kept moving for as long as they could, and when the desert defeated them they moved to cities or villages. Farmers were not so mobile. They had to watch as shifting sand dunes the size of houses moved with the wind. They saw houses buried and had to try to dig them out with no earth-moving machinery to help. People planted trees to hold back the sand, but the trees were also buried and died. They struggled on, growing more trees from seed and doing everything possible to reclaim their lands, but they also moved, and in some areas they started farming land that was formerly pasture.

Land Hunger

This sequence is not unique. There have been many occasions in European history when prolonged bad weather meant the land was unable to provide as much food as people needed or when the failure of alternative employment—in mines or factories, for example—left people with the choice between farming or starving. Then they started cultivating any land they could find that was not already being farmed. It was called *land hunger* and in Europe it led to the plowing of upland moors and other poor land that in better times would not have been thought worth farming. As in Africa, until it was enclosed and plowed that poor land was used for grazing animals.

In Africa land hunger drives the farmers onto the pasture used by pastoralists. In Niger, for example, nomads have been forced to move because their traditional grazing lands were enclosed by fences and turned into fields. The farmers allowed the pastoralists to graze their animals in the fields after the harvest, but they charged them for this. Unable to afford to pay the farmers, and in any case resentful at being charged for the use of land to which they formerly had free and unrestricted access, the nomads had no choice but to move on. In one case a group of them found another area where the pasture was adequate and free, and where there was also a water pump they could use. All was well for a time, but then farmers newly arriving in the area became interested in that land, too. They started enclosing fields and growing vegetables. These required much watering and the authorities introduced charges for water use that both the horticulturists and pastoralists had to pay.

Squeezing the Nomads

Several factors were now at work. Improved veterinary care and opening of markets for meat had led to increases in livestock numbers. The change in the composition of the herds altered the way the pasture was being utilized—it came to be grazed less efficiently. Drought had reduced the area and quality of the pasture, but it had also destroyed farmed land. This caused land hunger. Farmers expanded into what had formerly been pasture.

At a time when their herds were increasing in size, therefore, the pastoralists were being squeezed into ever smaller areas. As their animals began to die of hunger, many took those that remained and, with encouragement from the authorities, settled in permanent villages. There they had even closer access to veterinary care for their stock, as well as health care for them and their families, education for their children, and the possibility of paid employment.

The Tragedy of Overgrazing

As their crowding increased, the livestock became increasingly desperate. On the remaining pastures and most of all around the new settlements, the vegetation came under attack. Sheep that used to nibble the grass until it was short and then move on nibbled it a little lower. This destroyed the point, almost at ground level, from which grass plants grow. Eventually it killed the grass. Goats ate what they could find on the ground, then took to climbing into the shrubs and trees in search of food. Stripped bare of leaves, the trees and bushes died.

This is the tragedy of overgrazing and it extends even further. Once the pasture has been destroyed the land is left exposed to the wind. Where the degraded land lies close to a desert the desert is likely to claim it. Overgrazing can and often does contribute to desertification.

Some people blame the pastoralists. They accuse them of keeping too many animals out of greed, because they can sell meat to traders who supply city markets. In particular, they point to the harm caused by goats, which eat anything and everything until not a vestige of vegetation remains. They accuse the pastoralists of failing to comprehend the damage their way of life can cause. They blame them for the spread of deserts.

This is quite wrong. The pastoralists are not the perpetrators of damage, but its victims. Drought, due to entirely natural causes, has injured everyone living in and near the deserts and the nomads have suffered most of all. As their animals die or are sold, often it is only their goats that can survive. The goats did not destroy the pasture. They are the only survivors of the disaster. Their owners, meanwhile, have lost the way of life on which their culture was based. There are compensations and the promise of a better life in the future, but this loss is no small matter.

Providing Water

The Nile and Aswān Dams

Regardless of the advances and retreats of the Sahara, Egyptian farmers have always had access to water for irrigation. This has allowed them to feed and clothe a civilization that has existed for thousands of years. Theirs is the most sustainable agricultural system in the world, for it has maintained the fertility of the land throughout this long period.

It is the river Nile that delivers water to them. Although Egypt and Sudan have a desert climate, the lands to the east and south, through which the Nile flows, have abundant rainfall.

White Nile

There are two Nile rivers, the White Nile and the Blue Nile. The White Nile rises on the East African plateau, where two river systems drain water from the region around Lake Victoria and Lake Albert. Most of the plateau is more than 4,000 feet (1,220 m) above sea level and the equator crosses it. The rainfall is very high, but so is the rate of evaporation and in Lake Victoria the two almost balance. From Victoria, the water flows to Lake Kyoga and from there to Lake Albert. Lake Albert feeds the Al-Jabal River, which flows north, collecting more water from its tributaries and flowing through swamps and lakes known as *As-Sudd*. When the Al-Jabal water reaches the town of Malakāl, in southern Sudan, the river is known as the *White Nile*.

The flow from the Al-Jabal supplies about half the water in the White Nile. The other half comes from the highlands of southwestern Ethiopia. This water is carried mainly by the rivers Baro and Pibor, which unite to form the river Sobat. For about 200 miles (320 km) the Sobat crosses a level plain, joining the Al-Jabal at Malakāl.

Blue Nile

The Blue Nile differs from the White Nile in that its waters are not delayed by swamps or flooding. This also makes seasonal variations in the river level more extreme. During the Nile flood, about 70 percent of the water is from the Blue Nile.

South of Lake Tana, in northern Ethiopia, water flowing from a spring near Mount Amedamit becomes the Little Abbay River. *Abbay* is the Ethiopian name for the Blue Nile, and on November 4, 1770, the Scottish explorer

James Bruce (1730–94) identified the spring feeding the Little Abbay as the source of the Blue Nile. It flows north for about 85 miles (135 km) and is the biggest river flowing into Lake Tana, and so its reputation as the source of the river has endured, although the lake itself is the reservoir from which water flows to the Blue Nile.

Two tributaries, the Ar-Rahad and Ad-Dindar Rivers, join the Blue Nile in Sudan. These also rise in Ethiopia and together contribute much more of the water carried by the Blue Nile than Lake Tana does, although they cease to flow during the dry season. Other important tributaries join the river in Sudan. At Khartoum the Blue and White Niles merge. They are then simply the Nile, or *El Bahr en Nil*.

Atbara

The Blue Nile contributes about four-sevenths of the water in the Nile, the White Nile about three-sevenths, and the river Atbara the remaining one-seventh. Like the Blue Nile, the third major component of the Nile rises in Ethiopia, to the north of Lake Tana. It flows for about 500 miles (805 km), receiving water from two important tributaries, the Angareb and Satīt Rivers, and joins the Nile 200 miles (322 km) north of Khartoum, at the town of Atbara. It floods at the same time as the Blue Nile, but during the dry season the Atbara is reduced to a chain of pools.

There are farms, in some places, along a narrow strip to either side of the Nile from Khartoum to the north of Aswān, which is in Egypt. The Nile is navigable from the Mediterranean coast as far south as Aswān and from Aswān almost to Wadi Halfa, in the far north of Sudan, close to the Egyptian border—and in the ancient kingdom of Nubia.

Wadi Halfa is 6 miles (10 km) south of a waterfall. Between Aswān and Khartoum the Nile is interrupted by a series of six such waterfalls, known as the *cataracts,* and Wadi Halfa is close to the second cataract (the first is at Aswān). This stretch of the river is navigable only between the cataracts.

Flood Irrigation

The farms are irrigated by Nile water. North of Aswān the irrigation system is more elaborate and the cultivated area widens, eventually to a maximum width of 12 miles (19 km)—6 miles (9.5 km) on either side of the river. Until about

the beginning of the 20th century, all irrigation water was supplied by the Nile flood—as it had been since the days of the pharaohs. The cultivated land lay below the level the river surface reached during the flood. Earth embankments built at right angles to the river and extending as far as the edge of the desert divided the land into basins ranging in size from 2,000 to more than 50,000 acres (800–20,000 hectares).

Short canals, sealed by dikes for most of the year, led from the river to the basins. During the flood the dikes were opened and the canals carried water that inundated the land and deposited some of the mud the river was carrying. The mud was carried by the Blue Nile and Atbara, and it settled as a layer of richly fertile silt that grew thicker each year. As the flood subsided the water drained back to the river below ground and the seeds were sown.

As late as the 1960s this system of flood irrigation was still being used on about 700,000 acres (283,290 ha) of land. The method works especially well in Egypt because the land slopes from south to north, at a gradient of about 5 inches every mile (8 cm/km), and also slopes away from the river banks, so water overflowing the bank moves away from the river, not back toward it.

Predicting the Flood

It is May when the river level in the Blue Nile starts rising markedly at Khartoum. That is when water from the heavy Ethiopian rains reaches the junction of the two Niles, and the level continues to rise until the end of August or the first week in September. The total rise averages 20 feet (6 m). After that the level in the Blue Nile starts falling again. While the Blue Nile is in flood, however, it blocks the flow from the White Nile. This floods land to the south of Khartoum, where the Jabal al-Awliyā' Dam adds to the ponding effect. When the Blue Nile flood abates, water from the White Nile maintains a high water level for some time longer.

Nilometer

To help with predicting the flood the ancient Egyptians invented an instrument called the *nilometer* that measured the river level very accurately. Some have survived to the present day. The one at Aswān—on an island known in ancient Egyptian times as *Elephantine*—was restored in 1870. Nilometer records were kept and one series has survived. It covers most of the years from 622 to 1522 C.E. and comes from the nilometer at Roda Island, in Cairo.

The diagram shows how the nilometer works. A horizontal tunnel runs from a little way above the riverbed into a large cistern, the bottom of which is level with the bottom of the river. Water always finds its own level and so the depth of water in the cistern is the same as that in the river, but it is not moving, so it is much easier to observe. A graduated obelisk mounted in the center of the cistern allows an official to read the depth of water from an observation platform. In some nilometers there were graduations on the side of the cistern rather than an obelisk at the center. When the river level was clearly rising, a message was sent to stations downstream.

Perennial Irrigation

Predicting the flood did not control it. The nilometer record from Roda Island shows that in some years the flood level was high, in other years it was low, and sometimes it did not occur at all.

It was all very unsatisfactory and dependence on flood irrigation had a further disadvantage: it allowed only one crop a year to be grown. As the Egyptian population increased this was no longer sufficient and from about the middle of the 19th century flood irrigation began to be replaced by perennial irrigation.

Damming the Nile

Damming had always been practiced in those places where water could be lifted from the river by means of a shaduf or similar device (see page 000), but its use had to be extended. To achieve this it was decided in 1843 to build a series of dams across the river about 12 miles (19 km) downstream from Cairo, at the head of the delta. By holding back water, the dams would permanently raise the river level upstream, allowing river water to be fed into irrigation channels whenever it was needed. This would allow farms to grow two or even three crops each year.

The project was completed in 1861. Another dam was added in the delta in 1901 and in 1902 the Asyūt Barrage—barrage is another word for "dam"—was built near the town of Asyūt, about halfway between Cairo and Aswān. Later, two more dams were built upstream of Asyūt. The dam at Isnā was built in 1909 and the one at Naj' Hammādī in 1930.

A dam was completed in 1925 at Sannār, on the Blue Nile in Sudan. This made perennial irrigation possible on the land south of Khartoum between the Blue and White Niles.

The Aswān Dam

In 1902 a much bigger dam was completed at Aswān. This dam has four locks to allow ships to pass, and it was enlarged twice, between 1908 and 1911 and between 1929 and 1934. After the second enlargement the dam had a granite wall 1.5 miles (2.4 km) long with 180 sluices to allow surplus water to escape. This made it one of the biggest dams in the world. The Aswān Dam also houses a hydroelectric plant with an installed generating capacity of 345 megawatts that came into operation in 1960.

The lake behind the dam extended upstream for 150 miles (240 km). As the water level rose toward the flood peak the sluices were opened, allowing water to flow through the dam, taking its silt with it. When the flood peak passed the sluices were closed and water in the lake was used to irrigate crops through the dry season.

The Aswān High Dam

Work on a much bigger dam began in 1960, 4 miles (6.4 km) upstream of the Aswān Dam. This was the Aswān High Dam. Designed by West German and Soviet engineers, it was to allow perennial irrigation throughout the whole of Egypt. The project cost $1 billion and was completed in 1970, and the dam was inaugurated by President Sadat at a ceremony held on January 15, 1971.

The dam wall is rock-filled and its volume is 17 times that of the Great Pyramid at Giza. The dam is 364 feet (111 m) high, 3,280 feet (1,000 m) thick at its base, and 12,562 feet (3.8 km) long at its crest. Inside the dam there is a hydroelectric plant with an installed capacity of 2,100 megawatts that supplies nearly half of Egypt's electricity.

Behind the dam lies Lake Nasser, or to give it its Arabic name, Buheiret Nāsir, named after Gamal Abdel Nasser (1918–70), who was president of Egypt when the work began. Lake Nasser extends upstream for 310 miles (499 km)—125 miles (201 km) into Sudan—and averages 6 miles (9.6 km) in width. In 1959 Egypt and Sudan agreed on the maximal amount of irrigation water each country is allowed to draw from the lake each year, Egypt receiving three times more than Sudan. About one-quarter of the total capacity of the lake is held in reserve in anticipation of the highest flood likely to occur in a century, and the lake is designed to hold enough water to provide for the needs of both Egypt and Sudan during the most severe drought likely in a century.

Advantages and Disadvantages

Since the Aswān High Dam was completed and Lake Nasser filled, Egypt has been fully protected against damaging floods, has enjoyed a reliable water supply for all purposes even during prolonged drought, and has had a reliable power supply. These advantages greatly outweigh the disadvantages, but there have been disadvantages and the project was controversial from the moment it was proposed.

The lake has raised the water table beside the river. This has caused problems of waterlogging and salination (see page 124) in some areas. The reduced river flow downstream of the dam has led to the incursion of salt water from the Mediterranean into the delta, resulting in the salination of some delta soils. Water downstream of the dam carries no silt. Egyptian farmers now have to buy fertilizers to replace the nutrients formerly delivered by the flood. Previously, silt deposited in the delta protected the coastal region from erosion. Its loss has led to increased coastal erosion. Changes in the water discharged into the Mediterranean have increased the salinity there. This effect, combined with the loss of nutrient-rich silt entering the sea, has reduced the fish population, with adverse consequences for the fishing fleets working in the eastern Mediterranean.

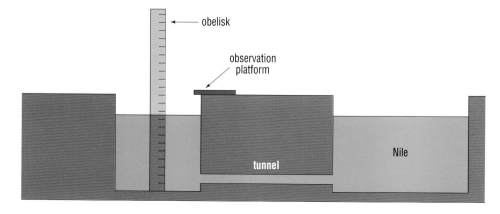

Nilometer

Diverting Rivers

It is the Nile that made the Egyptian civilization possible, just as the Tigris and Euphrates made possible the civilizations of the Fertile Crescent (see page 121) and the Indus sustained the cities of Mohenjo-Daro and Harappa (see page 116). By providing a fairly reliable supply of water for irrigation these rivers made the land fertile. Large urban populations could be fed and it is the concentration in cities of large numbers of people, most of whom are not engaged in food production, that triggers the emergence of civilization.

Rivers can make deserts habitable and nowadays it is sometimes possible to remedy a lack of rivers. If a river flows close to a desert, engineers are able to redirect its course, diverting it to where its water is needed. Unfortunately, the consequences of doing so can be catastrophic.

Ob and Irtysh

In September 1949, the Soviet Union detonated its first atomic bomb. Soon after that the chief Soviet delegate to the United Nations made a speech to the General Assembly in which he said that to further the development of his country's economy, atomic power would be used to move mountains and change the courses of rivers. He was referring to an article by V. O. Obruchev that had appeared recently in a geological journal published by the Academy of Sciences. In it, Obruchev suggested diverting rivers that flow into the Arctic Ocean to provide irrigation water to the deserts of Soviet Central Asia.

West of the river Yenisei and north of a ridge running east and west across Kazakhstan approx-imately along a line passing to the north of Karaganda and south of Magnitogorsk and Moscow, there lies one of the flattest plains on Earth. It is called the *Western Siberian Lowland* and it slopes very slightly from south to north, falling no more than about 2 inches every mile (2.4 cm per km). Nearly 2,000 rivers drain the plain, the most important being those constituting the Ob and Irtysh systems. These drain northward into the Kara Sea, which is part of the Arctic Ocean. The map shows their location.

As winter begins, water freezes at the mouth of the Ob. Farther south the rivers are not yet frozen, and so the water piles up behind an ice dam. Then the rivers freeze upstream. In spring the thaw sends vast torrents of water into the two rivers. This water is still held by the ice dam, and it floods a large area of the flat, low-lying land near the coast. Finally the ice dam breaks and all this freshwater flows into the Arctic Ocean.

South of the Irtysh and Ob, near where the river Tobol rises, there is a gap in the ridge that separates the Kirghiz Steppe from the Western Siberian Lowland. The Russian plan was to dam the Irtysh and Ob. This would flood an area of lowland to produce a lake, and a canal 1,500 miles (2,400 km) long would be constructed to carry water through the gap and into the river Volga.

Arctic Water to Irrigate the Desert

The plan would achieve two aims. The canal would bring water to irrigate the arid steppe and desert land to the north of the Caspian Sea and the increased flow in the Volga would replenish the Caspian Sea, the level of which had been falling for years. That fall was attributed to the excessive use of water from the Volga to irrigate farmland.

Those were heroic days in the Soviet Union, when children were taught in school that they must grow up to discover and conquer their country. It would become truly theirs, the textbooks told them, when columns of tractors drawing plows advanced to break soil that had never been cultivated. Diverting two mighty rivers was a project on an appropriately grand scale that would help increase Soviet agricultural output. Work was started on the diversion and although it was scaled down in 1953 the operation was still

River diversion

being defended as late as 1985, when Nikolai Basilyev, the minister for land reclamation and water resources, said the work was essential and would continue. The program finally died in 1991 with the collapse of the Soviet Union.

It had always been controversial. No one doubted that the diversion would carry water to the arid lands to the south, but there were fears of what might happen in the north. The Ob–Irtysh River system carries freshwater from the south into the Arctic Ocean. Without this flow the water in the partly enclosed Kara Sea would be cooler than it is. The ice that covers it in winter might persist longer into the spring, its white surface reflecting incoming sunlight and delaying the spring warming over a much wider area. There might be a marked effect on the climate throughout the Arctic. Soviet planners maintained this had been taken into account and their calculations showed the effect would be too small to be of any importance, but doubts remained.

There were also concerns about the ecological consequences of diverting so much water. The Kara Sea would become saltier, affecting marine organisms, and freshwater plants and animals would disappear from north of the dam.

Cotton from Central Asia

So water from the Ob and Irtysh never did reach the cotton fields in the parched lands of the south. Cotton had been grown in that part of Central Asia for a long time, but in the 1920s the Soviet authorities decided the USSR should become one of the world's leading cotton exporters. The farms expanded and the plan succeeded. Within a few years the Soviet Union was one of the top three cotton traders, along with the United States and China.

After about 30 years the irrigation system that had been installed to serve the cotton fields was running short of water. None was available from the northern rivers, so instead, in the 1960s the cotton crops began to be irrigated with water taken from the rivers Syr Dar'ya in Kazakhstan and Amu Dar'ya farther south in Uzbekistan. Mile after mile of canals led from these rivers into the fields—and the canals were unlined, so much of the water soaked away and so far as the farmers were concerned it was lost.

The Aral Sea

Until they were diverted to supply the farms these two rivers used to flow into the Aral Sea. Their diversion has produced one of the greatest environmental catastrophes ever recorded, with appalling damage to communities and to the health of local populations.

The sea derives its name from *Aral-denghiz*, also spelled *Aral Tengizi*, which means "Sea of Islands" in the Kyrgyz language. A thousand islands more than 2.5 acres (1 hectare) in extent once dotted its surface. In 1960, before the river diversion began, the Aral Sea was the fourth largest lake in the world, with a surface area of 26,300 square miles (68,000 sq km). For comparison, the surface area of Lake Huron is 23,000 square miles (59,570 sq km). The sea measured a maximum of nearly 270 miles (435 km) from north to south and a little more than 180 miles (290 km) from east to west. It is shallow. In 1960 the average depth was 53 feet (16 m), although it was 226 feet (69 m) deep in some places on the western side. Several large bays formed indentations along the northern shore. On the northern part of the eastern side the Syr Dar'ya formed a huge delta where it met the sea and the Amu Dar'ya formed a delta of similar size on the southern side. To the west the sea faced the high Plato Ustyurt (Ustyurt Plateau).

The sea is 175 feet (53 m) above sea level and the climate is that of a continental desert. In summer the water temperature averages 73–77°F (23–25°C). In winter the surface freezes. The overall result was that the amount of water evaporating from the surface each year was approximately equal to the amount entering from the two rivers. All rivers carry some salt. This entered the sea and was left behind when water evaporated. Consequently, salt accumulated in the sea over millions of years, raising the salinity to about 10 parts per thousand ($\permil$). The water was brackish, but much less salty than seawater, which has an average salinity of 35 parts per thousand.

The Disappearing Sea

Once water from the rivers was diverted into irrigation channels, the supply to the sea was reduced. Evaporation continued as formerly, of course, and so inevitably the sea began to shrink. Because it was so shallow over most of its area, reducing the volume of water also reduced the area the water covered. What was once a single sea is now two, the Large Aral Sea in the south and the Small Aral Sea in the north. Since 1960 the sea has lost 80 percent of its volume. Scientists have calculated that if it continues to shrink at the same rate, by about 2010 the Aral Sea will be reduced to three small "Aralet" lakes. The towns of Aral in the north and Mŭynoq in the south were once ports.

Mŭynoq used to be a busy town with a population of 25,000. As well as a fishing fleet it had a fish cannery processing 25,000 tons (22,700 tonnes) of fish a year and a tourist industry. Visitors came for the beaches, the swimming, and the therapeutic properties of the waters. Today the seashore is about 43 miles (69 km) to the north of Mŭynoq and it is still retreating. Fishing boats lie rusting in the sand. The cannery is still there, but now it processes no more than about 1,600 tons (1,450 tonnes) of fish a year, and there is very high unemployment. Up to 100,000 people have left the area.

Poisoned by Salt

As the sea shrank, so its salts became more concentrated and it is now much saltier than the ocean. Most of its fish have been killed. Salt from the dried-up bed has been blown by the wind and now covers a large area. The soil, too, has turned salty. Cotton growers were allowed as much water as they wanted. They used it wastefully and this waste, combined with seepage from the unlined canals, raised the water table. Water could no longer drain freely, and with the high surface evaporation salt accumulated (see page 124). The soil now contains about 280 tons of salt on every acre of land (628 tonnes per hectare) and salt contaminates the drinking water. Cotton is still grown, but yields are falling. They are now less than one-third of those in Israel, a country with a very similar climate.

Dust storms are common, but these are not ordinary desert storms. Mixed with the dust are salt from the sea and also fertilizer and pesticides that were spread and sprayed onto fields, then dried to a powder. The combination makes the dust poisonous. In the part of Uzbekistan close to the sea there were 167 deaths of respiratory illnesses for every 100,000 of the population in 1993. This is one of the highest levels in the world. Tuberculosis (TB) is common. In some towns there are 400 TB cases for every 100,000 people. Many people are anemic, including most pregnant women, and infant mortality rates are high.

It was because of the plight of the Aral Sea that Nikolai Basilyev believed it essential to divert the Ob and Irtysh. Their water was needed to flush the salt from the soil and replenish the sea. That plan was abandoned and if the sea is to recover the process will now be a very long one. Preventing or even reducing leaks in the irrigation system would mean less water would be needed from the rivers and at the same time would allow the water table to fall. Then—but it would probably take decades—salts could be flushed from the land. Scientists and engineers from many countries are working on solutions.

Diverting the Yangtze

There are also plans to divert a Chinese river, the Yangtze. The Yangtze rises in Tibet and flows in

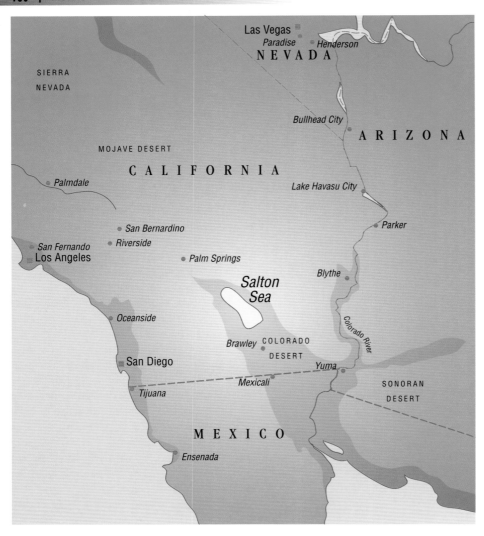

Salton Sea, California

ing into it has reduced its size. It now covers about 380 square miles (984 sq km), but since the 1960s the volume of inflowing water has exceeded the amount lost by evaporation and the water has risen. Nowhere is it more than 50 feet (15 m) deep.

It was called the *Salton Sea* and it lies in the Colorado Desert about 93 miles (150 km) east of San Diego, California. The map shows its location. It is a lake, but is called *sea* because the salinity of its water is about the same as that of seawater.

Like the Aral Sea, but on a much smaller scale and for entirely different reasons, the Salton Sea has turned into an ecological disaster. Vacationers used to visit the beaches to enjoy swimming, boating, and camping. Millions of birds spend the winter beside the sea, or call there to rest on their migratory journeys, so bird watchers were attracted from miles around. There were edible fish in the sea, providing sport for anglers.

Dying Birds and Fish

Then, in the late 1980s, visitors were warned not to eat fish from the sea. These were found to contain unacceptably high levels of selenium, a nonmetallic element resembling sulfur, which can cause liver damage in large doses. The water was also found to be contaminated with bacteria from sewage, entering from a polluted stream flowing north from Mexico.

After that matters went from bad to worse. As different algal species bloom the water changes color alarmingly. Birds began to die. Since 1992 more than 200,000 have been killed by avian cholera, botulism, and causes no one has been able to diagnose. One of the first species to succumb was the eared grebe, also known as the *black-necked grebe* (*Podiceps nigricollis*). In 1992, 150,000 of them died. No one knows why. A few years later botulism—bacterial food poisoning caused by *Clostridium botulinum*—killed thousands of American white pelicans (*Pelecanus erythrorhynchos*) and more than 1,000 brown pelicans (*P. occidentalis*). Double-crested cormorants (*Phalacrocorax auritus*) have died of Newcastle disease, caused by a virus. Fish are killed by ammonia and hydrogen sulfide released from rotting plants and animals, and by asphyxiation, because the decomposition of organic matter removes dissolved oxygen from the water. Fish also suffer because the sea has become saltier—it is now saltier than the ocean, with a salinity approaching 44 parts per thousand.

Curing the Problem

Scientists are debating how best to improve the condition of the Salton Sea, but the possible remedies create further problems. It might help if

an approximately northeasterly direction across southern China to Shanghai. It is China's longest river and carries a substantial proportion of the water draining from southern and central China.

More than half of all the cultivated land in China is in the north, however. Land there drains into China's second longest river, the Huang Ho, or Yellow River. This river also rises in Tibet and flows through Tsinghai Province in northwestern China, in a big loop around the Ordos Desert, and enters the sea at the Po Hai, or Gulf of Chihli. Lakes in Tsinghai feed rivers that flow into the Huang Ho, but in the 1990s drought dried out many of them, reducing by about 20 percent the amount of water entering the river. In some years the lower reaches of the Huang Ho run dry.

The proposed diversion would involve building a canal on the Tibetan Plateau to link the two rivers. At the point where the canal would leave the Yangtze that river is already large. The other end of the canal would enter the headwaters of the Huang Ho. The effect would be to send water from the Yangtze into the Huang Ho, so less water would flow into southern China and more into northern China. The Chinese diversion has not yet been built, so it is too early to tell whether it will prove successful.

The Salton Sea

America has its own example of a river diversion scheme that failed. In 1905–06 engineers attempted to divert part of the Colorado River into irrigation canals. They lost control and the entire river changed course. For 16 months it poured into the Salton Trough, a salt-covered depression that is part of the bed of a prehistoric lake. Finally, they managed to divert the river back into its original course. Levees were built in 1907 to prevent any more water from flowing in, at which time the lake was about 40 miles (60 km) long, 13 miles (21 km) wide, with a surface area of about 400 square miles (1,000 sq km). Since then the abstraction of irrigation water from rivers flow-the amount of plant nutrient flowing into the sea could be reduced, but this would be difficult, because it comes mainly from fertilizer used on nearby farms and wastewater from cities.

It might be possible to seal off part of the sea. Evaporation would maintain a constant level in the enclosed area, but its salinity would increase. Pumping water from the open area into the enclosed area would shift salt from one area to the other, steadily reducing the salinity in the open area. Then a channel could be constructed to carry in fresh water and another to allow the salt water to flow into the Gulf of California. There are fears, however, that releasing the salt water might harm a biosphere reserve in Mexico.

Diverting rivers to provide water for irrigation seems straightforward, but our experience so far shows that it can lead to serious ecological damage and, in the case of the Aral Sea, direct harm to the health of people living over a wide area. Once the damage has been done, remedying it is difficult, slow, and extremely expensive.

This is not to say that river diversions must invariably lead to disaster, but only that they must be planned with great care. Years ago we knew too little about the way natural ecosystems function to foresee harmful consequences. Scientists know much more now. It may still be impossible to predict in detail what side effects a major project will cause, but it is possible to recognize risks that are so serious it would be better not to take them.

Oasis Farming and Artificial Oases

Egypt depends heavily on the Nile, but not all Egyptian farmers use water from the river to irrigate their fields. Far to the west of Aswān farming thrives around Al-Khārijah, a town with more than 40,000 citizens. The town is in the northern part of the Al-Khārijah oasis and it has existed at least since about 700 B.C.E. Even earlier than that, around 1000 B.C.E., the oasis was a place to which political dissidents were exiled. Since the 1970s more land has been brought into cultivation around the oasis and the Egyptian government has encouraged farmers from the Nile Valley to settle there. As well as the farms, there are quarries and phosphate mines in the oasis.

Controlling rivers is one way to provide water for agriculture, but many desert farms, like those of Al-Khārijah, produce food far from the nearest river. They are located in oases and that is where about two-thirds of the population of the Sahara live settled lives in permanent towns.

Oases Can Be Large

Oases vary greatly in size. They are often depicted as no more than a few palm trees grouped around a pool, but this is misleading. It is true that some oases are no more than about 2.5 acres (1 ha) in extent, but others are very much bigger. About 40 miles (65 km) from the coast of the Persian Gulf in Saudi Arabia, for example, the Al-Hasa, or Al-Ahsā', oasis covers about 30,000 acres (12,000 ha). Siwa oasis, or Wāhat Sīwah, is between 4 and 5 miles (6–8 km) wide and about 6 miles (10 km) long. It is in the far west of Egypt and there was once a temple there with an oracle whom Alexander the Great consulted.

Oasis Farming

The ancient Egyptians knew the Siwa oasis as *Sekht-am,* which means "palm land," because, as in most oases, date palms grow there (see page 66). Dates are important for food, of course, but that is only one reason for growing them. They also provide shade, which is almost as important. Beneath the date palms the oasis farmers grow olives, figs, peaches, apricots, pomegranates, and citrus fruits, as well as cereal crops, especially millet, barley, and wheat. As well as supplying food, the leaves of the date palm are used as fuel, fibers from the leaves are twisted to make ropes or woven into a coarse cloth, and the timber is used for building. Oases also provide food for domesticated animals. There is pasture for cattle, sheep, goats, and camels, and chickens are raised.

At the center of an oasis there is usually a pool, and the cultivated land is worked by very labor-intensive methods, in what is almost a series of gardens. In Judaism, Christianity, and Islam—

Farming at the Dakhia oasis, Sahara Desert (Gerry Ellis/ENP Images)

religions developed in desert lands—paradise is conceived as a garden. The idea of that garden is based on the gardens around the center of an oasis. These represent islands of tranquillity, shade, fruit, and clean water in the midst of the harsh, hostile, unforgiving desert.

Where water is plentiful, however, salination often causes difficulties (see page 124). Some oases are surrounded by land contaminated by salt, where water evaporates rapidly.

Oases and Caravan Routes

Caravan routes across large stretches of desert take travelers from one oasis—one garden—to another (page 138). Consequently, in the days before modern rail and air transport many oases were commercially important, prosperous places. Sakākah oasis, for example, is on a caravan route leading from the Mediterranean coast to the interior of Arabia. It lies between the Syrian Desert to the north and the An-Nafūd Desert to the south. There is another oasis, Al-Jawf, some distance to the southwest of Sakākah.

Atar, in central Mauritania, built around an oasis on a route leading to the capital, Nouakchott, is an important town with a population of more than 20,000 people. It is the capital of Adrar, a region of the country, and it has an airstrip. Apart from agriculture, Atar is an important center for rug weaving and has a school for rug weavers.

Old routes across the Sahara fall from use and new ones are developed. Nafṭah, in western Tunisia, lies on one of the routes that are growing in importance. It is built around an oasis located near the shore of a saline lake, with a bigger oasis about 15 miles (24 km) away.

Artificial Oases

Oases are not confined to the Sahara. All deserts have them. Kattakurgan, in Uzbekistan, is an oasis town with a population of around 60,000. It was founded in the 18th century as a trade and handicraft center. Nearby a modern reservoir holds water from the Zeravshan River. This provides irrigation water and also recreational facilities.

Water from the reservoir increases the agricultural output and so, in a sense, creates an artificial oasis in the desert.

This is not unique. People in the Middle East learned long ago how to make artificial oases and at one time there were some regions where all the most important towns and villages received their water in this way. The method was probably invented in Iran around 4500 B.C.E. and spread to desert countries from Egypt eastward to Afghanistan. The system of water management on which the oases are based goes by various names. In Arabic it is called *qanāt* or *kanat,* in Persian *karez,* and in the Berber dialect of Arabic *foggara.*

Qanāt Irrigation

It is a system of underground channels—qanāts—that conveys water from the mountains to lower ground in the desert. No one is quite sure how these canals were made, but work probably began after an experienced individual had identified surface vegetation that suggested the presence of water below ground. This site would be in the mountains and on an alluvial fan—a fan-shaped deposit of gravel and other sediment that forms where the gradient of a stream abruptly decreases. Alluvial fans often occur where a mountain river emerges onto more gently sloping ground and the water table (page 38) is often higher there than it is elsewhere.

When a promising site had been identified a test well would be dug in the form of a vertical hole. The workers would dig downward—placing the soil they removed into a basket to be hauled to the surface by a windlass—until they reached the water table. Then they would measure the rate at which water was flowing. If the flow was strong enough, work would proceed to the next stage.

An expert would calculate the path for the underground canal, linking the well with the point where the water was needed. Digging would commence at the lower (outlet) end. Tunneling proceeded in a straight line, achieved by using lamps placed at intervals for sighting, and at a very gentle uphill slope. Typically, the gradient in a qanāt was between 1:500 and 1:1,500.

As the tunnel advanced, its depth below the ground surface increased, because the gradient in the tunnel was lower than that of the surface above. The sides and roofs of tunnels often needed support, just as the galleries of a mine do. Stone and clay were used for strengthening. More vertical shafts were dug at intervals along the route. These provided a means for checking the depth of the qanāt and they marked the line the tunnel followed. They also allowed air to reach the workers below ground.

Eventually, the tunnelers reached and penetrated the water table and water began to flow back along the canal they had made. By then the channel might be several miles long. Once one channel had been made, others might be made not far from the outlet, branching from it to distribute water over a wider area. At the outlets, water flowed from the qanāt as a stream.

Digging was always done during the dry season, when the flow was at a minimum. This was a safety measure. Heavy rain during the wet season could flood the tunnel and drown the diggers working in it.

At the outlet, the stream of mountain water would enter distribution ditches and begin to irrigate the fields. Crops would appear and an oasis would have been made where there had been no oasis in the past.

Some Qanāts Are Still Used

No one digs qanāt systems today. They are too expensive, both to install and to maintain, and there are cheaper ways to obtain water. Nevertheless, the fact that several thousand of them are still in use in Iran and Afghanistan shows their reliability.

As a way to supply water the method is distinctly attractive. The water is carried below ground all the way from its source to its outlet. This means there are no loss by evaporation and no opportunity for the water to become polluted. Nor is any power needed for pumping. The water flows by gravity. Finally, a qanāt delivers a very reliable water supply and in some cases continues to do so for centuries.

Conflicts over Water Resources

Isaac was a very successful farmer. He was so successful that the Philistines envied him and he and his followers had to move.

For all the wells which his father's servants had digged in the days of Abraham his father, the Philistines had stopped them, and filled them with earth.

And Abimelech said unto Isaac, Go from us; for thou art much mightier than we.

And Isaac departed thence, and pitched his tent in the valley of Gerar, and dwelt there.

And Isaac digged again the wells of water, which they had digged in the days of Abraham his father; for the Philistines had stopped them after the death of Abraham. . . .

And Isaac's servants digged in the valley, and found there a well of springing water.
(Genesis 26, 15–19)

Finding water was clearly only the start for people living in desert countries. They then had to keep it. The dispute over the ownership of wells between Abraham, then his son Isaac, and the Philistine king Abimelech arose when the envious Philistines denied Isaac and his people access to their wells. It was resolved after the king had asked Isaac to move, with his people, from the coastal plain of Gaza inland to somewhere near Beersheba, in the southern part of the Negev Desert. Isaac agreed, they all moved, and there they found a buried riverbed in which they were able to dig wells.

Lagash, Umma, and the Jordan River

They were fortunate. Had they failed to find freshwater they might have been compelled to fight the Philistines. On that occasion conflict was avoided, but in about 2500 B.C.E. two city-states, Lagash and Umma, located between the Tigris and Euphrates Rivers, went to war over access to water.

Disputes continue. Water in the Jordan River basin is shared among Lebanon, Syria, Israel, and Jordan. During the 1967 Six-Day War, Israeli forces attacked a dam built by Jordan and Syria on the Yarmūk River. This is a tributary of the Jordan, joining it a little way south of the Sea of Galilee, and it forms the border between Syria and Jordan. The dam had previously supplied hydroelectric power to Jordan as well as water for irrigation. Although the Gawr irrigation canal, completed in 1966, carries water from the Yarmūk to part of northern Jordan, Jordan is chronically and severely short of water, despite having the lowest water consumption per person of any Middle Eastern country—22 gallons (83 liters) per day. Israel controls most of the basin and headwaters of the river and takes so much that Jordan does not receive enough for its needs.

Jordan has not gone to war specifically over water, but Syria and Iraq came close to it in 1975. Syria and Turkey had built two new dams on the Euphrates. As the reservoirs filled behind them, the water level in the river fell, to the alarm of the Iraqi authorities. Later, during the 1991 Gulf War, Iraqi troops were ordered to dismantle desalination plants in Kuwait. Oil spilling from damaged refineries polluted the gulf and that also damaged desalination plants, in Saudi Arabia. In 1985, when he was Egyptian foreign minister, the former UN secretary general Boutros Boutros-Ghali warned that the next Middle Eastern war would be fought over water, not politics.

Water That Crosses Frontiers

Where water is scarce, a person who uses it denies its use to others. If an aircraft seeds a cloud to make rain fall (see page 172), that rain cannot fall somewhere else, as it might have. Abstract surface or groundwater for irrigation and there will be less for the people living downstream—and those people may live across an international frontier, in a different country, so that a dispute between neighbors becomes a dispute between nations. In the Middle East, most of the aquifers that supply the rivers and wells straddle the borders of two or more countries.

In the dry lands of Central Asia many of the international frontiers are new. The Aral Sea, for example, once lay inside the Soviet Union, so its problems could be addressed internally, by a single government. Now the sea lies between Kazakhstan and Uzbekistan, two independent nations. Theirs is only one of the new borders in the region that share water resources. The republics of Kirghistan, Tadzhikistan, and Turkmenistan could also find themselves drawn into disputes over water.

Some years ago there were plans for huge irrigation schemes fed by water from Lake Titicaca, which lies on the border between Peru and Bolivia. These could have led to conflict, because there was not enough water to maintain a reliable supply for both countries.

The Nile and Tigris

Egypt depends on the Nile, but it is not the only country to do so. The Nile flows through Ethiopia and Sudan (page 186) before entering Egypt and those countries also use its water for irrigation—potentially reducing the volume downstream. All three countries are already short of water and farther west so are Tunisia, Algeria, and Morocco.

There is competition for the waters of the Tigris, which rises in Turkey and flows through Iraq. Control of the river is based on diverting its water into storage reservoirs to protect against destructive flooding during the rainy season from March to May, and to provide water during the dry season, when no rain falls. This requires agreement between the two countries over the amount to store and how and when the store should be used.

"Virtual Water"

Despite the risks, competition for water has not been the primary cause of any war for thousands of years. This is remarkable, because water is an essential resource for manufacturing industry and domestic use as well as for agriculture. If there is insufficient water, economies falter and public health deteriorates through malnutrition and an inability to maintain standards of hygiene. Water is a resource for which nations might be expected to fight, yet they do not, even though many have access to less water than their industries and people need.

Part of the reason is that during the second half of the 20th century governments, even those of poor countries, have been able to import food they were unable to grow on their own land. A country that feeds its people with imported food reduces the pressure on its own farmers to maintain a high output, as they may be unable to do without more water. Water the farmers might have used can then be supplied to homes and factories. The imported food represents *virtual water*—the water that was used to grow it in another part of the world. In effect, countries in the deserts and semiarid lands were importing water. Americans and Europeans, for example, were sending water to the Middle East.

This worked because food—and in terms of international trade as well as diet, that means cereal grains—was often being sold for less than it cost to produce and governments were making up the difference by subsidizing agriculture. This practice generated huge grain surpluses and intense competition for markets among the producing countries. The competition reduced the price so much that in the 1980s grain was being bought and sold at half its production cost.

By 1996 grain prices had risen to above production cost. They then dropped back again, but they are not expected to fall to their 1980s levels. Governments are likely to find the import of "virtual water" in the form of food more expensive in years to come. Producing countries are struggling to reduce their surpluses, which are extremely costly in terms of agricultural support as well as storage. In the European Union (EU), the Common Agricultural Policy is a system of agricultural support and management that generates surpluses. It is by far the biggest item of EU expenditure, and is in the process of being reformed. The aim of the reforms is to reduce the cost, and that means trying to eliminate overproduction, and that will tend to keep world grain prices above the cost of production.

Treaties for Sharing Water

It was not until the second half of the 20th century that really large quantities of food began to be traded internationally, so the import of "virtual water" cannot explain the peaceful resolution of disputes over water earlier than that. The answer is probably that such disputes were familiar, easy to understand, and potentially catastrophic. There are many places where it would not be difficult for one country to divert or dam the river on which a neighboring country depended. This would have a devastating effect and no ruler could permit it to happen—or risk the furious retaliation that would follow. Conflicts had to be resolved peacefully and so, by and large, they were. There were fierce argument, ill feeling, and much hurling of insults, but over about the last 4,500 years there have been more than 3,500 international treaties regulating the sharing of water—not far short of one treaty every year.

Today such treaties are negotiated through the auspices of the United Nations, and especially the UN Environment Program (UNEP). UNEP works by identifying potential conflicts in advance and approaching the governments of the affected countries. It can then call on the appropriate experts to assess the situation and propose ways to resolve difficulties.

Despite the historic success in avoiding war, the need has never been more urgent. Experts have estimated that of all the freshwater resources in the world, about half are already being used to meet human needs and that by about 2030 this could rise to 70 percent. By 2050 between 1 billion and 2.4 billion people could be living in countries where water is in short supply. Across North Africa and the Middle East there are 45 million people without an adequate supply of drinking water. Of the 25 countries with the highest proportion of their population lacking access to safe drinking water, 19 are in Africa. Klaus Töpfer, UNEP executive director, has said that problems concerning the supply and quality of freshwater were at the top of the UNEP agenda.

Desalination and Mining Icebergs

When water evaporates, any substances dissolved in it are left behind. Consequently, evaporating seawater and then condensing the vapor yield drinkable freshwater. The process is called *distillation* and it has been known for thousands of years. According to Aristotle, sailors in ancient Greece were using distillation to obtain drinking water in the fourth century B.C.E., and in the eighth century C.E. an Arab writer published a detailed account of the process. In 1869 the British built the first modern distillation plant, at Aden in Yemen. It supplied freshwater to ships calling at the port.

Desalination Plants

Today more than 2 billion gallons (8 billion liters) of freshwater is produced by desalination plants every day. There are several thousand such plants. Some are huge. The one at Al-Jubayl, in Saudi Arabia, produces 1.2 billion gallons (4.7 billion liters) of water a day—more than half the world total. About 75 percent of all desalted water is produced in the Middle East, about 10 percent in the United States, about 5 percent in Africa, and about 5 percent in Europe.

Multistage Flash Evaporation

There are several ways to separate water from the salt dissolved in it. The most widely used method is multistage flash evaporation, illustrated in the diagram—the Al-Jubayl plant is of this type. The seawater enters along a pipe (from the right in the diagram) that passes through a series of chambers. This water is cold, so vapor will condense onto the pipes carrying it. After it leaves the final chamber, the pipe passes through a heater. There it is heated under pressure, to prevent it from starting to boil. In most multistage flash evaporation plants the temperature is raised to about 195°F (90°C).

From the heater the water is sprayed into the first of the series of chambers. The pressure in this chamber is lower than that in the pipe, so the water boils instantly—the technical term for instant boiling is *flashing,* hence the name of the process. Vapor released by flashing condenses on the cold pipe carrying incoming seawater and drips from there into a collector. The condensed water is fresh and it is piped away to a storage tank.

The salt water is now slightly saltier because of the freshwater that has been removed from it. It is carried to the next chamber, where the pressure is a little lower than it was in the previous one. Again, the water flashes and vapor condenses. The

process is repeated several times, with the pressure in each chamber lower than that in the preceding one so the water flashes in each chamber.

There are several alternatives to multistage flash evaporation, the most widely used of which is called the *long-tube vertical distillation process.* Again, the plant comprises a series of chambers. Steam is used to heat and vaporize salt water contained in long, vertical tubes. The vapor condenses and is carried away to a storage tank and the steam is used to heat salt water in the next chamber.

Distillation by Freezing

Freezing also separates water from substances dissolved in it. Distillation plants based on this principle also rely on the fact that latent heat is released or absorbed when water vaporizes, condenses, and freezes. In one type of plant seawater chilled almost to freezing is sprayed into a chamber where the pressure is very low. Some of the water vaporizes instantly because of the low pressure, absorbing the latent heat to do so from the water around it. This lowers the temperature of that water enough to freeze it. A mixture of salt water and ice falls to the bottom and is piped to a second chamber, where the salt water is drained off, leaving the ice. The vapor from the vacuum chamber is compressed and fed into the second chamber. Compression causes it to condense. It is freshwater and is used to wash the remaining brine from the ice and to melt it.

Alternatively, a refrigerant such as propane or butane is used. Cold seawater enters the first chamber and the refrigerant liquid is mixed with it. The refrigerant vaporizes, absorbing latent heat from the water and causing ice to form. The ice and remaining brine are separated. The ice is washed in a second chamber, then carried into a third chamber. The refrigerant vapor is piped from the top of the chamber through a compressor, which raises its boiling point, and into the third chamber. There, still contained in its pipe, the refrigerant condenses, giving up its latent heat and melting the ice. From there the refrigerant is returned to the first chamber, to vaporize again in a new batch of seawater.

The disadvantage of this method of freezing is that although the ice itself contains only freshwater, salt water becomes trapped between ice crystals. This must be washed out, and washing uses and contaminates an unacceptably large amount of freshwater.

Reverse Osmosis

It is also possible to use an entirely different method to desalinate water, which is based on the property that some very thin membranes have pores that allow certain molecules to pass but not others. A semipermeable membrane allows water molecules to pass but not molecules of substances dissolved in the water. If a semipermeable membrane separates two solutions of different strengths, water will pass through the membrane from the weaker to the stronger solution until the strengths of both solutions are equal. This process is called osmosis and it is an osmotic pressure that drives water molecules through the membrane.

This happens naturally in living cells, but it can be made to work in the opposite direction if the stronger solution is placed under sufficient pressure. Water will then flow from the stronger to the weaker solution. This is known as *reverse osmosis.*

Electrodialysis uses two semipermeable membranes. Ordinary salt is sodium chloride ($NaCl$), in which the sodium is positive (Na^+) and the chlorine negative (Cl^-). With electrodialysis, an electric current flowing through the salt water drives positive ions, such as the Na^+, through one membrane and negative ions, such as Cl^-, through the other. Freshwater is left between the membranes. Like reverse osmosis, this is used only with brackish water, not with seawater.

Improving Energy Efficiency

Clearly, all of these processes use a great deal of energy and the high cost of desalination is due to the fuel that is needed. This cost can sometimes be reduced, however, or even eliminated altogether.

The vapor compression distillation process uses the condensation of water vapor to boil more seawater. Incoming seawater is heated to about 200°F (93°C) and then piped into a chamber. It vaporizes and rises to the top of the chamber. There some of it condenses on the inside of vertical tubes, from which the freshwater is carried away, but at the top of the chamber there is a steam separator. This directs some of the water vapor into a pipe leading to a compressor. Compression heats the vapor and it is then fed back into the chamber, where it causes more salt water to vaporize.

Solar Power

Warm sunshine is one resource that is in plentiful supply in desert countries, and it can be used to

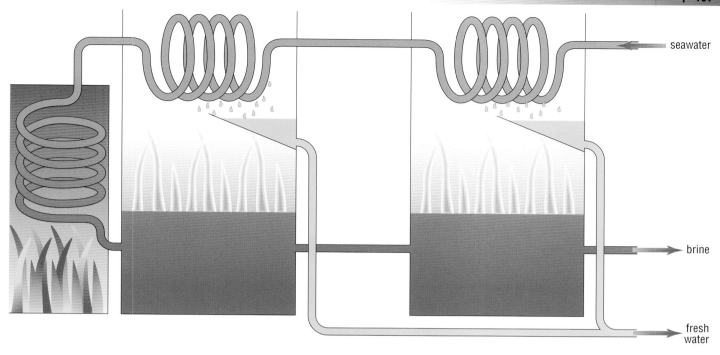

Multistage flash evaporation

power the simplest of all distillation plants. A transparent cover is placed over a tank of salt water with a large surface area. Solar heat passes through the transparent cover, heats and vaporizes water, and the vapor condenses as freshwater on the underside of the cover. If the cover is slightly inclined the water droplets will run down it to one end—like raindrops running down a window pane—where the water can be collected in a trough.

Membrane Distillation

Under ideal conditions solar power alone can supply enough energy to operate a small desalination plant. One design combines distillation with the properties of a microporous membrane. The membrane is no more than about 0.001 inch (30 μm) thick with pores averaging about 0.0004 inch (1 μm) in diameter, and pores cover about 80 percent of the surface. It allows water vapor to pass, but not liquid water, and the process works at ordinary atmospheric pressure—there is no need to compress vapor or create a partial vacuum—and at a temperature of only 176°F (80°C). It is because of the low operating temperature that solar heat or waste heat from a factory or generating plant is all it needs.

The membrane is arranged in a spiral inside a chamber. Hot seawater is in contact with one side of the membrane and water condenses on the

other, cold side. Energy is used to heat the seawater, but some of the energy is recovered, because the latent heat of condensation is used to preheat the incoming water.

It is known as the *membrane distillation* (MD) process and an MD plant running continuously will deliver up to about 5 gallons (20 liters) of freshwater a day.

Desalination plants produce drinkable freshwater, but their by-product is a brine much saltier than seawater. Some of the minerals this contains may be worth recovering, but finally the brine must be disposed of carefully if it is not to cause pollution. As seawater is heated, minerals are precipitated from it as scale on pipes and other surfaces the water contacts. Plant designers seek to minimize scaling, because it threatens to clog pipes and means that the operation must be shut down from time to time while the scale is removed.

Icebergs

Freeze seawater in a desalination plant and salt water remains trapped between the ice crystals. At sea, however, there is ice that is not contaminated. It is sold as bottled water in Newfoundland and is advertised as being "pure as the driven snow." This is not surprising, because the ice is made from driven snow. The Newfoundland ice comes mainly from western Greenland and drifts across the sea in the form of icebergs.

About 67 cubic miles (280 km³) of ice enters Arctic waters every year as icebergs and about 430 cubic miles (1,800 km³) breaks away from Antarctica. This is a vast amount of very pure

freshwater, and, not surprisingly, people sometimes imagine icebergs might be towed by ship into lower latitudes where water from them could be supplied to desert communities. So far no one has attempted this.

Can They Be Towed?

It might be feasible, but the water would be expensive. Icebergs big enough to be worth towing weigh between 100,000 and 200,000 tons (91,000–182,000 tonnes). Only the most powerful ships could attempt to tow them and once they were moving it would be extremely difficult to control or stop them. This is not to say it would be impossible, but it would consume a very large amount of fuel.

They would have to be towed fairly fast, because icebergs start melting as soon as they enter warm water. Although they can last for years as long as they remain in the Arctic Ocean or Antarctic Ocean, in water at 32–39°F (0–4°C) their height decreases at about 6.5 feet (2 m) a day. An iceberg 394 feet (120 m) long that once drifted into tropical waters, where the temperature was about 80°F (27°C), lasted only 36 hours before it disappeared completely.

Moored icebergs being mined for their water and seawater desalination plants suffer from one obvious geographic constraint: they depend on the sea. They may provide water for coastal regions, and may even produce enough water for some to be piped inland, but they have little to offer the deserts of Central Asia, thousands of miles from the nearest coast.

Food From the Arctic and Antarctic

There is no shortage of water in the polar deserts, most parts of which are covered by sheets of ice thousands of feet thick. Far from making the polar lands more hospitable to plants and animals, however, the ice sheets make conditions worse. Plants can utilize water only in its liquid form—ice and snow are useless to them—and the thick cover of ice makes it impossible for plant roots to find the mineral nutrients that lie in the soil beneath. So, despite all that water, far fewer plants grow in polar deserts than in hot deserts, where plants have easy access to such water as there is.

People living in the tundra region to the south of the Arctic desert in Europe and Asia are able to herd reindeer (caribou, *Rangifer tarandus*), and there is some sheep farming in Greenland (see page142). The wide expanses of the tundra resemble those of other deserts and make it possible to manage large herds of animals. Reindeer migrate between summer pastures on the tundra and the edge of the taiga to the south, where they spend the winter, and their herders move with them. Most of the reindeer are kept for their meat, fat, and skins, but some are trained to pull sledges, making them the equivalent of pack animals, such as the asses and camels used in other deserts. This Arctic way of life is very similar to that of the nomadic peoples of the Sahara, Middle East, and Central Asia. Like them, the reindeer herders live in tents, in their case conical tents covered with reindeer hides. The settled life of the Greenland sheep farmers also resembles that of many desert people dwelling around oases far to the south.

Whaling

Sheep farming and nomadic pastoralism are not the life-styles of most Arctic peoples. In the high Arctic, beyond the tundra, there is no food even for reindeer, but food is nevertheless plentiful in the sea—for those who know how to catch it. There are whales, seals, walruses, birds, and, most of all, fish.

It is not only the Inuit who hunt in the northern oceans, however. So do fleets of vessels from many other countries. At one time they hunted whales. Some countries still do so and it is likely that hunting for minke whales (*Balaenoptera acutorostrata*) will increase somewhat in years to come. Numbers of this species are now quite large and catching a strictly regulated number will not cause them to decline, although the number of catches that might be permitted is still being calculated. There are estimated to be

between 120,000 and 182,000 minkes in the North Atlantic, plus an unknown number off the eastern coast of Canada, and between 12,800 and 48,600 in the northwestern Pacific and Okhotsk Sea. In addition, between 510,000 and 1,140,000 are living in the Southern Hemisphere.

Minke whales are caught commercially by Norwegian whaling ships and for scientific research by Japanese and Icelandic ships. Until the size of whale populations is known more precisely and scientists understand better the breeding rate of these animals, the International Whaling Commission (IWC), which is the international body that regulates whaling, has set a quota of zero for all commercial whaling. Norway formally objected to some aspects of the way the quota was calculated, and under IWC rules it is not bound to obey the effective ban. Norwegian ships are therefore catching whales legally.

Aboriginal Subsistence Whaling

Inuit and other Arctic peoples whose way of life depends partly on the use of whale products are permitted to catch some whales. This is called *aboriginal subsistence whaling* and quotas are set by the IWC. In northern Canada and Alaska, for example, indigenous people are allowed to catch up to 67 bowhead whales, also known as *Greenland right whales* (*Balaena mysticetus*) a year. There are an estimated 6,400–9,200 bowhead whales in this area. Up to 40 gray whales (*Eschrichtius robustus*) may be caught each year in the eastern North Pacific, where there are 19,800–22,500 of them. Greenlanders are allowed to catch 19 fin whales (*Balaenoptera physalus*) a year, of which there are estimated to be between 27,700 and 82,000 in the North Atlantic, as well as 19 minkes each year off western Greenland and 175 off eastern Greenland.

Krill

Such large animals are able to thrive in Arctic and Antarctic waters because of the abundance of smaller animals on which they feed. The most important of these are krill (see page 114).

There are several species of krill, the most abundant of which is the Antarctic krill (*Euphausia superba*). Its numbers increase and decrease over a cycle, as do populations of lemmings and other small, land-dwelling animals in the Arctic (see page 108), but for a different reason. Along with many other small aquatic animals, krill feed

on the algae that grow on the underside of sea ice. While they are there they are also sheltered from predators. Consequently, krill numbers follow changes in the area of sea ice.

The extent of the ice varies according to changes in surface air pressure and temperature that move around Antarctica as the Antarctic Circumpolar Wave (ACW), taking about seven years to complete one circuit around the continent. It is the ACW that causes krill numbers to reach a maximum every seven years, then decline to a minimum over three to four years, after which they increase again. Female krill lay several batches of eggs each year with up to 10,000 eggs in each batch, so in good survival years the population builds rapidly.

Antarctic krill are caught for human consumption, although catches have declined in recent years, as a result of reduced demand (see page 114). Most of the krill that is caught is processed into food for farmed fish, bait for anglers, and fish products for human consumption. We do not eat krill directly, as we do prawns.

Antarctic Cod and Icefish

Fish are the really important food we obtain from the polar seas. Antarctic cod (*Notothenia coriiceps*) was once found in huge shoals, but it was fished almost to extinction. About 24 inches (60 cm) long when adult, the Antarctic cod is related to the perches (order Perciformes) rather than the cods (order Gadiformes), which occur only in the Northern Hemisphere.

Icefish (*Chaenocephalus aceratus*) have also been fished very heavily. The icefish is a member of the same order as the Antarctic cod, and about the same size; the name *icefish* refers to the fact that its blood is almost transparent, because it lacks the red pigment hemoglobin. Without hemoglobin the fish transports oxygen in its blood plasma. This is not very efficient and as a result icefish are very sluggish.

Cod, Capelin, and Their Relatives

It is in the Northern Hemisphere that fishing has been most intense and competition between national fleets is keenest. Some countries, most notably Iceland and Greenland, are economically heavily dependent on their fisheries. In Iceland fishing accounts for one-sixth of the gross domestic product and provides one-ninth of all jobs. Icelandic fishing is based mainly on cod

(*Gadus morhua*) and capelin (*Mallotus villosus*). Together these two species account for more than two-thirds of all the fish caught.

Cod has been an important food fish for centuries and for many years about 400 million of them were being caught every year in the North Atlantic. The cod is a big fish, up to 4 feet (1.2 m) long, that often swims in shoals. Its numbers have been greatly reduced by overfishing, but it is so prolific—a female can lay 60 million eggs a year—that, now that the fishing effort has been reduced, it should recover. A related species, the North Pacific cod (*G. macrocephalus*), occurs in the North Pacific.

The capelin is related to the smelts (order Salmoniformes, family Osmeridae). It is quite small, growing to no more than 8 inches (20 cm). Many smelts spawn in freshwater as do salmon, but the capelin is different. It spawns close inshore, sometimes laying its eggs on gravel beaches.

Most of the codlike fishes occur throughout the northern North Atlantic, from the latitude of northern Spain to the Arctic, and most of them are pursued by fishing fleets. They include the haddock (*Melanogrammus aeglefinus*) and saithe (*Pollachius virens*), both of which grow to about 30 inches (76 cm); whiting (*Merlangius merlangus*), which averages 14 inches (36 cm); and ling (*Molva molva*), a slim, almost eellike fish up to 6 feet (1.8 m) long.

Regulating Fishing Effort

Modern fishing boats are equipped with instruments to locate fish and have engines powerful enough to allow them to use immensely large nets. They can catch entire shoals. Over recent years the level of fishing effort has been so high that stocks of most of the commercially important species have been seriously reduced. Efforts are now made to regulate fishing, but this is difficult and often unpopular, because fishing communities are understandably reluctant to forgo opportunities to earn income—and even more

Whale skeleton, Antarctic Peninsula (Gerry Ellis/ ENP Images)

reluctant to decommission boats and reduce the size of their fleets.

Gradually the capacity of modern fishing fleets to catch fish will be brought into balance with the capacity of fish stocks to sustain a regular harvest. Once that balance is achieved fishing can continue indefinitely. Meanwhile, it is likely that an increasing number of sea fish will be raised in captivity.

At present sea fish, the principal food of the Arctic and Antarctic, are the only animals we still catch by hunting. If we are to continue to enjoy eating them, sooner or later hunting will have to give way to some kind of farming.

Appendix A

AREAS OF THE MAJOR WORLD DESERTS, BY CONTINENT

Continent	Desert	Area (square miles)	(square kilometers)
Africa			
	Kalahari	275,000	712,250
	Namib	97,000	251,000
	Sahara	3,513,530	9,100,000
Antarctica			
Asia		5,500,000	14,200,000
	Gobi	374,420	970,000
	Iranian	150,000	390,000
	Takla Makan	115,000	297,850
	Thar	231,600	600,000
	Turkestan	750,000	1,900,000
Australia			
	Australian	979,700	2,538,000
Central America			
	Chihuahuan	200,000	518,000
Middle East			
	Arabian	1,600,000	3,000,000
	Syrian	200,000	518,000
North America			
	Colorado	165,000	427,350
	Mojave	15,000	38,850
	Sonoran	120,000	310,000
	Greenland ice sheet	700,000	1,813,000
South America			
	Atacama	140,155	363,000
	Patagonian	300,000	777,000

Appendix B

CLIMATIC AVERAGES AND EXTREMES FOR MAJOR DESERTS

Desert	Place	Temperature °F(°C)			Rain fall inches (mm)
		Average	Maximum	Minimum	
Antarctic	Interior coast Vostok	-84 (-64)		-126.9 (-88.3)	2 (50) 15 (380)
Arabian	Riyadh	82 (28)	117 (47)	49 (9)	2.4 (61)
Atacama		65 (18)			0.4 (10)
	Antofagasta		85 (29)	41 (5)	
Chihuahuan					
	Durango	67.5 (20)			21 (536)
	El Paso	64 (18)	106 (41)	-6 (-21)	9 (229)
Colorado		90 (32.2)	115 (46.1)	32 (0)	4 (102)
	Death Valley	76 (24)	134 (57)		1.5 (38)
Gobi					1.5 (38)
	Ulan Bator	61 (16)	92 (33)	34 (1)	
Kalahari					17.5 (445)
	Francistown	69 (20)	107 (42)		
Mojave					4 (100)
	Las Vegas	65 (18)	115 (46)	8 (-13)	4.4 (112)
Namib					2 (51)
	Walvis Bay	62 (17)	104 (40)	25 (-4)	0.8 (20)
Patagonian					
	Sarmiento	52 (11)			5 (127)
Sahara					
	Al 'Aziziyah		136 (58)		
	In Salah	78 (26)	122 (50)	26 (-3)	0.6 (15)
Sonoran		55 (13)			5 (127)
	Phoenix	70 (21)	118 (48)	16 (-9)	7.5 (190)
Syrian					
	Deir ez Zor	68 (20)	114 (46)	16 (-9)	6.2 (157)
Takla Makan		41 (5)			1 (25)
	Kashgar	55 (13)	106 (41)	-15 (-26)	3.3 (84)
Thar					
	Jacobabad	81 (27)	127 (53)	32 (0)	3.5 (89)

Note: *Average temperatures are calculated from average daytime and average nighttime temperatures for each month. Temperature maxima and minima occur during the day and night, respectively.*

Appendix C

UNITS AND CONVERSIONS

Scientists usually use Système International d'Unités) (SI) units of measurement. These comprise seven base units plus two supplementary units, the radian (rad) and steradian (sr), as well as a number of derived units that are defined in terms of the base units. The base units, with their abbreviations, are as follows:

Length: meter (m)
Mass: kilogram (kg)
Time: second (s)
Electric current: ampere (A)
Thermodynamic temperature: kelvin (K)
Luminous intensity: candela (cd)
Amount of substance: mole (mol)

The most commonly used derived units include

Area: square meter (m^2)
Volume: cubic meter (m^3)
Frequency: hertz (Hz) = 1 cycle per second
Density: kilogram per cubic meter ($kg\ m^{-3}$)
Velocity: meter per second ($m\ s^{-1}$)
Angular velocity: radian per second ($rad\ s^{-1}$)
Angular acceleration: radian per second per second ($rad\ s^{-2}$)
Force: newton (N) = $m\ kg\ s^{-2}$
Pressure: pascal (Pa) = $N\ m^{-2}$
Energy, work, or quantity of heat: joule (J) = N m
Power: watt (W) = $J\ s^{-1}$
Electromotive force: volt (V) = $W\ A^{-1}$
Electric resistance: ohm (Ω) = $V\ A^{-1}$

Superscripted numbers (e.g., ^{2}) raise units to the power of the number indicated. A superscripted 2 means squared (multiplied by itself); a superscripted 3 means cubed (multiplied by itself twice). The minus sign attached to a superscripted number means per, so s^{-1} means per second, ft^{-2} means per square foot. This is the way scientific units are usually written.

Prefixes are used to increase or decrease the value of units by factors of 10. These are the following:

Factor	Name	Symbol
10^{12}	tera-	T
10^{9}	giga-	G
10^{6}	mega-	M
10^{3}	kilo-	k
10^{2}	hecto-	h
10	deca-	da
10^{-1}	deci-	d
10^{-2}	centi-	c
10^{-3}	milli-	m
10^{-6}	micro-	µ
10^{-9}	nano-	n
10^{-12}	pico-	p
10^{-15}	femto-	f
10^{-18}	atto-	a

Factors for converting between SI and everyday U.S. units are as follows:

Length

1 inch = 2.54 cm; 1 centimeter = 0.39 in
1 foot= 30.48 cm; 1 centimeter = 0.033 ft
1 yard = 0.914 m; 1 meter = 1.094 yd
1 mile = 1.609 km; 1 kilometer = 0.6214 mi
1 nautical mile = 1.852 km; 1 kilometer = 0.54 nm

Area

1 square inch = 6.45 cm^2; 1 square centimeter = 0.16 in^2
1 square foot = 9.29 dm^2; 1 square decimeter = 0.11 ft^2
1 square yard = 0.84 m^2; 1 square meter = 1.20 yd^2
1 acre = 0.4047 ha; 1 hectare = 2.471 acres
1 square mile = 2.59 km^2; 1 square kilometer = 0.39 mi^2

Volume

1 pint = 0.57 liter; 1 liter = 1.76 pints
1 quart = 1.14 liters; 1 liter = 0.88 quart
1 gallon (U.S.) = 3.785 liters; 1 liter = 0.264 gal
1 barrel = 0.159 m^3; 1 cubic meter = 6.29 bbl
1 cubic inch = 16.39 cm^3; 1 cubic centimeter = 0.061 in^3
1 cubic foot = 0.028 m^3; 1 cubic meter = 35.31 ft^3
1 cubic yard = 0.765 m^3; 1 cubic meter = 1.31 yd^3

Mass

1 ounce = 28.4 g; 1 gram = 0.035 oz
1 pound = 0.454 kg; 1 kilogram = 2.2 lb
1 ton = 0.91 t; 1 tonne = 1.1 ton

Force

1 pound force = 4.45 N; 1 newton = 0.225 lbf

Pressure

1 bar = 0.1 MPa; 1 megapascal = 10 bar
1 pound force per square inch = 6.89 kPa; 1 kilopascal = 0.145 $lbf\ in^{-2}$
1 pound force per square foot = 47.88 Pa; 1 pascal = 0.021 $lbf\ ft^{-2}$
1 inch of mercury = 3.38 kPa; 1 kilopascal = 0.29 in Hg
1 standard atmosphere = 0.1013 Mpa; 1 megapascal = 9.87 atm

Work, heat, or energy

1 calorie = 4.187 J; 1 joule = 0.239 cal
1 British thermal unit = 1.055 kJ; 1 kilojoule = 0.948 Btu
1 erg = 0.1 µJ; 1 microjoule = 10 erg

Speed

1 foot per second = 0.305 $m\ s^{-1}$; 1 meter per second = 3.28 $ft\ s^{-1}$
1 foot per second = 1.097 $km\ h^{-1}$; 1 kilometer per hour = 0.911 $ft\ s^{-1}$
1 mile per hour = 1.609 $km\ h^{-1}$; 1 kilometer per hour = 0.6214 mph
1 knot = 1.852 $km\ h^{-1}$; 1 kilometer per hour = 0.54 knot

Temperature

°F = (°C ÷ 5 x 9) + 32; °C = (°F - 32) x 5 ÷ 9

Web Sites

The following sites are arranged in alphabetical order by topic.

Ant-Plant Interactions are described by Matthew E. Fyles at

    www.colostate.edu/Depts/Entomology/Courses/en507/papers_1999/fyles.htm

Arid lands: International Arid Lands Consortium is at

    ag.arizona.edu/OALS/IALC/home.htm

Purdue University held a symposium, the proceedings of which were published in 1990 as *Advances in New Crops* by Timber Press, Portland, OR. One chapter, "The New Crops Era" by Noel Vietmeyer, is especially relevant to arid lands. It can be seen at

    newcrop.hort.purdue.edu/newcrop/proceedings1990/Vl-forwd.html

Aswan High Dam: Information about the High Dam can be found at

    www.vol.it/mirror/egypt/Wonders/Modern/aswandam.html
    geography.miningco.com/library/weekly.aa012698.htm

Information about the temples at *Abu Simbel* is at

    www.ccer.ggl.ruu.nl/abu_simbell.html

Bedouin are described at

    www.premier.net/~bethany/profiles/clusters/8086.html

Bedouin of Burkina Faso are described at

    www.premier.net/~bethany/profiles/p_code1/1073.html

Bedouin of Saudi Arabia are described at

    www.premier.net/~bethany/profiles/p_code1/1640.html

Chaamba Bedouin of Algeria are described at

    www.premier.net/~bethany/profiles/p_code/1934.html

"Live Chat on Sinai Bedouin Women with Ann Gardner," part of the transcript of an on-line discussion on AOL, is at

    www.sherryart.com/women/bedouinchat.html

"Reflections on Fieldwork Among the Sinai Bedouin Women" by Ann Gardner is at

    www.sherryart.com/women/bedouin.html

Bellingshausen, Fasbian Gottlieb von, is described at

    www.southpole.com/p0000073.htm

Central American Swollen-Thorn Acacias are described at

    http://daphne.palomar.edu/wayne/acacia.htm

Chaco Culture National Historical Park is described at

    www.nps.gov/chcu/

Cheetahs are described at

    http://africam.xoom.com/glossary/animals/cheetah.html

Chihuahuan Desert is described at

    www.desertusa.com/du_chihua.html

Chinampas: "Don't Float by the Gardens" by Phil Crossley is at

    www.txinfinet.com/mader/planeta/0895/0895chinampa.html

"Floating Gardens of Mexico" is at

    www.agnr.umd.edu/users/mg/schfloa.htm

Climate control: Project Stormfury is described at

    www.aoml.noaa.gov/hrd/nhurr97/SFURY.HTM

Colorado Desert is described at

    ceres.ca.gov/geo_area/bioregions/Colorado_Desert/about.html

Desertification: The Convention to Combat Desertification is described by authors from the World Bank, with a list of links to other relevant sites at

    ag.arizona.edu/OALS/ALN/aln43/ccd.html

Dumont d'Urville, Jules-Sebastien, is described at

    www.south-pole.com/p0000077.htm

ENSO: information is abundantly available from the NOAA at

    www.pmel.noaa.gov/toga-tao/el-nino-report.html

Gobi Desert: The wildlife is described at

    www.nomads.mn/gobi.htm

Greenland: General information is available at

    www.greenland-guide.dk/gt/green-10.htm

And at

    www.platinova.com/1-1-glance.html

Greenland Ice Sheet is described at

    www.uwin.siu.edu/announce/press/atlas.html

Inuit diet is described by Rachel A. Qitsualik at

www.cyberus.ca/~stinsley/qfaqs6.htm

Krill are described at

www-aadc.antdiv.gov.au/data/ten_facts/ten_facts_krill.html

And at

www.k2net.co.uk/ef/dt/krlxtra.html

Antarctic fishing, for krill and fish, is described by the Scientific Committee of the Convention on the Conservation of Antarctic Marine Living Resources at

www.ccamlr.org/English/e_scientific_committee.../
e_fisheries_monitoring_intro.ht

Locusts: The Desert Locust Information Service of the Migratory Pests Group, part of the United Nations Food and Agriculture Organization, answers FAQs at

www.fao.org.NEWS/GLOBAL/LOCUSTS/LOCFAQ.htm

University of Florida Book of Insect Records: "Largest Swarm" by Hussein Sanchez-Arroyo is at

www.ifas.ufl.edu/~tjw/chap27.htm

University of Florida Book of Insect Records: "Longest Migration" by Christopher Tipping is at

gnv.ifas.ufl.edu/~tjw/chap11.htm

Melpa: This Native American farming system is described at

hammock.ifas.ufl.edu/txt/fasirs/12048

Membrane distillation is described at

www2.hawaii.edu/~nabil/solar.htm

Mesa Verde National Park is described at

www.nps.gov/meve/

Mongolia: Nomad life is described at

www.nomads.mn/culture/htm

And at

lcweb2.loc.gov/cgi-bin/query/r?frd/cstdy:@field(DOCID+mn0053)
lcweb2.loc.gov/cgi-bin/query/r?frd/cstdy:@field(DOCID+mn0054)
lcweb2.loc.gov/cgi-bin/query/r?frd/cstdy:@field(DOCID+mn0055)
lcweb2.loc.gov/cgi-bin/query/r?frd/cstdy:@field(DOCID+mn0056)

Nunavut: General information is at

npc.nunavut.ca/eng/nunavut/general.html

General history of northern Canada leading to Nunavut is described at

www.arctic-travel.com/history.html

Political history is described at

npc.nunavut.ca/eng/nunavut/govern.html

Oil supplies: Whether we are running out of oil is discussed by the American Petroleum Institute at

www.api.org/oilsup.htm

Panos Institute: The Panos Institute is at

www.oneworld.org/panos

The Institute of Development Studies, associated with Panos, is at

www.ids.ac.uk/ids/

Qanats: "The Qanats of the Middle Eastern Arid Lands":

www.bae.ncsu.edu/bae/courses/bae472/perspectives/1995/
jdcarrol.html

Ross, James Clerk, is described at

www.south-pole.com/0000081.htm

Sahel: Conditions for people living in the Sahel region are described in the FEWS Bulletin at

www.info.usaid.gov/regions/afr/fewsfb970326/sh970326.html.

Silk Road is described by Oliver Wild at

www.ess.uci.edu/~oliver/silk.html

"Following Ancient Footprints: Exploring the Northern Silk Road" by Pamela Logan:

www.alumni.caltech.edu/~pamlogan/srart.html

Introduction by Jeannette Mirsky to "On Ancient Central-Asian Tracks" by Sir Aurel Stein is at

www.physics.wisc.edu/~shalizi/reviews/
on-ancient-central-asian-tracks/

Solar cells:

www.soton.ac.uk/~ajdw/solar/tech6.htm

is a site at the University of Southampton providing a full explanation of how solar cells work, with enough technical detail but not so much as to make it hard to understand.

Solar chimneys are explained

design.gateway.net.hk/gluck/SolarChimney.html

and at

www.argonet.co.uk/users/bobsier/sola6.html

Solar energy: The David Ben-Gurion National Solar Energy Center has developed many solar-energy installations suitable for desert climates. It is at

ramat-negev.org.il/solar.htm.

Solar ponds

www.ncsc.ncsu.edu/11overvw.htm

is a site maintained by North Carolina University. It provides general explanations of how solar ponds and other solar-energy devices work.

Southern Oscillation: Explained in "The Southern Oscillation: Historical Origins" by Donald R. Mock at

www.cdc.noaa/gov/~drm/pubs/mock81-1a.html

Tuareg: "Blue Men of the Desert: Mali's Tuareg Give Up the Nomadic Life" by Anton Foek is at

www.worldandi.com/article/clfeb99.htm

Walrus is described at

www.greenchannel.com/tec/species/walrus.htm

Water conflicts: "Environment: Trying to Pre-Empt Water Wars" by Moyiga Nduru, in *World News* at

www.oneworld.org/ips2/feb98/water.html

"History of Water Disputes Is Cooperation, Not Conflict" by David Stauth. *OSU News,* Oregon State University, at

osu.orst.edu/Dept/ncs/newsarch/1998/Oct98/water.htm

"Strategies for Water Resources Management in Emergency and Conflicting Situations" at

www.pangea.org/orgs/unesco/conflictsub.html

"Water and Conflict":

www.cnie.org/pop/pai/water-25.html

"Watersheds and Problemsheds: Explaining the Absence of Armed Conflict Over Water in the Middle East" by Tony Allan. *MERIA (Middle East Review of International Affairs),* vol. 2, # 1, March 5, 1998, at

www.biu.ac.il/SOC/besa/jour5a7.html

Whaling: The New Bedford Whaling Museum, in Massachusetts, has information at

www.newbedford.com/whalingmuseum.html

and at

www.whalingmuseum.org/arctic.htm

The home page of the International Whaling Commission is at

ourworld.compuserve.com/homepages/iwcoffice/IWC/htm

Weddell, James, is described at

www.south-pole.com/0000075.htm

Wilkes, Charles, is described at

www.south-pole.com/p0000079.htm

Books

Allaby, Michael. *Dangerous Weather: Droughts.* New York: Facts On File, 1998.
A general description of dry climates that includes an account and explanation of the Dust Bowl.

———. *Dangerous Weather: A Chronology of Weather.* New York: Facts On File, 1998.
A general account that also includes two chronological lists, one of climatic disasters and the other of significant events in the development of the sciences of climatology and meteorology, as well as brief descriptions of some of the persons involved.

———. *Air, the Nature of Atmosphere and the Climate.* New York: Facts On File, 1992. Includes a discussion on wind power.

———. *Biomes of the World: Deserts* (Vol. 2) and *Tropical Grasslands* (Vol. 9). Danbury, Conn.: Grolier Educational, 1999.
These short books (part of a nine-volume series) provide a simple explanation of the problems of erosion and ways of reducing them.

———. *Dangerous Weather: Floods.* New York: Facts On File, 1998.
Contains descriptions of nilometers and the Aswan Dams.

Banister, Keith, and Andrew Campbell. *The Encyclopedia of Aquatic Life.* New York: Facts On File, 1985.

Brewer, Richard. *The Science of Ecology,* 2nd ed. Fort Worth: Saunders College Publishing. 2nd ed. A comprehensive textbook on all aspects of ecology.

Cross, Nigel, and Rhiannon Barker, eds. *At the Desert's Edge.* London: Panos Publications Ltd., 1992.
Interviews from the Sahel Oral History Project in which people living in the region talk about their own lives.

Halliday, Tim, and Kraig Adler, eds. *The Encyclopedia of Reptiles and Amphibians.* New York: Facts On File, 1986.

Henderson-Sellers, Ann, and Peter J. Robinson. *Contemporary Climatology.* London: Longman, 1986.
A textbook that is well written, not too mathematical, and makes the subject easy to understand.

Heywood, V. H. *Flowering Plants of the World,* rev. ed. New York: Oxford University Press, 1993.

Hidore, John J., and John E. Oliver. *Climatology: An Atmospheric Science.* New York: Macmillan, l993.
An introductory textbook, written very simply and clearly.

Lamb, H. H. *Climate, History and the Modern World,* 2nd ed. New York: Routledge, 1995.
A clear, simply written and highly readable account of the history of climate by one of the leading world authorities on the subject.

Macdonald, David. *The Encyclopedia of Mammals.* New York: Facts On File, 1984.

McIlveen, Robin. *Fundamentals of Weather and Climate.* New York: Chapman & Hall, 1992.
A textbook on climatology and meteorology written for more advanced students, but containing simple explanations of many phenomena.

More, David M., ed. *Green Planet: The Story of Plant Life on Earth.* New York: Cambridge University Press, 1982.

O'Toole, Christopher, ed. *The Encyclopedia of Insects.* New York: Facts On File, 1986.

Perrins, Christoper M., and Alex L. A. Middleton. *The Encyclopedia of Birds.* New York: Facts On File, 1985.

Articles

Glenn, Edward P., Brown, J. Jed, and O'Leary, James W. "Irrigating Crops With Seawater." *Scientific American,* August 1998, pp. 56–61. The article describes research into the use of seawater for growing farm crops.

Hattersley, Lia. "Electric Dreams." *New Scientist,* March 6, 1999, pp. 30–33. Describes solar chimneys.

Kerr, Richard E. "Big El Niños Ride the Back of Slower Climate Change." *Science,* **283,** 1108–09, February 19, 1999.